STRUGGLE ALLIANCE

MIDDLE EAST INSTITUTE POLICY SERIES

The Middle East Institute (MEI) Policy series aims to inform policy debates on the most pressing issues that will shape the future of the Middle East. The series publishes manuscripts that provide cutting-edge analysis and recommendations to policymakers in the Middle East and to international actors as they work toward solutions to some of the most searing problems facing the region.

Seeking to contribute to policy debates that will influence the Middle East in the future, the MEI Policy series promotes innovative and incisive work that focuses on issues that cut across the various countries of the region and span the areas of politics, culture, economics, society, the state, climate, health, gender and any other issue that meets the above policy impact criteria.

STRUGGLE FOR ALLIANCE

Russia and Iran in the Era of War in Ukraine

Edited by
Abdolrasool Divsallar

I.B. TAURIS
LONDON • NEW YORK • OXFORD • NEW DELHI • SYDNEY

I.B. TAURIS
Bloomsbury Publishing Plc
50 Bedford Square, London, WC1B 3DP, UK
1385 Broadway, New York, NY 10018, USA
29 Earlsfort Terrace, Dublin 2, Ireland

BLOOMSBURY, I.B. TAURIS and the I.B. Tauris logo are trademarks of Bloomsbury Publishing Plc

First published in Great Britain 2024

Copyright © Abdolrasool Divsallar, 2024

Abdolrasool Divsallar and Contributors have asserted their rights under the Copyright, Designs and Patents Act, 1988, to be identified as Authors of this work.

For legal purposes the Acknowledgments on p. ix constitute an extension of this copyright page.

Series design by Charlotte Daniels
Cover image © Alexandr Demyanchuk/SPUTNIK/AFP/Getty Images

All rights reserved. No part of this publication may be reproduced or transmitted in any form or by any means, electronic or mechanical, including photocopying, recording, or any information storage or retrieval system, without prior permission in writing from the publishers.

Bloomsbury Publishing Plc does not have any control over, or responsibility for, any third-party websites referred to or in this book. All internet addresses given in this book were correct at the time of going to press. The author and publisher regret any inconvenience caused if addresses have changed or sites have ceased to exist, but can accept no responsibility for any such changes.

A catalogue record for this book is available from the British Library.

Library of Congress Cataloging-in-Publication Data
Names: Divsallar, Abdolrasool, editor.
Title: Struggle for alliance : Russia and Iran in the era of war in Ukraine / edited by Abdolrasool Divsallar.
Description: London, UK ; New York, NY : I.B. Tauris, 2024. | Series: Middle East Institute policy series | Includes bibliographical references and index. | Summary: "This book analyzes Russo-Iranian relations from the perspective of the emerging literature on authoritarian regionalism, exploring the role domestic politics and common threat perceptions play in these states' decisions to adjust to the systemic changes caused by the war in Ukraine. Chapters address how changes in the strategic environment are affecting Moscow and Tehran's perception of each other, what factors contribute the most to both states' decision to pursue greater cooperation and how they manage the new conflicts of interest raised by the war"–Provided by publisher.
Identifiers: LCCN 2024005742 (print) | LCCN 2024005743 (ebook) | ISBN 9780755653515 (hardback) | ISBN 9780755653508 (paperback) | ISBN 9780755653522 (ebook) | ISBN 9780755653539 (epub)
Subjects: LCSH: Russia (Federation)–Foreign relations–Iran. | Iran–Foreign relations–Russia (Federation) | Russia (Federation)–Foreign relations–21st century. | Iran–Foreign relations–21st century. | Alliances–History–21st century. | Strategy–History–21st century. | Russian Invasion of Ukraine, 2022–Influence.
Classification: LCC DK68.7.I7 S77 2024 (print) | LCC DK68.7.I7 (ebook) | DDC 327.47055–dc23/eng/20240301
LC record available at https://lccn.loc.gov/2024005742
LC ebook record available at https://lccn.loc.gov/2024005743

ISBN: HB: 978-0-7556-5351-5
PB: 978-0-7556-5350-8
ePDF: 978-0-7556-5353-9
eBook: 978-0-7556-5352-2

Typeset by Newgen KnowledgeWorks Pvt. Ltd., Chennai, India
Printed and bound in Great Britain

To find out more about our authors and books visit www.bloomsbury.com and sign up for our newsletters.

CONTENTS

List of Figures vii
List of Tables viii
Acknowledgments ix

Introduction: Russia and Iran: A Continuity of the Past or a Historical Juncture? 1
  Abdolrasool Divsallar

PART ONE DOMESTIC DEBATES: BETWEEN STATE ENTHUSIASM AND PUBLIC UNCERTAINTY

1 Iran's Ascent in Russian Foreign Policy Thinking: The Emergence of a New Paradigm 33
  Nicole Grajewski

2 The Ukraine War and Internal Debates in Iran 73
  Mahmood Shoori

3 Identity, Statehood, and Strategic Sympathy 103
  Diana Galeeva

PART TWO GEOSTRATEGIC FACTORS: CONSTRAINTS OR AN ENABLER?

4 The Ukraine War and Russian Policy in the MENA and Mediterranean Region: Implications for Iran 127
  Mark N. Katz

5 The Principle of Strategic Stability: Has the War Changed Russia's Nuclear Policy toward Iran? 149
Anastasia Malygina

6 An Authoritarian Alliance: Systemic Factors That Bring Russia and Iran Together 179
Abdolrasool Divsallar

PART THREE A HYBRID STATUS: COMPETITION AMID COOPERATION

7 Anti-Americanism and the Dream of a Non-Western Order 209
Jeffrey Mankoff and Mahsa Rouhi

8 Prospects for Russo-Iranian Economic Relations: Competition over Cooperation 253
Esfandyar Batmanghelidj

9 Will Iran Challenge Russia's Position as a Major Global Energy Player? 281
Jakub M. Godzimirski

10 Iran and Russia in Syria: A Changing Alliance amid the War in Ukraine 317
Hamidreza Azizi

Conclusion 347
   Abdolrasool Divsallar

List of Contributors 355
Index 359

FIGURES

- **2.1** Poll on the extent of news consumption on the war 94
- **2.2** Poll on the reasons for Western support of Ukraine 94
- **2.3** Poll on the concerns about the war's impact on Iran 95
- **2.4** Poll on the parties Iran ought to support in the war 95
- **8.1** Russian trade with Iran 263
- **8.2** Weekly calls at Iran's Caspian ports 265
- **8.3** Russian and Iranian exports to China 270
- **8.4** Russian and Iranian imports from China 272
- **8.5** Russian and Iranian exports to Turkey 273
- **8.6** Russian and Iranian imports from Turkey 274
- **9.1** The relative importance of Iran in the broader MENA context on the Russian map of interests as measured by the references to Iran-related documents on the Russian MFA (MID Hierarchy) and the president of the Russian Federation (Kremlin Hierarchy) websites 288

TABLES

8.1 Top Fifteen Categories of Russian and Iranian Goods Exports, 2020 267

8.2 Top Fifteen Categories of Russian and Iranian Goods Imports, 2020 268

9.1 Key Indicators of Russia's Trade with Iran in 2011–20 290

9.2 Russia and Iran as Global Energy Players 293

9.3 Key Developments in Russian-Iranian Relations, 2022 304

ACKNOWLEDGMENTS

This volume is the collaborative effort of a number of colleagues and friends. My deepest thanks go, first and foremost, to the contributors to this volume, who have been particularly generous in sharing their knowledge and patiently accompanying me through various stages of this research. The Middle East Institute (MEI) in Washington and its leadership provided invaluable support on many dimensions, without which this book would not have been produced. I owe a special debt to Ross Harrison, director of research at the MEI, for his advice, mentorship, and friendship throughout this project. Alistair Taylor, the editorial director at the MEI, and Alex Vatanka, the director of the Iran Program at the MEI, generously supported the project. The Iran Program at the MEI allowed me to organize two panels on the topic between May and June 2022, which helped the initial concept of the chapters to grow. I am grateful to Tatiana Ozhereleva for her kind support and marvelous job in finding Russian sources and translations. Cecilia Deleo deserves special thanks for taking the time to assist me in editing references. Gaden James generously dedicated his time to read and edit earlier versions of the chapters. I am also indebted to the I.B. Tauris and Bloomsbury Press team for their enthusiastic support. Finally, I acknowledge the debt to my family for their support while I focused too much attention to this work.

—Abdolrasool Divsallar

INTRODUCTION
RUSSIA AND IRAN: A CONTINUITY OF THE PAST OR A HISTORICAL JUNCTURE?

Abdolrasool Divsallar

The Russian invasion of Ukraine on February 24, 2022, has not only shaken European security and Moscow's relations with the West, but it has also had profound implications on its partnership with the Middle East and particularly with Iran. The war has caused massive geopolitical waves and has shifted strategic environments in which Russo-Iranian relations operated. The two countries' perception of each other seems to be changing in the aftermath of the war. At first glance, the war led Moscow and Tehran to initiate a complex dynamic of readjustment and upgradation of relations. The officials of both countries met each other at different levels more than at any other time in 2022, showing how the war has revitalized ties between the countries. At the same time, Tehran's military assistance to Moscow was perceived in the West as an unprecedented intervention in European security affairs and a clear sign of Iranian siding in the war. Indeed, more than anything else, the military

---

The views expressed in this chapter are those of the author and are not an official policy or position of the UNIDIR (United Nations Institute for Disarmament Research) or the United Nations.

dimension of Russo-Iranian relations brought the issue to the spotlight, attracting security officials, media outlets, and expert communities. However, the two countries' relations have also transformed in many other ways, making an updated study of Russo-Iranian ties necessary. This book attempts to see how the war in Ukraine has impacted Moscow and Tehran's strategies for bilateral relations.

The book will address the following critical questions: How has the war changed Moscow and Tehran's perception of each other? What factors contribute the most to both states' decision for greater cooperation after a collective Western response to the war? How has the war affected previously existing regional and domestic constraints that set limits to the relations? Given both capitals' past experiences of transactional interest-based behaviors, how have they managed new conflicts of interest raised by the outbreak of war? Will the relations continue based on a tactical partnership, or is a stronger alliance between Moscow and Tehran unfolding? What are the implications of closer Russo-Iranian relations on the Persian Gulf region?

Mapping the Debates

At least three narratives can be identified in the debates about the impact of the war on Russo-Iranian relations. The first narrative argues that war is a historical juncture and has profoundly changed the relationship, setting new levels in bilateral ties. There is a counternarrative to this argument, branding recent developments as mere optics with less content, thus asserting that the relationship is continuing to be business as usual. In this view, the true impacts of the war remain to be seen. Finally, a third narrative asserts that the war is only initiating a process that may give a strategic characteristic to the Russian-Iranian partnership, implying that the relationship is in progressive transition.

The first narrative supports the idea of war as a historical juncture. It focuses on a strong political will that has emerged as a vehicle to elevate the state of the relationship. Adlan Margoev, for example, argues that "as the conception of Iran in Russia has changed greatly, so too the intention on both sides to raise the relations to the strategic level."[1] One Iranian

---

[1] Adlan Margoev (researcher at the Moscow State Institute of International Relations, MGIMO University), in discussion with the author, March 31, 2023.

scholar who claims the relationship has become strategic writes that "the fundamental reason that the ties have become strategic for Iran is that Russia, a nuclear power state and a member of [the] UN Security Council, is not seeking a regime change in Tehran. For Russia, however, it is critical to keep Iran out of the Western sphere of influence."[2] The rhetoric coming out of Moscow and Tehran seems to support these claims. In September 2022, Russian President Vladimir Putin, after meeting with his Iranian counterpart, Ebrahim Raisi, announced that "work on a new big agreement between Russia and Iran, which will mark the elevation of relations to the level of strategic partnership, is in its final phase."[3] Hossein Amir-Abdollahian, the current Iranian foreign minister, also made a similar claim. On a visit to Moscow in March 2023, he said, "Iran and Russia are finalizing a long-term strategic cooperation agreement."[4] Officials in Washington and many European capitals joined by some experts point out that the rising military cooperation between Moscow and Tehran is at the core of this historical change. Anna Borshchevskaya states that "the relation is taking on a more strategic character."[5] A similar view has also been reflected by US government officials from the State Department and the CIA, which characterized the relations as "transforming into a full-fledged defense partnership."[6]

This view is a logical continuation of literature that describes Russia and Iran as natural allies.[7] Ghonche Tazmini, an expert on Iran-Russia relations, believes that "the Moscow-Tehran axis is not an ad-hoc alliance; rather, it is based on a careful calibration of strategic, geopolitical, and

---

[2]Mahmood Sariolghalam, "chera ravabet e iran va russiye estrategic shode ast? [Why Iran's Relations with Russia Have Become Strategic?]," May 11, 2023, https://telegra.ph/sariolghalam-05-11-2 (accessed January 29, 2024; note that the accessed date for all URLs mentioned across the book is January 29, 2024, unless otherwise specified).
[3]"Russia, Iran Wrapping Up Work on New Strategic Partnership Deal, Says Putin," Tass News Agency, September 15, 2022, https://tass.com/politics/1508011.
[4]"Iranian, Russian FMs Hold Talks in Moscow," Mehr News, March 29, 2023, https://en.mehrnews.com/news/198885/Iranian-Russian-FMs-hold-talks-in-Moscow.
[5]"Transactional or Strategic? The Future of Russo-Iranian Relations," Middle East Institute, April 13, 2023, https://www.mei.edu/events/transactional-or-strategic-future-russo-iranian-relations.
[6]"Iran's Deepening Strategic Alliance with Russia," The Iran Primer, April 25, 2023, https://iranprimer.usip.org/blog/2023/feb/24/iran's-deepening-strategic-alliance-russia.
[7]Parham Ghani and Abbasgholi Asgarian, "Manehaye sheklgiri etelafe rahbordi iran va russiye: Motale moredi jange suriye [Barriers to the Formation of the Strategic Alliance between the Islamic Republic of Iran and Russia: Case Study, Iran-Russia Alliance in the Syrian Crisis]," *Journal of Central Eurasia Studies* 14 (2021), 229–49.

economic priorities."[8] She adds: "Connective tissue that binds Russia and Iran is embedded within a broader assemblage of shared principles, priorities, and preoccupations."[9] Another Iranian scholar calls the relation a "strategic alignment," saying "the relation is deeply rooted and constant … based on calibration of strategic preferences and priorities informed by similar perceptions of the international order."[10] Even before the war, the foreign policy directions of the Ebrahim Raisi administration approved this perception. Raisi, on a visit to Moscow in January 2022, said, "We have no limits on the development of relations with Russia, and the excellent Tehran-Moscow relations are at the level of strategic relations and will be upgraded."[11]

On the contrary, the second narrative argues that it is too soon to judge the implication of the war on Russo-Iranian relations, given the historical complexities, limitations, and costs of the bilateral ties. Mehdi Sanaei, former Iranian ambassador to Moscow, supports this view. He believes that "except for the military cooperation that has raised to the next level, there are no other major developments in the relations. The interest-based nature of relation has not shifted."[12] He refers to the fact that most agreements on nonmilitary areas of cooperation have been discussed before the war. At the same time, these prewar challenges that prevented the implementation of accords have not yet been resolved. Therefore, no noticeable new developments can be expected. Sanaei adds, "No big state project has been started between the two countries since 2022. Instead, limitations persisted and were reinforced. For example, Iran's non-admission of Russian territorial claims reveals Iranians' concerns about fully backing the war, while the public view of relations inside Iran has worsened after the war."[13]

---

[8]Ghonche Tazmini, "Russian and Iran: Strategic Partners or Provisional Counterweights?" in *Russian Foreign Policy towards the Middle East: New Trends, Old Traditions*, edited by Nikolay Kozhanov (London: Hurst, 2022), 139.
[9]Tazmini, "Russian and Iran," 140.
[10]Ali Omidi, "Russian-Iranian Ties: Strategic Alliance, Strategic Coalition, or Strategic Alignment (Partnership)," *Russian Politics* 7 (2022), https://doi.org/10.30965/24518921-00604023.
[11]"Ayatollah Raisi: The Excellent Relations between Iran and Russia Are on the Path of Strategic Relations," dolat.ir, January 19, 2022, https://dolat.ir/detail/378458.
[12]Mehdi Sanaei (former Iranian Ambassador to Russia) in discussion with the author, April 2, 2023.
[13]Sanaei, 2023.

Nikolay Kozhanov thinks along the same lines and writes, "Iran's readiness to pay the price for better relations with Russia might gradually weaken ... As such, despite an improved overall dialogue between Moscow and Tehran, and obvious positive shifts in bilateral and regional trade and economic cooperation, current relations are far from constituting a full-fledged axis of allies."[14] Similarly, Hamidreza Azizi asserts, "When it comes to the methods for opposing the US role in the Middle East, the Iranian and Russian approaches reflect fundamental differences that act as a brake on developing a close partnership between the two. So, the foundations of Iran-Russia relations in the Middle East have remained largely intact since the Russian invasion of Ukraine began."[15] Another prominent Iranian Russologist, Alireza Noori, argues that "the relation after the war in Ukraine is still derived by pragmatic opportunism, and remains to be transactional for both capitals. The war in Ukraine has not changed the prominence of the US factor that is at the core of Russia-Iran relations. Thus future changes in this factor will largely modify the relations."[16]

These arguments are rooted in a large body of literature that has elaborated on structural limitations and divergence in foreign policy strategies of the two states. Scholars have shown that Russia-Iran relations have always been sensitive to external and situational factors, which have often justified short-lived transactional, interest-based decisions.[17] The war in Ukraine can be only one of these situations that creates opportunities and necessities that might fade over time. Such a conception of relations makes forming any principle-based partnership between Moscow and Tehran difficult.[18] Ariane Tabatabai and Dina

---

[14] Nikolay Kozhanov, "Putin's War in Ukraine and Prospects for Russian-Iranian Relations," Chatham House, April 4, 2023, https://kalam.chathamhouse.org/articles/putins-war-in-ukraine-and-prospects-for-russian-iranian-relations?s=35.
[15] Hamidreza Azizi, "Close but Complicated: Iran-Russia Relations in the Middle East amid the War in Ukraine," Friedrich-Ebert-Stiftung, February 2023, https://library.fes.de/pdf-files/international/20084.pdf.
[16] Alireza Noori (professor at Shahid Beheshti University), in discussion with the author, July 24, 2023.
[17] See Elaheh Koolaee, Hamed Mousavi, and Afifeh Abedi, "Fluctuations in Iran-Russia Relations during the Past Four Decades," *Iran and the Caucasus* 24, no. 2 (2020): 216–32, https://doi.org/10.1163/1573384X-20200206.
[18] See Hossein Asgarian, *Outlook of Iran–Russia Relations* (Tehran: Tehran International Studies and Research Institute, 2015); Nikolay Khozhanov, "Russian-Iranian Relations through the Prism of the Syrian Crisis," *Insight Turkey* 19, no. 41 (2017), 105–24.

Esfandiary write that "the relationship is based on mutual interests and necessities. This means that as long as their goals are aligned, the alliances will hold, but it also ensures that there will come a time when the alliances break apart."[19] In addition, the differences in the two countries' strategic cultures, as some analysts put it, have made any strategic partnership impossible.[20] The opponents of Moscow and Tehran's strategic partnership believe that even factors such as anti-Americanism, often portrayed as the core of relations, cannot bring a strategic character to the relations. Noori writes: "Revisionism cannot make them [Russia and Iran] reliable partners since Russia's version appears to be less risk-taking than Tehran's apparent desire to oppose the US openly."[21]

The bottom line is that both sides' nonideological and pragmatic foreign policies have led to strategies that complicate the application of classical alliance and alignment concepts. Ebrahim Motaghi, a professor at the University of Tehran and a prominent figure in the strategic circles in Tehran, argues that pragmatism has forced "Russia's modern colonial approach towards Iran to be characterized by 'balance of weakness' based on Russian interests."[22] This fact can be best traced through Russia's position toward the US-Iran confrontation. Moscow's interests are maximized by the sustained Iranian crisis with the United States, a gray area between open conflict and US-Iran reconciliation.[23] Besides, in the post-Soviet era, the Kremlin often saw Tehran as a leverage in its relationship with the United States. But so did the Iranians. Tehran has historically used Russia to counterweight relations with other powers. At

---

[19] Ariane Tabatabai and Dina Esfandiary, *Triple Axis: Iran's Relations with Russia and China* (London: I.B. Tauris, 2021), 191.
[20] Akbar Valizadeh and Somayeh Kazemi, "tasire moalefehaye farhange rahbordi bar ravabete dujanebe va mantaghaei iran va russiye [The Influence of Strategic Culture Components on Bilateral and Regional Relations between Iran and Russia]," *Journal of Central Eurasia Studies* 15, no. 1 (2022), 402, https://doi.org/10.22059/jcep.2022.337629.450051.
[21] Alireza Noori, "Mahiyat tajdide nazar talabi rusiye va chin: siyasat va manafe Iran [The Nature of Russian and Chinese Revisionism: Iran's Policy and Interests]," *Journal of Central Eurasia Studies* 14, no. 2 (2021), https://www.doi.org/10.22059/jcep.2021.328326.450023.
[22] Ebrahim Mottaghi, Zohreh Postinchi, Saeed Mojaradi, and Amir Hayat Moghadam, "amalgaraei rahbordi dar ravabete iran va russiye [Strategic Pragmatism in I.R. Iran–Russia Relations]," *Scientific Quarterly Journal of Defense Strategy* 12, no. 2 (2014), 127, https://ds.sndu.ac.ir/article_660.html?lang=en.
[23] Abdolrasool Divsallar and Pyotr Kortonuv, "The Fallout of the US-Iran Confrontation for Russia: Revisiting Factors in Moscow's Calculus," Robert Schuman Centre for Advanced Studies and Russian International Affair Council Research (Florence: European University Press, 2020), 18, https://doi.org/10.2870/678655.

least as long as the 17th century, Russia was seen by Iranian leaders as a card to manage relations with foes—once in connection with the Ottoman Empire and later with Western powers. For example, Mohammad Reza Pahlavi, the last monarch of Iran, adopted a pragmatic policy of using the Soviets as a pressure point to extract concessions from the United States and its regional foe, Iraq. His trip to Moscow in October 1972 and attempts to purchase Soviet arms and involve the Russians in Iran's development project had this logic in mind.[24] The criticism that Tehran has often received in Moscow is that for Iranians, Tehran's relations with Russia are a pure reflection of the state of interactions with the West.

This book, however, puts forth a third narrative about the state of Russo-Iranian relations after the outbreak of the war in Ukraine, which takes a more cautious middle ground. This narrative confirms that the war has unfolded systemic changes in Russo-Iranian relations, and Iran, in particular, has gained considerable importance in Russia's foreign policy. However, a series of limitations still prevents the formation of a meaningful strategic partnership in the short term. In this context, a process has been initiated by the war, which, if it persists, may end up giving relations a strategic character. As Andrey Kortunov explains, "the war was a catalyst for Russia-Iranian relations, and it is making the relations more mature. If current trends continue, strategic ties may emerge."[25] He adds: "But Russian mistrust of Iran and fear of eventually an Iranian shift towards the West, decisive role of external factors in the relations, and opportunistic pragmatism of both sides remain major obstacles in this process."[26] In the aftermath of the war, regime security concerns, immediate interests, and opportunity costs have formed trends of protective integration and interdependence between Moscow and Tehran.[27] These trends might initiate a gradual process of strategic partnership. The authors in this volume mostly embark on this group,

---

[24]Mohamda Javad Javadi and Arjmand Abdolrasool Divsallar "rabeteye amniyat va tose-e: mored ravabete iran va shoravi [Security-Development Nexus in Foreign Policy: The Case of Soviet-Iran relations]," *Politics Quarterly* 49, no. 2 (2019), https://doi.org/10.22059/jpq.2019.228045.1007024.

[25]Andrey Kortunov (former director of the Russian International Affairs Council), in discussion with the author, April 7, 2023.

[26]Kortunov, 2023.

[27]Abdolrasool Divsallar, "Protective Integration and Rising Interdependency: Making Sense of Iranian Response to Russian Invasion of Ukraine," *The Chinese Journal of International Politics* (forthcoming).

showing how the war has fed into an integration process between Moscow and Tehran.

So, according to this last narrative, the war may have embarked on a transitory period in Russo-Iranian relations. While the international environment and political willingness of the two countries' leadership substantially favored cooperation since 2015, the relations have remained free from any commitment and, as a whole, cannot be characterized as an alliance.[28] The war in Ukraine might turn into an opportunity to transform relations formerly known by pragmatic opportunism into a more principally guided relationship in which both sides have a clearer normative commitment toward each other. As Russian foreign minister Sergey Lavrov puts it: "The document [that both sides are finalizing] will be strategically important. It will establish basic guidelines for further expanding Russian-Iranian relations in the coming decades." But still, the views of the two sides have important points of divergence. For example, Iran's refusal to recognize Russian territorial gains in Ukraine does not satisfy the Kremlin. Moscow perceives such an Iranian stand as a reluctance to fully support and commit to Russian objectives. Similarly, Russian support of UAE claims about Iranian islands in the Persian Gulf has had deep negative impacts on the perception of Russia as a future ally. So, Elena Dunaeva is right in saying that "the success of this process seems complicated as it depends on if both countries can mutually benefit from relations; otherwise, such process of rapprochement will not necessarily succeed."[29]

Russia and Iran before the War in Ukraine

The turning point in Russo-Iranian modern history goes back to the Russian conquer of Kazan (1552) and Astrakhan (1556), which made the two then empires neighbors. It started hundreds of years of geopolitical

---

[28]Lana Ravandi-Fadai, "Partnerstvo bez obyazatelstv: osobennosti rossiysko-itanskikh otnosheni v poslednie desyatiletiya [Partnership without Commitments: Features of Russian-Iranian Relations in Recent Decades]," *Russia and the World: Scientific Dialogue* 1, no. 1 (2021), 42–50, https://doi.org/10.53658/RW2021-1-1-42-50.

[29]Elena Dunaeva (senior research fellow with the Russian Academy of Sciences Institute of Oriental Studies), in discussion with the author, May 1, 2023.

disputes that ended with massive Iranian loss of land. However, what changed this geography-centered view was the collapse of the Soviet Union, which ended the era of the two states being direct neighbors. The collapse of the Soviet Union and the formation of newly independent states that functioned as buffer zones between Russia and Iran provided an opportunity in which Russians were no longer seen as a direct threat to Iranian borders. This geographical distance plays a key role in Iranian psyche and the perception of Russia as a threat. Jahangir Karami argues, "Russia was no more a direct threat, but a powerful potential partner that can balance the West."[30]

The Islamic Republic of Iran's relations with the Soviet Union started with tensions over Moscow's support of Saddam's war of aggression against Iran and Tehran's support of Afghan Mujaheddin. Saddam's bombing of Tehran with Soviet-made bombers and Scud-B missiles infuriated Iranians, resulting in Ali Akbar Hashemi Rafsanjani's anti-Soviet statement in a public prayer and protests in front of the Soviet embassy in Tehran. As then foreign minister Ali Akbar Velayati argues, "[the] Kremlin armed Saddam to persuade Tehran to cease its support of Afghan resistance to Soviet invasion."[31] According to Karami, Ayatollah Khomeini's controversial letter to Gorbachev in 1989, in which he welcomed the Soviet leader's reforms, followed by Gorbachev's positive response, opened a new window for the states' engagement.[32] Shortly thereafter, Hashemi Rafsanjani traveled to Moscow to sign a ten-year agreement that same year, providing the basis for bilateral ties in the coming years.

Moscow and Tehran's relations in the 1990s remained limited but better regulated through the ten-year agreement. The relations were a mix of cautious collaboration and disagreements. Russian policy was influenced by competing foreign policy narratives, Moscow's pro-Western foreign policy orientations, and suspicions of Iran's influence in the South Caucasus and Central Asia. Both sides cooperated in the 1993 Tajikistan peace talks and the anti-Taliban policies of 1996–2001. In addition, Russia sold arms to Iran and agreed to build the Bushehr

---

[30]Jahangir Karami, "ravabete iran va rusiye az 1369–1388: zamineha, avamel va mahdodiyatha [Iran-Russia Relations from 1989–2009: Grounds, Factors and Constraints]," *Journal of Iran and Central Eurasia Studies* 6 (2010), 111–36.

[31]"Sali ke ba mooshakhaye doshman shoro shod [A Year Started with Enemy's Missile]," IBNA News Agency, March 27, 2022, https://www.ibna.ir/fa/rep ort/319 625/ سالی-موشک-های-دشمن-شروع-صدام-تهران.

[32]Karami, "Iran-Russia Relations from 1989–2009."

Nuclear Power Plant (NPP). But even these positive developments had a flavor of mutual suspicion and mistrust. The Gore-Chernomyrdin secret agreement in which Russia pledged to the United States to limit its arms sales to Tehran and the Iranian criticism of Russia's slow progress in the Bushehr NPP were two areas that disturbed relations. By the beginning of the year 2000, bilateral trade was as low as $700 million.

With President Putin in power, things started to change. President Mohammad Khatami traveled to Moscow in 2001. He signed a ten-year agreement known as the "Mutual Relations and Principles of Cooperation between Iran and Russia," which was later renewed for two five-year terms. The two sides started some of their most critical projects, such as the North-South Transit Corridor (NSTC), and more serious negotiations on the division of the Caspian Sea. By 2008, trade had grown five times and had reached $3.5 billion. However, Iran's nuclear program brought the country under major international sanctions. Russia decided to adhere to the binding sanctions against Iran, and thus, bilateral trade dropped below $1 billion by 2012. Between 2008 and 2015, Russian-Iranian relations faced multiple political challenges. Russia supported all six of the UN Security Council resolutions against Iran. In a bid for closer ties with the United States, Russian President Dmitry Medvedev decided to ban the delivery of five S-300 systems that Iran had paid for. The decision sparked diplomatic tensions and also raised public sensitivity to Russian actions. But both sides' pragmatism, marked by Moscow's willingness to play the role of the responsible member of the international community and its contribution to nuclear negotiations, and Tehran's power deficit and its need for Russian support, kept the working relations intact. In general, in this period, sanctions and the Kremlin's desire for rapprochement with Washington fundamentally limited Russo-Iranian bilateral ties.

By 2015, a new era of bilateral relations had started. The Russian position on the key aspects of Iran's security strategy, such as the nuclear file and regional presence, was a mix of diplomatic support, coordination, and behind-the-scenes influence. Russia remained a key partner in implementing Iran's nuclear deal, the Joint Comprehensive Plan of Action (JCPOA). Despite criticism of Russia's negative role in finalizing the JCPOA by former Iranian top diplomat Mohammad Javad Zarif, the general perception, including those held by European and US officials,[33]

---

[33] Anonymous EU official, in discussion with the author, February 15, 2023.

highlighted Moscow's positive role in the deal. Russia's collaboration with Iran and other signatories of the JCPOA was instrumental in the implementation phase of the deal.[34] Besides, the Kremlin emerged as the main political supporter of Tehran after Trump's withdrawal from the JCPOA and played an active role in shielding the country in international fora. But also, Moscow, along with E3, the UK, France, and Germany, took great care to advocate talks for the restoration of the nuclear deal, which was initiated after the Biden administration, known as the Vienna Talks. On several occasions, Russian diplomacy was instrumental in averting a collapse of these talks by providing technical solutions and pressuring Tehran for concessions.[35]

No doubt, Moscow's partnership with Tehran in support of the Assad regime was a turning point in bilateral relations. It initiated military-security relations that were unprecedented in the history of the two neighbors. Cooperation in Syria pushed Moscow and Tehran's partnership beyond a simple arms transfer. It added extensive bilateral intelligence-sharing, coordination for military operations, and joint efforts to shape regional security architecture. The Syrian case allowed top military-security leadership in Moscow and Tehran to establish personal bonds and institutional links. The result was a better understanding of each other's threat perceptions and military strategy, especially in spaces beyond Syria, such as the Caspian Sea, and perception of NATO as a threat. For example, the parties have been actively participating since 2015 in the military war games, also organizing the Sea Cup competition, and conducting joint drills in the Caspian Sea in 2017, 2019, and 2022.[36] In another example of supporting each other's defense policies, in February 2019, Russia vetoed a resolution against Iran's arms transfer to Yemen, avoiding open criticism of Iranian-backed military groups across the Middle East. At the same time, the Russian military had taken a pragmatic stand of maintaining a

---

[34]Anton Khlopkov and Anna Lutkova, "The Bushehr NPP: Why It Take So Long?" Center for Energy and Security Studies, August 1, 2010, http://ceness-russia.org/data/doc/TheBushehrNPP-WhyDidItTakeSoLong.pdf.
[35]Hanna Notte, "Don't Expect Any More Russian Help on the Iran Nuclear Deal," War on the Rocks, November 3, 2022, https://warontherocks.com/2022/11/dont-expect-any-more-russian-help-on-the-iran-nuclear-deal/.
[36]V. Sadchenko, "Sadchenko V. Yuzhni Kavkaz V peresechenii nazionalnikh interesov Rossii i Irana (2014-2022 gg.) [South Caucasus at the Intersection of National Interests Russia and Iran (2014–2022)]," in *Russia and Iran: Five Centuries of Cooperation*, edited by Bezborodov Alexander, Vitaly Naumkin, and Alikberov Alikber, 74–85 (Moscow: Russian State University for the Humanities, 2022).

good working relationship with these groups, including in Iraq, Lebanon, and Syria, as part of its broader coordination efforts with Iran.[37] Besides, Russia has consistently recognized Iran's right to develop a combined missile and proxy-based deterrence model. Russia has remained one among a handful of states with none or fewer threat perception regarding Iran's missile programs and armed militias.

By 2022, Iran was increasingly seeing offensive Russian foreign policy toward the West as an opportunity to fill some of its strategic gaps in the military and security sectors. Research published by Iran's General Staff of Armed Forces based on a content analysis of Russian military-security concepts argues that Russia is becoming more and more willing to make strategic offensive decisions against the West. The research identifies it as an opportunity and recommends a more proactive defense collaboration with Russia, initiating joint military-industrial projects and strengthening mutual capabilities.[38]

Looking at the Iranian policy toward Russia after the end of the Iran-Iraq War, it is safe to argue that almost every president since Hashemi Rafsanjani sought to improve ties with Moscow. Both reformist and conservative presidents perceived Russia as an important pole of power and source of sensitive technologies that could help the Islamic Republic resist US pressures. Reformists, moderates, and hardliner presidents were all common in their cautiousness to avoid a crisis with Moscow. Iran's criticism of Russia remained mild and calculated even in times of political discontent toward Russian politics, such as between 2006 and 2010 over Russian UN Security Council voting or disputes over the Caspian Sea divisions. Thus, one Iranian writer argues, "notwithstanding all doubts and challenges, Russia's position in Iran's foreign policy steadily grows."[39] On the Russian side, however, as Nicole Grajewski argues in her chapter, Russia's perception of Iran has undergone significant changes over the years. Iran initially featured

---

[37]Abdolrasool Divsallar and Yulia Roknifard, "Iran, Russia, and the Militias: Seeds of Tactical Cooperation," ISPI, March 23, 2023, https://www.ispionline.it/en/publication/iran-russia-and-the-militias-seeds-of-tactical-cooperation-121968.

[38]Ehsan Fallahi, "Seire tahavol rahbord defaei rusie az 1991 ta 2021 bar asase olgohaye rahbordi SWOT [The Evolution of Russia's Security Defense Strategy 1991–2021 based on SWOT Strategic Models]," *Strategic Management Studies of National Defense* 21 (2022), 186, https://dorl.net/dor/20.1001.1.74672588.1401.6.21.6.3.

[39]Farshad Roomi, "Russia's Place in Foreign Policy of Islamic Republic of Iran," *The Politics Quarterly* 50 (2020), 591, 589–610, https://doi.org/10.22059/jpq.2020.264709.1007300.

in Russian foreign policy thinking as a potential source of instability in Central Asia and the South Caucasus. Later, Moscow's view shifted to see Tehran as a potential partner to exhibit autonomy in foreign policy. Yet, what impacted the Russian view of Iran most was Moscow's relations with the West. The position of Iran changed depending on Moscow's decision to integrate with the West, to counterbalance it, or to rebuild its great power position in the Middle East. In all these phases, a combination of pragmatism and strategic opportunism was a dominant feature of Russian policy.

Immediate Impacts of the War in Ukraine on Russo-Iranian Relations (2022–24)

It is not surprising that the West's simultaneous containment of Russia and Iran has convinced both sides to become closer. Moscow and Tehran are leaving behind their differences despite the discord in mentality, culture, religion, historical experience, and even philosophy of life, notwithstanding conflicts of interest and rivalries.[40] In the last decade, the two capitals have signed dozens of cooperation agreements, but as a consequence of the war in Ukraine, efforts to implement these agreements have been sped up. Also, sanctions on Russia have created new areas of cooperation that were previously perceived as less urgent. In this way, the political will on both sides has translated into actions for expanding and deepening bilateral relations in less-developed areas of cooperation. This section outlines the most important developments between February 2022 and 2024.

With Western sanctions imposed on Russia, Moscow replaced Tehran in March 2022 as the most sanctioned state. In the aftermath of the war, the two capitals faced similar operational requirements in resisting Western sanctions. Learning from each other's successful experiences and best practices was among the first reactions. One *Kommersant* report said, "Iran can teach Russia the art of parallel import and gray

---

[40]Vladimir Sazhin, "Rossisko-iranskie otnoshenia v svete vizita v Mosckvu glavi MID Irana [Russian-Iranian Relations in the Light of the Visit of the Iranian Foreign Minister to Moscow]," *Interaffirs*, September 7, 2022, https://interaffairs.ru/news/show/36897.

zone operations."[41] Reports claimed that Ali Shamkhani, the then chief of Iran's Supreme National Security Council, in his meeting with Putin in early February 2023, held an hour-long talk focused on initiatives to offset the impact of Western sanctions on Iran and Russia.[42] Shamkhani followed this agenda in a conversation with Putin's aide Igor Levitin, who traveled to Tehran to oversee joint transit and de-dollarization project advancements.[43] Ali Akbar Velayati, advisor to Iran's supreme leader, acknowledged the importance of sanctions and said, "the sanctions have become the context which facilitates Russia-Iran collaborations."[44] Despite new efforts, the two states encountered difficulties in initiating any major project or investment in the short term.

Iranian goods, such as agricultural products, pharmaceuticals, building materials, cosmetics, dairy products, and even industrial products like gas turbines, started to enter the Russian market on a larger scale in the immediate aftermath of the war. In July 2022, the two sides agreed to double their trade volume to $8 billion in the short term and $15 billion in the mid-term.[45] But trade volume between Russia and Iran grew only about 20 percent, from $4 billion in 2021 to $4.9 billion in 2022.[46] It was only a modest increase compared to the Turkey-Russia trade, which doubled, reaching $68.19 billion in 2022, and the Russian-Indian trade, which surged to $39.8 billion in 2022. As a strategy to resolve obstacles to trade, Moscow and Tehran focused on forming the financial infrastructure needed for trade under sanction. Several monetary and memorandums on interbank cooperation were signed

---

[41]"Moskva i Tegeran uglublyaut svyazi [Moscow and Tehran Deepen Ties]," *Kommersant*, November 2, 2022, https://www.kommersant.ru/doc/5646418.

[42]"Iran Security Chief Had Extensive De-dollarization Talks with Putin," Press TV, April 6, 2012, https://www.presstv.ir/Detail/2023/04/06/701086/Iran-Shamkhani-Putin-de-dollrization-talks.

[43]"Top Iranian Official Hails Global De-dollarization Bids," IRNA, April 9, 2023, https://en.irna.ir/news/85078116/Top-Iranian-official-hails-global-de-dollarization-bids.

[44]Ali Akbar Velayati, "aghle che migoyad? Be samte gharberavim che hamvare doshmani karde ya rusiye che ta tavaneste komak karde [What Is the Logic? Going toward the West That Has Always Animosity or Russia That Helped As Much As It Could]," Khabar Online, June 22, 2022, https://www.khabaronline.ir/news/1653867/ولایتی-مشاور-رهبری-عقل-چه-می-گوید-به-سمت-غرب-برویم-که-همواره

[45]"Iran, Russia Bid to Wipe Dollar Off Their Trades," IRNA News Agency, July 19, 2022, https://en.irna.ir/news/84825899/Iran-Russia-Bid-to-wipe-dollar-off-their-trades.

[46]"Trade Volume between Iran, Russia Has Increased by More than 30%," Iran Press, August 26, 2022, https://iranpress.com/content/64768/trade-volume-between-iran-russia-has-increased-more-than-30.

by the Iranian Central Bank governor with his Russian counterpart in July 2022.[47] Accordingly, the Tehran Stock Exchange launched the Iranian rial/Russian ruble trading, and activities for replacing SWIFT (Society for Worldwide Interbank Financial Telecommunications) with national financial messaging instruments, aiming to de-dollarize mutual trade, began.[48] By the end of 2023, payments between the two countries that use rial and ruble became operational. In parallel, the Russian-led Eurasian Economic Union (EAEU) signed a permanent full-scale free trade agreement (FTA) with Iran in December 2023. The new deal will eliminate customs duties on almost 95 percent of mutual Russia-Iran trade. The regulatory facilitation and the cost savings granted by the FTA could potentially boost Russia-Iran trade.

Also, the two sides signed a $40 billion memorandum of understanding (MOU) between Gazprom and the National Iranian Oil Company. In their sixteenth Joint Economic Commission held in Moscow on October 31, 2022, officials seemed determined to move forward with contracts and the operationalization of the signed MOU. In these meetings, several areas received particular attention, including activating the North-South Transit Corridor (NSTC), establishing free trade zones, coordination on standardization of industrial and agricultural products, and agreement between state export credit guarantees.[49] And finally, efforts aimed to activate region-to-region trade, especially in the Russian North Caucasus and Middle Volga regions, found momentum as they were seen to be candidates for grassroots trade and tourism with Iran.[50]

As Jakub Godzimirski argues in his chapter, the war in Ukraine seemed to intensify competition between Moscow and Tehran to keep their energy share in Chinese and Indian markets with little prospect of cooperation. Some skeptics in Tehran argue that Russia pledges to invest in Iran's oil

---

[47]"Tehran Stock Exchange Launches Ruble-Rial Pair Trades," Tass News Agency, July 19, 2022, https://tass.com/economy/1481927.
[48]"Iran and Russia Agreed for Monetary and Banking Cooperation," IRNA News Agency, July 9, 2022, https://www.irna.ir/news/84815 /329-همک-برای-توسعه-توافق-ایران-و-روسیه-های-پولی-و-بانکی.اری.
[49]"amadegi 10 milyard dolari russiye baraye tamine maliye projehaye eghtesadiye iran [Russian Readiness for $10 Billion Financing of Projects in Iran]," Petro Energy Information Network, November 5, 2022, https://www.shana.ir/news/463985/۱-آمادگی%B0%DB--میلیارد-دلاری-روسیه-برای-تأمین-مالی-پروژه-های-اقتصادی.
[50]"Vizit v Grozniy pokazal zaintetesovannost Irana v regionakh Severnogo Kavkaza (Istochnik) [A Visit to Grozny Showed Iran's Interest in the Regions of the North Caucasus]," Caucasian Knot, November 3, 2022, https://www.kavkaz-uzel.eu/articles/382714/.

and gas projects but only to gain control over them. Such control would allow Moscow to slow the emergence of Iran as an alternative oil and gas exporter to European markets and thus replace Russia.[51] Some Iranian oil and gas industry officials even propose exporting oil to Europe as the only way that Iran can deal with the Russian threat to capture Tehran's oil export markets in Asia.[52] Despite these critiques, the dominant view in Tehran and Moscow seems to be leaning toward energy cooperation. Russian economists have argued that the two countries can manage and avoid competition in the energy sector. Hossein Hosseinzadeh, a member of the Energy Commission of Iran's parliament, thinks, "Iranian Ministry of Petroleum is shifting from competing to interactively cooperating with Russia."[53] He believes that "such a cooperation can help us reach our objective from energy diplomacy." On the ground and in the absence of a Western presence, with even the Chinese reluctant to invest because of US sanctions, Russia emerged as Iran's top foreign investor with a $2.76 billion investment in 2022. Iran's oil and gas industry signed contracts worth $6.5 billion, with projects progressing between 7 and 35 percent.[54]

Cooperation on transit routes was an area that received the most attention from Moscow. This development was because the war and sanctions interrupted Russia's westward logistical corridors. Suddenly, a twenty-year-long NSTC project was found to have strategic value for the Kremlin. The NSTC passes through Iran and Azerbaijan and links Russia to the Arab states in the Persian Gulf, India, and Bangladesh. While Tehran was pushing for the project for decades, it became Moscow's priority only after the war in Ukraine. The NSTC counterweights Russian dependency on the Turkish route and the Chinese Belt and Road projects, helping Moscow to balance them. Moscow and Tehran intensified works on a two-axis strategy to activate the NSTC. The first axis linked the Iranian railway system to Azerbaijan and then Russia. Both sides boosted

---

[51] Alex Vatanka and Abdolrasool Divsallar, "Can the West Stop Russian-Iranian Convergence?" Middle East Institute, April 3, 2023, https://mei.edu/publications/can-west-stop-russian-iranian-convergence.
[52] Vatanka and Divsallar, "Can the West Stop Russian-Iranian Convergence?."
[53] Hossein Hosseinzadeh, "fasli no az monasebate iran va russiye aghaz shode ast [A New Chapter Has Begun in the Relations between Iran and Russia in the Field of Energy]," Tahlil Bazaar, November 6, 2022, http://bitly.ws/xyzE.
[54] Javad Owji, "Doran e talaei: Panjerehaye iran va russiye goshode shod [The Golden Time: Windows for Russian-Iranian Trade Is Opening," *Mashal* (Iran's Oil Industry Magazine), November 5, 2022, http://files.mashal.ir/249.pdf.

efforts to finance the Astra-Rasht railway project, which is the critical unfinished segment of this route. In what can only be interpreted as a Russian commitment to invest in the project, President Putin's aide, Igor Levitin, visited the project on several occasions. Also, first deputy prime minister Andrei Belousov proposed establishing a joint railway operator for Russia-Azerbaijan-Iran. He added that "[the operator] will provide end-to-end service and a high level of logistics services."[55]

Despite technical challenges, the second axis was revitalized in 2022, which entailed a sea-based segment of the NSTC, linking Iran and Russia directly through the Caspian Sea. The trans-Caspian route was able to resolve the bottlenecks of the NSTC's land segment and secure the project from each side's political turbulences with third parties—in this case, Iran-Azerbaijan tensions. To this end, and for the first time, Moscow allowed the passage of Iranian ships through the Volga-Caspian Seaway Canal and agreed to build container carrier ships for Iran's Caspian Sea fleet.[56] At the same time, Iran also joined China in helping Russia to dredge the canal.[57] Besides, along the port of Solyanka, Iranian shipping lines started to operate in three new ports, including the port of Makhachkala, the ports of the VTS group of companies, as well as the port of Olya in Astrakhan.[58]

The implications of war were likely stronger on the bilateral security ties than anywhere else. Three core areas, including the nuclear field, the military sector, and the regional policies, were each affected by the war uniquely but more or less in important ways. Less than two weeks

---

[55]Polina Pisareva, "V Rossii obsuzhdaut vozmozhnost sozdaniya edinogo logisticheskogo operatora mezhdu Rossiei, Azerbaijanom i Iranom [Russia Is Discussing the Possibility of Creating a Single Logistics Operator between Russia, Azerbaijan and Iran]," Transport News, October 31, 2022, https://www.transport-news.ru/counseling/v-rossii-obsuzhdayut-vozmozhnost-sozdanie-edinogo-logisticheskogo-operatora-mezhdu-rossiej-azerbajdzhanom-i-iranom/.

[56]"Gharardade sachet yek farvand kashti mian iran va rusiye emza shod [The Contract for Building One Ship Signed between Iran and Russia]," Fars News Agency, January 4, 2023, https://www.farsnews.ir/news/140 1101 4000 471/قرار داد-ساخت-یک-فروند-کشتی-میان-ایران-و-روسیه-امضا-شد

[57]Paul Goble, "Iran Joins China in Dredging Russia's Volga River, Further Solidifying Anti-Western Axis," The Jamestown Foundation, February 24, 2023, https://jamestown.org/program/iran-joins-china-in-dredging-russias-volga-river-further-solidifying-anti-western-axis/.

[58]"Iran budet exportirovat svii tovari v Rossiu cherez porti Olya, Astrakhan, Makhachkala [Iran Will Export Its Goods to Russia through the Ports of Olya, Astrakhan, Makhachkala]," Morvesti, December 6, 2022, http://www.morvesti.ru/news/1679/99677/.

after the Russian invasion of Ukraine, Iran's nuclear file was the first to be impacted. Russian foreign minister Sergey Lavrov said, "We need a guarantee that these [US] sanctions will not in any way touch the regime of trade, economic, and investment relations which is laid down in the JCPOA."[59] Russian demand created dissatisfaction in Tehran and was perceived by the Iranians as instrumentalizing the Vienna Talks to secure Russian interests elsewhere.[60] Iran's foreign minister, Hossein Amir-Abdollahian, traveled to Moscow to urge Lavrov to step back—a meeting he later described as "serious and heavy discussions."[61] However, in the following months, the Kremlin leaned toward shielding the Iranian nuclear position in the Vienna Talks and the IAEA board of governors. This fact eventually contributed to a tougher Iranian stand that rejected giving concessions, thus contributing to the standstill of nuclear talks.

Russia vetoed the June 2022 resolution, which called on Iran to cooperate fully with the agency's investigation into undeclared sites. At least since June 2022, Moscow has placed a premium on Iran's partnership with Russia and on the utility of Iran's nuclear hedge in serving Russia's broader geopolitical aims.[62] This policy opposed Russia's approach toward the JCPOA between January 2021 and February 2022, when Moscow was willing to criticize Iran and urge it to show restraint. As Anastasia Malygina argues in her chapter, Russia's official position toward nuclear nonproliferation commitments did not change in this period. However, judging based on the implications of the JCPOA revival, Moscow might be less comfortable with a scenario in which successful talks end important parts of US sanctions on Iran at a time when international sanctions on Russia have just begun.[63] This will boost Tehran's leverage over the Kremlin and may even disincentivize the Islamic Republic

---

[59]Parisa Hafezi and Francois Murphy, "Russia's Demand for US Guarantees May Hit Nuclear Talks, Iran Official Says," Reuters, March 5, 2022, https://www.reuters.com/world/middle-east/iran-nuclear-official-kamlavandi-says-god-willing-there-will-be-an-understanding-2022-03-05/.
[60]"Iranian Official Says Russia Could Harm Nuclear Talks by Linking Sanctions against It to Deal," RFE/RL, March 5, 2022, https://www.rferl.org/a/iran-iaea-grossi-visit/31737358.html.
[61]Hossein Amir-Abdollahian, Closed-Door Speech at Italian Institute of International Affairs (IAI), July 12, 2022.
[62]Hanna Notte, "Russia's Invasion of Ukraine: The Iran Nuclear Price Tag," Friedrich-Ebert-Stiftung, February 2023, 4–10, https://library.fes.de/pdf-files/international/20083.pdf.
[63]Sazhin, "Russian-Iranian Relations"; Elena Dunaeva, in discussion with the author, May 1, 2023.

from deepening ties with Moscow. In this context, the US Intelligence Community's claims become meaningful when they said, "Moscow may provide assistance to Tehran for acquiring additional nuclear materials, potentially further shortening Iran's so-called 'breakout time' to create a nuclear weapon."[64]

In the military sector, the war certainly caused the biggest shifts. It put Russia on the receiver side of military assistance for the first time in the history of bilateral relations. Moscow's need for Tehran's assistance proved urgent and significant after Russia ran uncomfortably low on missile stocks, given the heavy expenditure from February to June 2022 and the requirements to maintain a contingency stockpile to deter NATO.[65] Moscow turned to Tehran to buy thousands of Shahed-136, Shahed-129, Shahed-191, and Mohajer-6 drones and received operational training. By mid-2022, the Russian Army became critically reliant on Iranian drones to maintain its long-range strike capability, implementing the strategy of hitting Ukrainian infrastructures and depleting Ukrainian missile defense stockpiles. Other reports by *The Wall Street Journal* claimed that between November 2022 and April 2023, cargo ships through the Caspian Sea had carried more than 300,000 artillery shells and a million rounds of ammunition from Iran to Russia.[66]

Tehran's security assistance to Russia led to harsh European criticism and was seen as a destabilizing intervention in European security affairs through supporting the aggressor side. Europe, in response, imposed several rounds of sanctions on Iran, and the Brussels-Tehran relationship hit its lowest by the winter of 2022. Except for direct costs, most of what Iran received as payoff for its security assistance to Russia seems unclear. Ironically, some in Tehran accused Russia of leaking the news about drone export to complicate US-Iran nuclear talks. Conversely, Iranian sources announced that Russia has agreed to deliver advanced SU-35 fighter jets

---

[64]Natasha Bertrand, "Exclusive: Iran Is Seeking Russia's Help to Bolster Its Nuclear Program, US Intel Officials Believe," CNN, November 4, 2022, https://edition.cnn.com/2022/11/04/politics/iran-russia-nuclear-program.
[65]Justin Bronk, Nick Reynolds, and Jack Watling, "The Russian Air War and Ukrainian Requirements for Air Defense," Royal United Service Institute (RUSI), November 7, 2022, https://rusi.org/explore-our-research/publications/special-resources/russian-air-war-and-ukrainian-requirements-air-defence.
[66]Dion Nissenbaum and Benoit Faucon "Iran Ships Ammunition to Russia by Caspian Sea to Aid Invasion of Ukraine," *The Wall Street Journal*, April 24, 2022, https://www.wsj.com/articles/iran-ships-ammunition-to-russia-by-caspian-sea-to-aid-invasion-of-ukraine-e74e8585.

to Iran. A claim that Russian authorities have not confirmed by 2024 and former officials involved in the previous rounds of the Moscow-Tehran defense talks declined states that "discussions over SU-35 delivery was on the table since 2020 and had nothing to do with the war in Ukraine. The delays were due to financial problems."[67] While it remained largely unclear what Tehran will likely receive from Moscow in military terms, Western sources claimed that Russia had facilitated the transfer of some of the captured Western technologies to Iran, such as the Javelin anti-tank missiles and the Stinger antiaircraft systems.[68]

On the regional front, Moscow's continued dependency on Iranian drone provisions for what seems to be a prolonged war created new leverages for Tehran. In Syria, for example, Anton Mardasov observes Moscow's reluctance to strongly impede Iranian actions, although previously it could oppose them, if not publicly, then covertly.[69] Hamidreza Azizi, in his chapter, shows that a year after the war in Ukraine, Moscow neither had enough bandwidth nor had the political will to contain Tehran in Syria. Moscow's reliance on Iranian forces to keep the status quo increased, while Russian troops favored concentrating on more strategic areas in the East Mediterranean. This situation was because of the Russian deficit in military resources and the challenges of projecting power in the long term as the war in Ukraine prolonged, as well as Moscow's confusion in revising its strategy in the Middle East.[70] These assessments led to a new division of labor between Tehran and Moscow, according to which the Iranian forces confronted the revival of radical armed groups and maintained pro-Assad positions in eastern and central Syria.[71] In addition, Russia gradually leaned toward the Iranian standpoint on the Israeli strikes in Syria, especially as new complications

---

[67] Mehdi Sanaei (former Iranian ambassador to Russia), in discussion with the author, April 2, 2023.
[68] Joe Saballa, "Russia Sending Captured US Weapons to Iran to Reverse-Engineer," The Defense Post, March 13, 2023, https://www.thedefensepost.com/2023/03/13/russia-us-weapons-iran/.
[69] Anton Mardasov comments in https://www.al-monitor.com/originals/2023/02/ukraine-war-year-1-russia-iran-alignment-threatens-delicate-middle-east-balance#ixzz7vjwFqYAi.
[70] Anonymous speaker, "Chatham House and UCLA Burkle Centre Closed-Door Discussion on 'The Ukraine Effect: Great Power Relations and the Middle East,'" October 18, 2022.
[71] Hamidreza Azizi, "The Impact of the Ukraine War on Iran-Russia Relations in Syria," Al-Sharq Strategic Forum, June 17, 2022, https://research.sharqforum.org/2022/06/17/iran-russia-relations-in-syria/.

emerged in Moscow-Tel Aviv relations. Iran benefited from more operational freedom and assisted the Assad regime in boosting its air-defense capabilities while improving its early warning assets across Syria.

Russo-Iranian relations in this period included many more important areas, such as participating in multilateral formats to resolve security concerns in Afghanistan, official accession of Iran to the Shanghai Cooperation Organization (SCO) in July 2023, BRICS bloc[72] invitation to Iran to join its ranks, and closer dialogue between Moscow and Tehran on Azerbaijan-Armenia peace talks. But it is important to note that many of these areas of cooperation were initiated before the war in Ukraine and influenced in minor ways by war dynamics. For example, Iran submitted its application for a full SCO membership in 2008, and negotiations at the 2021 summit in Dushanbe led to the approval of the Iranian request before the Ukraine war. In general, the overall improvement of Russo-Iranian political dialogues indirectly contributed to closer cooperation in other regional files like in Afghanistan. That being said, the gap between Russia and Iran on certain regional issues, for example, the divergence of perceptions about the peace talks between Azerbaijan and Armenia, was not resolved notwithstanding Moscow and Tehran's closer interactions after the Ukraine war. This means that important aspects of the Russo-Iranian interactions remained outside the impacts of the war in Ukraine.

Content of This Volume

This book is organized into three parts. Part 1 focuses on Moscow and Tehran's mutual expectations and assessment of each other's role and power in the international system after the war in Ukraine. Nicole Grajewski begins the book with a discussion of domestic debates in Russia about its relations with Iran after the outbreak of war in Ukraine. She focuses on two critical questions: What are Moscow's expectations from its partnership with Tehran? Has the war impacted the Russian assessment of Iran's position in its foreign policy agenda? She explores domestic political debates, especially in foreign policy establishments, and argues whether Russian public opinion has any role in Moscow's decisions toward Iran. Grajewski's analysis provides a framework to understand the role of elite

---

[72] The bloc consists of Brazil, Russia, India, China, and South Africa.

discussions in defining Russian interests and objectives in interacting with Tehran, especially during crises, and advances our understanding of how partners' perceptions of commitments and expectations amid international crises have impacted the process of alliances. In particular, it expands on the themes of strategic empathy, Eastern orientation, and resilience and resistance.

Internal debates in Iran about the country's response to the Russian invasion of Ukraine are what Mahmood Shoori discusses in Chapter 2. Two centuries after the Russo-Iranian wars, Iranians still remember the war's memories and the Soviet invasion of Iran in post–Second World War. Sensitivities to any decision that involves Russia have dominated political debates in Tehran and interfere with how the Islamic Republic elites view Russia. To elaborate on these aspects, the chapter investigates what the Iranian social media and public reactions to the Russian war in Ukraine were. How did different political groups react to the war? How did social mistrust and fear of Russian political interference and infiltration impact the Islamic Republic leaders' decisions about their partnership with Russia? How do internal debates among various actors inside Iran's foreign policy institutions shape Tehran's decisions toward Russia? The chapter conducts an in-depth examination of both public and political elite perceptions of Russia through news articles, speeches, and social media posts and explores particular common threads among ideologically divergent groups. Shoori shows that contrary to the government's best efforts, public opinion in Iran influences even the most conservative administrations' foreign policy goals and behaviors.

Chapter 3 makes a deep dive into a less-discussed dimension of the relations. Diana Galeeva explores the role of identity in Iranian and Russian relations and the two states' shared perception of a so-called cultural cancelation and denial of rights by the West. The Western response to the Russian invasion of Ukraine made Russian elites feel a similar experience that Iran had under the US Maximum Pressure campaign and decades of crisis over its nuclear program. Galeeva looks at the ways these experiences and the threat of colliding with the West's coercive soft power impact the Russian and Iranian elites' worldviews toward each other. What is the role of a shared experience of confronting the liberal order and common threat perception in strengthening the two political systems' mutual strategic sympathy and understanding? Given Russia's sizeable Muslim population, what role does the shared Muslim identity play? Based on considerable fieldwork observations in Russia, and learning from ongoing discourse of bilateral relations, in addition to primary and secondary sources, Galeeva's chapter effectively combines the role of identity politics, shared threat perception, and strategic sympathy between Moscow and Tehran as an analytical perspective on relations.

Part 2 moves forward to focus on the impact of geostrategic factors on relations. The chapters in this part explain whether geostrategic factors play a limiting role that constrains relations or act as drivers of relations. Mark N. Katz begins this part with a chapter on the implications of Russian policy for Iran in the MENA and Mediterranean regions. His chapter addresses the following questions: Will Russian Middle East policy remain intact after the war in Ukraine? How can Arab states' strategic neutrality in the war and growingly bumpy relations with Israel impact Moscow's regional policy? What is Russia's preferred balance of forces in the Middle East, and can the war in Ukraine change the Russian perspective? Katz compares Russian Middle East policy and power instruments before and after the war to track shifts and changes in tools, objectives, and interests of Russian policy in the region. He explores different scenarios regarding how the outcome of the war in Ukraine might affect Russian policy toward MENA and the Mediterranean and how this might impact Iran, in particular, given Russia's commitment to its invasion of Ukraine. The chapter concludes that while Putin will likely continue to try to expand Russia's influence in the MENA region, the war in Ukraine will inevitably impact Moscow's ability to conduct foreign policy in the Middle East.

Anastasia Malygina in Chapter 5 investigates shifts in Russia's nuclear policy toward Iran based on the principle of strategic stability. One of the first areas impacted by the war in Ukraine was the two countries' nuclear collaborations, including the negotiations to restore the JCPOA. It remains an open question whether the war would minimize the possibility of nuclear cooperation between Moscow and Tehran, including on civilian reactors and international commitments. Can the deterioration of US-Russia relations create new incentives and spaces for Moscow to accommodate a nuclear-armed Iran? Can the growing tensions with the West and the prospects of a stronger anti-Western partnership alter Russian nonproliferation principles? How will Russia's perception of nuclear proliferation and strategic stability in the Middle East limit its relations with Iran? Malygina attempts to answer these questions using Russian official narratives, and documents and strategic principles governing these narratives. She argues that the Ukrainian war has not altered Russia's assessments of the Iranian nuclear program, and it is not going to make Moscow more tolerant of nuclear proliferation risks. According to Malygina's findings, Moscow seems to have no intention of making the JCPOA a victim of the intensified confrontation between Russia and the West and continues to see the Vienna Talks as a critical procedure for maintaining Russia's role as a facilitator.

In Chapter 6, Abdolrasool Divsallar examines the impact of systemic factors on the strategies of alliance between Moscow and Tehran. He explains that developments and shifts at the domestic and international levels have factored in new drivers that are increasing interdependence between the two states. Divsallar argues that developments after February 24, 2022, have eroded the structure of some of the past limits, while both sides resort to more normative dispute resolution mechanisms because of the benefits they see in interdependence. Using an authoritarian integration model, the chapter presents regime survival as the fundamental factor that has caused the leadership in both capitals to overcome existing limits. In this perspective, the overall contribution of closer ties in making both political systems resistant to hybrid internal and external pressures justifies some losses that they may encounter in some areas.

Part 3 contextualizes the war's implications on specific bilateral issues. In particular, the chapters here aim to see how stronger cooperation on military-security issues and sanction evasion meet with new forces of divergence that are also strengthened by the war—especially divergence over new strategic vacuums and conflicts of interest in Syria and the energy market. In Chapter 7, Jeffrey Mankoff and Mahsa Rouhi engage with the idea of anti-Americanism and a dream for the non-Western order as the driver of Russo-Iranian ties. The chapter aims to help understand the ways strategic changes in great power competitions might influence Moscow's calculus toward its relations with Iran. The chapter deals with one fundamental question: Has the war strengthened Moscow and Tehran's revisionist stands, creating stronger shared values and threat perceptions to boost cooperation? Mankoff and Rouhi suggest that Russia and Iran believe norms underpinning the "liberal international order" reflect not just US policy preferences but also US historical experiences and are, therefore, not relevant for states whose rulers self-identify as non-Western. The authors argue that to the extent that the Kremlin and Tehran perceive US centrality to the global order as a threat to their core interests, they are ready to put away differences and competition.

Chapter 8 looks at the prospects for Russia-Iran economic relations. As Western sanctions on Russia become more comprehensive, Moscow and Tehran are seeing new interests in facilitating trade and business. Esfandyar Batmanghelidj looks at economic initiatives that took place after the war to see what the long-term impacts of the war on economic and trade relations between Iran and Russia can look like. Despite political willingness on both sides, he identifies two factors that influence trade between the two countries the most. First, there are a number of constraints that have long dogged economic ties. These include banking constraints, logistical constraints, and institutional constraints. Second, Batmanghelidj argues that cooperation between Russia and Iran should be sealed from increased competition in other areas. The chapter provides a detailed analysis of the structure of the two countries' economies and the fact that they export and import many of the same goods, thus making the intensified competition a natural reaction of the forces of the market. Accordingly, both sides have the same partners, and so far, Russia seems to be expanding trade with those partners, including China and Turkey, at the expense of Iran.

Jakub M. Godzimirski in Chapter 9 examines the energy relations between Moscow and Tehran. His research shows the extent to which Iran can challenge Russia's position as a major global energy player. Based on official documents and statistics, the chapter shows that a mix of overlapping and contradicting strategic energy interests causes a conflict of interest between the two countries. Godzimirski claims that this conflict of interest has expanded in the energy sector as a result of the war in Ukraine. He further tries to explore whether the two countries' inability to resolve such disputes can cause divergence and contradicting strategic energy interests. Godzimirski's main argument is that given Moscow and Tehran's close mutual political support and their anti-Western narrative, Iranian leaders are not willing to help the West in the challenges raised due to the Russian energy policy, and so the top leadership in Tehran does not opt to replace Russia in the EU market. In addition to structural- and market-related factors, given the EU and Iran's difficult relations, the Europeans also do not see Iran as a reliable substitute for Russian energy.

Finally, the last chapter deals with the impact of the war in Ukraine on the strategic vacuums in the Middle East. Hamidreza Azizi, in this chapter, studies the implications of the Ukraine war on Moscow and Tehran's cooperation in Syria. The chapter looks at the following questions: How will the Ukraine war influence the two countries' collaboration in Syria? Will Russia's calculus toward Syria and appetite to play a role be expected to shift? Will Russian readjustments of its external power projection likely affect Iranian decisions? And from a long-term perspective, can a new power-sharing dynamic between Iran and Russia be expected in Syria?

Bibliography

Amir-Abdollahian, Hossein. "Closed-Door Speech at Italian Institute of International Affairs (IAI)," July 12, 2022.

Anonymous speaker, "Chatham House and UCLA Burkle Centre Closed-Door Discussion on 'The Ukraine Effect: Great Power Relations and the Middle East,'" October 18, 2022.

Asgarian, Hossein. *Outlook of Iran–Russia Relations*. Tehran: Tehran International Studies and Research Institute, 2015.

Azizi, Hamidreza. "Close but Complicated: Iran-Russia Relations in the Middle East Amid the War in Ukraine." Friedrich-Ebert-Stiftung, February 2023. https://library.fes.de/pdf-files/international/20084.pdf.

Azizi, Hamidreza. "The Impact of the Ukraine War on Iran-Russia Relations in Syria." Al-Sharq Strategic Forum, June 17, 2022. https://research.sharqforum.org/2022/06/17/iran-russia-relations-in-syria/.

Bertrand, Natasha. "Exclusive: Iran Is Seeking Russia's Help to Bolster Its Nuclear Program: US Intel Officials Believe." CNN, November 4, 2022. https://edition.cnn.com/2022/11/04/politics/iran-russia-nuclear-program.

Bronk, Justin, Nick Reynolds, and Jack Watling. "The Russian Air War and Ukrainian Requirements for Air Defense." Royal United Service Institute (RUSI), November 7, 2022. https://rusi.org/explore-our-research/publications/special-resources/russian-air-war-and-ukrainian-requirements-air-defence.

Caucasian Knot. "Vizit v Grozniy pokazal zaintetesovannost Irana v regionakh Severnogo Kavkaza (Istochnik) [A Visit to Grozny Showed Iran's Interest in the Regions of the North Caucasus]." November 3, 2022. https://www.kavkaz-uzel.eu/articles/382714/.

Divsallar, Abdolrasool. "Protective Integration and Rising Interdependency: Making Sense of Iranian Response to Russian Invasion of Ukraine." *The Chinese Journal of International Politics* (forthcoming).

Divsallar, Abdolrasool, and Pyotr Kortonuv. "The Fallout of the US-Iran Confrontation for Russia: Revisiting Factors in Moscow's Calculus." Robert Schuman Centre for Advanced Studies and Russian International Affair Council Research. Florence: European University Press, 2020. https://doi.org/10.2870/678655.

Divsallar, Abdolrasool, and Yulia Roknifard. "Iran, Russia, and the Militias: Seeds of Tactical Cooperation." ISPI, March 23, 2023. https://www.ispionl

ine.it/en/publication/iran-russia-and-the-militias-seeds-of-tactical-cooperation-121968.

Dolat.ir. "Ayatollah Raisi: The Excellent Relations between Iran and Russia Are on the Path of Strategic Relations." January 19, 2022. https://dolat.ir/detail/378458.

Fallahi, Ehsan. "Seire tahavol rahbord defaei rusie az 1991 ta 2021 bar asase olgohaye rahbordi SWOT [The Evolution of Russia's Security Defense Strategy 1991-2021 based on SWOT Strategic Models]." *Strategic Management Studies of National Defense* 21 (2022): 162–89. https://dorl.net/dor/20.1001.1.74672588.1401.6.21.6.3.

Fars News Agency. "Gharardade sachet yek farvand kashti mian iran va rusiye emza shod [The Contract for Building One Ship Signed between Iran and Russia]." January 4, 2023. https://www.farsnews.ir/news/14011014000471/قرارداد-ساخت-یک-فروند-کشتی-میان-ایران-و-روسیه-امضا-شد.

Ghani, Parham, and Abbasgholi Asgarian. "Manehaye sheklgiri etelafe rahbordi iran va russiye: Motale moredi jange suriye [Barriers to the Formation of the Strategic Alliance between the Islamic Republic of Iran and Russia: Case Study, Iran-Russia Alliance in the Syrian Crisis]." *Journal of Central Eurasia Studies* 14 (2021): 229–49.

Goble, Paul. "Iran Joins China in Dredging Russia's Volga River, Further Solidifying Anti-Western Axis." The Jamestown Foundation, February 24, 2023. https://jamestown.org/program/iran-joins-china-in-dredging-russias-volga-river-further-solidifying-anti-western-axis/.

Hafezi, Parisa, and Francois Murphy. "Russia's Demand for US Guarantees May Hit Nuclear Talks, Iran Official Says." Reuters, March 5, 2022. https://www.reuters.com/world/middle-east/iran-nuclear-official-kamlavandi-says-god-willing-there-will-be-an-understanding-2022-03-05/.

Hosseinzadeh, Hossein. "fasli no az monasebate iran va russiye aghaz shode ast [A New Chapter Has Begun in the Relations between Iran and Russia in the Field of Energy]." Tahlil Bazaar, November 6, 2022. http://bitly.ws/xyzE.

IBNA News Agency. "Sali ke ba mooshakhaye doshman shoro shod [A Year Started with Enemy's Missile]." March 27, 2022. https://www.ibna.ir/fa/report/319625/سالی-موشک-های-دشمن-شروع-صدام-تهران.

Iran Press. "Trade Volume between Iran, Russia Has Increased by More Than 30%." August 26, 2022. https://iranpress.com/content/64768/trade-volume-between-iran-russia-has-increased-more-than-30.

The Iran Primer. "Iran's Deepening Strategic Alliance with Russia." April 25, 2023. https://iranprimer.usip.org/blog/2023/feb/24/iran's-deepening-strategic-alliance-russia.

IRNA News Agency. "Iran and Russia Agreed for Monetary and Banking Cooperation." July 9, 2022. https://www.irna.ir/news/84815329/توافق-ایران-و-روسیه-برای-توسعه-همکاری-های-پولی-و-بانکی.

IRNA News Agency. "Iran, Russia Bid to Wipe Dollar Off Their Trades." July 19, 2022. https://en.irna.ir/news/84825899/Iran-Russia-bid-to-wipe-dollar-off-their-trades.

IRNA News Agency. "Top Iranian Official Hails Global De-Dollarization Bids." April 9, 2023. https://en.irna.ir/news/85078116/Top-Iranian-official-hails-global-de-dollarization-bids.

Javadi Arjmand, Mohamda Javad, and Abdolrasool Divsallar. "rabeteye amniyat va tose-e: mored ravabete iran va shoravi [Security-Development Nexus in Foreign Policy: The Case of Soviet-Iran Relations]." *Politics Quarterly* 49, no. 2 (2019): 311–32. https://doi.org/10.22059/jpq.2019.228045.1007024.

Karami, Jahangir. "ravabete iran va rusiye az 1369-1388: zamineha, avamel va mahdodiyatha [Iran-Russia Relations from 1989-2009: Grounds, Factors and Constraints]." *Journal of Iran and Central Eurasia Studies* 6 (2010): 111–36.

Khlopkov, Anton, and Anna Lutkova, "The Bushehr NPP: Why It Take So Long?" *Center for Energy and Security Studies*, August 1, 2010. http://ceness-russia.org/data/doc/TheBushehrNPP-WhyDidItTakeSoLong.pdf.

Kommersant. "Moskva i Tegeran uglublyaut svyazi [Moscow and Tehran Deepen Ties]." November 2, 2022. https://www.kommersant.ru/doc/5646418.

Koolaee, Elaheh, Hamed Mousavi, and Afifeh Abedi, "Fluctuations in Iran-Russia Relations during the Past Four Decades." *Iran and the Caucasus* 24, no. 2 (2020): 216–32. https://doi.org/10.1163/1573384X-20200206.

Kozhanov, Nikolay. "Putin's War in Ukraine and Prospects for Russian-Iranian Relations." Chatham House, April 4, 2023. https://kalam.chathamhouse.org/articles/putins-war-in-ukraine-and-prospects-for-russian-iranian-relations?s=35.

Kozhanov, Nikolay. "Russian-Iranian Relations through the Prism of the Syrian Crisis." *Insight Turkey* 19, no. 41 (2017): 105–24.

Lana Ravandi-Fadai. "Partnerstvo bez obyazatelstv: osobennosti rossiysko-itanskikh otnosheni v poslednie desyatiletiya [Partnership without Commitments: Features of Russian-Iranian Relations in Recent Decades]." *Russia and the World: Scientific Dialogue* 1, no. 1 (2021): 42–50. https://doi.org/10.53658/RW2021-1-1-42-50

Mardasov, Anton. Comments in Jared Szuba, "Ukraine War at Year 1: Russia-Iran Alignment Threatens Delicate Middle East Balance." Al-Monitor, February 24, 2023. https://www.al-monitor.com/originals/2023/02/ukraine-war-year-1-russia-iran-alignment-threatens-delicate-middle-east-balance#ixzz7vjwFqYAi.

Mehr News. "Iranian, Russian FMs Hold Talks in Moscow." March 29, 2023. https://en.mehrnews.com/news/198885/Iranian-Russian-FMs-hold-talks-in-Moscow.

Middle East Institute. "Transactional or Strategic? The Future of Russo-Iranian Relations." April 13, 2023. https://www.mei.edu/events/transactional-or-strategic-future-russo-iranian-relations.

Morvesti. "Iran budet exportirovat svii tovari v Rossiu cherez porti Olya, Astrakhan, Makhachkala [Iran Will Export Its Goods to Russia through the Ports of Olya, Astrakhan, Makhachkala]." December 6, 2022. http://www.morvesti.ru/news/1679/99677/.

Mottaghi, Ebrahim, Zohreh Postinchi, Saeed Mojaradi, and Amir Hayat Moghadam. "amalgaraei rahbordi dar ravabete iran va russiye [Strategic

Pragmatism in I.R. Iran–Russia Relations]." *Scientific Quarterly Journal of Defense Strategy* 12, no. 2 (2014): 117–47. https://ds.sndu.ac.ir/article_660.html?lang=en.

Nissenbaum, Dion, and Benoit Faucon. "Iran Ships Ammunition to Russia by Caspian Sea to Aid Invasion of Ukraine." *The Wall Street Journal*, April 24, 2022. https://www.wsj.com/articles/iran-ships-ammunition-to-russia-by-caspian-sea-to-aid-invasion-of-ukraine-e74e8585.

Noori, Alireza. "Mahiyat tajdide nazar talabi rusiye va chin: siyasat va manafe Iran [The Nature of Russian and Chinese Revisionism: Iran's Policy and Interests]." *Journal of Central Eurasia Studies* 14, no. 2 (2021): 371–96. https://www.doi.org/10.22059/jcep.2021.328326.450023.

Notte, Hanna. "Don't Expect Any More Russian Help on the Iran Nuclear Deal." War on the Rocks, November 3, 2022. https://warontherocks.com/2022/11/dont-expect-any-more-russian-help-on-the-iran-nuclear-deal/.

Notte, Hanna. "Russia's Invasion of Ukraine: The Iran Nuclear Price Tag." Friedrich-Ebert-Stiftung, February 2023, 4–10. https://library.fes.de/pdf-files/international/20083.pdf.

Omidi, Ali. "Russian-Iranian Ties: Strategic Alliance, Strategic Coalition, or Strategic Alignment (Partnership)." *Russian Politics* 7 (2022): 341–65. https://doi.org/10.30965/24518921-00604023.

Owji, Javad. "Doran e talaei: Panjerehaye iran va russiye goshode shod [The Golden Time: Windows for Russian-Iranian Trade Is Opening," *Mashal* [Iran's Oil Industry Magazine]." November 5, 2022. http://files.mashal.ir/249.pdf.

Petro Energy Information Network. "amadegi 10 milyard dolari russiye baraye tamine maliye projehaye eghtesadiye iran [Russian Readiness for $10 Billion Financing of Projects in Iran]." November 5, 2022. https://www.shana.ir/news/463985/۱۰-میلیارد-دلاری-روسیه-برای-تأمین-مالی-پروژه-های-DB%B0%آمادگی-اقتصادی.

Pisareva, Polina. "V Rossii obsuzhdaut vozmozhnost sozdaniya edinogo logisticheskogo operatora mezhdu Rossiei, Azerbajjanom i Iranom [Russia Is Discussing the Possibility of Creating a Single Logistics Operator between Russia, Azerbaijan and Iran]." Transport News, October 31, 2022. https://www.transport-news.ru/counseling/v-rossii-obsuzhdayut-vozmozhnost-sozdanie-edinogo-logisticheskogo-operatora-mezhdu-rossiej-azerbajdzhanom-i-iranom/.

Press TV. "Iran Security Chief Had Extensive De-dollarization Talks with Putin." April 6, 2012. https://www.presstv.ir/Detail/2023/04/06/701086/Iran-Shamkhani-Putin-de-dollrization-talks.

RFE/RL. "Iranian Official Says Russia Could Harm Nuclear Talks by Linking Sanctions Against It to Deal." March 5, 2022. https://www.rferl.org/a/iran-iaea-grossi-visit/31737358.html.

Roomi, Farshad. "Russia's Place in Foreign Policy of Islamic Republic of Iran." *The Politics Quarterly* 50 (2020): 589–610. https://doi.org/10.22059/jpq.2020.264709.1007300.

Saballa, Joe. "Russia Sending Captured US Weapons to Iran to Reverse-Engineer." The Defense Post, March 13, 2023. https://www.thedefensepost.com/2023/03/13/russia-us-weapons-iran/.

Sadchenko, V. "Sadchenko V. Yuzhni Kavkaz V peresechenii nazionalnikh interesov Rossii i Irana (2014-2022 gg.) [South Caucasus at the Intersection of National Interests Russia and Iran (2014–2022)]," in *Russia and Iran: Five Centuries of Cooperation*, edited by Bezborodov Alexander, Vitaly Naumkin, and Alikberov Alikber, 74–85, Moscow: Russian State University for the Humanities, 2022.

Sariolghalam, Mahmoud. "chera ravabet e iran va russiye estrategic shode ast? [Why Iran's Relations with Russia Have Become Strategic?]." May 11, 2023. https://telegra.ph/sariolghalam-05-11-2.

Sazhin, Vladimir. "Rossisko-iranskie otnoshenia v svete vizita v Mosckvu glavi MID Irana [Russian-Iranian Relations in the Light of the Visit of the Iranian Foreign Minister to Moscow]." *Interaffirs*, September 7, 2022. https://interaffairs.ru/news/show/36897.

Tabatabai, Ariane, and Dina Esfandiary. *Triple Axis: Iran's Relations with Russia and China*. London: I.B. Tauris, 2021.

Tass News Agency. "Russia, Iran Wrapping Up Work on New Strategic Partnership Deal, Says Putin." September 15, 2022. https://tass.com/politics/1508011.

Tass News Agency. "Tehran Stock Exchange Launches Ruble-Rial Pair Trades." July 19, 2022. https://tass.com/economy/1481927.

Tazmini, Ghonche. "Russian and Iran: Strategic Partners or Provisional Counterweights?" in *Russian Foreign Policy Towards the Middle East: New Trends, Old Traditions*, edited by Nikolay Kozhanov, 117–40, London: Hurst, 2022.

Valizadeh, Akbar, and Somayeh Kazemi. "tasire moalefehaye farhange rahbordi bar ravabete dujanebe va mantaghaei iran va russiye [The Influence of Strategic Culture Components on Bilateral and Regional Relations between Iran and Russia]." *Journal of Central Eurasia Studies* 15, no. 1 (2022): 387–410. https://doi.org/10.22059/jcep.2022.337629.450051.

Vatanka, Alex, and Abdolrasool Divsallar. "Can the West Stop Russian-Iranian Convergence?" Middle East Institute, April 3, 2023. https://mei.edu/publications/can-west-stop-russian-iranian-convergence.

Velayati, Ali Akbar. "aghle che migoyad? Be samte gharberavim che hamvare doshmani karde ya rusiye che ta tavaneste komak karde [What Is the Logic? Going toward the West That Has Always Animosity or Russia That Helped as Much as It Could]." Khabar Online, June 22, 2022. https://www.khabaronline.ir/news/1653867/-که-برویم-غرب-سمت-به-گوید-می-چه-عقل-رهبری-مشاور-ولایتی
.همواره

PART ONE

DOMESTIC DEBATES: BETWEEN STATE ENTHUSIASM AND PUBLIC UNCERTAINTY

1 IRAN'S ASCENT IN RUSSIAN FOREIGN POLICY THINKING: THE EMERGENCE OF A NEW PARADIGM

Nicole Grajewski

Introduction

Vacillations, unmet expectations, and historical tensions have long marred Russia's relationship with Iran. In February 2022, Russia's invasion of Ukraine highlighted the changing nature of Russia-Iran relations as Tehran emerged as one of Moscow's most prominent partners. Russia's war in Ukraine has elevated the importance of Iran in Moscow's domestic calculations. Yet, since the war in Ukraine, the growth and intensity of Russia's ties to Iran have been unprecedented, considering the historical tensions between the two countries. To fully understand the nature and evolution of this relationship, this chapter seeks to elucidate the place of Iran within Russian foreign policy thinking. By doing so, it evaluates the historical trajectory of Russia's view of Iran and the changes since the onset of the war in Ukraine.

Russia's interests in Iran stem from various factors, including economic, political, and security considerations. Russia has long viewed Iran as a critical player in the Middle East, one that holds significant strategic, geopolitical, and economic importance. The relationship between Russia and Iran has been shaped by a complex history, marked by periods of collaboration, as well as competition and mutual suspicion. Despite these challenges, Russia and Iran have continued to cooperate in areas of overlapping interests ranging from Central Asia to the Middle East while collaborating on a larger effort to counterbalance Western hegemony.

Vladimir Putin's return to the presidency in 2012 led to the strengthening of Russia's ties to Iran as Moscow adopted a more assertive foreign policy posture. Several years later, in 2015, Russia's intervention in Syria elevated the extent of Russian and Iranian cooperation as Moscow relied on Iranian and Iranian-backed forces to support its air campaign. The downturn in US-Russia relations coincided with heightened animosity between the United States and Iran when the Trump administration withdrew from the Iran nuclear deal and pursued maximum pressure.

This chapter begins with an exploration of the various intellectual currents and bureaucratic interests that have shaped Russia's views of Iran. Next, the chapter contextualizes the evolution of Iran within Russian foreign policy thinking, examining the salient themes surrounding Iran that pervaded the Russian foreign discourse over time. After contextualizing the historical evolution of Iran in Russian foreign policy, the chapter shifts to the developments in Russia-Iran relations since the onset of Russia's war in Ukraine. It argues that the war in Ukraine has contributed to the formation of strategic empathy between Russia and Iran, illuminating the extent to which they have shaped Russia's expectations of Iran. By providing a comprehensive overview of the evolution of Iran in Russian foreign policy thinking, this chapter sheds light on the complex and dynamic nature of the Russia-Iran relationship in the context of the war in Ukraine.

Historical Evolution of Iran in Russian Foreign Policy Thinking

Moscow's foreign policy toward Tehran has reflected many of the more extensive debates and intellectual "turns" in Russian foreign policy thinking. Akin to Russian ideas about its relationship with India, China, or the Global South, Iran has frequently represented an alternative to

Western integration and symbolized the country's independence in foreign relations. By the nature of Iran's unique position in regional and international society, the ideas and principles that have shaped and constrained Russian foreign policy in the post–Cold War era have manifested prominently in the country's foreign policy toward Iran.

Russian ideas about Iran operate as part of a broader system of ideas, which shapes and guides Russia's foreign policy toward Iran. However, the study of Russian ideas and foreign policy has overwhelmingly centered on Europe as an external Other or the West in shaping Russian identity.[1] As a result, little scholarship has been devoted to the role of the East (*Vostok*) in Russia's international thought. Russian debates have been studied at length by scholars who focused on the role of ideologically bound groups in reorienting Russian foreign policy away from the so-called Atlanticist or Western path toward a more statist and pragmatic variant of foreign policy.[2] By categorizing officials and elites into ideological subgroups, these scholars argue that the shift in Russian foreign policy emerged due to the increasing prominence of certain ideological groupings. Such a method closely resembles the work of liberal scholars who consider state preferences to be determined by the representation of the interests and ideals of individuals and groups of individuals rather than rational choice institutionalists who view ideas as epiphenomenal.[3] Scholarship on the competing identity discourses and ideological groupings in Russia typically offer a similar typology that organizes ideational groups along a spectrum reflecting the intellectual cleavages between the "Slavophiles"

---

[1] Iver B. Neumann, *Russia and the Idea of Europe: A Study in Identity and International Relations* (New York: Routledge, 2016); Ted Hopf, *Russia's European Choice* (New York: Palgrave Macmillan, 2008); Andrei Tsygankov, *Russia's Foreign Policy: Change and Continuity in National Identity*, fourth edition (Lanham: Rowman & Littlefield, 2016).
[2] Neil Malcolm et al., *Internal Factors in Russian Foreign Policy* (New York: Oxford University Press, 1996); Jeffrey T. Checkel, *Ideas and International Political Change: Soviet/Russian Behavior and the End of the Cold War* (New Haven: Yale University Press, 1997); Nicole J. Jackson, *Russian Foreign Policy and the CIS: Theories, Debates and Actions*, Routledge Advances in International Relations and Politics (London: Routledge, 2003); Anne L. Clunan, *The Social Construction of Russia's Resurgence: Aspirations, Identity, and Security Interests* (Baltimore: Johns Hopkins University Press, 2009).
[3] Judith Goldstein and Robert O. Keohane, *Ideas and Foreign Policy: Beliefs, Institutions, and Political Change*, Cornell Studies in Political Economy (Ithaca, NY: Cornell University Press, 1993); Andrew Moravcsik, "Taking Preferences Seriously: A Liberal Theory of International Politics," *International Organization* 51, no. 4 (October 1, 1997), 513–53, https://doi.org/10.1162/002081897550447.

and "Westernizers."[4] For the sake of this chapter, the precision of these intellectual cleavages matters less than the means by which Iran has been situated across Russian thinking.

Andrei Tsygankov advances the most comprehensive analysis of the intellectual traditions in Russian international thought, ranging from the imitation of the West (*zapadnichestvo*), the preservation of independent statehood or "statism" (*derzhavnichestvo*), and the country's unique system of cultural values (*samobytnost'*).[5] Tsygankov contends that each tradition illustrates different identifications of the "Russian Self," rooted in the debates on the "Russian idea" and the country's external relations. This chapter broadly follows Tsygankov's categorization to situate the place of Iran within Russian international schools of thought.

Within Tsygankov's typology, the discussions of Iran have varied across each tradition and over time. In general, the *zapadnichestvo* or Westernizing tradition has been the most reticent of a closer relationship with Tehran due to its adverse impact on Russian ties to the West.[6] The *samobytnost'* and *derzhavnichestvo* traditions generally advocate for closer relations with Iran. Even the elements within the statist or *derzhavnichestvo* tradition that support Russian engagement with the West, albeit in terms acceptable to Russia, considered ties with Iran beneficial to Russia as both a "bargaining chip" and an expression of independence in foreign policy.[7] During periods of increasing discontent

---

[4] Ted Hopf, *Social Construction of International Politics: Identities and Foreign Policies, Moscow, 1955 and 1999* (Ithaca: Cornell University Press, 2002); Stephen White and Valentina Feklyunina, *Identities and Foreign Policies in Russia, Ukraine and Belarus: The Other Europes* (Basingstoke: Palgrave Macmillan, 2014).
[5] Andrei P. Tsygankov, *Mezhdunarodnye otnosheniya: traditsii russkoi politicheskoi mysli* [*International Relations: Traditions of Russian Political Thought*] (Moscow: Al'fa-M, 2013), 17.
[6] Tor Bukkvoll, "Arming the Ayatollahs: Economic Lobbies in Russia's Iran Policy," *Problems of Post-Communism* 49, no. 6 (November 2002), 29–41, https://doi.org/10.1080/10758 216.2002.11656010.
[7] Vladimir Lukin, "Rossiya i Ee Interesy [Russia and Its Interests]," *Nezavisimaya Gazeta*, October 20, 1992, 202 (373) edition, Arkhivy federal'nykh SMI, Nezavisimaya Gazeta (1990–2005): ZAO Redaktsiya "Nezavisimoi Gazety," Integrum Digital Archive; Alexei Arbatov, "Natsional'naia Bezopasnost' Rossii v Mnogopoliarnom Mire [Russia's National Security in a Multipolar World]," *Mirovaya Ekonomika i Mezhdunarodnie Otnoshenia* 10, no. 4 (2000), 21–8; Pavel Felgenhauer, "Stoiat Li Rossiiskie Postavki Oruzhiya Iranu Ssory s Amerikoi [Are Russian Arms Deliveries to Iran a Quarrel with America]," *Moskovskiye Novosti*, November 28, 2000; Yevgeny Primakov, *Mir Posle 11 Sentyabrya* [*The World after September 11th*] (Moscow: Mysl', 2002).

with US policy, Iran has factored into mainstream Russian foreign policy discussions on the creation of a geopolitical union consisting of the major power centers on the Eurasian landmass—a union including the idea of a "Eurasian quadrangle" consisting of China, Russia, India, and Iran, which broadens foreign minister Evgeniy Primakov's proposal for the Moscow-Beijing-Delhi "strategic triangle."[8] Across each tradition, ideas about Iran operate as part of a broader system of ideas attached to the social practices and discourses inherent in the formation of foreign policy.

Since the mid-2000s, the *siloviki*—a prominent cohort of influential officials and politicians in Russia whose professional experience lies predominantly within the realm of the country's security structures— has held considerable sway in shaping the contours of Russia's foreign policy decisions. These individuals possess extensive backgrounds in military, intelligence, police, and prosecutorial offices. They are known for their staunch advocacy of a firm and an unyielding foreign policy agenda that seeks to advance Russia's strategic interests on the global stage. The *siloviki* tend to represent the more assertive variant of the *derzhavnichestvo* tradition, which has dominated Russian foreign policy thinking. Under Putin, the Russian elite convergence around the *derzhavnichestvo* tradition has emphasized the importance of Russia's great power status and, more recently, the rejection of the West. Within the *derzhavnichestvo* tradition, there has been an emphasis on *maintaining* good ties with Iran to achieve Russian foreign policy goals of augmenting its power and status. As Moscow found itself increasingly reliant on the non-West, the emphasis shifted from *maintaining* good ties to consciously *strengthening* ties with Iran predicated on the belief that Russia could strengthen its position in the Middle East and assert

---

[8]Mikhail Karpov and Dmitrii Gornostayev, "Rossiya i SShA Soglasilis', Chto Ne Soglasny Drug s Drugom Na Rasshirenie Severoatlanticheskogo Soyuza Moskva Otvetit Svoim Prodvizheniem Na Vostok [Moscow and the USA Agreed to Disagree on the Enlargement of the North Atlantic Alliance, Moscow Will Respond with Its Advance to the East]," *Nezavisimaya Gazeta*, March 22, 1997, Integrum Digital Archive ; S. E. Blagovolin, *Evoluzia struktur voennoi bezopasnosti: rol i mesto Rossii (geopoliticheski aspect)* [*Evolution of Military Security Structures: The Role and Place of Russia (Geopolitical Aspect)*] (Moscow: IMÈMO RAN, 1997), https://catalog.hathitrust.org/Record/007592 635; Stanislav Khatuntsev, "Zapad i 'Evraziiskaya Kvadriga' (Rossiya, Kitai, Indiya, Iran) [The West and the 'Eurasian Quadriga' (Russia, China, India, Iran)]," *Polis. Politicheskie Issledovaniya*, no. 6 (2015), 45–52.

its influence in the region by forming a strategic alliance with Iran. As a result, the relationship between Russia and Iran has become increasingly important in Russia's foreign policy, with the country being viewed as a key partner in achieving Russia's strategic objectives.

Bureaucratic and Institutional Foundations

The extent of cooperation with Iran varies within Russia due to the nature of the different perspectives, priorities, and responsibilities of Russian bureaucratic and institutional structures. The modern structure of Russian foreign policy-making decisions bears the impact of the institutional experience of the Soviet Union. The creation of the Inter-Agency Foreign Policy Commission of the Security Council in December 1992 and the Presidential Council in February 1993 contributed to the progressive centralization of foreign policy in Russia.[9] Under Putin, the diminution of the role of institutions and their parallel replacement with personal networks of relationships have increased the importance of the unique role of the country's leadership and the Security Council in the decision-making process.[10]

During Vladimir Putin's tenure as president of the Russian Federation, the *siloviki* have come to play a prominent role in shaping the country's foreign policy. Central to the *siloviki* worldview is the restoration of Russia's status as a great power or "*velikaya derzhava*," a conviction within the *derzhavnichestvo* tradition.[11] In addition, the *siloviki* are known to advocate for a strong state and centralized control, focusing on maintaining domestic stability and security. In practice, these policy principles often translate into assertive actions on the international stage, such as Putin's 2007 Munich speech, the assassination of dissidents

---

[9]In the early 1990s, the Russian Supreme Soviet's Committee on Foreign Affairs and Foreign Economic Relations ascended the main institutional rival to Andrei Kozyrev's Ministry of Foreign Affairs, challenging key decisions and basic principles.
[10]Viktor Averkov, "Prinyatie vneshnepoliticheskikh reshenii v Rossii [The Adoption of Foreign Policy Decisions in Russia]," *Mezhdunarodnye protsessy* 10, no. 2 (2012), 110–23.
[11]Brian D. Taylor, *The Code of Putinism* (Oxford: Oxford University Press, 2018); Michael McFaul, "Putin, Putinism, and the Domestic Determinants of Russian Foreign Policy," *International Security* 45, no. 2 (October 1, 2020), 95–139, https://doi.org/10.1162/isec_a_00390.

abroad, or the annexation of Crimea in 2014. Furthermore, the *siloviki* are known to harbor a general skepticism and opposition toward Western-style democracy and have been instrumental in suppressing political opposition and media censorship in Russia.

Within the Russian government, the *siloviki* dominate Russia's security services, namely the SVR (Russia's Foreign Intelligence Service) and FSB (Federal Security Service), which have played a significant role in the country's foreign policy under Putin. These organizations are closely tied to the Kremlin and have been involved in a variety of actions, including election interference, cyberattacks, and espionage. The SVR is responsible for Russia's foreign intelligence gathering, while the FSB is responsible for domestic security and counterintelligence. Both organizations are closely tied to the Kremlin and have been known to act as the main instruments of Putin's foreign policy.

When it comes to the question of Iran, the *siloviki* and security services are known to adopt a pragmatic approach, viewing Iran as an important partner in the region, particularly in terms of counterbalancing the influence of the United States and its allies. The *siloviki* share a similar worldview to many of the elites within Iran, especially in terms of foreign policy priorities. Coincidentally, central figures within the *siloviki*, like Nikolai Patrushev, have played an essential role in forging ties between the Russian and Iranian elite establishments.[12]

The Russian Foreign Ministry has largely been marginalized in forming the Russian policy, often relegated to implementing rather than creating policy. Within the Foreign Ministry, Iran is placed in the Second Asia Department, along with countries such as Afghanistan, Pakistan, and India, rather than in the Middle East and North Africa Department. This placement reflects the broader focus of Russian foreign policy in the region, which seeks to maintain balance and stability. However, it is important to note that the Second Asia Department is not the department involved in Iran affairs, as other departments also

---

[12]Nikolai Patrushev, "Interv'yu Sekretarya Soveta Bezopasnosti Rossiiskoi Federatsii N.P.Patrusheva [Interview with Secretary of the Security Council of the Russian Federation N.P. Patrushev]," *Kommersant*, January 12, 2012, 3 (4788) edition, Integrum Digital Archive; "Glava Sovbeza Patrushev Rasskazal Iranskomu Kollege Ob Organizatorah Himataki v Sirii [Security Council Chief Patrushev Told His Iranian Counterpart about the Organizers of the Chemical Attack in Syria]," *Parlamentskaia Gazeta*, April 8, 2017, Integrum Digital Archive.

play a role in implementing policy toward the country. For example, the Arms Control and Disarmament Department has traditionally wielded more influence than the Second Asia Department, given the importance of issues such as nonproliferation and arms control in the relationship between Russia and Iran.

The shifts in the global geopolitical landscape have not only redefined the contours of Russian foreign policy but have also heralded a transformation in the balance of power between various departments and ministries. The decline of the Foreign Ministry's influence in the policy formulation process has been a defining feature of this changing landscape. This has been particularly pronounced in the case of Iran, where the Ministry of Defense and the Ministry of Energy have emerged as critical players in shaping policy toward the country. The Russian Ministry of Defense's growing involvement in Iran's foreign policy can be traced back to the Syrian Civil War, when Russia and Iran found themselves on the same side of the conflict. This shared strategic objective led to a natural alignment between the Russian Ministry of Defense and its Iranian counterparts, which culminated in an increased role for the former in shaping Russia's policy toward Iran. This shift has inevitably led to a decrease in the Foreign Ministry's influence on Iranian policy as the Ministry of Defense takes on a more significant role in defining Russia's strategic priorities in the region. Similarly, under the stewardship of former minister Alexander Novak, the Ministry of Energy played a pivotal role in forging closer coordination between Russia and Iran in areas such as sanctions evasion and trade.

The intricate fabric of Russia's perception of Iran is woven from a multitude of threads, both within and beyond the corridors of power. The pragmatic approach of the *siloviki* and security services, coupled with a shared worldview with many elites in Iran, has underscored Iran's strategic importance as a counterbalance to the United States and its regional allies. Meanwhile, the marginalization of the Russian Foreign Ministry in the policy formulation process, and the ascendancy of the Ministry of Defense and Ministry of Energy, reflect the fluidity of Russia's foreign policy dynamics. The roles played by various bureaucratic actors in the formulation of policy toward Iran have evolved over time, underscoring the importance of comprehending the historical trajectory of Russia's understanding of Iran.

Evolution of the Russian Elite's Views of Iran

Russia's perception of Iran has undergone significant changes over the years. To fully comprehend the broader transformations in Russian foreign policy since the war in Ukraine, it is crucial to examine the evolution of Russia's comprehension of Iran. The following section delves into the historical trajectory of Russia's outlook toward Iran, encapsulating the nuanced shifts in attitude and perspective.[13]

In the 1990s, Russian policy toward Iran was characterized by political uncertainty, economic collapse, and a fractured national identity. This policy reflected the broader issues of deep disorganization and incoherence in Moscow's approach to the world. As the Yeltsin administration oscillated erratically between integration with the West and pragmatic balancing in a multipolar international system, the implementation of foreign policy reflected the tension between the principal ideological schisms of the Russian elite. The intellectual diversity and presence of multiple schools of thought actively influencing Russian foreign policy distinguishes the 1990s from subsequent periods where the statist tradition dominated among the elite and officials. During this time, Russian discussions of Iran were primarily concerned with Iran as a country along the periphery of "near abroad" (*blizhnee zarubezh'e*), the region encompassing the Soviet successor states of the Commonwealth of Independent States (CIS). At the same time, Iran was also considered a source of revenue for Russia's civilian nuclear industry and the military-industrial complex.[14]

Until the fall of 1992, Russian foreign policy was driven by the conviction that success in international affairs depended entirely on the

---

[13]This chapter features data collected from databases of Russian and Persian materials, such as EastView, Integrum, Magiran, and Sid.ir. These databases offer access to major journals, news reports, and government statements in both Russian and Persian.
[14]Maxim Yusin, "Moskva Predlagaet Tegeranu Strategicheskoe Partnerstvo [Moscow Offers Tehran a 'Strategic Partnership']," *Izvestiya*, April 1, 1993, Integrum Digital Archive; Aleksandr Koretskii, "Voennoe Sotrudnichestvo Rossii i Irana [Military Cooperation of Russia and Iran]," *Kommersant*, October 1, 1994; "Otnosheniya Mezhdu Rossiei i Iranom [Relations between Russia and Iran]," *Kommersant*, December 25, 1996, Integrum Digital Archive ; Konstantin Zatulin, "Moskva i Tegeran Gotovy Ob"edinit' Usiliya [Moscow and Tehran Are Ready to Join Forces]," *Nezavisimaya Gazeta*, November 4, 1995, 114 edition, Integrum Digital Archive.

country's integration into the "community of civilized Western nations," which referred to "the West" and the group of industrialized democratic nations.[15] Whereas Russia initially focused on strengthening ties with the West, domestic opposition and regional instability prompted Moscow to make a more concerted effort to assert its interests in the near abroad. The near abroad grew to occupy a distinctive point of focus in Russian foreign policy as the prominent "statist" voices viewed the country's national interests as inextricably tied to maintaining "a sphere of Russia's vital interests" along "the entire geopolitical space of the former USSR."[16] Even more moderate and liberal voices in the political establishment argued that countries in the West needed to offer "the recognition of [Russia's] legitimate interests in the 'near abroad.'"[17] As a state along the periphery of the near abroad, Iran initially featured in Russian foreign policy thinking as a potential source of instability in Central Asia and the South Caucasus.[18] Early skepticism of Iranian proselytization in the Muslim republics of the former Soviet Union was also tied to the situation in Afghanistan and Moscow's fear of the ensuing instability emanating from Islamic extremism.[19]

The shift in the Russian discourse toward a more constructive view of Iran occurred at a time of increasing pressure from more hardline voices in Russia to manage its interests in the near abroad while diversifying its relations with the non-Western powers.[20] More importantly, the early

---

[15] Andrei Kozyrev, *Preobrazhenie [Transfiguration]* (Moscow: Mezhdunarodnye Otnosheniya, 1995).

[16] Andranik Migranyan, "Podlinnye i Mnimye Orientiry vo Vneshnei Politike [The Real and Imaginary Directions of Foreign Policy]," *Rossiyskaya Gazeta*, August 4, 1992, Integrum Digital Archive.

[17] "Interv'iu c Poslom RF v SShA Vladimirom Lukinym [Interview with the Ambassador of the Russian Federation in the USA Vladimir Lukin]," *Segodnya*, September 3, 1993, 48 edition, Arkhivy federal'nykh SMI, Segodnya 1994–1999: ZAO, Integrum Digital Archive.

[18] For example, the 1993 Russian foreign policy doctrine explicitly mentions Iran as

> a source of dangerous unpredictability and instability in the region, rendering vague the prospects of its general political development … Having ceased to be a US partner, yet coming no closer to us, Iran represents a tangible factor of uncertainty in regional international affairs. The region in question is directly linked with some internal conflicts in the CIS, which is clearly visible in the way Tajikistan is being directly influenced by Iran and Afghanistan.

[19] Although Russia and Iran supported the Northern Alliance, there were genuine fears in Moscow that Iranian influence in Tajikistan would create a protracted conflict akin to the ongoing Afghan Civil War, which would necessitate Russia's involvement.

[20] Sergei Stankevich, "Derzhava V Poiskah Sebia [A Power in Search of Itself]," *Nezavisimaya Gazeta*, March 28, 1992, Integrum Digital Archive.

efforts of peacekeeping or "peacemaking" (*mirotvorchestvo*) in the near abroad revealed that Iran had no desire to promote "the export of the revolution" (*ṣudūr-i inqilāb*) in either Nagorno-Karabakh or Tajikistan.[21] The idea that Iran posed a challenge to Russian interests in Central Asia and the South Caucasus eventually evolved into an emphasis on the importance of a stable Iran as a country directly adjacent to the frontiers of the CIS since it "contributes to stabilization on the southern borders of Russia and the near abroad."[22] Moreover, by the mid-1990s, proponents of an independent foreign policy argued in favor of alignment with Iran since it "prevents the transformation of Russia's near abroad to the south in the buffer zones of NATO."[23] The conception of Iran as a source of stabilization and as a bulwark against the West in a region where Moscow asserts special entitlements has persisted in the Russian discourse. Russian elites began to laud the mutual understanding between Russia and Iran regarding an implicit agreement over "spheres of influence" in which Russia and Iran respect each other's interests and aspirations in the Middle East, Central Asia, and the Caucasus.

Starting in the 1990s, the interest in Iran among the Russian elite was closely tied to the statist belief that Russia should reemerge as a great power. The growing popularity of the *derzhavnichestvo* tradition led to a wider embrace of the goals of maintaining a strong state and augmenting Russia's international standing through diverse partnerships.[24] Though

---

[21] Unlike Moldova or Georgia, Tajikistan and Nagorno-Karabakh were two conflicts in which Iranian linguistic and minority ethnic ties could have potentially exacerbated these conflicts. Instead, Iran used Tajikistan as a means of portraying itself as a constructive actor in Central Asia and demonstrating that it favored relations with Russia over the revolutionary spread of Islam in the region. See, generally, Akram Ḥusayn'pūr et al., *Māhīyat-i Taḥavvulāt Dar Āsiyā-Yi Markazī va Qafqāz* [*The Nature of Changes in Central Asia and the Caucasus*], chapter 1 (Tehran: Mu'assasah-i chāp va intishārāt-i Vizārat-i umūr-i khārijah, 1994); Elena Dunaeva and Nina Mamedova, ed., *Politika RF I IRI v Regional'nom Kontekste: TsA, Kavkaz, Blizhnii Vostok* [*The Policy of the Russian Federation and the Islamic Republic of Iran in the Regional Context: Central Asia, the Caucasus, the Middle East*] (Moscow: Institut Vostokovedeniya RAN, 2011).

[22] Aleksandr Umnov, "Strategicheskie Interesy RF Na Blizhnem i Srednem Vostoke [Strategic Interests of the Russian Federation in the Near and Middle East]," *Nezavisimaya Gazeta*, December 20, 1996, Integrum Digital Archive.

[23] Aleksei Gromyko, "Rossiya i Iran: Novaya Real'nost'" [Russia and Iran: New Reality]," *Nezavisimaya Gazeta*, June 26, 1998, Integrum Digital Archive.

[24] See, for example, Yevgeny Bazhanov, *Rossiya Kak Velikaya Derzhava: Traditsii I Perspektivy* [*Russia as a Great Power: Traditions and Perspectives*], Moscow: Nauchnaya kniga, 1999; SVOP, "Strategiya Dlya Rossii: Povestka Dnya Dlya Prezidenta-2000 [Strategy for Russia: Agenda for the President-2000]," Moscow, 2000; Sergei Karaganov, "Novye Vyzovy

the dominance of the *derzhavnichestvo* tradition was solidified under Putin, the idea of a strong state to secure Russia's international position became more prominent in light of changes in the relationship between Russia and the West, particularly the expansion of NATO and the inclusion of former Warsaw Pact states. As a means of demonstrating the country's independence from the West, the Russian leadership saw Iran as a potential partner where it could exhibit its autonomy in foreign policy from the West and strengthen the power of the state through both sales of arms and peaceful nuclear energy.[25]

The early consensus around Russian self-perception as an independent great power (*velikaya derzhava*) in the post-Soviet period initially emerged as a reaction to the failure of the Atlanticist or pro-Western trend in foreign policy, and further intensified through the Putin era. During this time, similar views on Russia's future as a great power were also held by nationalist-minded elite members who opposed the Yeltsin regime but still held important positions in various segments of Russian society. These individuals, referred to as imperial nationalists, saw an alliance with Iran as crucial for Russia's future as a great power. Many of them viewed the relationship between Russia and the West, particularly the United States, in purely geopolitical terms, believing that Russia was in a mortal conflict with the West regardless of political makeup.

With the resignation of President Boris Yeltsin in December 1999, Vladimir Putin assumed office with the desire to restore authority through a strong state (*gosudarstvennost*) that could maintain internal order and assert the country's interests abroad. Throughout Putin's first term as president (2000–4), Russia's relationship with Iran experienced considerable moments of cooperation alongside frequent moments of tension. From the outset, it appeared that Putin would strengthen relations with Iran; however, Russian discontent over revelations of Iran's nuclear program, as well as the conflict surrounding the Caspian Sea

---

Bezopasnosti: Rossiya i Zapad [New Security Challenges: Russia and West]," *Sovremennaya Evropa* 9, no. 1 (2002), 38–46; Alexei Pushkov, "Rossiya i SShA: Predely Sblizheniya [Russia and the USA: Limits of Convergence]," *Nezavisimaya Gazeta*, December 27, 2001, Integrum Digital Archive .

[25]Nina Mamedova, "Vzaimnye Interesy Rossii I Irana: Istoricheskaia Evoliutsiya I Nyneshnii Etap [Mutual Interests of Russia and Iran: Historical Evolution and the Present Stage]," in *Rossiya i Islamskii Mir: Istoricheskaia Retrospektiva i Sovremennye Tendentsii*, edited by Viacheslav Belokrenitskii, Il'ia Zaitsev, and Natalia Ul'chenko (Moscow: Institut Vostokovedeniya RAN, 2010), 27–29.

delimitation, demonstrated the underlying tensions in the relationship. By June 2000, Putin's first foreign policy concept identified "the growing trend towards establishing a unipolar world order" dominated by the United States as a primary threat to global stability. The concept stated that "it is important to develop further relations with Iran" to achieve a "multipolar system" that would "genuinely reflect the diversity of the contemporary world and its great variety of interests."[26]

Russia's relationship with Iran continued to evolve in the following years, with both cooperation and tension present. The nuclear issue was a key area that demonstrated this tension in Russia's balance between the West and Iran. In the 1990s, Moscow's position toward Iran's nuclear activities was ambiguous, but the revelation of Iran's covert nuclear program in 2002, including uranium enrichment facilities in Natanz and weapons-grade plutonium production facilities in Arak, strengthened Moscow's resolve to support international efforts for a diplomatic solution.[27] Despite evidence of Iranian violations of its obligations under the Nuclear Non-Proliferation Treaty (NPT), the Russian government argued that Iran had the right to use civilian nuclear energy, contingent on the International Atomic Energy Agency (IAEA) oversight. Iran's rejection of the 2006 Russian-brokered fuel swap proposal, however, provoked a shift in Russian elite thinking that culminated in Moscow's support for the IAEA board of governors' decision to refer the Iranian nuclear file to the UN Security Council.[28] During the brief period of

---

[26] It also emphasized the primacy Russia placed on the UN and preservation of pluralist norms. Russian Foreign Policy Conception asserts: "All attempts to introduce into international language such concepts as 'humanitarian intervention' and 'limited sovereignty' in order to justify unilateral force that bypasses the UN Security Council are unacceptable." "Kontseptsiya Vneshnei Politiki Rossiiskoi Federatsii [Foreign Policy Conception of the Russian Federation]," *Diplomaticheskii Vestnik* 8 (2000), 3–11.

[27] Georgi Mirsky, "Iran i SShA: protivostoyanie na fone 'yadernogo krizisa' [Iran and the US: Confrontation against the Backdrop of the 'Nuclear Crisis']," *Mirovaya Ekonomika I Mezhdunarodnye Otnosheniya*, no. 7 (2006), https://elibrary.ru/item.asp?id=9220234; Sevak Norairovich Sarukhanyan, "Iranskaya Atomnaya Bomba. Byt' Ili Ne Byt'? [Iranian Atomic Bomb: To Be or Not to Be?]," *Polis. Politicheskie Issledovaniya*, no. 4 (2005), 109–16.

[28] "Glava MID Rossii Primet Uchastie vo Vstreche Glav Vneshnepoliticheskikh Vedomstv 'Shesterki' Po Yadernoi Probleme Irana [Head of the Russian Foreign Ministry Will Participate in the Meeting of Foreign Ministers 'Six' on the Iranian Nuclear Problem]," *RIA Novosti*, June 1, 2006, Integrum Digital Archive; Vitaly Naumkin, "Yadernye Ambitsii Tegerana: Mif I Real'nost' [Nuclear Ambitions of Iran: Myth or Reality]," *Trud*, October 12, 2005, Integrum Digital Archive; Aleksei Georgievich Arbatov, "Iranskii Yadernyi Uzel [Iran's Nuclear Knot]," *Aziya I Afrika Segodnya* 631, no. 2 (2010), https://elibrary.ru/item.asp?id=16901349; Andrei Baklanov, "Rossiiskoe posrednichestvo na peregovorakh

improved US-Russia relations under the "reset" in 2009 under then president Barack Obama, Russian cooperation with the United States on the Iranian nuclear program elicited US reciprocity on the removal of Rosoboronexport sanctions and the ratification of the 1-2-3 Nuclear Cooperation Agreement for closer cooperation between Moscow and Washington in the nuclear sphere.[29]

At the time, Russia pursued a policy that adversely impacted its relations with Iran in Moscow's attempt to integrate with the West and join major Western institutions. Following the 9/11 terrorist attacks, Vladimir Putin's famous phone conversation with George W. Bush symbolized Russia's ambition to become a Western partner. Still, this partnership never fully materialized as the United States swiftly lost interest in Moscow. Still, Moscow cooperated with Washington on curbing Iran's ambitions through various sanctions resolutions and delays in the Bushehr Nuclear Power Plant. Even after the Color Revolution and the Khodorkovsky case, Russia still strove to achieve parity with its Western allies with a more assertive foreign policy. For Russia, Iran was a major area where its leverage provided reciprocity with the West and underscored its importance. However, Russia's endeavor to achieve an equal partnership with the West ultimately proved unsuccessful. Putin's Munich speech in 2007 and subsequent actions, such as increased air force patrols near US and NATO borders and the suspension of Russia's participation in the Treaty on Conventional Forces in Europe, indicated the Kremlin's determination to coerce the West into recognizing an

---

vokrug yadernoi programmy Irana [Russian Mediation in the Negotiations on Iran's Nuclear Program]," *Etnosotsium I Mezhnatsional'naya Kul'tura* 41 no. 9 (2011), https://elibrary.ru/item.asp?id=18813647; Anna Igorevna Filimonova, "'Iranskaya yadernaya problema'—istoki i istoriya razvitiya ["The Iranian Nuclear Problem"—Origins and History of Development]," *Uchenyi Sovet*, no. 2 (2021), https://doi.org/10.33920/nik-02-2102-04.

[29]Vladimir Orlov, Roland Makhmutovich Timberbaev, and Anton Khlopkov, *Problemy yadernogo nerasprostraneniya v rossiysko-amerikanskikh otnosheniyakh: istoriya, vozmozhnosti i perspektivy dal'neishego vzaimodeistviya* [*Nuclear Non-proliferation Issues in Russian-American Relations: History, Opportunities, and Prospects for Further Interaction*] (Moscow: PIR-Tsentr politicheskikh issledovanii, 2001), https://russiancouncil.ru/library/library_rsmd/problemy-yadernogo-nerasprostraneniya-v-rossiysko-amerikanskikh-otnosheniyakh-istoriya-vozmozhnosti-i-perspektivy-dalneyshego-vzaimodeystviya/ (accessed January 30, 2024); Alexei Arbatov, "Iranskii Yadernyi Uzel [Iranian Nuclear Knot]," *Sovremennaya Evropa* 29, no. 1 (2007), 24–36; Vladimir Ivanenko, "Iranskaia Iadernaia Programma i Rossiisko-Iranskie Otnosheniya [Iranian Nuclear Program and Russian-Iranian Relations]," *Mezhdunarodnaia Politika* 34, no. 1 (2016), 109–31.

equitable partnership.[30] Whereas Russia previously supported sanctions resolutions over Iran in 2011, growing discontent toward the West led to a reexamination of the role of Iran in Russian foreign policy. This intensified with the 2011–12 domestic protests, disagreements around missile defense, and the Magnitsky Act. With the return of Vladimir Putin to the presidency in May 2012, Russian foreign policy toward Iran resulted in an overall shift.

Iran's importance as a counterbalance to the West appeared in Russian assessments of its great power status project, under which alignment with centers of power opposed to US hegemony would contribute to the decline in Western dominance. Russian observers continued to stress the Sino-Russian relationship regarding the "building structures" of a world order due to the closeness of the two countries' visions of a multipolar order.[31] Countries like Iran, India, and Brazil were frequently mentioned as potential countries to support the Sino-Russian vision for multipolarity.[32] The growth of new centers of influence, which "acquire an increasing share in world affairs, change the usual balance of power and, on this basis, objectively claims a role commensurate to the weight of traditional world centers, previously represented by the countries of the West."[33]

Russia's belief in the limitations of Western hegemony was accompanied by ambitious policy proclamations that hailed the propensity of a multipolar world. Official Russian foreign policy statements continued to emphasize the emergence of new poles due to the growing integration process in Latin America, Asia, Africa, and the

---

[30] Fyodor Lukyanov, "Rossiya i Ne-Zapad [Russia and the Non-West]," *Nezavisimaya Gazeta*, June 24, 2014: 162–85, Integrum Digital Archive; Igor Istomin, "Sravnitel'nyi Analiz Prioritetov Rossiiskoi Vneshnei Politiki i Nauchno-Obrazovatel'nogo Soobshchestva Spetsialistov Po Mezhdunarodnym Otnosheniyam [Comparative Analysis of the Russian Foreign Policy Priorities and Research Interests of the National Academic Community]," *Vestnik RUDN Mezhdunarodnye Otnosheniya* 18, no. 1 (2018).
[31] Aleksandr Nikitin, "Novaia sistema otnoshenii velikikh derzhav XXI veka: 'kontsert' ili konfrontatsiya? [New System of Relations between Great Powers for the XXI Century: 'Concert' or Confrontation?]," *Polis. Politicheskie issledovaniya*, no. 1 (January 25, 2016), 44–59.
[32] Alexander Lukin and Tamara Troyakova, "Mnogopolyarnaya Vostochnaya Aziya: Tendentsiya Ili Uzhe Real'nost'? [Multipolar East Asia: A Trend or Already a Reality?]," *Problemy Dal'nego Vostoka*, December 31, 2010, 168–73.
[33] Mikhail Titarenko and Vladimir Petrovskii, *Rossiya, Kitai i Novyi Mirovoi Poryadok [Russia, China and the New World Order]* (Moscow: Ves' Mir, 2016), 9, https://www.vesmirbooks.ru/book/9785777706201/ (accessed January 30, 2024).

Middle East. Such a sentiment is captured in the 2014 Strategy for Russia issued by the influential Council on Foreign and Defense Policy that characterizes the period from the Iraq War to the Arab Spring with the erosion of Western influence—a period that coincided with the rapid rise of China and India, Russia's recovery, and the rise of non-Western powers with alternative views on the world order. The report notes that "growing dissatisfaction with rising powers" and ongoing "processes of redistribution of power and influence" have "undermined the credibility of the Western model" of international order, necessitating the development of a polycentric system that accounts for the diversity of views.[34]

At the regional level, Iran remained a crucial pillar of Russia's regional projection of its great power status in the Middle East.[35] The Syrian Civil War demonstrated the importance of engagement with regional powers to elevate Russia's diplomatic profile and, by extension, its status as a great power.[36] Russia and Iran's campaign in Syria not only demonstrated the growth in the effectiveness of Russia's armed forces but also elevated Moscow's indispensable role as a leader in a multipolar world.[37] On the

---

[34] "Rossii v XXI Veke: Analiz Situatsii i Nekotorye Predlozheniya (Strategiya-3) [Russia's Strategy in the 21st Century: Analysis of the Situation and Some Suggestions (Strategy-3)]," *Sovet po vneshnei i oboronnoi politike*, Moscow. June 19, 2014.

[35] Vladimir Baranovsky and Vitaly Naumkin, "Blizhnii Vostok V Menyayushchemsya Global'nom Kontekste: Klyuchevye Trendy Stoletnego Razvitiya [The Middle East in a Changing Global Context: Key Centenary Trends]," *Mirovaya Ekonomika I Mezhdunarodnye Otnosheniya* 62, no. 3 (2018), https://doi.org/10.20542/0131-2227-2018-62-3-5-19; Aleksandr Aksenenok and Viktoriya Fradkova, "Blizhnii Vostok vo vneshnei politike SShA posle Trampa i interesy Rossii [Post-Trump US Foreign Policy in the Middle East and the Interests of Russia]," *Mirovaya Ekonomika I Mezhdunarodnye Otnosheniya* 66, no. 1 (2022), 8–50, https://doi.org/10.20542/0131-2227-2022-66-1-38-50.

[36] Ivan Safranchuk and Fyodor Lukyanov, "Sovremennyi Mirovoi Poryadok: Strukturnye Realii i Sopernichestvo Velikikh Derzhav [Modern World Order: Structural Realities and Great Power Rivalries]," *Polis. Politicheskie Issledovaniya*, no. 3 (2021), 57–76.

[37] Alexei Fenenko, "Mezhderzhavnaia Konkurentsiya Na Blizhnem Vostoke [International Conflict in the Middle East]," *Mezhdunarodnye Protsesi* 12, no. 3 (2014), 34–54; Boris Dolgov, "Siriiskii Konflikt [The Syrian Conflict]," in *Konflikty i Voiny XXI Veka: Blizhnii Vostok i Severnaia Afrika*, edited by Vitaly Naumkin and Dina Malysheva (Moscow: Institut Vostokovedeniya RAN, 2015), 401–22; Alexei Vasil'ev, *Ot Lenina Do Putina: Rossiya Na Blizhnem i Srednem Vostoke [From Lenin to Putin: Russia in the Near and Middle East]* (Moscow: Tsentrpoligraf, 2018); Alexander Yakovlev, "Perebalansirovka sistemy mezhdunarodnykh otnoshenii na Blizhnem Vostoke v XXI v. [Rebalancing the System of International Relation in the Middle East in the 21st Century]," *Vostok. Afro-aziatskie obshchestva: istoriya i sovremennost*, no. 2 (2020), 119, https://doi.org/10.31857/S08691908 0009061-4.

eve of Russia's invasion of Ukraine, Russian elites tied its military success in Syria as an essential condition for the country's recognition as a great power in the multipolar world.

The understanding of Iran in Russian elite calculations has evolved considerably over the past three decades. The oscillations in Russian foreign policy often corresponded with changing assessments of the country's place in the world and the direction of its national interests. The war in Ukraine served as a catalyst in the trend toward a greater appreciation of Iran in Russian elite thinking. Whereas these changes have materialized discursively, they have not materialized in practice.

Ukraine and the Russian Ideological Shift

The Russian discourse on Iran has generally corresponded with broader trends in Russian thinking; however, the war in Ukraine has led to a more in-depth examination of the significance of Iran in Russian elite understanding. Amid growing international isolation, Russia has steadfastly pursued avenues to bolster its economic and political alliances with like-minded nations. Among these partners, Iran has emerged as a crucial ally, offering a diverse array of economic and political prospects amenable to mutually advantageous cooperation.[38]

Already in 2014, the imposition of Western sanctions after the annexation of Crimea on Russia not only drew parallels to the situation in Iran but illustrated that both states "refused to play according to the old Western rules."[39] The Speaker of the State Duma Sergei Naryshkin described Iran as a "reliable, promising partner" and noted that Iran and Russia are "equally critical of the toxic actions of Western countries" that pursue "geopolitical interests" without consideration of "the norms of international law" by intervening in the "internal affairs of sovereign states."[40] In an op-ed for *Rossiyskaya Gazeta*, former foreign minister Igor

---

[38]"Na Zapade Zakryvayut, Na Vostoke Otkryvayut [They Close in the West, They Open in the East]," *Sankt-Peterburgskie Vedomosti*, March 5, 2022, Integrum Digital Archive .
[39]Sergei Karaganov, "Mir stanovitsa vse menee prozapadnym [The World Is Becoming Less Pro-Western]," *Rossiyskaya Gazeta*, April 24, 2014, 2, Integrum Digital Archive .
[40]Alexander Levchenko and Alexei Tsypin, "RF Vidit v Irane Nadezhnogo, Perspektivnogo Partnera [Russia Sees a Reliable, Promising Partner in Iran]," *ITAR-TASS*, November 18, 2014, Integrum Digital Archive.

Ivanov highlighted "Russia's interest to maintain current friendly relations with our southern neighbor" and to intensify relations to a "qualitatively new level" as a means of corresponding to the "new realities" of the world.[41] One year later, Russian and Iranian military cooperation in Syria allowed for the realization of a closer partnership.

Amid Moscow's embattlement with the collective West, Iran emerged as a focal point of deliberations concerning the necessity of resilience and resistance in the face of Western pressures.[42] The fundamental premise of Moscow's global narrative posits that Russia, Iran, and other nations consigned to the margins of the Western-dominated global paradigm share a unifying aspiration to realign the global balance of power and assert their own interests on the world stage. As such, states like Russia and Iran represent natural allies in this endeavor.

The war in Ukraine has precipitated a notable transformation in Russia's perception of Iran, as evinced by the concept of strategic empathy that posits that Russia and Iran share parallel strategic interests and confront similar challenges, particularly in the context of perceived Western hostility. The notion of strategic empathy has forged a sense of solidarity between Russia and Iran, fueling a conviction that Moscow and Tehran must collaborate to counter the perceived threats emanating from the West. Strategic empathy implies that by acknowledging and comprehending each other's strategic interests and challenges, Russia and Iran can form a powerful alliance, effectively countering Western pressures. The concept of strategic empathy between Russia and Iran transcends numerous domains, encompassing diverse aspects such as reciprocal backing in times of domestic turmoil and coordination in global forums.

Russian discussions surrounding Iran frequently highlight the crucial need for mutual assistance in the face of Western influence. This emphasis implicitly presupposes a degree of alignment between Iran and Russia's political undertakings, which include the promotion of a multipolar

---

[41]Igor Ivanov, "Vozvrashchenie Irana [Return of Iran]," *Rossiyskaya Gazeta*, July 17, 2014, Integrum Digital Archive.
[42]Lukyanov, "Rossiya i Ne-Zapad [Russia and the Non-West]"; Anatolii Torkunov and Nodari Simonia, "Novyi Mirovoi Poryadok: Ot Bipolyarnosti k Mnogopolyusnosti [New World Order: From Bipolarity to Multipolarity]," *Polis. Politicheskie Issledovaniya*, no. 3 (2015), 27–37; Mikhail Margelov, "Rossiya i Ne-Zapad. Paradoksy Mul'tipolyarnosti [Russia and Non-West: Paradoxes of Multipolarity]," *Rossiyskaya Gazeta*, August 25, 2022, Integrum Digital Archive.

global order and the repudiation of Western hegemony.[43] Moscow anticipates that Tehran will spurn Western overtures and embrace Russia's vision of an alternative global order, which would entail Iran's active involvement in international organizations and forums that hold significant importance in the eyes of Moscow, while also championing principles that are believed to effectively counter Western pressures. Even prior to the onset of the Ukraine crisis, the shared experiences of domestic protests and perceived Western meddling engendered a profound sense of solidarity between the two countries in the face of what Russia and Iran regarded as unjust interference.[44]

In transactional areas impacted by international pressure and sanctions, Russia has placed a greater emphasis on Russian and Iranian cooperation in order to offset the negative effects of sanctions and maintain their respective domestic industries.[45] Russia sees Iran as a country that shares a similar experience of being subject to sanctions and therefore may be inclined to resist them in conjunction with Russia.[46]

---

[43]"Sanktsii Ne Pomeshayut Sotrudnichestvu Rf I Irana, Tegeran Pomozhet Rossiiskim Kompaniyam Vyiti Na Novye Rynki—Zamministra Nefti Irana Ria No 9 [Sanctions Will Not Hinder Cooperation between Russia and Iran, Tehran Will Help Russian Companies Enter New Markets—Deputy Minister of Oil of Iran RIA Novosti]," *RIA Novosti. Vse Novosti*, October 14, 2022, Integrum Digital Archive; "V Irane Nashli Prichinu Provala Antirossiiskikh Sanktsii [In Iran, the Reason for the Failure of Anti-Russian Sanctions Was Found]," *URA.Ru*, May 30, 2022, Integrum Digital Archive.

[44]For the Iranian discourse on domestic interference, see Mohammad Ali Khosravi and Davoud Bayat, "Qālbod Shekāfi Enqelābhā-Ye Rangi va Taasiri Ān Dar Irān [Anatomy of Colored Revolutions and Its Effect in Iran]," *Moṭāla'āt Ravābeṭ-e Bayn al-Melali* 3, no. 13 (2011); Farhad Dimashqee, "Negāh-ye Takāpu-Ye Doshmanān Barā-Ye Ijād-e Enqelāb-e Makhmalin Dar Irān [Enemies Trying to Look for a Velvet Revolution in Iran]," *Irān*, July 2, 2009; "Barrandāzi-ye Rangin [Colorful Overthrow]," *Jām-e Jam*, June 29, 2009, 10; Habibollah Abolhassan Shirazi, "Ta'ṣīrāt-i Bahār-i 'Arabī va Inqilābha-Yi Rangi Dar Āsiyā-Yi Markazī va Qafqāz [Influences of Arabic Spring and Color Revolutions in Central Asia and the Caucasus]," *Muṭāla'āt Ravābiṭ-i Bayn al-Milal* 5, no. 19 (2012), 9–36; Mohammed Kashafi, "Ingilistān va Ru'yā-yi Mujaddid-i Dikhālat dar Īrān [The UK and the Repeated Dream of Interference in Iran]," *Jam-i Jam*, September 21, 2009, http://jamejamonline.ir/fa/news/282081; Amīr Hūshang Ṭahmāsbī'pūr and Humāyūn Ārāmish, *Abzārhā-yi jang-i narm 'alayh-i Jumhūrī-i Islāmī-i Īrān [Soft War Tools Against the Islamic Republic of Iran]* (Tehran: Nashr-i Sāqī, 2011).

[45]"Iran Predlozhil Rossii Sotrudnichestvo i Pomoshch' v Ukhode Ot Amerikanskikh Sanktsii [Iran Proposed Cooperation and Help to Russia in Avoiding US Sanctions]," *Komsomol'skaya Pravda*, April 1, 2022, Integrum Digital Archive.

[46]"Peskov: Rossiya, Kak Iran, Mozhet Desyatiletiyami Zhit' Pod Sanktsiyami Radi Suvereniteta [Peskov: Russia, like Iran, Can Live under Sanctions for Decades for the Sake of Sovereignty]," *IA Rosbalt*, July 18, 2022, Integrum Digital Archive; Nikolay Kozhanov and Leonid Isaev, "Iran I Sanktsii: Opyt Preodoleniya I Vliyanie Na Sotsial'no-Ekonomicheskoe

From Russia's vantage point, Iran represents a promising alternative source of goods, capable of supporting the Kremlin's import substitution initiatives aimed at curbing Russia's dependence on Western imports.[47] Moscow has also highlighted the potential for deepening economic cooperation with Iran, particularly in the pursuit of alternative export routes and infrastructure projects. Although this may not necessarily equate to a full-fledged strategic partnership, the war in Ukraine has served as an impetus in elevating the importance of Iran in Russian foreign policy.

The development of strategic empathy between Russia and Iran is intimately connected with Moscow's emphasis on resilience and resistance. Similar to strategic empathy, resilience and resistance indicate the nations' domestic capacity to withstand and counter external pressures and influences, particularly emanating from the West. Russian and Iranian state-narratives claim victimhood, stemming from the idea that Russia and Iran are excluded from the dominant Western-led global order and are thus natural allies in resisting this order. The sense of strategic empathy between the two countries leads to forming a coalition of the excluded and resistant, and both of these elements are crucial for their resilience and resistance amid Western pressure. Strategic empathy provides the foundation for the cooperation and understanding necessary for this coalition to be successful. Indeed, resilience and resistance are what allow the coalition to effectively counter external pressures and assert its own interests on the global stage.

Russia's statements toward Iran not only reflect a deepened bilateral relationship but also carry certain expectations of mutual understanding and cooperation in areas of strategic importance. To demonstrate this, the following section evaluates the salient areas of the Russian discourse surrounding Moscow's ties to Iran: (1) greater Eurasia and geo-economics connectivity, (2) normative alignment, (3) resistance economics, and (4) defense.

Razvitie [Iran and Sanctions: Experience of Overcoming and Impact on Socio-Economic Development]," *Aziya i Afrika Segodnya*, 2019, 24–31, Integrum Digital Archive.

[47]"Iran Parkuetsya v Rossii [Iran Is Parking in Russia]," *Kommersant" [Prilozhenie]*, October 20, 2022; "Iran Otomstit SShA Za Suleimani s Pomoshch'yu Rossii [Iran Will Avenge Soleimani with the Help of Russia against the US]," *Pravda.Ru*, July 19, 2022, Integrum Digital Archive.

Constructing Greater Eurasia

As Moscow shifted further away from Europe after the Crimea annexation in 2014, the leadership pursued a policy of the Turn to the East (*Povorot na Vostok*) and later the notion of Greater Eurasia. Iran formed a critical juncture in Moscow's vision for Eurasian integration and a like-minded partner who sought to induce a more significant transition to the East.[48] The Turn to the East was viewed through the prism of three global processes: Russia's participation in the reconfiguration of the world, Russia's implementation of the strategy for the reintegration of the post-Soviet space, and Russia's building of alternative political and economic ties to the Western direction. From Russia's perspective, Iran can serve as an influential center of gravity by connecting Eurasia to the surrounding regions and broadening opportunities for transcontinental trade.[49] One of the leading architects of Greater Eurasia, Sergey Karaganov, argues that "Iran is almost destined to become a dynamic centre of the new supercontinent, unless it falls victim to new aggression ... Iran can connect the Persian Gulf and India with the continent's north."[50] Though heavily conditioned by geographic determinism, the Russian narrative corresponds to Iran's messianic view of its historical role in Eurasia and the future potential for its reemergence as a formidable power in the region. Iran tends to portray its participation in regional initiatives as a testament to the country's centrality in promoting regional connectivity and shaping the emerging "multipolar" world order.[51] Proponents of Greater Eurasia contend that Russia, China, India, and Iran have similar

---

[48]Mohesen Pak Ayeen, "Ūrāsiyā, Quṭb-i Nū Ẓuhūr I'tilāf'hā-Yi Jahānī [Eurasia, the Emerging Pole of Global Integration]," *Jām-i Jam*, September 24, 2017; Morteza Damanpak Jami and Jalal Dihghani Firoozabadi, "Diplomāsi-ye Eqteṣādi-ye Jomhuri-ye Eslāmi-ye Irān Dar Āsiyā-Ye Markazi [Economic Diplomacy of the Islamic Republic of Iran in Central Asia]," *Faslnāmah-ye Motāla'āt-e Āsiyā-ye Markazi va Qafqāz* 22, no. 96 (February 1), 25–66.

[49]Andrei Volodin and Mariya Volodina, "Proekt mezhdunarodnogo transportnogo koridora 'Sever—Yug' kak faktor vozmozhnogo ukrepleniya vneshneekonomicheskikh svyazei Rossii [The International Transport Corridor Project 'North-South' as a Possible Factor for Strengthening Russia's Foreign Economic Ties]," *Kontury Global'nykh Transformatsii: Politika, Ekonomika, Pravo* 12, no. 6 (2019), https://doi.org/10.23932/2542-0240-2019-12-6-2.

[50]Sergey Karaganov, "The New Cold War and the Emerging Greater Eurasia," *Journal of Eurasian Studies* 9, no. 2 (July 1, 2018), 85–93, https://doi.org/10.1016/j.euras.2018.07.002.

[51]Volodin and Volodina, "Proekt mezhdunarodnogo transportnogo koridora 'Sever—Yug' kak faktor vozmozhnogo ukrepleniya vneshneekonomicheskikh svyazei Rossii [The International Transport Corridor Project 'North-South' as a Possible Factor for Strengthening Russia's Foreign Economic Ties]."

geopolitical challenges and goals, including creating a multipolar world and opposing American hegemony.[52]

Moscow's ambitions to develop the International North-South Transit Corridor (INSTC)—a multimodal network of railways, roads, and shipping routes to connect Eurasia to the Persian Gulf and South Asia—grew following the inception of the Chinese Belt and Road Initiative. Although Russia, India, and Iran formalized an agreement on the INSTC in 2002, the development corridor faced substantial setbacks in its first decade owing to domestic economic weaknesses, lack of political will, and international constraints. Russia's vision for its future economic relations implicitly relies on Iran's port infrastructure and inland road and rail networks to expand Russian exports into the Persian Gulf and South Asian markets.

Sanctions imposed on Russia after its invasion of Ukraine further elevated the importance of INSTC in Russia's domestic discourse. Russian authorities viewed INSTC as a way to solve logistical problems resulting from sanctions.[53] The development of this route is seen as necessary not only because of sanctions but also due to changes in world markets, specifically the shifting of economic activity centers to China, Southeast Asia, and the Persian Gulf.[54] Russia has not only viewed Iran as a desirable trade route due to the urgency of circumventing Western markets but has also been trying to intensify cooperation with Iran under the auspices of geo-economic ambitions. In November, Deputy Prime Minister Alexander Novak reported that Russia and Iran have agreed to sign an agreement on a free trade zone with the Eurasian Economic Union (EAEU) in the near future. Both Russia and Iran highlight the

---

[52]Maxim Braterskii, "Kontseptsii Bol'shoi Evrazii tri goda [The Concept of Greater Eurasia over Three Years]," *Aktual'nye Problemy Evropy* 109, no. 1 (2021), https://www.elibrary.ru/item.asp?id=44721591; Aleksandr Vladimirovich Lukin, "Rossiya i Kitai v Bol'shoi Evrazii [Russia and China in Greater Eurasia]," *Polis. Politicheskie Issledovaniya*, no. 5 (2020), https://doi.org/10.17976/jpps/2020.05.04; Aleksandr Aleksandrovich Dynkin, Elena Aleksandrovna Telegina, and Gyul'nar Osmanovna Khalova, "Rol' Evraziiskogo Ekonomicheskogo Soyuza V Formirovanii Bol'shoi Evrazii [The Role of the Eurasian Economic Union in the Formation of Greater Eurasia]," *Mirovaya Ekonomika I Mezhdunarodnye Otnosheniya* 62, no. 4 (2018), https://doi.org/10.20542/0131-2227-2018-62-4-5-24.

[53]"Mezhdunarodnyi Transportnyi Koridor 'Sever-Yug' Mozhet Stat' Real'nym Konkurentom Suetskomu Kanalu [International Transport Corridor 'North-South' Could Become a Real Competitor to the Suez Canal]," *Agentstvo Biznes Novostei [Sankt-Peterburg]*, November 3, 2022, Integrum Digital Archive.

[54]"Cherez Zapad Na Vostok [Through the West to the East]," *Izvestiya [Izvestiya]*, August 8, 2022, Integrum Digital Archive.

potential benefits of cooperation under the EAEU under the assumption that the EAEU would open up new avenues for trade and investment while solidifying their strategic partnership.[55]

Although Russia and Iran have developed a number of geo-economic visions and strategic plans aimed at deepening their cooperation and expanding their influence, the practical implementation of these initiatives has been limited. Nonetheless, the rhetorical emphasis on these plans has allowed Russia and Iran to project an image of closer cooperation, lending credence to their strategic partnership and enhancing their geopolitical ambitions. However, the slow progress in realizing these visions highlights the intricate and multifaceted challenges associated with economic integration in the modern geopolitical landscape, particularly in the face of ongoing sanctions and international pressure. As such, while the geo-economic visions of Russia and Iran remain an important component of their strategic calculus, their ability to transform these plans into tangible economic gains and lasting geopolitical influence remains to be seen.

Normative Partners

The formation of solidarity between Russia and Iran has been captured by a mutual contestation of the rights and rules underpinning a more ambitious normative order. Russia's relationship with Iran is evolving to reflect a shared concern for changing the norms of the international order, similar to Russia's relationship with China. Russia is incorporating aspects of its relationship with China and India into its ties with Iran, particularly in international law, as seen in the similar language used in the 2016 Russia-China and 2020 Russia-Iran declarations promoting international law. These declarations emphasize equal sovereignty, noninterference,

---

[55]Hojjat Mahkavi and Mahnaz Goodarzi, "Ta'sīr-i Ittiḥādīyah-i Iqtiṣādī-i Ūrāsiyā Bar Mawqi'īyat-i Zhi'ūikūnūmīk-i Jumhūrī-i Islāmī-i Īrān [The Impact of the Eurasian Economic Union on the Geoeconomic Position of the Islamic Republic of Iran]," *Muṭāla'āt-i Ūrāsiyā-i Markazī* 12, no. 2 (September 23, 2019), 519–38, https://doi.org/10.22059/jcep.2019.267 106.449803; Nina Mamedova, "Mezhdunarodnyi Transportnyi Koridor 'Sever-Yug' Kak Sovremennyi Analog Velikogo Volzhskogo Puti [International North-South Transport Corridor as a Modern Analogue of the Great Volga Route]," *Vostochnaya Analitika*, no. 3 (2018), 149–56; Masoud Hamiani and Mohammad Kazem Sajjadpour, "Zhi'ūpulītīk va Huviyat-i Ūrāsiyā: Īrān va Sāzmān-i Hamkārī-i Shānghāy [Geopolitics and the Identity of Eurasia: Iran and the Shanghai Cooperation Organization]," *Faslnāmah-Ye Motāla'āt-e Āsiyā-Ye Markazī va Qafqāz* 28, no. 117 (May 22, 2022), 71–98.

and the nonuse of force while opposing the extraterritorial application of national law, unilateral sanctions, and regime change under the guise of human rights. This convergence demonstrates Russia's attempt to unite with states dissatisfied with Western-led liberal norms by transferring elements of its relationship with China to Iran.[56]

Several months after the Russian invasion of Ukraine in February 2022, Iran demonstrated its support for Russia in international forums and in rhetoric. Iran was among the few countries that opposed the United Nations General Assembly resolution suspending Russia's membership in the UN Human Rights Council (UNHRC).[57] Iran publicly denounced the resolution and asserted that human rights should not be subordinated to manipulation for the benefit of certain nations.[58] Since Russia's invasion, Iranian officials have conveniently avoided censure of Moscow's actions by ardently castigating the West for exploiting human rights as a mere tool for political maneuvers. The unwavering commitment of Iran toward considering Russia as a crucial ally, coupled with its staunch advocacy for Russia's interests in the global arena, has exemplified the deep-rooted normative ties that bind Russia and Iran.[59] Even so, Iran's demonstration of support for Russia's stance against the West in the war has not translated into formal recognition of the Donetsk People's Republic or the Luhansk People's Republic. Consistent with Iran's positions on Georgia in 2008 and Crimea in 2014, Tehran has neglected to support Moscow's challenges to Ukraine's territorial integrity—an outgrowth of Iran's concerns about separatism and irredentism with its Kurdish, Baloch, and Ahvaz Arab minorities.

---

[56]Nicole Grajewski, "An Illusory Entente: The Myth of a Russia-China-Iran 'Axis,'" *Asian Affairs* 53, no. 1 (January 3, 2022), 164–83, https://doi.org/10.1080/03068374.2022.2029076.
[57]"Okolo 40 Stran Ne Vyderzhali Davleniya Zapada Pered Golosovaniem v GA OON [About 40 Countries Couldn't Withstand Pressure from the West before the Vote at the UN General Assembly]," *RIA Novosti. Vse Novosti*, October 13, 2022, Integrum Digital Archive.
[58]Sayyid Ibrāhīm Ra'īsī, "Hamkārī-i Irān bā Rusiyah, Chīn va A'ẓā-yi Shānghāy mītavānad Qodrat-hā-i Jadīdī Pāydā āvarad [Collaboration of Iran with Russia, China, and the Members of the Shanghai Cooperation Organisation Can Create New Powers]," *Pāyegāh-i Etlā' Rassānī-i Sayyid Ibrāhīm Ra'īsī*, October 5, 2022.
[59]"Glava MID Irana Osudil Postavki Zapadnogo Oruzhiya Ukraine [Iranian Foreign Minister Condemns Western Arms Supplies to Ukraine]," *URA.Ru*, September 27, 2022, Integrum Digital Archive; "Iran Napugal Zapad Zayavleniem, Kotoroe Moglo Byt' Mest'yu Rossii [Iran Scared the West with a Statement that Could Have Been Russia's Revenge]," *Pravda.Ru*, November 11, 2022, Integrum Digital Archive.

Russia's international isolation and acrimonious relations with the West offer Tehran and Moscow further incentives to strengthen their ties as both face strategic loneliness in the international arena.[60] Short of full recognition of Russia's territorial claims in Ukraine, Iran will likely remain one of the few states willing to outwardly support Moscow's narrative and political justifications for invading its neighbor.[61] In November, during a visit to Tehran with Ali Shamkhani, Nikolia Patrushev, the secretary of the Security Council of Russia, emphasized that "Russia and Iran today are at the forefront of the struggle for the establishment of a multipolar world order." He added that this "is confirmed by the unprecedented pressure on our countries from Washington and its satellites."[62] Iran's rhetoric has paralleled the Russian discourse, describing the Russia-Iran partnership as "the realization of the west's nightmare," since the world undergoes a "transfer of the axis of global power to the east from the west."[63] The common narratives of triumph over the West provide Russia and Iran with an area of bonding. Even if simply rhetorical, Moscow and Tehran's shared narratives on broader long-term processes in global affairs, such as the role of non-Western powers, provide a common discursive frame to contested concepts emanating from the West.

Russia's Resistance: Economics

The 2014 Ukraine crisis and the imposition of sanctions on Russia resulted in the country's outward challenge toward the West. The concept

---

[60]Sara Farahmand, "Jang-i Rusiyah–Ukrāin va Āyandah-Yi Niẓam-i Bayn al-Milalī [The Russia-Ukraine War and the Future of the International System]," *Faslnāmah-i Mutāla'āt-i Āsiyā-Yi Markazī va Qafqāz* 28, no. 118 (August 23, 2022), 87–113.
[61]"Iran Zanimaet Vzveshennuyu Pozitsiyu Po Ukraine, Vpolne Priemlemuyu Dlya Rossii Posol RF [Iran Takes a Balanced Position on Ukraine, Which Is Quite Acceptable for Russia—RF Ambassador]," *TASS—Mirovye Novosti*, July 13, 2022, Integrum Digital Archive.
[62]"Patrushev: Rossiya Schitaet Vazhnym Dlya Svoei Natsbezopasnosti Vzaimodeistvie s Iranom [Patrushev: Russia Considers Interaction with Iran Important for Its National Security]," *VPS-Monitoring "Banki i Birzhi Segodnya,"* November 11, 2022, Integrum Digital Archive; "Patrushev Nazval Vazhnym Dlya Natsbezopasnosti Rossii Vzaimodeistvie s Iranom [Patrushev Called Interaction with Iran Important for Russia's National Security]," *Komsomol'skaya Pravda [Msk.Kp.Ru]*, November 9, 2022, Integrum Digital Archive.
[63]"Āyatollāh Ra'īsī dar Bist-o-Dovvomīn Ajlās-i Sarān-i Sāzmān-i Hamkārī-i Shānghāy [Ayatollah Raisi at the 22nd Summit of the Shanghai Cooperation Organization Leaders]," *Pāyegāh-i Etlā' Rassānī-i Sayyid Ibrāhīm Ra'īsī*, September 16, 2022.

of self-sufficiency (*samoobespechennost'*) in the face of pressure was first articulated by Putin in 2014 when he stated, "Russia is not going to get all worked up, get offended or come begging at anyone's door. Russia is a self-sufficient country."[64] Moreover, the shared experience of punitive sanctions prompted Russian elites to look to Iran for lessons in mitigating the effects on the economy. As a result, the Russian elite began to study Iran's "resistance economy" (*Eghtesad e-Moghavemati*) as an inspiration for Russian self-sufficiency.[65] Iran's own experience of sanctions, particularly those imposed by the United States, has led to a shared understanding and inclination to resist sanctions with Russia. From Moscow's view, the common experience of sanctions has further strengthened the bond between Russia and Iran, which has served as the motivation to cooperate in the policy domain.

In addition to studying Iran's experience under sanctions, Russian officials have argued that Iran has the potential to offset sanctions pressures in areas such as industrial services, trade, and export routes.[66] In May 2022, the former Russian ambassador to Iran argued that international sanctions imposed on Moscow after its invasion of Ukraine presented an opportunity for closer economic ties with Iran.[67] Similarly, in October 2022, Russian Prime Minister Mikhail Mishutshin noted that the two states intend to strengthen their cooperation in all areas, regardless of the external situation, referring to the "illegitimate economic sanctions that unfriendly states imposed on both Russia and Iran."[68]

---

[64] Vladimir Putin, "Meeting of the Valdai International Discussion Club," *President of Russia*, October 24, 2014, http://en.kremlin.ru/events/president/transcripts/46860.
[65] Vladimir Yuratev, "Iran v Situatsii Transformatsii Sanktsionnogo Rezhima [Iran in the Situation of Sanction Regime Transformations]," *Kontury Global'nyh Transformatsii: Politika, Ėkonomika, Pravo* 10, no. 2 (2017); A. I. Salitskii, Xin Zhao, and V. I. Yurtaev, "Sanktsii i Zameshchenie Importa Na Primere Opyta Irana i Kitaia [Sanctions and Import Substitution as Exemplified by the Experience of Iran and China]," *Vestnik Rossiiskoi Akademii Nauk* 87, no. 3 (March 1, 2017), 263–72; Ivan Timofeev, "A Pyrrhic Victory: The History of the Sanctions War Against Iran" (Russian International Affairs Council, April 20, 2018).
[66] "V Usloviyakh Ekonomicheskoi Voiny s Kollektivnym Zapadom Pereorientatsiya Vneshneekonomicheskikh Svyazei Rossii Na Global'nyi Yug Stanovitsya Bezal'ternativnoi Strategiei [In the Conditions of Economic War with the Collective West, Reorientation of Russia's External Economic Ties to the Global South Becomes the Only Strategy]," *VPS-Monitoring "Banki i Birzhi Segodnya*," May 30, 2022, Integrum Digital Archive.
[67] "Rossiya i Iran Ob"edinilis' Dlya Preodoleniya Bespretsedentnykh Sanktsii [Russia and Iran Joined Forces to Overcome Unprecedented Sanctions]," *Pravda.Ru*, May 16, 2022, Integrum Digital Archive.
[68] "Sotrudnichestvo Irana I Rossii Posle Ukrainskikh Sobytii I Vvedeniya Sanktsii Stalo Rasshiryat'sya [Cooperation between Iran and Russia Has Been Expanding after the

Since the war in Ukraine, Russia and Iran have signed several agreements in which Iran would provide Russia with the much-needed resources and offer a reliable alternative to Western imports.[69] Russia and Iran agreed on barter cooperation, with Russia looking to receive auto parts and gas turbines. In reality, gas turbines remain one of the few areas in which Iran could feasibly support Russia's domestic needs. For example, Russia looked to Iran in response to the imposition of restrictions on flights of Russian airlines by the West as well as a ban on the supply of goods and technologies to Russia in the aviation and space sectors.[70] Yet, the ability of Iran to replace Western goods is marginal given the impact of economic sanctions on Iran's aviation industry.[71]

Grandiloquent statements from Russian officials continue to overstate the economic and trade opportunities with Iran. For example, Vladimir Obydenov, chairman of the Russian-Iranian Business Council, stated that Iran could "replace a number of Western goods in [Russian] markets" and serve as "an alternative to certain Western products."[72] Similarly, during a visit to Iran in May, Deputy Prime Minister Alexander Novak expressed optimism stating that Tehran and Moscow could "use the existing potential of our trade and economic relations to the fullest."[73] Yet, the absence of reliable banking channels has limited trade between Russia and Iran for decades with little progress on mitigation measures. Moreover, due to US sanctions and the difficulty of conducting trade in

---

Ukrainian Events and the Introduction of Sanctions]," *RIA Novosti. Vse Novosti*, October 13, 2022, Integrum Digital Archive.

[69]Mamedova, "Mezhdunarodnyi Transportnyi Koridor 'Sever-Yug' Kak Sovremennyi Analog Velikogo Volzhskogo Puti [International North-South Transport Corridor as a Modern Analogue of the Great Volga Route]"; "Pashinyan: Sever-Yug Blagodarya Razblokirovke Kommunikatsii Stanovitsya Proektom Sever-Yug-Vostok-Zapad [Pashinyan: North-South Becomes a Project of North-South-East-West Thanks to the Unblocking of Communications]," *VZGLYaD.AZ [Vzglyad.Az]*, February 17, 2022, Integrum Digital Archive.

[70]"Iran Ne Ustupit Zapugivaniyu so Storony SShA Prezident [Iran Will Not Yield to US Intimidation, Says President]," *TASS—Mirovye Novosti*, September 16, 2022, Integrum Digital Archive.

[71]"Rossiya i Iran Idut Na Vzlet [Russia and Iran Are Taking Off]," *Kommersant" FM (Kommersant.Ru)*, July 27, 2022, Integrum Digital Archive.

[72]"Tegeran-2022 [Tehran-2022]," *Trud—Moskva [Trud—Moscow]*, August 19, 2022, Integrum Digital Archive.

[73]"Sanktsii Zapada Pobuzhdayut Moskvu Diversifitsirovat' Marshruty Postavok Uglevodorodnykh Resursov [Sanctions from the West Encourage Moscow to Diversify Hydrocarbon Supply Routes]," *VPS-Monitoring "Biznes-Neft'*," November 8, 2022, Integrum Digital Archive.

dollars, Iran and Russia have been forced to attempt to trade with rubles and rials in bilateral trade and to integrate their financial messaging services to handle two-way banking transactions.[74]

Defense

The ongoing conflict in Ukraine has brought to the fore the extent of military cooperation between Russia and Iran, revealing a significant shift in the nature of their strategic partnership. This transformation has been made evident by Iran's provision of advanced drone technology to Russia, which has played a crucial role in the conflict. Prior to Russia's incursion into Ukraine, the military-technical relationship between Moscow and Tehran was primarily characterized by a patron-client dynamic, with Russia providing Iran with weapons and military equipment. However, the ongoing conflict has showcased the deepening of defense ties between the two nations, marked by a shared commitment to bolstering their military capabilities and safeguarding their respective strategic interests.[75]

Since the 1990s, Russia has served as a major supplier of military equipment and weaponry to Iran, providing the country with access to a range of advanced technologies, including fighter jets, missile defense systems, and other cutting-edge military hardware. Notably, the 2007 arms deal between Russia and Iran, which included the provision of advanced S-300 missile defense systems, represented a significant milestone in the history of their defense cooperation. However, the cancellation of the S-300 deal in 2010 marked a period of tension in Russia-Iran relations, driven in part by pressure from Western nations seeking to limit Iran's access to advanced military technology. It was only following the signing of the Iran nuclear deal in 2015 that Russia lifted the ban on arms sales to Iran, leading to a renewed period of military cooperation between the two nations.[76]

---

[74]Iman Samadi, "Tijārat-i Īrān va Rūsīyah Az Mavāni' Tā Furṣat'hā [Iran-Russia Trade: From Barriers to Opportunities]," *Daftar-i Muṭāla'āt-i Dīplumāsī-i Iqtiṣādī-i*, November 30, 2019, https://eco-dip.ir/تراجت-ناریا-و-هیسور-زا-عناوم-ات-تفرصت%8C%80%E2/ (accessed January 30, 2024).
[75]"Iran Zayavil o Gotovnosti Postavlyat' Oruzhie 'Druzhestvennym Stranam' [Iran Declares Readiness to Supply Weapons to 'Friendly Countries']," *VZGLYaD.AZ [Vzglyad.Az]*, July 22, 2022, Integrum Digital Archive.
[76]Vladimir Sazhin and Vladimir Evseev, *Iran, Uran i Rakety* [*Iran, Uranium and Rockets*] (Moscow: Institut Vostokovedeniya RAN, 2009).

The Syrian Civil War transformed the military-technical relationship into one characterized by interoperability and military coordination. The military campaign to preserve Assad's regime in Syria compelled Russia and Iran to adapt to the challenges of joint military cooperation on the battlefield by establishing bureaucratic channels and command structures. The experience of closer coordination in Syria and the overall improvement of Russia-Iran relations enabled the exchange of advanced military technology and weaponry, along with joint military training and operations.[77] However, Iran was often the beneficiary of Russian military technology. This changed with the war in Ukraine.

If the Syrian Civil War exhibited this growing cooperation, then the war in Ukraine demonstrated the elevated importance of Iran in Russian defense calculations. Iran has become Russia's key military supplier, providing drones that have been utilized in attacks against Ukrainian cities and energy facilities. According to Western governments, Iranian personnel have also been sent to Crimea to instruct Russian troops on how to operate the drones to target Ukrainian cities and civilian infrastructure. Russia obtained weaponized drones from Iran in a deal in late 2022, when Iran agreed to provide hundreds of drones to Russia. Both parties have sought to keep this cooperation confidential, with Iran denying involvement in the conflict.[78]

Within Russia, the question of Iran's technological capacity has been a topic of much debate and speculation. Many have doubted the country's ability to develop and produce advanced technologies, including in the realm of military hardware and weaponry. Such a trend has appeared despite the provision of Iranian drones to Russia as Moscow has continued denying its reliance on Iranian technology, emphasizing its extensive research and development capabilities. In February 2023, for example, amid reports about plans for joint production of drones by Russia and

---

[77]Aleksandr Dvornikov, "Formy boevogo primeneniya i organizatsiya upravleniya integrirovannymi gruppirovkami vooruzhennykh sil na teatre voennykh deistvii [Forms of Combat Use and the Organization of the Management of Integrated Groups of the Armed Forces at the Theater of Military Operations]," *Vestnik AVN* 63, no. 2 (2018), 37–41.
[78]"Lavrov: Zapad Ne Smog Dokazat' 'postavki' Iranom Bespilotnikov Rossii—IA REGNUM [Lavrov: The West Failed to Prove Iran's 'Deliveries' of Russian Drones]," *IA REGNUM*, December 29, 2022, Integrum Digital Archive.; "Polyanskii Otreagiroval Na Obvineniya Zapada v Poluchenii Rossiei Iranskikh Bespilotnikov [Polyansky Reacts to Accusations from the West that Russia Has Received Iranian Drones]," *URA.Ru*, October 20, 2022, Integrum Digital Archive.

Iran, Kremlin spokesman Dmitry Peskov stated, "Russia has a number of its own programs to create unmanned aerial vehicles for a variety of purposes." Moreover, the Russian leadership remains hesitant to supply Iran with its requested military technology as many in Moscow fear that advanced aircraft could fundamentally change the regional balance of power. Moreover, within the Middle East, Russia is unlikely to sacrifice its own regional ambitions for the sake of a more formal defense pact with Iran.

The war in Ukraine has transformed the military-technical relationship between Moscow and Tehran, formerly defined by a patron-client dynamic through Russia's provision of military technologies to Iran. However, despite the strengthening defense ties, a full-fledged defense pact between Russia and Iran remains unlikely.

Conclusion

The deepening of the Russia-Iran relationship since the onset of the war in Ukraine signifies the culmination of various factors that have bound the two countries together during periods of strain. Russia and Iran have recognized the value of strengthening their partnership as a way to counterbalance their ostracism and assert their influence on the global stage. The partnership is not simply a transactional alliance of convenience but a complex and multifaceted relationship with a long and, at times, fraught history.

After two decades of increasing assertiveness in their self-proclaimed spheres of influence, Russia's difficulties in Ukraine and the unabating wave of protests in Iran have brought the two partners even closer and have contributed to rebalancing a relationship that has historically been skewed in Russia's favor. The conflict in Ukraine altered this dynamic, propelling Moscow to acknowledge Iran as one of its leading international partners to obtain the necessary military supplies and to provide relief for its economy burdened by sanctions, despite the absence of a formal alliance.

The common bonding between Russia and Iran has been reflected in the increased military and political cooperation between the two countries, as well as their coordination with international organizations to promote their policy agendas. The idea of strategic empathy has become central to the way in which the Russian elite understand and approach their relationship with Iran and has played a significant role in their foreign policy decision-making. Russia and Iran have espoused perspectives on broader long-term global affairs processes such as the role of non-Western powers in shaping international order and respect for the internal diversity of states. Whereas the ostensible commitment to a "multipolar world order" has been employed to express grievances toward US structural primacy, it also reflects Russian and Iranian synergies around global politics.

Bibliography

Aksenenok, Aleksandr, and Viktoriya Fradkova. "Blizhnii Vostok vo vneshnei politike SShA posle Trampa i interesy Rossii [Post-Trump US Foreign Policy in the Middle East and the Interests of Russia]." *Mirovaya Ekonomika I Mezhdunarodnye Otnosheniya* 66, no. 1 (2022): 8–50. https://doi.org/10.20542/0131-2227-2022-66-1-38-50.

Arbatov, Alexei. "Iranskii Yadernyi Uzel [Iranian Nuclear Knot]." *Sovremennaya Evropa*, no. 1 (29) (2007): 24–36.

Arbatov, Alexei. "Natsional'naia Bezopasnost' Rossii v Mnogopoliarnom Mire [Russia's National Security in a Multipolar World]." *Mirovaya Ekonomika i Mezhdunarodnie Otnoshenia* 10, no. 4 (2000): 21–8.

Arbatov, Aleksei Georgievich. "Iranskii Yadernyi Uzel [Iran's Nuclear Knot]." *Aziya I Afrika Segodnya*, no. 2 (2010): 2–7. https://elibrary.ru/item.asp?id=16901349.

Averkov, Viktor. "Prinyatie vneshnepoliticheskikh reshenii v Rossii [The Adoption of Foreign Policy Decisions in Russia]." *Mezhdunarodnye protsessy* 29, no. 2 (2012): 110–23.

Ayeen, Mohesen Pak. "Ūrāsiyā, Quṭb-i Nū Ẓuhūr I'tilāfʿhā-Yi Jahānī [Eurasia, the Emerging Pole of Global Integration]." *Jām-i Jam*, September 24, 2017. www.magiran.com.

Baklanov, Andrei. "Rossiiskoe posrednichestvo na peregovorakh vokrug yadernoi programmy Irana [Russian Mediation in the Negotiations on Iran's Nuclear Program]." *Etnosotsium I Mezhnatsional'naya Kul'tura* 41, no. 9 (2011). https://elibrary.ru/item.asp?id=18813647.

Baranovsky, Vladimir, and Vitaly Naumkin. "Blizhnii Vostok V Menyayushchemsya Global'nom Kontekste: Klyuchevye Trendy Stoletnego Razvitiya [The Middle East in a Changing Global Context: Key Centenary Trends]." *Mirovaya Ekonomika I Mezhdunarodnye Otnosheniya* 62, no. 3 (2018). https://doi.org/10.20542/0131-2227-2018-62-3-5-19.

"Barrandāzi-ye Rangin [Colorful Overthrow]." *Jām-e Jam*, June 29, 2009, 10.

Bazhanov, Yevgeny. *Rossiya Kak Velikaya Derzhava: Traditsii I Perspektivy* [*Russia as a Great Power: Traditions and Perspectives*]. Moscow: Nauchnaya kniga, 1999.

Blagovolin, S. E. *Evoluzia struktur voennoi bezopasnosti: rol i mesto Rossii [Evolution of Military Security Structures: The Role and Place of Russia (Geopolitical Aspect)]*. Moscow: IMĖMO RAN, 1997. https://catalog.hathitr ust.org/Record/007592635.

Bukkvoll, Tor. "Arming the Ayatollahs: Economic Lobbies in Russia's Iran Policy." *Problems of Post-Communism* 49, no. 6 (November 2002): 29–41. https://doi.org/10.1080/10758216.2002.11656010.

Checkel, Jeffrey T. *Ideas and International Political Change: Soviet/Russian Behavior and the End of the Cold War*. New Haven: Yale University Press, 1997.

"Cherez Zapad Na Vostok [Through the West to the East]." *Izvestiya [Izvestiya]*, August 8, 2022. Integrum Digital Archive.

Clunan, Anne L. *The Social Construction of Russia's Resurgence: Aspirations, Identity, and Security Interests*. Baltimore: Johns Hopkins University Press, 2009.

Dimashqee, Farhad. "Negāh-ye Takāpu-Ye Doshmanān Barā-Ye Ijād-e Enqelāb-e Makhmalin Dar Irān [Enemies Trying to Look for a Velvet Revolution in Iran]." *Irān Newspaper*, July 2, p. 5, 2009.

Dolgov, Boris. "Siriiskii Konflikt [The Syrian Conflict]." In *Konflikty i Voiny XXI Veka: Blizhnii Vostok i Severnaia Afrika*, edited by Vitaly Naumkin and Dina Malysheva, 401–22. Moscow: Institut Vostokovedeniya RAN, 2015.

Dunaeva, Elena, and Nina Mamedova, eds. *Politika RF I IRI v Regional'nom Kontekste: TsA, Kavkaz, Blizhnii Vostok [The Policy of the Russian Federation and the Islamic Republic of Iran in the Regional Context: Central Asia, the Caucasus, the Middle East]*. Moscow: Institut Vostokovedeniya RAN, 2011.

Dvornikov, Aleksandr. "Formy boevogo primeneniya i organizatsiya upravleniya integrirovannymi gruppirovkami vooruzhennykh sil na teatre voennykh deistvii [Forms of Combat Use and the Organization of the Management of Integrated Groups of the Armed Forces at the Theater of Military Operations]." *Vestnik AVN* 63, no. 2 (2018): 37–41.

Farahmand, Sara. "Jang-i Rusiyah–Ukrāin va Āyandah-Yi Niẓam-i Bayn al-Milalī [The Russia-Ukraine War and the Future of the International System]." *Faslnāmah-i Mutāla'āt-i Āsiyā-Yi Markazī va Qafqāz* 28, no. 118 (August 23, 2022): 87–113.

Felgenhauer, Pavel. "Stoiat Li Rossiiskie Postavki Oruzhiya Iranu Ssory s Amerikoi [Are Russian Arms Deliveries to Iran a Quarrel with America]." *Moskovskiye Novosti*, November 28, 2000. Integrum Digital Archive.

Fenenko, Alexei. "Mezhderzhavnaia Konkurentsiya Na Blizhnem Vostoke [International Conflict in the Middle East]." *Mezhdunarodnye Protsesi* 12, no. 3 (2014): 34–54.

Filimonova, Anna Igorevna. "'Iranskaya yadernaya problema'—istoki i istoriya razvitiya ["The Iranian Nuclear Problem"—Origins and History of Development]." *Uchenyi Sovet*, no. 2 (2021). https://doi.org/10.33920/ nik-02-2102-04.

Goldstein, Judith, and Robert O. Keohane. *Ideas and Foreign Policy: Beliefs, Institutions, and Political Change*. Cornell Studies in Political Economy. Ithaca, NY: Cornell University Press, 1993.

Grajewski, Nicole. "An Illusory Entente: The Myth of a Russia-China-Iran 'Axis.'" *Asian Affairs* 53, no. 1 (January 3, 2022): 164–83. https://doi.org/10.1080/03068374.2022.2029076.

Gromyko, Aleksei. "Rossiya i Iran: Novaya Real'nost' [Russia and Iran: New Reality]." *Nezavisimaya Gazeta*, June 26, 1998. Integrum Digital Archive.

Hamiani, Masoud, and Mohammad Kazem Sajjadpour. "Zhi'ūpulītīk va Huviyat-i Ūrāsiyā: Irān va Sāzmān-i Hamkārī-i Shānghāy [Geopolitics and the Identity of Eurasia: Iran and the Shanghai Cooperation Organization]." *Faslnāmah-Ye Motāla'āt-e Āsiyā-Ye Markazi va Qafqāz* 28, no. 117 (May 22, 2022): 71–98.

Hopf, Ted. *Russia's European Choice*. New York: Palgrave Macmillan, 2008.

Hopf, Ted. *Social Construction of International Politics: Identities and Foreign Policies, Moscow, 1955 and 1999*. Ithaca, NY: Cornell University Press, 2002.

Ḥusayn'pūr, Akram, Manīzhah Turāb Zādah, Fahīmah Vazīrī, and Farībā Shahīdīfar. *Māhīyat-i Taḥavvulāt Dar Āsiyā-Yi Markazī va Qafqāz* [The Nature of Changes in Central Asia and the Caucasus]. Chapter 1. Tehran: Mu'assasah-i chāp va intishārāt-i Vizārat-i umūr-i khārijah, 1994.

"Iran Otomstit SShA Za Suleimani s Pomoshch'yu Rossii [Iran Will Avenge Soleimani with the Help of Russia against the US]." *Pravda.Ru*, July 19, 2022. Integrum Digital Archive.

"Iran Parkuetsya v Rossii [Iran Is Parking in Russia]." *Kommersant" [Prilozhenie]*, October 20, 2022. Integrum Digital Archive.

"Iran Predlozhil Rossii Sotrudnichestvo i Pomoshch' v Ukhode Ot Amerikanskikh Sanktsii [Iran Proposed Cooperation and Help to Russia in Avoiding US Sanctions]." *Komsomol'skaya Pravda*, April 1, 2022. Integrum Digital Archive.

"Iran Zanimaet Vzveshennuyu Pozitsiyu Po Ukraine, Vpolne Priemlemuyu Dlya Rossii Posol RF [Iran Takes a Balanced Position on Ukraine, Which Is Quite Acceptable for Russia—RF Ambassador]." *TASS—Mirovye Novosti*, July 13, 2022. Integrum Digital Archive.

"Iran Zayavil o Gotovnosti Postavlyat' Oruzhie 'Druzhestvennym Stranam' [Iran Declares Readiness to Supply Weapons to 'Friendly Countries']." *VZGLYaD.AZ [Vzglyad.Az]*, July 22, 2022. Integrum Digital Archive.

Istomin, Igor. "Sravnitel'nyi Analiz Prioritetov Rossiiskoi Vneshnei Politiki i Nauchno-Obrazovatel'nogo Soobshchestva Spetsialistov Po Mezhdunarodnym Otnosheniyam [Comparative Analysis of the Russian Foreign Policy Priorities and Research Interests of the National Academic Community]." *Vestnik RUDN Mezhdunarodnye Otnosheniya* 18, no. 1 (2018).

Ivanenko, Vladimir. "Iranskaia Iadernaia Programma i Rossiisko-Iranskie Otnosheniya [Iranian Nuclear Program and Russian-Iranian Relations]." *Mezhdunarodnaia Politika* 34, no. 1 (2016): 109–31.

Ivanov, Igor. "Vozvrashchenie Irana [Return of Iran]." *Rossiyskaya Gazeta*, July 17, 2014. Integrum Digital Archive.

Jackson, Nicole J. *Russian Foreign Policy and the CIS: Theories, Debates and Actions*. Routledge Advances in International Relations and Politics. London: Routledge, 2003.

Jami, Morteza Damanpak, and Jalal Dihghani Firoozabadi. "Diplomāsi-ye Eqteṣādi-ye Jomhuri-ye Eslāmi-ye Irān Dar Āsiyā-Ye Markazi [Economic Diplomacy of the Islamic Republic of Iran in Central Asia]." *Faslnāmah-ye Motālaʿāt-e Āsiyā-ye Markazi va Qafqāz* 22, no. 96 (February 2017): 25–66.

Karaganov, Sergei. "Mir stanovitsia vse menee prozapadnym [The World Is Becoming Less Pro-Western]." *Rossiiskaia Gazeta*, April 24, 2014. Integrum Digital Archive.

Karaganov, Sergei. "Novye Vyzovy Bezopasnosti: Rossiya i Zapad [New Security Challenges: Russia and West]." *Sovremennaya Evropa*, no. 1 (9) (2002): 38–46.

Karaganov, Sergey. "The New Cold War and the Emerging Greater Eurasia." *Journal of Eurasian Studies* 9, no. 2 (July 1, 2018): 85–93. https://doi.org/10.1016/j.euras.2018.07.002.

Karpov, Mikhail, and Dmitrii Gornostayev. "Rossiya i SShA Soglasilis', Chto Ne Soglasny Drug s Drugom Na Rasshirenie Severoatlanticheskogo Soyuza Moskva Otvetit Svoim Prodvizheniem Na Vostok [Moscow and the USA Agreed to Disagree on the Enlargement of the North Atlantic Alliance, Moscow Will Respond with Its Advance to the East]." *Nezavisimaya Gazeta*, March 22, 1997. Integrum Digital Archive.

Kashafi, Mohammed. "Ingilistān va Ru'yā-yi Mujaddid-i Dikhālat dar Īrān [The UK and the Repeated Dream of Interference in Iran]." *Jam-i Jam*, September 21, 2009. http://jamejamonline.ir/fa/news/282081.

Khatuntsev, Stanislav. "Zapad i 'Evraziiskaya Kvadriga' (Rossiya, Kitai, Indiya, Iran) [The West and the 'Eurasian Quadriga' (Russia, China, India, Iran)]." *Polis. Politicheskie Issledovaniya*, no. 6 (2015): 45–52.

Khosravi, Mohammad Ali, and Davoud Bayat. "Qālbod Shekāfi Enqelābhā-Ye Rangi va Taasiri Ān Dar Irān [Anatomy of Colored Revolutions and Its Effect in Iran]." *Moṭālaʿāt Ravābeṭ-e Bayn al-Melali* 3, no. 13 (2011): 57–94.

Kommersant. "Otnosheniya Mezhdu Rossiei i Iranom [Relations between Russia and Iran]." December 25, 1996.

"Kontseptsiya Vneshney Politiki Rossiyskoy Federatsii [Foreign Policy Conception of the Russian Federation]." *Diplomaticheskii Vestnik* 8 (2000): 3–11.

Koretskii, Aleksandr. "Voennoe Sotrudnichestvo Rossii i Irana [Military Cooperation of Russia and Iran]." *Kommersant*, October 1, 1994. Arkhivy federal'nykh SMI, Kommersant 1991–1999: ZAO Kommersant Izdatel'skii dom. Integrum Digital Archive.

Kozhanov, Nikolay, and Leonid Isaev. "Iran I Sanktsii: Opyt Preodoleniya I Vliyanie Na Sotsial'no-Ekonomicheskoe Razvitie [Iran and

Sanctions: Experience of Overcoming and Impact on Socio-Economic Development]." *Aziya i Afrika Segodnya*, 2019, 24–31.

Kozyrev, Andrei. *Preobrazhenie [Transfiguration]*. Moscow: Mezhdunarodnye Otnosheniya, 1995.

"Lavrov: Zapad Ne Smog Dokazat' 'postavki' Iranom Bespilotnikov Rossii—IA REGNUM [Lavrov: The West Failed to Prove Iran's 'Deliveries' of Russian Drones]." *IA REGNUM*, December 29, 2022. Integrum Digital Archive.

Levchenko, Alexander, and Alexei Tsypin. "RF Vidit v Irane Nadezhnogo, Perspektivnogo Partnera [Russia Sees a Reliable, Promising Partner in Iran]." *ITAR-TASS*, November 18, 2014. Integrum Digital Archive.

Lukin, Alexander, and Tamara Troyakova. "Mnogopolyarnaya Vostochnaya Aziya: Tendentsiya Ili Uzhe Real'nost'? [Multipolar East Asia: A Trend or Already a Reality?]." *Problemy Dal'nego Vostoka*, December 31, 2010, 168–73.

Lukin, Vladimir. "Rossiya i Ee Interesy [Russia and Its Interests]." *Nezavisimaia Gazeta*, October 20, 1992, 202 (373) edition. Arkhivy federal'nykh SMI, Nezavisimaia Gazeta (1990–2005): ZAO Redaktsiya "Nezavisimoi Gazety." Integrum Digital Archive.

Lukyanov, Fyodor. "Rossiya i Ne-Zapad [Russia and the Non-West]." *Nezavisimaia Gazeta*, June 24, 2014. Integrum Digital Archive.

Mahkavi, Hojjat, and Mahnaz Goodarzi. "Ta'sīr-i Ittiḥādīyah-i Iqtiṣādī-i Ūrāsiyā Bar Mawqi'īyat-i Zhi'ūikūnūmīk-i Jumhūrī-i Islāmī-i Īrān [The Impact of the Eurasian Economic Union on the Geoeconomic Position of the Islamic Republic of Iran]." *Muṭāla'āt-i Urāsiyā-i Markazī* 12, no. 2 (September 23, 2019): 519–38. https://doi.org/10.22059/jcep.2019.267106.449803.

Malcolm, Neil, Margot Light, Roy Allison, and Alex Pravda. *Internal Factors in Russian Foreign Policy*. New York: Oxford University Press, 1996.

Mamedova, Nina. "Mezhdunarodnyi Transportnyi Koridor 'Sever-Yug' Kak Sovremennyi Analog Velikogo Volzhskogo Puti [International North-South Transport Corridor as a Modern Analogue of the Great Volga Route]." *Vostochnaya Analitika*, no. 3 (2018): 149–56.

Mamedova, Nina. "Vzaimnye Interesy Rossii I Irana: Istoricheskaia Evoliutsiya I Nyneshnii Etap [Mutual Interests of Russia and Iran: Historical Evolution and the Present Stage]." In *Rossiya i Islamskii Mir: Istoricheskaia Retrospektiva i Sovremennye Tendentsii*, edited by Viacheslav Belokrenitskii, Il'ia Zaitsev, and Natalia Ul'chenko, 27–29. Moscow: Institut Vostokovedeniya RAN, 2010.

Margelov, Mikhail. "Rossiya i Ne-Zapad. Paradoksy Mul'tipolyarnosti [Russia and Non-West: Paradoxes of Multipolarity]." *RossiyskayaGazeta*, August 25, 2022. Integrum Digital Archive.

McFaul, Michael. "Putin, Putinism, and the Domestic Determinants of Russian Foreign Policy." *International Security* 45, no. 2 (October 1, 2020): 95–139. https://doi.org/10.1162/isec_a_00390.

"Mezhdunarodnyi Transportnyi Koridor 'Sever-Yug' Mozhet Stat' Real'nym Konkurentom Suetskomu Kanalu [International Transport Corridor 'North-South' Could Become a Real Competitor to the Suez Canal]." *Agentstvo*

Biznes Novostei [Sankt-Peterburg], November 3, 2022. Integrum Digital Archive.

Migranyan, Andranik. "Podlinnye i Mnimye Orientiry vo Vneshnei Politike [The Real and Imaginary Directions of Foreign Policy]." *Rossiyskaya Gazeta*, August 4, 1992. Integrum Digital Archive.

Mirsky, Georgi. "Iran i SShA: protivostoyanie na fone 'yadernogo krizisa' [Iran and the US: Confrontation against the Backdrop of the 'Nuclear Crisis']." *Mirovaya Ekonomika I Mezhdunarodnye Otnosheniya*, no. 7 (2006). https://elibrary.ru/item.asp?id=9220234.

Moravcsik, Andrew. "Taking Preferences Seriously: A Liberal Theory of International Politics." *International Organization* 51, no. 4 (October 1, 1997): 513–53. https://doi.org/10.1162/002081897550447.

"Na Zapade Zakryvayut, Na Vostoke Otkryvayut [They Close in the West, They Open in the East]." *Sankt-Peterburgskie Vedomosti*, March 5, 2022. Integrum Digital Archive.

Naumkin, Vitaly. "Yadernye Ambitsii Tegerana: Mif I Real'nost' [Nuclear Ambitions of Iran: Myth or Reality]." *Trud*, October 12, 2005. Integrum Digital Archive.

Neumann, Iver B. *Russia and the Idea of Europe: A Study in Identity and International Relations*. London: Routledge, 2016.

Nikitin, Aleksandr. "Novaia sistema otnoshenii velikih derzhav XXI veka: 'kontsert' ili konfrontatsiya? [New System of Relations between Great Powers for the XXI Century: 'Concert' or Confrontation?]." *Polis. Politicheskie issledovaniya*, no. 1 (January 25, 2016): 44–59.

"Okolo 40 Stran Ne Vyderzhali Davleniya Zapada Pered Golosovaniem v GA OON [About 40 Countries Couldn't Withstand Pressure from the West before the Vote at the UN General Assembly]—Polyanskii." *RIA Novosti. Vse Novosti*, October 13, 2022.

Orlov, Vladimir, Roland Makhmutovich Timberbaev, and Anton Khlopkov. *Problemy yadernogo nerasprostraneniya v rossiisko-amerikanskikh otnosheniyakh: istoriya, vozmozhnosti i perspektivy dal'neishego vzaimodeistviya [Nuclear Non-proliferation Issues in Russian-American Relations: History, Opportunities, and Prospects for Further Interaction]*. Moscow: PIR-Tsentr politicheskikh issledovanii, 2001. https://russiancouncil.ru/library/library_rsmd/problemy-yadernogo-nerasprostraneniya-v-rossiysko-amerikanskikh-otnosheniyakh-istoriya-vozmozhnosti-i-perspektivy-dalneyshego-vzaimodeystviya/ (accessed January 30, 2024).

Parlamentskaia Gazeta. "Glava Sovbeza Patrushev Rasskazal Iranskomu Kollege Ob Organizatorah Himataki v Sirii [Security Council Chief Patrushev Told His Iranian Counterpart about the Organizers of the Chemical Attack in Syria]." April 8, 2017. Integrum Digital Archive.

"Pashinyan: Sever-Yug Blagodarya Razblokirovke Kommunikatsii Stanovitsya Proektom Sever-Yug-Vostok-Zapad [Pashinyan: North-South Becomes a Project of North-South-East-West Thanks to the Unblocking of

Communications]." *VZGLYaD.AZ [Vzglyad.Az]*, February 17, 2022. Integrum Digital Archive.

"Patrushev Nazval Vazhnym Dlya Natsbezopasnosti Rossii Vzaimodeistvie s Iranom [Patrushev Called Interaction with Iran Important for Russia's National Security]." *Komsomol'skaya Pravda [Msk.Kp.Ru]*, November 9, 2022. Integrum Digital Archive.

Patrushev, Nikolai. "Interv'yu Sekretarya Soveta Bezopasnosti Rossiiskoi Federatsii N.P.Patrusheva [Interview with Secretary of the Security Council of the Russian Federation N.P. Patrushev]." *Kommersant*, January 12, 2012, 3 (4788) edition. Integrum Digital Archive.

"Patrushev: Rossiya Schitaet Vazhnym Dlya Svoei Natsbezopasnosti Vzaimodeistvie s Iranom [Patrushev: Russia Considers Interaction with Iran Important for Its National Security]." *VPS-Monitoring "Banki i Birzhi Segodnya,"* November 11, 2022. Integrum Digital Archive.

"Peskov: Rossiya, Kak Iran, Mozhet Desyatiletiyami Zhit' Pod Sanktsiyami Radi Suvereniteta [Peskov: Russia, like Iran, Can Live under Sanctions for Decades for the Sake of Sovereignty]." *IA Rosbalt*, July 18, 2022. Integrum Digital Archive.

"Polyanskii Otreagiroval Na Obvineniya Zapada v Poluchenii Rossiei Iranskikh Bespilotnikov [Polyansky Reacts to Accusations from the West that Russia Has Received Iranian Drones]." *URA.Ru*, October 20, 2022. Integrum Digital Archive.

Pravda.Ru. "Iran Napugal Zapad Zayavleniem, Kotoroe Moglo Byt' Mest'yu Rossii [Iran Scared the West with a Statement that Could Have Been Russia's Revenge]." November 11, 2022. Integrum Digital Archive.

Pravda.ru. "Rossiya i Iran Ob"edinilis' Dlya Preodoleniya Bespretsedentnykh Sanktsii [Russia and Iran Joined Forces to Overcome Unprecedented Sanctions]." May 16, 2022. Integrum Digital Archive.

Primakov, Yevgeny. *Mir Posle 11 Sentyabrya [The World after September 11th]*. Moscow: Mysl', 2002. Integrum Digital Archive.

Pushkov, Alexei. "Rossiya i SShA: Predely Sblizheniya [Russia and the USA: Limits of Convergence]." *Nezavisimaya Gazeta*, December 27, 2001. Integrum Digital Archive.

Putin, Vladimir. "Meeting of the Valdai International Discussion Club." *President of Russia*, October 24, 2014. http://en.kremlin.ru/events/president/transcripts/46860.

RIA Novosti. "Glava MID Rossii Primet Uchastie vo Vstreche Glav Vneshnepoliticheskikh Vedomstv 'Shesterki' Po Yadernoi Probleme Irana [Head of the Russian Foreign Ministry Will Participate in the Meeting of Foreign Ministers 'Six' on the Iranian Nuclear Problem]." June 1, 2006. Integrum Digital Archive.

"Rossiya i Iran Idut Na Vzlet [Russia and Iran Are Taking Off]." *Kommersant" FM (Kommersant.Ru)*, July 27, 2022. Integrum Digital Archive.

Safranchuk, Ivan, and Fyodor Lukyanov. "Sovremennyi Mirovoi Poryadok: Strukturnye Realii i Sopernichestvo Velikikh Derzhav [Modern World

Order: Structural Realities and Great Power Rivalries]." *Polis. Politicheskie Issledovaniya*, no. 3 (2021): 57–76.

Salitskii, A. I., Xin Zhao, and V. I. Yurtaev. "Sanktsii i Zameshchenie Importa Na Primere Opyta Irana i Kitaia [Sanctions and Import Substitution as Exemplified by the Experience of Iran and China]." *Vestnik Rossiiskoi Akademii Nauk* 87, no. 3 (March 1, 2017): 263–72.

Samadi, Iman. "Tijārat-i Īrān va Rūsīyah Az Mavāni' Tā Furṣat'hā [Iran-Russia Trade: From Barriers to Opportunities]." *Daftar-i Muṭāla'āt-i Dīplumāsī-i Iqtiṣādī-i*, November 30, 2019. https://eco-dip.ir/-تجارت-ایران-و-روسیه-از-موانع-تا-فرصت%E2%80%8C‎/ (accessed January 30, 2024).

"Sanktsii Ne Pomeshayut Sotrudnichestvu Rf I Irana, Tegeran Pomozhet Rossiiskim Kompaniyam Vyiti Na Novye Rynki—Zamministra Nefti Irana Ria No 9 [Sanctions Will Not Hinder Cooperation between Russia and Iran, Tehran Will Help Russian Companies Enter New Markets—Deputy Minister of Oil of Iran RIA Novosti]." *RIA Novosti. Vse Novosti*, October 14, 2022. Integrum Digital Archive.

"Sanktsii Zapada Pobuzhdayut Moskvu Diversifitsirovat' Marshruty Postavok Uglevodorodnykh Resursov [Sanctions from the West Encourage Moscow to Diversify Hydrocarbon Supply Routes]." *VPS-Monitoring "Biznes-Neft'*," November 8, 2022. Integrum Digital Archive.

Sarukhanyan, Sevak Norairovich. "Iranskaya Atomnaya Bomba. Byt' Ili Ne Byt'? [Iranian Atomic Bomb: To Be or Not to Be?]." *Polis. Politicheskie Issledovaniya*, no. 4 (2005): 109–16.

Sayyid Ibrāhīm Ra'īsī. "Hamkārī-i Irān bā Rusiyah, Chīn va A'ẓā-yi Shānghāy mītavānad Qodrat-hā-i Jadīdī Pāydā āvarad. [Collaboration of Iran with Russia, China, and the Members of the Shanghai Cooperation Organisation Can Create New Powers.]" *Pāyegāh-i Etlā' Rassānī-i Sayyid Ibrāhīm Ra'īsī*, October 5, 2022. https://raisi.ir/news/5336/-همکاری-ایران-با-روسیه-چین-و-اعضای-شانگ‌های-می‌تواند-قدرت‌های-جدیدی-پدید-آورد.

Sazhin, Vladimir, and Vladimir Evseev. *Iran, Uran i Rakety [Iran, Uranium and Rockets]*. Moscow: Institut Vostokovedeniya RAN, 2009.

Segodnya. "Interv'iu c Poslom RF v SShA Vladimirom Lukinym [Interview with the Ambassador of the Russian Federation in the USA Vladimir Lukin]." September 3, 1993, 48 edition. Arkhivy federal'nykh SMI, Segodnya 1994–1999: ZAO. Integrum Digital Archive.

Shirazi, Habibollah Abolhassan. "Ta'ṣīrāt-i Bahār-i 'Arabī va Inqilābha-Yi Rangi Dar Āsiyā-Yi Markazī va Qafqāz [Influences of Arabic Spring and Color Revolutions in Central Asia and the Caucasus]." *Muṭāla'āt Ravābiṭ-i Bayn al-Milal* 5, no. 19 (2012): 9–36.

"Sotrudnichestvo Irana I Rossii Posle Ukrainskikh Sobytii I Vvedeniya Sanktsii Stalo Rasshiryat'sya [Cooperation between Iran and Russia Has Been Expanding after the Ukrainian Events and the Introduction of Sanctions]." *RIA Novosti. Vse Novosti*, October 13, 2022. Integrum Digital Archive.

Sovet po vneshnei i oboronnoi politike. "Rossii v XXI Veke: Analiz Situatsii i Nekotorye Predlozheniya (Strategiya-3) [Russia's Strategy in the 21st

Century: Analysis of the Situation and Some Suggestions (Strategy-3)]." Moscow, June 19, 1998.
Sovet po vneshnei i oboronnoi politike. "Strategiya Dlya Rossii: Povestka Dnya Dlya Prezidenta-2000 [Strategy for Russia: Agenda for the President-2000]." Moscow, 2000. https://www.svop.ru/files/meetings/m026013379414301.pdf.
Stankevich, Sergei. "Derzhava V Poiskah Sebia [A Power in Search of Itself]." *Nezavisimaya Gazeta*, March 28, 1992. Integrum Digital Archive.
Ṭahmāsbī'pūr, Amīr Hūshang, and Humāyūn Ārāmish. *Abzārhā-yi jang-i narm ʿalayh-i Jumhūrī-i Islāmī-i Īrān* [*Soft War Tools Against the Islamic Republic of Iran*]. Tehran: Nashr-i Sāqī, 2011.
TASS—*Mirovye Novosti*. "Iran Ne Ustupit Zapugivaniyu so Storony SShA Prezident [Iran Will Not Yield to US Intimidation, Says President]." September 16, 2022. Integrum Digital Archive.
Taylor, Brian D. *The Code of Putinism*. Oxford: Oxford University Press, 2018.
"Tegeran-2022 [Tehran-2022]." *Trud—Moskva* [*Trud—Moscow*], August 19, 2022. Integrum Digital Archive.
Timofeev, Ivan. "A Pyrrhic Victory: The History of the Sanctions War against Iran." Russian International Affairs Council, April 20, 2018. http://russiancouncil.ru/en/analytics-and-comments/analytics/a-pyrrhic-victory-the-history-of-the-sanctions-war-against-iran/.
Titarenko, Mikhail, and Vladimir Petrovskii. *Rossiya, Kitai i Novyi Mirovoi Poryadok* [*Russia, China and the New World Order*]. Moscow: Ves' Mir, 2016. https://www.vesmirbooks.ru/book/9785777706201/ (accessed January 30, 2024).
Torkunov, Anatolii, and Nodari Simonia. "Novyi Mirovoi Poryadok: Ot Bipolyarnosti k Mnogopolyusnosti [New World Order: From Bipolarity to Multipolarity]." *Polis. Politicheskie Issledovaniya*, no. 3 (2015): 27–37.
Tsygankov, Andrei P. *Mezhdunarodnye otnosheniya: traditsii russkoi politicheskoi mysli* [*International Relations: Traditions of Russian Political Thought*]. Moscow: Al'fa-M, 2013.
Tsygankov, Andrei. *Russia's Foreign Policy: Change and Continuity in National Identity*. Fourth edition. Lanham: Rowman & Littlefield, 2016.
Umnov, Aleksandr. "Strategicheskie Interesy RF Na Blizhnem i Srednem Vostoke [Strategic Interests of the Russian Federation in the Near and Middle East]." *Nezavisimaya Gazeta*, December 20, 1996. Integrum Digital Archive.
URA.Ru. "Glava MID Irana Osudil Postavki Zapadnogo Oruzhiya Ukraine [Iranian Foreign Minister Condemns Western Arms Supplies to Ukraine]." September 27, 2022. Integrum Digital Archive.
"V Irane Nashli Prichinu Provala Antirossiiskikh Sanktsii [In Iran, the Reason for the Failure of Anti-Russian Sanctions Was Found]." *URA.Ru*, May 30, 2022. Integrum Digital Archive.
"V Usloviyakh Ekonomicheskoi Voiny s Kollektivnym Zapadom Pereorientatsiya Vneshneekonomicheskikh Svyazei Rossii Na Global'nyi Yug Stanovitsya Bezal'ternativnoi Strategiei [In the Conditions of Economic War

with the Collective West, Reorientation of Russia's External Economic Ties to the Global South Becomes the Only Strategy]." *VPS-Monitoring "Banki i Birzhi Segodnya,"* May 30, 2022. Integrum Digital Archive.

Vasil'ev, Alexei. *Ot Lenina Do Putina: Rossiya Na Blizhnem i Srednem Vostoke [From Lenin to Putin: Russia in the Near and Middle East].* Moscow: Tsentrpoligraf, 2018.

Volodin, Andrei, and Mariya Volodina. "Proekt mezhdunarodnogo transportnogo koridora 'Sever—Yug' kak faktor vozmozhnogo ukrepleniya vneshneekonomicheskikh svyazei Rossii [The International Transport Corridor Project 'North-South' as a Possible Factor for Strengthening Russia's Foreign Economic Ties]." *Kontury Global'nykh Transformatsii: Politika, Ekonomika, Pravo* 12, no. 6 (2019). https://doi.org/10.23932/2542-0240-2019-12-6-2.

White, Stephen, and Valentina Feklyunina. *Identities and Foreign Policies in Russia, Ukraine and Belarus: The Other Europes.* Basingstoke: Palgrave Macmillan, 2014.

Yakovlev, Alexander. "Perebalansirovka sistemy mezhdunarodnykh otnoshenii na Blizhnem Vostoke v XXI v. [Rebalancing the System of International Relation in the Middle East in the 21st Century]." *Vostok. Afro-aziatskie obshchestva: istoriya i sovremennost,* no. 2 (2020): 119. https://doi.org/10.31857/S086919080009061-4.

Yuratev, Vladimir. "Iran v Situatsii Transformatsii Sanktsionnogo Rezhima [Iran in the Situation of Sanction Regime Transformations]." *Kontury Global'nyh Transformatsii: Politika, Ėkonomika, Pravo* 10, no. 2 (2017). Integrum Digital Archive.

Yusin, Maxim. "Moskva Predlagaet Tegeranu Strategicheskoe Partnerstvo [Moscow Offers Tehran a 'Strategic Partnership']." *Izvestiya,* April 1, 1993. Integrum Digitial Archive.

Zatulin, Konstantin. "Moskva i Tegeran Gotovy Ob"edinit' Usiliya [Moscow and Tehran Are Ready to Join Forces]." *Nezavisimaia Gazeta,* November 4, 1995, 114 edition. Arkhivy federal'nykh SMI, Nezavisimaia Gazeta (1990–2005): ZAO Redaktsiya "Nezavisimoi Gazety." Integrum Digitial Archive.

2 THE UKRAINE WAR AND INTERNAL DEBATES IN IRAN

Mahmood Shoori

Introduction

Despite the obvious reluctance of the Islamic Republic toward interference of public opinion in the process of foreign policy decisions, ordinary Iranians' reactions and approaches often find a way to influence decision-making. Such influences should be traced not necessarily in the decisions that the Islamic Republic has made, but also in the decisions that the political system avoids due to possible popular negative reactions. In the beginning, Russia's invasion of Ukraine in February 2022 may not have been as shocking and problematic for ordinary Iranians as it was for the West, but immediately, the question of what position should be taken against this invasion regardless of government and official policies, or what consequences this issue could have for Iran, became a popular question for many elites and even ordinary people. Beyond the confrontation between ethnicities and politics, which has affected an important part of the approaches to this international event, the concern of falling into the Russian trap emerged. Public opinion immediately compared the negative consequences of the Ukraine war for Iran under the lens of unpleasant historical memories of Russia's treasons. In this way, the war in Ukraine became a tangible and sensitive issue in Iran too.

This chapter focuses on how the perceptions and approaches of domestic actors in Iran, including public opinion, media, and political elites, have affected the process of decision-making and policies related to the cooperation between Iran and Russia. The chapter argues that, at best, public opinion has prevented the dominance of extreme approaches regarding open and all-around support for Russia and prevented Iran from publicly joining Russia against NATO.

Domestic Level of Analysis

The study and monitoring of domestic debates and public opinion is considered one of the key variables influencing foreign policy decisions.[1] In recent decades, theories of foreign policy analysis have paid greater attention to the relationship between public opinion and government policies, as it is assumed that there is a causal relationship between the two and that the citizens' collective preferences serve as a catalyst for the policies of the state.[2]

A relatively large set of research in recent years has sought to explain and confirm the claim that the domestic political configurations of national governments broadly influence, or modify, their involvement in international affairs.[3] Leaders are viewed as coping simultaneously with the pressures and constraints of their own domestic political systems as well as with those of the international environment.[4]

On the contrary, it assumes that all foreign policy decisions occur based on specific domestic contexts such as values, national character, political culture, and historical traditions of a society, its structural attributes, and the specific political issues that are important at any given time.[5] Perspectives that emphasize domestic sources of foreign policy

---

[1] See Rose Gideon, "Neoclassical Realism and Theories of Foreign Policy," *World Politics* 51, no. 1 (1998), 144–72.
[2] Cale D. Horne, "The Structure and Significance of Public Opinion in Non-Democratic Contexts" (PhD dissertation, University of Georgia, 2010); Joe D. Hagan, "Domestic Political Explanations," in *Foreign Policy Analysis: Continuity and Change in Its Second Generation*, edited by Laura Neack, Jeanne A. K. Heyand, and Patrick J. Haney (Englewood Cliffs: Prentice Hall, 1995), 319; Douglas C. Foyle, "Public Opinion and Foreign Policy: Elite Beliefs as a Mediating Variable," *International Studies Quarterly* 41, no. 1 (March 1997), 141–69.
[3] Juliet Kaarbo, "A Foreign Policy Analysis Perspective on the Domestic Politics Turn in IR Theory," *International Studies Review* 17, no. 2 (June 2015), 189–216.
[4] Hagan, "Domestic Political Explanations," 117.
[5] Deborah Gerner, "The Evolution of the Study of Foreign Policy," in *Foreign Policy Analysis: Continuity and Change in Its Second Generation*, edited by Laura Neack, Jeanne A. K. Heyand, and Patrick J. Haney (Englewood Cliffs: Prentice Hall, 1995), 21.

highlight different internal voices and conflicts over foreign policy. These many voices originate from various levels of actors and institutions—the public, societal groups, government organizations, and leaders.[6]

Despite the more serious attention of foreign policy theorists to the subject of public opinion in recent years, the study of the relationship between public opinion and foreign policy is faced with two serious ambiguities: first, ambiguity about the nature and manner of formation of public opinion, and second, the uncertainty about the extent and how effective it is. Public opinion is accused of lacking structure, stability, and coherence, especially in the context of foreign policy issues, and may be directed or instigated by governments, elites, or the media. The influence process is often portrayed as running from the top down.[7]

Some realist theorists argue, based on conventional wisdom, that public opinion is not only irrelevant to shaping foreign policy but that it should also not do so.[8] However, in recent decades, due to various reasons, including the expansion of democracy and demands for accountability, the importance of public opinion in foreign policy has increased. The expansion of social networks has practically made it impossible to ignore public opinion in the policy-making process. Indeed, new approaches emphasize that not only are domestic audiences capable of understanding and rationally responding to global events, but that even these opinions also influence policy outcomes. However, the influence of social debates and public opinion on foreign policy decisions depends on various factors, among them the status of democracy, the government's commitment and obligation to free elections, the government's accountability, its need for legitimacy, and regional and international conditions. Thus, the sensitivity of political systems to public opinion in foreign policy issues is subject-centric, which means that sensitivity can be different from one subject matter to another. Even democratic systems may advance policies

---

[6]Juliet Kaarbo, Jeffrey S. Lantis, and Ryan K. Beasley, "The Analysis of Foreign Policy in Comparative Perspective," in *Foreign Policy in Comparative Perspective: Domestic and International Influences on State Behavior*, edited by Ryan K. Beasley, Juliet Kaarbo, Jeffrey S. Lantis, and Michael T. Snarr (London: SAGE, 2013), 13.
[7]Thomas Knecht and M. Stephen Weatherford, "Public Opinion and Foreign Policy: The Stages of Presidential Decision Making," *International Studies Quarterly* 50, no. 3 (September 2006), 705, https://doi.org/10.1111/j.1468-2478.2006.00421.x.
[8]Joshua D. Kertzer, "Public Opinion and Foreign Policy," in *The Oxford Handbook of Political Psychology*, edited by Huddy, Leonie, David O. Sears, and Jack S. Levy, 3rd edn (Oxford: Oxford Academic, September 21, 2021), 1.

without the proper inclusion of public opinion on some issues,[9] while nondemocratic systems might be forced to notice public opinion on certain sensitive matters. This approach is what helps us in this chapter to understand better the fluid nature of domestic debates' impacts on Iran's decisions toward Russia.

Domestic Debates and Iranian Foreign Policy

In the case of Iran, regardless of discussions on the nature of the political system, foreign policy issues have been the subject of elite debates, public scrutiny, and discussion. This fact relates to a number of foreign policy challenges that the country faces that directly impact society, such as sanctions and risks of military conflict. In the past four decades, most of the regional and international developments have influenced Iran's internal politics in one way or another. Among them are the occupation of Afghanistan by the Soviet Union in December 1979, the Arab-Israeli peace talks, the collapse of the Soviet Union in 1991, the September 11 terrorist attack and the subsequent US invasion of Afghanistan in 2001 and Iraq in 2003, the Arab Spring, the emergence of ISIS in 2014, and finally the Russian invasion of Ukraine in February 2022. In addition, the eight-year war between Iran and Iraq and the endless conflict between the Islamic Republic and the major world powers over Iran's nuclear activities should be added to the long list of events that have had a direct impact on the economic and social life of Iranians. Just for the nuclear dispute, during the years 2006–9, six Security Council resolutions were approved, which imposed a significant number of international sanctions against Iran.

People are continuously influenced by foreign policy decisions; thus, foreign policy has been elevated to the central issue in social discourse in Iran. According to the available evidence, in the presidential elections of 2013 and 2017, the hopes for solving the nuclear issue and improving Iran's external relations were one of the most important issues that helped Hassan Rouhani win the election.[10] Compared to other presidential

---

[9] For example, see Foyle, "Public Opinion and Foreign Policy."
[10] For example, look at the report from World Public Opinion, March 31, 2016, https://worldpublicopinion.net/iran-poll-shows-rouhani-comes-out-of-election-with-broad-based-support/.

candidates, Rouhani's election slogan was characterized by an emphasis on foreign policy challenges, including resolution of the nuclear issue through negotiations with the world powers and normalization of the country, as well as improving relations with neighboring countries such as Saudi Arabia.

However, public debates on foreign policy issues in a country like Iran, where the identity of the political system is linked to specific foreign policy orientations, have clear borders and boundaries, which means it is less likely that public debates engage with issues that are considered as the state's red lines. Notwithstanding such limits, to analyze better the social debates on foreign policy issues in Iran, several points should be considered.

First, the political system has never been fully closed to public debate, even on sensitive areas of foreign policy, such that no dialogue or comment is tolerated. Even in the most difficult circumstances, serious debates on sensitive foreign policy issues took place at a limited level in the media. Second, non-state-owned media and social media platforms, despite increasing pressures and restrictions, still play an active role in the Iranian political scene, and important political issues, including those that are considered as red lines, can be seriously criticized and challenged by different factions.

Third, restrictions and closure of public debates, imposing the feeling of fear and worry about freely expressing an opinion, which can cause self-censorship or putative measures, are not the same in different times and conditions. For example, close to election times, especially presidential elections, and during political crises, the Islamic Republic shows a higher level of tolerance to opposing views. Finally, apart from sensitive security issues or issues that affect the ontological security of the political system in terms of identity, in other foreign policy issues, the media and public opinion have more relative freedom to express their views.

On the contrary, there are many reasons and signs that the political system in Iran is not indifferent to the views and approaches that are raised at the public level. Although, in the end, public opinion may not have an influential role in foreign policy decisions, attracting the support of people and elites, especially on issues that can have direct impacts on economic and social conditions, has been one of the most important concerns of the Islamic Republic.

For example, the state media and the propaganda machine have been continuously trying to persuade public opinion in different ways and means regarding the reasons for enmity with the United States and Israel. This can be best seen in the slogans "Death to America" and "Death to Israel," which are often repeated in political and religious ceremonies since the 1979 revolution. A similar situation can be seen regarding the public perception of Iran's nuclear program. Between 2007 and 2015, during the presidency of Mahmoud Ahmadinejad and during the peak of nuclear tensions between Iran and the Western powers, the slogan "Nuclear Energy Is Our Inalienable Right" became a central slogan in every official ceremony due to the Islamic Republic's need to attract public support for its policies.

The relationship between the political system and public opinion in Iran has been a very complex and intertwined one due to various factors ranging from religiosity, political efficacy, and exogenous shocks. For at least the first two decades after the 1979 Islamic Revolution and during the Iran-Iraq War, the state-society gap on foreign policy issues was minimal. However, as we move away from the early years of the revolution, the gap between the parts of society and the political elites grew on several issues that gradually became the Islamic Republic's main foreign policy red lines.

As an example, Attaullah Mohajerani, the parliamentary deputy of the then president Akbar Hashemi Rafsanjani, wrote an article in the *Etteleaat* newspaper on May 28, 1991, a year after the death of Ayatollah Khomeini, in which Mohajerani broke the taboo and spoke about the necessity of direct negotiations with the United States. In fact, the article echoed the voices of a part of the elites and society for whom the prohibition of direct talks with the United States was not understandable. In another case, although Mohammad Khatami was elected as president in 1997 by an overwhelming majority of voters, mostly due to internal reasons, his election was also largely influenced by foreign policy issues. Khatami clearly presented a more modern and harmonious vision for Iran's relations with the world, which attracted the Iranian youth. Another manifestation of the conflict between public opinion and official foreign policy directions can be seen during the 2009 protests in which, for the first time, some protesters chanted the slogan "No Gaza, No Lebanon, Sacrifice My Life to Iran." These chants were in opposition to the official policy of supporting movements such as Hezbollah in Lebanon and Hamas in Gaza. In the same protests, the slogan "Death to Russia" was chanted by some protesters to reject the state-promoted slogan of "Death to America." Protesters believed that hostilities with the United States had intensified Iran's dependency on Russia, which has led to Russian interference in Iran's internal affairs.

Having said that, it is difficult to capture the influence of public opinion on foreign policy issues through standard tools such as polling. This is because polling in Iran presents unique challenges that can lead to inaccuracies and misunderstandings given the fact that conducting a survey can touch on politically sensitive topics and block respondents from revealing their views.[11] Nonetheless, an appraisal of public viewpoints and their impact on foreign policy cannot be definitively ascertained through a mere examination of the correlation between public attitudes and the formulation of official policies, as derived from the structure of polling methods. In this context, this chapter aims to study the role of public opinion in the formulation of Iran's Russia policy by identifying core debates and the process of their expansion across the public sphere and among elite debates.

Iran and Russia: Historical Mistrust

For Iranians, Russia holds a distinct significance beyond being a mere formidable neighboring power that intermittently poses threats to its territory. Over the past two centuries, the Russians have played an important role, directly or indirectly, not only in shaping Iran's foreign policy but also in its domestic politics and economic development. At the dawn of the 19th century, Russia began its all-encompassing interaction with Iran, which spanned the conclusion of two extensive wars. The outcome of this encounter witnessed the Russians becoming the primary nation to secure favorable trade privileges with Iran through the imposition of the Golestan (1813) and Turkmenchay (1828) treaties. Furthermore, the Russians extended their support to Abbas Mirza, the Iranian political leader, and consequently solidified their influence within the country. Moscow also acquired extraterritorial rights that undermined Iranian sovereignty through capitulation. In the following years, Russia resisted the construction of a railway by other countries

---

[11]Despite these difficulties, a series of domestic and international surveys have been conducted since 2003, which make it possible to broadly estimate popular perceptions. Among these polls are the World Public Opinion.org (WPO) at the University of Maryland, Terror Free Tomorrow (TFT), and Iranian Students' Opinion Polling Center, which is one of the few reliable opinion polling centers in Iran.

in Iran due to a fear of British access to the north of Iran and pushed to postpone the construction of the railway in Iran for at least fifty years.[12]

The intervention in the Constitutional Revolution in Iran and the assistance in suppressing the freedom fighters in the years leading up to the First World War were the last attempts of the Tsarist government to maintain its superior position within the Iranian political system. Although much of Russia's colonial behavior in Iran came to an end following the 1917 Bolshevik Revolution, Russian influence manifested in Iranian domestic politics in new forms through the ideology of Marxism and leftist parties. Despite Lenin's commitment to abandon colonial policies and agreements of past governments, Joseph Stalin reversed this course and pursued its predecessors' policies. During the Second World War, the Red Army occupied Iran together with the UK, which paved the way for more Soviet intervention in Iran's internal affairs through the establishment of the Tudeh Party. After the end of the Second World War and the withdrawal of British and American forces from Iran, the Soviet Army refused to evacuate the northern areas and, after facing the American ultimatum, attempted to disintegrate Iran by supporting internal separatist groups. Soviet plots formed two short-term autonomous governments, the Republic of Mahabad and the autonomous government of Azerbaijan. In addition, after the establishment of the Tudeh Party in 1941, it remained one of the important players in Iran's domestic politics until years later, under the direct guidance of the Soviet Union. During the Iranian oil nationalization movement, the Tudeh Party was one of the opponents of the nationalization and the National Front of Iran because it wanted to preserve the possibility of giving the northern oil privilege to the Soviet Union.[13]

After the victory of the Islamic Revolution, the new regime's foreign policy slogan "Neither East, Nor West" not only rejected reliance on either of the two world powers during the Cold War but also obligated itself to confront the imperialist policies of these powers, especially in the surrounding regions of Iran. For this reason, the newly established Islamic Republic was not only opposed to America's interventions but also

---

[12] See Zhand Shakibi, *Rousyeh va gharbengari* [*Russia and Politics of Occidentalism*] (Tehran: IRAS, 2018), 558–9.

[13] Hamid Shokat, *Negahi az daroon be jonbesh chp Iran, goftegoo ba Mahdi khanbabaei* [*An Inside Look at Iran's Leftist Movement, a Conversation with Mehdi Khan Babaei*] (Tehran: Sherkat Sahami Entesha, 2001), 61, quoted by Mohammadali Movahed, *Khabe ashofteh naft* [*Oil Disturbed Dreams*] (Tehran: Nashre Karnameh, 2013), 144–7.

objected to the Soviet Union's military intervention in Afghanistan. Over the course of nearly nine years of Soviet presence in Afghanistan, Iran even organized and supported the Mujahideen against the Soviet Union.

In the aftermath of the revolution, the Soviet Union resumed its role in Iranian domestic affairs by reviving the Tudeh Party and supporting some leftist groups. However, the suppression of these groups by the newly established Islamic Republic largely limited the Soviet tools for influencing Iran's domestic politics. During the war between Iran and Iraq, the transfer of long-range missiles by the Soviets to Iraq enabled Saddam to target various cities, including Tehran,[14] and left a lasting negative impression among the Iranians, solidifying yet another negative image of the Soviet Union in public memory. However, the final years of the Soviet Union, the end of the Iran-Iraq War, and the withdrawal of the Soviet Union from Afghanistan brought about a change in the two countries' perspectives toward each other. The improvement in relations between the Soviet Union and Iran culminated in Hashemi Rafsanjani's, the then speaker of the Iranian Parliament and future president, visit to Moscow, during which the two countries signed several agreements to strengthen bilateral cooperation. Upon returning to Tehran, Rafsanjani even removed the slogan "Death to the Soviet Union" from use in official ceremonies. He emphasized, "Until yesterday, the Russians were against us and [the Death to the Soviet Union] slogan was defensible, but I went to Moscow and it was decided that we will be good neighbors and respect each other, so please do not chant the slogan of death to the Soviet Union."[15] In reality, the phrase "Death to the Soviet Union" never truly gained traction as a prevailing discourse unlike the prevalence of the slogan "Death to America." Instead, the slogan "Death to the Soviet Union" served more as a means of articulating the Islamic identity of the revolution and maintaining a balance through nonalignment with either superpower in Iran's foreign policy.

Throughout the past two centuries, Russia has played a complex role in shaping the collective memories and aspirations of the Iranian people, engendering a paradoxical mix of positive and negative impressions.

---

[14]Kamran Taremi, "Ballistic Missiles in Iran's Military Thinking," Wilson Center, October 14, 2003, https://www.wilsoncenter.org/event/ballistic-missiles-irans-military-thinking.
[15]"Dastane hazfe shoare marg bar shoravi bar asase ravayate safire iran dar Moscow [The Story of the Removal of the Slogan 'Death to the Soviet Union' According to the Narrative of the Former Iranian Ambassador in Moscow]," Iran History, May 24, 2011, http://tarikhirani.ir/fa/news/825.

Despite the historical mistrust, Russia is not solely associated with unpleasant memories. Moscow's positive impact has been felt in a variety of spheres, from the economic realm, where trade with Russia has often been seen as a rare source of benefit for many, particularly in the northern regions of the country, to the ideological sphere, where the ideas of Lenin and Marxism were once seen as the only way to overcome the country's internal and external difficulties. Thus, Russia's historical significance for Iran remains a multifaceted and often ambivalent subject of reflection and contemplation.[16]

After the collapse of the Soviet Union, Russia's place in Iran's internal debates has experienced at least two distinct periods before the start of the war in Ukraine, mainly influenced by the beginning of Iran's nuclear case in the early years of the 2000s and Russia's role in this matter. In general, these periods can be named as (1) the period of optimism and hope and (2) the period of doubt and increased pessimism.

The first period consists of the early 1990s and the early years of Vladimir Putin's presidency, during which Russia occupied a peripheral role in foreign policy discussions beyond transactional issues like economic and military cooperation. Due to various reasons, Russia did not receive much attention from the major segments of Iranian society, except for a small group of traders and economic activists who viewed Russia and the former Soviet republics as presenting new economic opportunities. At the same time, both within elite and public opinion, discussions about Russia were accompanied by a combination of fear and hope. The dissolution of the Soviet Union and the abandonment of Marxist ideology alleviated the traditional concerns and suspicions toward Moscow. During this time, the most important issue for many elites and influential interest groups pertaining to Russia was Moscow's burgeoning cooperation with the West, which Tehran viewed as a tool to pressure Iran. Yet, at the same time, the deep-seated suspicion and concern about Russian intentions was also accompanied by a sense of opportunity as Tehran increasingly looked toward Moscow to enhance its economic, technological, and military development.

---

[16]Mohammad Jafar Javadi Arjmand and Abdolrasool Divsallar, "rabeteh amniyat—toseeh dar syasat khareji: motaleh moredi ravabet iran va shoravi 1340–1357 [Security-Development Nexus in Foreign Policy: The Case of Iranian-Soviet Relations]," *Politics Quarterly* 49, no. 2 (2019), 311–32, https://doi.org/10.22059/jpq.2019.228045.1007024.

The second period covers the time from the beginning of the nuclear tensions between Iran and the West in the early 2000s until the onset of the war in Ukraine. During this time, the most salient area where Russia was evaluated by the Iranian public and elite was its involvement in the Iranian nuclear issue. For many, Russia's intervention and meddling in the nuclear issue was a major area of discord and mistrust. Moreover, a litany of grievances formed the basis of Iranian popular opinion toward Russia. In particular, the most important indicators that the Iranian public used in its judgment of Russia were related to the delays in the construction of the Bushehr Nuclear Power Plant, the decision to refer Iran to the Security Council, the support for anti-Iranian resolutions in the Security Council, the role of Russia in the Joint Comprehensive Plan of Action (JCPOA) negations, and the Russian reaction to the US withdrawal from the JCPOA. In this regard, there was no precise demarcation between the views in favor or against Russia in terms of their attribution to power positions or ordinary people, and even reformist, conservative, or other political factions.

Russia's delays over the construction of the Bushehr Nuclear Power Plant stoked harsh criticism across Iranian elite circles. Moderate and pragmatic figures like Hashemi Rafsanjani, former president and then head of the Expediency Council, stated during Friday prayer in March 2009 that "the Russians and others should know that today Iran has reached a point where if [the Russians] don't come, we can complete the Bushehr nuclear power plant ourselves, but [the Russians] must keep their promise."[17] Three years later, this sentiment was echoed by hardline president Mahmoud Ahmadinejad who criticized Russia's cooperation with the West on Iran's nuclear program for the first time in a public speech, warning to Moscow to refrain from "making the Iranian nation one of [Russia's] ... historical enemies."[18] Moreover, Ahmadinejad stated:

> Russian officials should not take a measure which causes Iranian nation [to] regard it as its historic enemy ... . Iran and Russia are neighbors, and two neighbors cannot avoid keeping friendly relations, but the

---

[17] "Russha ham naiayand niroogah boushehr ra takmil mikonim [We Will Complete the Bushehr Power Plant so that the Russians Don't Come Either]," *Mehrnews*, March 1, 2009, mehrnews.com/x993h.

[18] "Tehran Declaration, 'Historic Opportunity' for Obama," ISNA, May 26, 2010, https://en.isna.ir/news/8903-03745/Tehran-declaration-historic-opportunity-for-Obama-Ahmadinejad.

friendly ties necessitate that the two sides respect each other's rights .... We do not like to see that our neighbor stands behind countries which have been Iran's enemy for 30 years.[19]

Mohammad Javad Zarif, Iran's foreign minister in Hassan Rouhani's government, in a confidential private conversation that was disclosed in May 2021 regarding Russia's role in the JCPOA negotiations, emphasized that "when the JCPOA was signed, Russia did its utmost in the last week of the negotiations to prevent the deal from coming to fruition."[20] According to Zarif, "it is not in Russia's interest to normalize our [Iran's] relations with the West."[21] These comments, which were expressed by various officials with different tendencies in a period of fifteen years, actually reflect the views that have been raised in various forms in Iran's public opinion and elite debates about Russia. These statements were made while the same officials spent a lot of effort in expanding cooperation between Iran and Russia during their tenure.
Referring to the close and extensive cooperation between Iran and Russia in various fields, doubt about the sincerity of the Russians has become a pervasive issue among at least a portion of the public and political leadership in Iran. After three decades of a tumultuous relationship, phrases such as "Russia's unreliability," "Russia playing with Iran's card," or "Russia stabbing Iran in the back" have become frequent propositions in public discourse regarding this relationship. Interestingly, these propositions are voiced not solely by ordinary people but also by experts and political officials.[22] The withdrawal of the United States from the JCPOA and Russia's cooperation with Saudi Arabia to fill Iran's void in the energy market was another case that amplified such sentiments. In an interview, Falahatpisheh, the former head of the National Security and Foreign Policy Commission of the Iranian Parliament, emphasized that Iranians have repeatedly become pawns of Russia's interest-oriented policies. These developments have further reinforced the notion that Iran

---

[19]"Tehran Declaration," 2010.
[20]"Enteshar faile soti zarif darbareh Solimani va karshekani rusiieh dar barjam [The Release of a Sensitive Audio File about Soleimani and Russia's Sabotage of the JCPOA]," BBC Persian, April 25, 2021, https://www.bbc.com/persian/iran-56878595.
[21]"Enteshar faile soti zarif," 2021.
[22]"Iraniha barha bazicheh siasathaye manfat talabaneh rosssha ghara greftand [Iranians Have Become the Toys of Russia's Self-interested Policies Many Time]," ISNA, June 24, 2018, isna.ir/xd3ffZ.

cannot count on Russia to be a reliable partner—a view shared by many Iranians across different sectors of the society. Another member of the parliament also spoke about the betrayal of the Russians to Iran and the fact that Russia cannot be a strategic partner for Iran.[23] Ali Khorram, a retired diplomat, also wrote in a note in the *Shargh* newspaper that Russia has repeatedly stabbed Iran in the back.[24]

A remarkable point is that all those who analyze and describe the relations between Iran and Russia with such phrases and propositions do not look at this issue from the same approach and starting point. Despite the verbal similarities, for some parts of them, these expressions and statements describe a less thought-out feeling that has historical and cultural roots and represents a kind of phobia from relations with great powers. But for others, these statements are a tool for criticizing the entirety of Iran's foreign policy discourse in the last few decades. For the second group, the main problem is not the relations between Iran and Russia but the policy of using conflicts between Russia and the West as a means to take advantage of Russia in supporting Iran's confrontation with the West. So, these phrases and propositions are often mentioned with the aim of condemning this approach to the relationship and not explaining or analyzing it.

Distrust toward official policies and, even in some cases, the desire to create a distance with the current policies have also been among the reasons for opposition to Russia. Some political elites, assuming the gap between the official and public discourse toward Russia, consider criticism of Russia and its relations with Iran as a kind of alignment with the public and as a way to attract public support. In other cases, rather than being analyzed and evaluated in the text of the foreign policy discourse, the issue of Iran-Russia relations has been the subject of factional politics and the conflict between internal policy sub-discourses. In fact, being a member of a political faction is a highly effective factor in distinguishing one's view toward Russia without paying proper attention to the detailed aspects of the relations. In the meantime, some political analysts and experts also use these expressions and statements as part of

---

[23]"neshast OPEC va baz ham esbat daghal bazi rosha [OPEC Meeting and Proof of the Russians' Cheating Again]," *Etedal*, June 23, 2018, https://etedaldaily.ir (accessed January 30, 2024).

[24]"rosieh barha be iran az posht khanjar zadeh ast [Russia Has Repeatedly Stabbed Iran in the Back]," Khabaronline, July 1, 2018, khabaronline.ir/x8HP5.

critical thinking within the discourse of Iran's foreign policy.[25] For these people, Russia is an actor that should always be handled with caution, and Iran should avoid getting too close to it.

Fragmentation of the Internal Debates after the Ukraine War: From Condemnation to Strategic Solidarity

The Russian invasion of Ukraine has put Iranian leaders in a political and moral paradox, much like many countries close to Russia. Iranian leaders had neither the desire to condemn Russia's actions nor the legal and moral justification to support them openly. On the one hand, opposing Western policies, particularly NATO's expansion and its continued hegemony, has sparked a kind of strategic solidarity with Russia and has made Moscow's claims of self-defense understandable to Iranian leaders and even the public. On the other hand, Russia's actions, which amounted to aggression and disregard for international norms and laws, were incompatible with Iran's basic principles of foreign policy that oppose unilateralism, oppression of nations, and the use of force to resolve disputes.

Amid a palpable sense of confusion regarding the appropriate course of action and stance to be taken toward the ongoing war, Iranian television found itself under the sway of Russian media on the first day of the conflict, referring to it as "Russia's Special Operation in Ukraine." However, in light of criticisms, the network subsequently altered the title to "Ukraine War." In response to this disorientation, an expert on international affairs highlighted during an interview with Iran's official television news network on the first day of the war that concerns over NATO's expansion ought not to translate into support for Russia's military intervention in Ukraine, as the policy of military action could potentially expose Iran to the risk of Russian military aggression.[26] Ali

---

[25] For example, see Elahe Kolaei and Afifeh Abedi, "faraz vz forod ravabet iran va rosyieh [Ups and Downs of Iran-Russia Relations 1990–2016]," *International Relations Studies* 10, no. 40 (2018), 135–64, https://sid.ir/paper/247535/fa.
[26] "Beheshtipour: az rosyieh hamayat nakonid, tazmini nist be Iran ham haml-e nakonad [Beheshtipour: Do Not Support Russia, There Is No Guarantee that It Will Not Attack Iran as Well]," *Entekhab*, February 24, 2022, https://www.entekhab.ir/002mok.

Motahari, a former representative of the Iranian Parliament, also wrote in a tweet to protest the way news was being reported about the war in Ukraine, stating that "state TV reports the news of the Ukraine war like one of Russia's colonies."[27]

Given the international significance of the war in Ukraine and the potential implications it could have for Iran, media outlets and political elites in Iran reacted quickly to the issue in various ways, offering opinions on the causes of the war, its consequences for Iran and the world, and the implications of Iran's position toward the war. Almost all Iranian media outlets shared their viewpoints on the war with their audiences on the first working day following its outbreak, with the *Etemad* newspaper devoting more than ten notes and reports to the subject, surpassing other media outlets in coverage. In analyzing the different reactions of various media outlets, it is important to note the similarities and differences in these responses. It was clear that almost all analysts from various political currents condemned the start of the war in different tones and intensities. However, in the next step, these analysts emphasized different issues in accordance with their political views and affiliations. For example, the *Kayhan* newspaper, the most important and powerful platform of the conservatives in Iran, in its first editorial on the war, entitled "The Final Scene of Mr. Comedian," attributed the outbreak of the war to Zelensky's wrong policies and his trust in Western powers. The paper wrote:

> The US and NATO played with Ukraine and sent it to the slaughterhouse, leaving it alone on the day of the incident. Perhaps Zelensky thought this was another one of those exciting TV programs and he was the protagonist whom the audience applauded, but soon he realized that he might be a star in the world of acting, but in the game of politics, he is just another delusional amateur.[28]

The conservative newspaper *Hamshahri*, affiliated with the principlist camp in Iran, dedicated its editorial to justifying Russia's military attack on Ukraine and wrote:

---

[27] "enteghad tond motahhari az nahveh poshesh khabari hamleh nezami putin be ukrine [Motahari Criticized the Way Putin's Military Attack on Ukraine Was Covered]," Khabaronline, February 24, 2022, khabaronline.ir/xhG5b.

[28] Mohammad Sarfi, "Sekans-e Akhar-e Aghaye Komediyan, List Ra Biavarid! [The Last Sequence of Mr. Comedian: Bring the List!]," *Kayhan* (newspaper), February 26, 2022, https://kayhan.ir/fa/news/237393/.

Surely, Russia did not have a desire for a war or an unwanted conflict with Ukraine, but when Putin, as the leader who must defend his country's interests, observes future developments and sees the risks of delay and hesitation, he decided to accept sanctions and economic pressure against security interventions and intrusions that impose much heavier costs on his country. Russia could not retreat on the issue of Ukraine, because any retreat meant a retreat from the guarantee and preservation of Russia's security and survival.[29]

Abdullah Ganji, the editor-in-chief of this newspaper, also mocked Volodymyr Zelensky in a tweet and wrote: "If the Ukrainian comedian president knew the ABCs of politics, he would have realized that when he visited NATO headquarters last year and sought to join it, he started a war with Russia."[30]

On the opposite side, reformist newspapers such as *Shargh* and *Etemad* focused on criticizing Russia's policies instead of criticizing the West and Zelensky. The *Shargh* newspaper, with headlines such as "Reviving Russian Nationalism" and "Bloody Expansionism of the Kremlin," reacted to the start of the war in Ukraine by condemning Russian aggression.[31] In *Etemad*, the newspaper emphasized that "now, Ukraine is burning in the flames of a one-sided war, and the world is witnessing this war crime moment by moment, which has been prepared by the Russian military down to the last detail, but effective action has not been taken to repel aggression from the world and especially Europe."[32]

Regardless of factional positions on the issue of Ukraine—which seem to have emanated from domestic schisms—sensitivities and concerns regarding the war in the media and public opinion in Iran include various dimensions. It is crucial to note that if we address these concerns and

---

[29]Hassan Rashvand, "Amniat va Manafe'e Melli Harfe Avval va Akhar [Security and National Interests First and Last Words]," *Hamshahri* (newspaper), February 26, 2022, https://newspaper.hamshahrionline.ir/id/154974/.
[30]"osolgrayan be donbal manafe jenahi [Conservatives Looking for Factional Interests?]," *Shargh* (newspaper), February 26, 2022, https://www.sharghdaily.com/fa/tiny/news-841651.
[31]Mohammad Javad Lesani,"tezarism va taghir didgah oropa [Tsarism and the Change of Europe's Perspective]," *Sharq* (newspaper), February 26, 2022, https://static2.sharghdaily.com/servev2/GR2GP0TAxzlB/i1kub06DEUw,/01.pdf.
[32]Mohammad Hossein Lotfollahi, "oropa zire potinhaye sarbazan tezar [Europe under the Bras of the Tsar's Soldiers]," *Etemad* (newspaper), February 26, 2022, https://www.etemadnewspaper.ir/fa/main/detail/181877/.

sensitivities from this standpoint, a clear delineation between various political currents in Iran may not be observable in certain cases. Based on this, the main points of attention in the media and public opinion include the following trends that run the gamut from criticism of the West to lessons for Iran.

First, criticism of the West and NATO's actions is a common theme among media outlets and commentators affiliated with the principled conservative movement. However, many analysts and media outlets close to the reformist movement, or in other words, nonprincipled conservative perspectives, also offer numerous criticisms of Western policies toward Russia. For example, Hossein Mousavian, a former Iranian diplomat, emphasized in an interview with the *Shargh* newspaper one day after the start of the war that "the West is also to blame for the emergence of this situation because they have insulted Russia in various fields and matters and by insisting on expanding NATO to newly independent countries and Russia's neighbors, they have made Russians believe that their national security is threatened by Western hegemony."[33] Abbas Abdi, a reformist political activist, also wrote in the *Etemad* newspaper: "Countries do not accept provocative actions against themselves in proportion to their power. In the current situation, the accession of Ukraine to NATO is clearly perceived as provocative."[34]

Second, alongside the prevalence of the critique of the West, the criticism of Russia has appeared as well. Criticism of Russia's invasion of an independent country, like criticism of the West, to some extent, has taken on cross-sectional dimensions in the opinions of various analysts, and even some conservative figures have explicitly criticized Russia's behavior in the days following the start of the war. For example, Nasser Noobari, Iran's former ambassador to the Soviet Union, said in a television program affiliated with hard-line currents: "People! What Mr. Putin did in Ukraine, the Russians did to Iran before. The mind of the Russian body was that if necessary, they had to cross Iran's borders and come inside, just like they did in Ukraine."[35] Heshmatollah Falahatpisheh, with tendencies

---

[33] Hossein Mousavian, "ehyaye nasionalism roosie [Revival of Russian Nationalism?]," interview by Ahmed Gholami, *Sharq* (newspaper), February 26, 2022, https://static2.sharghdaily.com/servev2/MrBrr6nH8Re7/i1kub06DEUw,/04.pdf.
[34] Abbas Abdi, "vaghegaraei va jang [Realism and War]," *Etemad* (newspaper), February 26, 2022, https://www.etemadnewspaper.ir/fa/main/detail/181866/.
[35] "nagoftehaie safir iran dar shoravi [Unsaid Stories of Iran's Ambassador to the Soviet Union]," *Tarikh Iran*, March 15, 2022, http://tarikhirani.ir/fa/news/8752.

close to the conservatives, also wrote on Twitter: "Hitler, Stalin, Reagan, Bush, Trump, and Putin are bloodthirsty politicians who did not allow humanity to live in peace. The attack on Ukraine is the beginning of a new Cold War, global anarchy, and the domination of authoritarian and oppressive rulers in countries."[36] Gholamali Jafarzadeh Aymanabadi, a member of the parliament for several terms, also expressed his view on the war in Ukraine as follows: "Aggression is condemned and condemned in any form, whether it is Saudi aggression against Yemen or Russia's military aggression against Ukraine."[37]

Third, the war underscored the importance of learning from Ukraine and the necessity of increasing national power. After the start of the war, many analysts affiliated with the conservatives argued along this line emphasizing the importance of relying on domestic capabilities to ensure national security. In a rare moment of factional unity, reformist commentators expressed similar views. Abbas Abdi, a reformist political activist, believes that

> they [the Ukrainians] should have relied on their own resources and capabilities. It is a lesson that we should also learn, otherwise we will inadvertently find ourselves in a military crisis ... The main issue is that while war is terrible and should be avoided, it is not going to disappear because many policies pursued under the banner of peace ignore the balance of power and are indeed catalysts of war.[38]

Fourth, criticism of Iran's position in not explicitly condemning the war materialized across the spectrum. The officials' ambiguous position regarding the war in Ukraine in the days following its outbreak was one of the issues that attracted media attention and public opinion in the country. Mohammad Mokhberi, a conservative activist with views close to the reformists, wrote in the *Etemad* newspaper a few days after the start of the war that:

---

[36]Heshmatollah Falahatpisheh, Twitter post, February 24, 2022, https://twitter.com/drfalahatpishe/status/1496924201181192201?ref_src=twsrc%5Etfw.
[37]Gholamali Jafarzadeh Aymanabadi, "ma mostamere rosyie nistim [We Are Not a Russian Colony]," Etemad Online, March 17, 2022, https://www.etemadonline.com/tiny/news-543862.
[38]Abdi, "vaghegaraei va jang."

for fifty years, my generation has heard that the correct policy is neither East nor West. But now we see how wishy-washy they are when it comes to the slaughter of the Ukrainian people. My generation sees that Biden, Trump, Obama, Bush, Clinton, Reagan, and Carter are all liars and dishonorable (which they are), but when it comes to Putin, they turn a blind eye. My generation sees that some who claimed to follow values and revolutionary principles have remained silent toward Russians who their expansionist Tzara have shelled our parliament, have violated our dignity and raped our women, destroyed Iran and Iranians with their weapons and imposing wars, been in a love affair with Israel, and have voted against us in the UN Security Council ... Meanwhile, the fault of Ukrainians is not just about pleasing the West, but is about handing over their entire nuclear arsenal to the Russians.[39]

The newspapers *Sharq* and *Etemad* have criticized Iran's ambiguous and flexible stance toward the war in various editorial notes and emphasized the need for a clearer position in condemning aggression. An article in *Etemad* criticizes the Iranian foreign minister's position, who attributed the war to NATO's provocations, saying:

How does Amirabdollahian not know that even despite of NATO provocations, no country can attack an independent country with cannons and tanks. Above all, does he not know that such a sympathetic statements to Russia will have a negative impact on Iran's nuclear negotiations and foreign policy? ... Learn neutrality at least from Taliban officials! ... Gentlemen! In this situation, we must think of our own interests. When the crisis subsides tomorrow, Russia will use all these cards to its advantage and to the detriment of others' interests.[40]

---

[39] Fayaz Zahed, "laaghal az taleban biamozid [At Least Learn from the Taliban!]," *Etemad* (newspaper), February 26, 2022, https://www.etemadnewspaper.ir/fa/Main/Detail/181867/.

[40] Mohammad Mohajeri, "nasl man, bomb roosie va shoare marg bar amrika [My Generation, the Russian Bomb, and the Slogan of Death to America]," *Etemad* (newspaper), February 28, 2022, https://www.etemadnewspaper.ir/fa/main/detail/181982.

Hossein Mousavian, a former Iranian diplomat, also refers to this issue in an interview with the *Sharq* newspaper, stating that "creating a perception that Iran is an ally of Russia in this war is not in favor of the country and will have a cost."[41] Gholamali Jafarzadeh Esmailabad, a parliament member for several terms, also expresses similar views in an interview, saying, "President Raisi's untimely and inappropriate call to Vladimir Putin and the lack of a strong position in this regard was a mistake; at least we should learn from the Taliban to declare neutrality."[42] Abbas Abdi also wrote this on Twitter: "The main criticism of Iran's foreign policy is not why it did not condemn this attack. The main problem is that they did not leave another option for themselves toward Russia. If they could have condemned but did not, it would have been at least debatable."[43] Even the moderate and centrist newspaper *Ettela'at* criticized the state's position in a note and wrote, "But what is Iran's position? A dual position, if not a dual-sided one! While Iran is negotiating in Vienna on the future of relations with the Western governments, adopting a dual-sided position will only bring harm to country's foreign relations."[44]

Fifth, concern about Iran being dragged into the war in Ukraine, especially after revelations about Iranian drones being used by Russia in the war, was another topic that emerged at the center of public debates for months. Former commander of the Revolutionary Guard, Hossein Alaei, said in an interview:

> There is a view that Russia has been seeking to drag Iran into this war from the very beginning, in order to prevent Tehran from remaining isolated, to increase pressure on Iran with sanctions, to make it harder to resolve the nuclear issue, to take Iran's foreign policy hostage, and to somehow undermine Iran's independent behavior. Perhaps that's

---

[41] Mousavian, "ehyaye nasionalism roosie."
[42] Aymanabadi, "ma mostamere rosyie nistim."
[43] Abbas Abdi, Twitter post, February 24, 2022, 8:48 p.m., https://twitter.com/abb_abdi/status/1496897433875456006.
[44] Abbas Najari Sisi, "bitarafi faal [Active Impartiality]," *Ettelaat* (newspaper), Monday, March 9, 2022, https://fa.shafaqna.com/news/1328376/الطاع‌تاشنون‌بی‌طرفی‌فعال/ (accessed January 30, 2024).

why Russia made a media issue out of buying drones from Iran and promoted it regularly.[45]

Sixth, there are concerns about the impact of the Ukraine war on nuclear negotiations. Immediately after the start of the war, one of the questions that received more attention in public opinion was about the consequences of this war on nuclear negotiations. According to many analysts, it was possible that "Russia could disrupt the Vienna negotiations or weaken Iran's positions in negotiations to gain scores from Washington in its crisis over Ukraine."[46] For many, the primary concern was that the Russian war in Ukraine could have a negative impact on Iran's position in nuclear negotiations. The statements of Russian leaders requesting US guarantees to secure Russian interests from the JCPOA revival initially confirmed these concerns. However, in the following days, public opinion in Iran was convinced that the differences between Iran and the United States on the nuclear issue were so huge that Russia's positive or negative role would not have much influence on the outcome.

Despite the intense discussions and arguments among the intellectual and political spheres, public opinion seems to have been less attentive and reactive to the news and ramifications of the Ukrainian conflict, particularly during the initial stages of the hostilities. In fact, the sole survey carried out about the war in Ukraine, roughly a month after the outbreak of the conflict, revealed rather lukewarm and apathetic responses. The Iranian Student Polling Agency (ISPA) survey of Iranians' attitudes about the war between Russia and Ukraine in March 2022 depicts the complex public reaction. The survey was conducted on a national scale and by telephone interview method—the statistical population included all citizens aged eighteen and over living in urban and rural areas (see Figures 2.1 and 2.2).

Based on the survey, it appears that a majority of the respondents who were aware of the war—53.2 percent of respondents—believe that the West supports Ukraine for its own interests. Only 20.6 percent believe that Western support for Ukraine is for the defense of human rights.

---

[45]Hossein Alaei, "roosie be donbal keshandan paye iran be jang ukrine ast [Russia Seeks to Drag Iran's Foot into the War in Ukraine]," *Shafqna*, October 26, 2022, https://fa.shafaqna.com/?p=1466014.
[46]Armin Montazeri, "dorahi ukrine pish paye iran [Ukraine's Dilemma before Iran]," *Etemad* (newspaper), February 26, 2022, https://www.etemadnewspaper.ir/fa/main/detail/181884/.

ISPA Poll on the extent of news consumption on the War between Russia and Ukraine

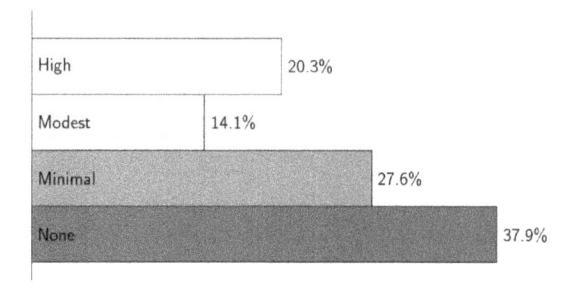

Category	Percentage
High	20.3%
Modest	14.1%
Minimal	27.6%
None	37.9%

Figure 2.1 Poll on the extent of news consumption on the war.

ISPA Poll on Reasons for Western Support of Ukraine

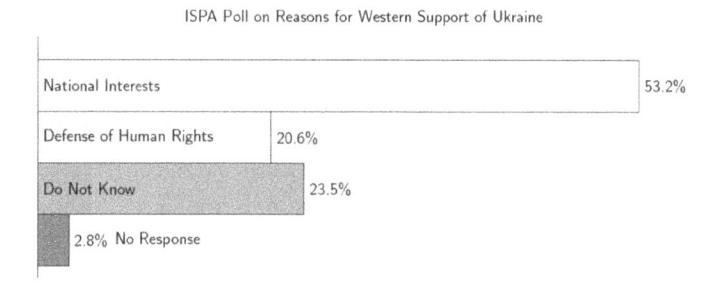

Category	Percentage
National Interests	53.2%
Defense of Human Rights	20.6%
Do Not Know	23.5%
No Response	2.8%

Figure 2.2 Poll on the reasons for Western support of Ukraine.

Additionally, a significant portion of respondents (23.5 percent) stated that they did not know about this issue. It is worth noting that 2.8 percent of respondents did not answer the question, so their opinion is unknown. Overall, the survey suggests that there is skepticism about the motivations behind Western support for Ukraine, with many believing that it is driven by self-interest rather than a commitment to human rights (see Figure 2.3).

Citizens who were aware of the war between Russia and Ukraine were asked, "How worried do you feel about the possible consequences of this war for Iran?" A significant proportion of citizens—39.7 percent of the respondents—expressed high levels of concern about the potential consequences of the war for Iran, while 8.3 percent feel somewhat worried. On the contrary, nearly half of the respondents, 47.9 percent, do not feel worried at all or have only minor concerns regarding the impact of the

ISPA Poll on concerns about the War's impact on Iran

Not Concerned	47.9%
Somewhat	8.7%
Very/Extremely Concerned	39.7%

Figure 2.3 Poll on the concerns about the war's impact on Iran.

Neutral	64.5%
Ukraine	14%
Russia	6.6%
No Opinion/No Response	15%

Figure 2.4 Poll on the parties Iran ought to support in the war.

conflict on Iran. These results suggest that a considerable proportion of the population believes that the ongoing conflict in Ukraine may have negative consequences for Iran. There may be several reasons behind this sentiment, including Iran's proximity to the region of conflict, potential economic and geopolitical ramifications, and the possibility of increased tensions and conflict in the Middle East. However, it is also important to note that a significant proportion of the respondents do not express high levels of concern regarding the impact of the conflict on Iran. This may be due to a lack of awareness about the potential implications for the country or a belief that the conflict will not directly affect Iran (see Figure 2.4).

Also, the survey suggests that a significant proportion of the Iranians believes that Iran should remain neutral regarding the ongoing conflict between Russia and Ukraine. Specifically, 64.5 percent of the respondents believe that Iran should not take sides. This may be due to concerns about the potential implications of taking sides, including potential economic and geopolitical consequences. Interestingly, a smaller proportion of the respondents, 14 percent, believed that Iran should support Ukraine, while 6.6 percent believed that Iran should support Russia. These findings reflect the complex geopolitical landscape in the region, with some Iranians potentially viewing Russia as an important ally against Western influence, while others see Ukraine as a fellow victim of Western intervention. It is worth noting that 15 percent of the respondents did not express a specific opinion on how Iran should react to the conflict, indicating a level of uncertainty or lack of interest in the issue. However, the fact that the majority of respondents believe that Iran should remain neutral suggests a cautious approach to the conflict that prioritizes stability and avoids potentially damaging entanglements.[47]

The survey results provide a snapshot of public opinion at a specific moment in time, less than a month after the start of the conflict between Russia and Ukraine. However, it is important to note that the situation on the ground, as well as the various factors influencing public opinion, may have evolved since then. For instance, in the months following the survey, the goals and motivations of Russia and the West in the conflict, as well as the position of Iran, may have become clearer. This could potentially lead to a shift in public opinion regarding Iran's stance on the conflict and whether the policy of neutrality is being practically respected. Indeed, discussions about Iran's military aid to Russia, which occurred after the time the survey was conducted, may have influenced public opinion on this issue. As a result, if another poll were to be conducted in the following months, a decisive question could be whether the Iranian population believes that the country's policy of neutrality is still appropriate, given its military involvement in the conflict.

Conclusion

The present circumstances of Iran's relations with the West, coupled with its limited foreign policy options, suggest that the influence of public sentiment and internal deliberations on foreign policy, particularly with regard to the nature of its association with Russia, may not carry

---

[47]"negaresh mardom iran darbareh jang roosie va ukrine [Iranian People's Attitude about the War between Russia and Ukraine]," Iranian Student Opinion Center (ISPA), April 13, 2022, http://www.ispa.ir/Default/Details/fa/3372/.

significant weight. Nevertheless, it can be asserted with greater conviction that the Iranian public opinion has effectively acted as a bulwark against the bellicosity espoused by certain elements of the Iranian government concerning the appropriate response to the ongoing conflict in Ukraine. Despite the tacit support of Iran's leadership for Putin's actions, a year into the conflict, Iran's foreign policy apparatus has consistently underscored the country's neutrality in the war and refused to take responsibility for dispatching drones to Russia's war in Ukraine. In summary, several factors have historically influenced the special attention of public opinion to the type of relations between the Islamic Republic of Iran and the Russian Federation.

The first factor, as mentioned earlier, relates to the existence of unpleasant historical memories between the two countries. To elaborate on the historical tensions between Iran and Russia, it is important to note that the first factor contributing to public attention on the nature of their relationship is rooted in a history of strained relations between the two nations. Iran has experienced several difficult episodes with Russia, including the Russian empire's occupation of northern Iran in the early 19th century and the Soviet Union's invasion and annexation of Iranian territory during the Second World War. These events have left a lasting impact on the collective memory of Iranians, leading to a degree of caution and suspicion toward Russia. This historical context has undoubtedly played a role in shaping public opinion regarding Iran's relations with Russia.

The second influential factor in the approach of public opinion and the views of elites in Iran toward Russia is doubts about the sincerity of the Kremlin in cooperation with Iran in regional and international arenas. Russia's contradictory behavior at various junctures of Iran's relations with the Western powers over the past three decades has turned "Russia's game with Iran's card" or "Russia's dagger in Iran's back" into one of the main statements in public discourse regarding Russia. Issues such as deliberate delays in completing and launching the Bushehr Nuclear Power Plant, the Gore-Chernomydrin agreement, Russia's positive vote on the Security Council resolutions against Iran, the type of reaction of the Russians to US sanctions against Iran, Russia's game in the energy market, and Russia's game with Iran's regional rivals and enemies are among the issues that have contributed to the prominence of these statements in the public opinion of Iran as well as the views of elites and even some official authorities.

The third factor that has influenced public views toward Russia in the past three decades is the type of cooperation that Russia has extended to Iran in confronting American unilateralism. Given Russia's claims about opposing US unilateralism, in fact, Tehran's expectations from Moscow were higher than what Moscow delivered. This fact was especially noticeable in supporting and mitigating the costs of Iranian confrontation with the United States. Indeed, Tehran's expectations from Moscow in mitigating the costs of sanctions and the expansion of economic cooperation were mostly not met. Despite Russia's various assistance to Iran in the fields of nuclear industry, iron smelting, steel, thermal power plants, and energy-related sectors, public opinion in Iran is still not convinced that in the process of an all-out confrontation between Iran and the West, Russia can provide at least a part of Iran's needs for capital and new technologies. For many Iranian businessmen, industrialists, and even economic officials, cooperation with Western companies and governments in these fields is still a priority.

Finally, and fourth, from the perspective of a significant portion of Iranian public opinion and elites, the expansion of cooperation with Russia in recent decades has been primarily the result of the anti-Western policies of the Islamic Republic, rather than an inherent value of Russia for Iran. Therefore, for all those who oppose these policies for any reason and at any level, opposition to Russia is perceived as the flip side of opposition to anti-Western policies. Of course, opposition to Iran's policy toward Russia varies among individuals and groups depending on the intensity and weakness of their opposition to Iran's anti-Western policies. Besides, the general anti-Russian propaganda and historical influences of the West inside Iran have helped the formation of such negative attitudes toward Russia.

The combination of these different reasons has practically made interaction with Russia in Iran's foreign policy a challenging and complex matter. At the top leadership level, due to the centrality of confronting the West in strategic thinking, cooperation and expansion of relations with Russia has always been an unchanging priority. Thus, issues such as Russia's violation of moral and humanitarian norms and international law in Ukraine or lack of public interest have not affected this policy negatively. But at the lower political and bureaucratic levels, doubts about the sincerity, willingness, and ability of Russia to cooperate with Iran have manifested itself in various ways. It has generated a cautious attempt to cooperate with Moscow and refrain from putting all the eggs in the Russian basket. This is best seen in strategic issues such as the nuclear program and the Syrian crisis. In addition, it has constantly caused a point of coercion manifested in the expression of often open and hidden complaints of Russian policies by executive officials, from the president to the ministers and officials at the lower level. Examples can be seen in Ahmadinejad's criticism of Russia in a public speech after Russia's positive vote on Resolution 1929, or in the subtle criticisms in the leaked Zarif conversation, and so on.

Bibliography

Abdi, Abbas. "vaghegaraei va jang [Realism and War]." *Etemad* (newspaper), February 26, 2022. https://www.etemadnewspaper.ir/fa/main/detail/181866/.

Abdi, Abbas. Twitter post, February 24, 2022, 8:48 p.m. https://twitter.com/abb_abdi/status/1496897433875456006.

Alaei, Hossein. "roosie be donbal keshandan paye iran be jang ukrine ast [Russia Seeks to Drag Iran's Foot into the War in Ukraine]." *Shafqna*, October 26, 2022. https://fa.shafaqna.com/?p=1466014.

BBC Persian. "Enteshar faile soti zarif darbareh Solimani va karshekani rusiieh dar barjam [The Release of a Sensitive Audio File about Soleimani and Russia's Sabotage of the JCPOA]." April 25, 2021. https://www.bbc.com/persian/iran-56878595.

Deborah, Gerner. "The Evolution of the Study of Foreign Policy." In *Foreign Policy Analysis: Continuity and Change in Its Second Generation*, edited by Laura Neack, Jeanne A. K. Heyand, and Patrick J. Haney, 21, Englewood Cliffs: Prentice Hall, 1995.

Entekhab. "az rosyieh hamayat nakonid, tazmini nist be Iran ham hamle nakonad [Do Not Support Russia, There Is No Guarantee That It Will Not Attack Iran As Well]." February 24, 2022. https://www.entekhab.ir/002mok.

Etedal News Agency. "neshast OPEC va baz ham esbat daghal bazi rosha [OPEC Meeting and Proof of the Russians' Cheating Again]." June 23, 2018. https://etedaldaily.ir (accessed January 30, 2024).

Fazli, Mohammad, and Janadele, Ali. "Tahlil ejtemaei nesbat afkar-e- omomi, parvandeh hastehei va barjam [Social Analysis of Public Opinion, the Nuclear Case, and the JCPOA]." In *Brjam; syastha, dstavrdha va alzamat [JCPOA; Policies, Achievements, and Requirements]*, 223–54, Tehran: Research Institute for Strategic Studies, 2015.

Foyle, Douglas C. "Public Opinion and Foreign Policy: Elite Beliefs as a Mediating Variable." *International Studies Quarterly* 41, no. 1 (1997): 141–69. http://www.jstor.org/stable/2600910.

Hagan, Joe D. "Domestic Political Explanations in the Analysis of Foreign Policy." In *Foreign Policy Analysis: Continuity and Change in Its Second*

Generation, edited by Laura Neack, Jeanne A. K. Heyand, and Patrick J. Haney, 117–43, Englewood Cliffs: Prentice Hall, 1995.

Hamid, Shokat. "Negahi az daroon be jonbesh chp Iran, goftegoo ba Mahdi khanbabaei [An Inside Look at Iran's Leftist Movement, A Conversation With Mehdi Khan Babaei]." Tehran: Sherkat Sahami Enteshar, 2001.

Heshmatollah Falahatpisheh Twitter post. February 24, 2022, 10:35 p.m. https://twitter.com/drfalahatpishe/status/1496924201181192201?ref_src=twsrc%5Etfw.

Horne, Cale D. "The Structure and Significance of Public Opinion in Non-Democratic Contexts." PhD dissertation, University of Georgia, 2010.

Iranian Student Opinion Center (ISPA). "negaresh mardom iran darbareh jang roosie va ukrine [Iranian People's Attitude about the War between Russia and Ukraine]." April 13, 2022. http://www.ispa.ir/Default/Details/fa/3372/.

ISNA News Agency. "Iraniha baarha bazicheh siasathaye manfat talabaneh rosssha gharar greftand [Iranians Have Become the Toys of Russia's Self-Interested Policies Many Time]." June 24, 2018, isna.ir/xd3ffZ.

ISNA News Agency. "Tehran Declaration, "Historic Opportunity" for Obama." May 26, 2010. https://en.isna.ir/news/8903-03745/Tehran-declaration-historic-opportunity-for-Obama-Ahmadinejad.

Jafarzadeh Aymanabadi, Gholamali. "ma mostamere rosyie nistim [We Are Not a Russian Colony]." Etemad Online, March 17, 2022. https://www.etemadonline.com/tiny/news-543862.

Javadi Arjmand, Mohammad Jafar, and Abdolrasool Divsallar. "rabeteh amniyat—toseeh dar syasat khareji(motalerh moredi ravabet iran va shoravi 1340–1357) [Security-Development Nexus in Foreign Policy: The Case of Iranian-Soviet Relations]." *Politics Quarterly* 49, no. 2 (2019): 311–32. https://doi.org/10.22059/jpq.2019.228045.1007024.

Joshua D. Kertzer. "Public Opinion and Foreign Policy." In *The Oxford Handbook of Political Psychology*, edited by Huddy, Leonie, David O. Sears, and Jack S. Levy, Oxford: Oxford Academic, September 21, 2021.

Kaarbo, Juliet. "A Foreign Policy Analysis Perspective on the Domestic Politics Turn in IR Theory." *International Studies Review* 17, no. 2 (2015): 189–216. http://www.jstor.org/stable/24758357.

Kaarbo, Juliet, Jeffrey S. Lantis, and Ryan K. Beasley. "The Analysis of Foreign Policy in Comparative Perspective." In *Foreign Policy in Comparative Perspective: Domestic and International Influences on State Behavior*, edited by Ryan K. Beasley, Juliet Kaarbo, Jeffrey S. Lantis, and Michael T. Snarr, London: SAGE, 2013, 1–26.

Khabaronline. "rosieh barha be iran az posht khanjar zadeh ast [Russia Has Repeatedly Stabbed Iran in the Back]." July 1, 2018, khabaronline.ir/x8HP5.

Khabaronline. "enteghad tond motahhari az nahveh poshesh khabari hamlehnezami putin be ukrine [Motahari Criticized the Way Putin's Military Attack on Ukraine Was Covered]." February 24, 2022, khabaronline.ir/xhG5b.

Knecht, T., and M. S. Weatherford. "Public Opinion and Foreign Policy: The Stages of Presidential Decision Making." *International Studies Quarterly* 50, no. 3 (2006): 705–27. https://doi.org/10.1111/j.1468-2478.2006.00421.x.

Kolei, Elahe, and Afifeh Abedi. "faraz vz forod ravabet iran va rosyieh [Ups and Downs of Iran-Russia Relations 1990–2016]." *International Relations Studies* 10, no. 40 (2018): 135–64. https://sid.ir/paper/247535/fa.

Lesani, Mohammad Javad. "tezarism ve taghir didgah oropa [Tsarism and the Change of Europe's Perspective]." *Sharq* (newspaper), February 26, 2022. https://static2.sharghdaily.com/servev2/GR2GP0TAxzlB/i1kub06DEUw,/01.pdf.

Lotfollahi, Mohammad Hossein. "oropa zire potinhaye sarbazan tezar [Europe Under the Bras of the Tsar's Soldiers]." *Etemad* (newspaper), February 26, 2022. https://www.etemadnewspaper.ir/fa/main/detail/181877/.

Mehrnews (News Agency). "Russha ham naiayand niroogah boushehr ra takmil mikonim." [We Will Complete the Bushehr Power Plant so that the Russians Don't Come Either]." March 1, 2009. mehrnews.com/x993h.

Mohajeri Mohammad. "nasl man, bomb roosie va shoare marg bar amrika." [My Generation and the Russian Bomb and the Slogan of Death to America]." *Etemad* (newspaper), February 28, 2022. https://www.etemadnewspaper.ir/fa/main/detail/181982.

Mohammad Javad Lesani. "tezarism ve taghir didgah oropa." [Tsarism and the Change of Europe's Perspective]." *Sharq* (newspaper), February 26, 2022. https://static2.sharghdaily.com/servev2/GR2GP0TAxzlB/i1kub06DEUw,/01.pdf.

Montazeri, Armin. "dorahi ukrine pish paye iran [Ukraine's Dilemma before Iran]." *Etemad* (newspaper), February 26, 2022. https://www.etemadnewspaper.ir/fa/main/detail/181884/https://www.etemadnewspaper.ir/fa/Main/Page/2065/6/.

Mousavian, Hossein. "ehyaye nasionalism roosie [Revival of Russian Nationalism?]." Interview by Ahmed Gholami, *Sharq* (newspaper), February 26, 2022. https://static2.sharghdaily.com/servev2/MrBrr6nH8Re7/i1kub06DEUw,/04.pdf.

Movahed, Mohammadali. *Khabe ashofteh naft* [*Oil Disturbed Dreams*]. Tehran: Nashre Karnameh, 2013.

Najari Sisi, Abbas. "bitarafi faal [Active Impartiality]." *Ettelaat* (newspaper), Monday, March 9, 2022. https://fa.shafaqna.com/news/1328376/الطاعات-نوشت-بیطرفی-فعال/ (accessed January 30, 2024).

Rashvand, Hassan. "Amniat va Manafe'e Melli Harfe Avval va Akhar [Security and National Interests First and Last Words]." *Hamshahri* (newspaper), February 26, 2022. https://newspaper.hamshahrionline.ir/id/154974/.

Rose, Gideon. "Neoclassical Realism and Theories of Foreign Policy." *World Politics* 51 no. 1 (1998): 144–72.

Sarfi, Mohammad. "Sekans-e Akhar-e Aghaye Komediyan, List Ra Biavarid! [The Last Sequence of Mr. Comedian: Bring the list!]." *Kayhan* (newspaper), February 26, 2022. https://kayhan.ir/fa/news/237393/.

Shakibi, Zhand. *Rousiyeh va gharbengari* [*Russia and Politics of Occidentalism*]. Tehran: IRAS, 2018.

Shargh. "osolgrayan be donbal manafe jenahi [Conservatives Looking for Factional Interests?]." February 26, 2022. https://www.sharghdaily.com/fa/tiny/news-841651.

Taremi, Kamran. "Ballistic Missiles in Iran's Military Thinking." Wilson Center, October 14, 2003. https://www.wilsoncenter.org/event/ballistic-missiles-irans-military-thinking.

Tarikh Irani. "nagoftehaie safir iran dar shoravi [Unsaid Stories of Iran's Ambassador to the Soviet Union]." March 15, 2022. http://tarikhirani.ir/fa/news/8752.

Tarikh Irani. "Dastane hazfe shoare marg bar shoravi bar asase ravayate safire iran dar Moscow [The Story of the Removal of the Slogan 'Death to the Soviet Union' according to the Narrative of the Former Iranian Ambassador in Moscow]." May 24, 2011. http://tarikhirani.ir/fa/news/825.

World Public Opinion. "Iranian Public Opinion on Governance, Nuclear Weapons and Relations with the United State." August 27, 2008. https://worldpublicopinion.net/iranian-public-opinion-on-governance-nuclear-weapons-and-relations-with-the-united-state/.

World Public Opinion. "Iran Poll Shows Rouhani Comes Out of Election with Broad-Based Support." March 31, 2016. https://worldpublicopinion.net/iran-poll-shows-rouhani-comes-out-of-election-with-broad-based-support/.

Zahed, Fayaz. "laaghal az taleban biamozid [At Least Learn from the Taliban!]." *Etemad* (newspaper), February 26, 2022. https://www.etemadnewspaper.ir/fa/Main/Detail/181867/.

3 IDENTITY, STATEHOOD, AND STRATEGIC SYMPATHY

Diana Galeeva[1]

Iran and Russia share a common experience of what they call a "cultural cancelation and denial of their rights by the West." The Western response to the Russian invasion of Ukraine has given Russian elites a similar experience to that which Iran had under the maximum US pressure and decades of crisis regarding its nuclear program. How has this shared experience of colliding with the West's coercive power impacted the Russian and Iranian elite's views toward each other? What is the role of a shared experience of confronting the liberal order and common threat perception in strengthening the two political systems' mutual strategic sympathy and understanding? Given Russia's sizeable Muslim population, what role does shared Muslim identity play in this matter? Based on considerable engagement with primary and secondary sources, fieldwork in Russia, and monitoring ongoing developments in bilateral relations, this chapter explains the combined roles of identity politics, shared threat perception, and strategic sympathy in Moscow and Tehran's decision.

---

[1] The author would like to express gratitude to Professor Abdolrasool Divsallar for offering valuable and useful comments over the review process, in addition to kind support over the publication process.

Theoretical Foundations of Russia-Iran Identity Formations

This chapter brings into analysis the propositions of Iver Neumann "Uses of the Other 'The East' in European Identity Formation,"[2] in which he builds a well-recognized model on identity formation.[3] Specifically, the theme of self-alienation[4]—what constitutes "'the Other,' and the otherness of 'the Other'—has been at the very heart of the work of every major twentieth-century Continental philosopher," according to Richard Bernstein. Neumann distinguishes four paths to identity formation based on relations and considerations between "self" and "other." These can be named the ethnographic path, the psychological path, the Continental philosophical path, and the "Eastern excursion."[5]

The ethnographic path is built on the approaches of international relations academics toward nationalism "and may therefore be, as it were, closest to home."[6] For the purpose of this chapter, it is specifically worth considering Neumann's examinations of works of social anthropology to carry this view of "self"/"other." In Fredrik Barth's *Ethnic Groups and Boundaries*,[7] the proposition is that ethnicity could most productively be learned by taking the boundaries of ethnic groups as a point of departure. Barth suggested that the self/other nexus be analyzed through the boundary markers of identity, which he named "diacritica." Given examples, he reminds the reader that diacritica is focused on the markets of history, language, and religion, and offers two main propositions: certain diacritica can be highly culture-specific, while others can be interpreted by understandings that may strike an outside observer as being highly esoteric. Among such examples is language, a crucial bearer of national identity. In the context of this chapter, observing the role of identities in

---

[2] Iver B. Neumann, *Uses of the Other: "The East" in European Identity Formation* (Manchester: Manchester University Press, 1999).
[3] Georg Wilhelm Friedrich Hegel, *Phenomenology of Spirit* (Delhi: Shri Jainendra Press, 1977), 112; Garth J. Thomas and D. M. Gash, "Differential Effects of Posterior Septal Lesions on Dispositional and Representational Memory," *Behavioural Neuroscience* 101, no. 1 (1986), 101.
[4] Karl Marx, *Economic and Philosophic Manuscripts of 1844* (Moscow: Progress Publishers, 1959), 83–93.
[5] Neumann, *Uses of the Other*.
[6] Neumann, *Uses of the Other*, 4.
[7] Fredrik Barth, *Ethic Groups and Boundaries* (Long Grove, IL: Waveland Press, Inc., 1969).

Russia-Iran relations is crucial. The ethnographic path considers the role of existing shared Muslim identities, particularly whether the existing Shia communities act as a contributing factor for bilateral relations or serve as a limitation for Russia due to the multinational and multiethnic structure and fears of Iran's use of the Shia population to gain further influence.

The psychological path is based on the boundary between "us" and "them," which is a concept from social psychology. Here, Neumann focuses on the Lacanian psychoanalytical literature of learning about identity formation as an attempt to overcome a lack, or as a process of desire for the power of the other, that produces an image of the self. Abrams and Hogg[8] argue that

> a differentiation arises between oneselves, the we-group, or in-group. And everybody else, or the other-groups, out-groups. The insiders in a we-group are in a relation of peace, order, law, government, and industry to each other. Their relation to all outsiders, or other-groups is one of war and plunder, except so far as agreements have modified it.

In this regard, the chapter is considered particularly relevant to observing at a psychological level how the shared anti-Western view among the leadership has prevailed, especially in the current Ukraine war, and contributed further to the Russia-Iran alliance. In other words, attempting to read the mindsets of policymakers and to identify to what extent decisions based on their anti-Western views have made this alliance stronger.

The third proposed path is the Continental philosophical path, which Neumann calls the high road of modernity. He argues that Habermasian "discourse ethics" of the self and other are still ideologically rooted in "ideal speech situations"—abstracted from power and the multiplicities of social bonds other than the bond of reasoned discourse. Further, the author quotes Charles Taylor's book *Sources of the Self*[9] to demonstrate "a magisterial overview of ideas of the self in the Western tradition."[10]

---

[8]Dominic Abrams and Michael A. Hogg, *Social Identifications: A Social Psychology of Intergroup Relations and Group Processes* (Abingdon: Routledge, 1998), 17.
[9]Charles Taylor, *Sources of the Self: The Making of the Modern Identity* (Cambridge: Cambridge University Press, 1989).
[10]Neumann, *Uses of the Other*, 10.

By contrast, to achieve the objectives of this chapter, the Russia-Iran dyad can be considered as self, based on a shared anti-Western tradition, and their consequent view of the global international system. In other words, what is the international world order they aim to build based on this shared anti-Western agenda? What measures and policies are being undertaken to achieve this?

This can be linked to Neumann's proposal of the "Eastern excursion," which considers the importance of the margin of the collective self, what he refers to as "the stranger." In regard to the Continental philosophical path, this chapter aims to analyze the policies of the two states, which aim to challenge the prevailing Western-dominated world order. In contrast, the fourth level of analysis, based on Neumann's proposition on the "Eastern excursion," can be considered in terms of the extent to which Western policies against these two states brought this alliance to a new level. In other words, as Alex Vatanka puts it, when Iran and Russia became "the two most sanctioned states," to what extent did this shape their alliance?[11] Given the principal themes, the role of the shared identities between Russia and Iran and their relations since the start of the Ukraine war are primarily developed at two levels—shared Muslim identities and shared anti-Western agendas. The chapter will first look at the ethnographic path of relations and then unite the main themes discussed in the psychological path, the continental philosophical path, and "the Eastern excursion," under the umbrella of their anti-Western collaborations, and the role of the Ukraine war in this. As the anti-Western agenda plays a more important role in Russia-Iran relations, this second factor will be more in focus in the chapter after the discussion of the role of shared Muslim identities.

The Ethnographic Path: The Role of Shared Muslim Identities

Russia and Iran share Muslim identities, as Russia is home to 20–25 million Muslims. Based on this shared Islamic identity, several paths for engagement can be identified: through the existing shared Shia factor, as Shia communities are represented in the North Caucasus in

---

[11]"The War in Ukraine and Its Impact on Russia-Iran Relations," Middle East Institute, May 26, 2022, https://www.mei.edu/events/war-ukraine-and-its-impact-russia-iran-relations.

addition to the Azerbaijani diaspora, along with Shia among the Tajiks of Gorno-Badakhshan.[12] The second dimension can be summarized in pragmatic terms as building dialogue with Russian Muslims (both Sunni and Shia) for geopolitical, economic, and other reasons, which will be discussed further.

The Role of Shared Shia Muslim Identities

It is estimated that Shia Muslims make up 3 percent of the Muslim population in Russia.[13] The majority of Russia's Shia population lives on the northwestern shore of the Caspian Sea. It is estimated that the city of Derbent has the largest concentrated Shia community, and in the Kizlyar region, there are an estimated two thousand Shia Muslims.[14] Due to its geographic proximity to the North Caucasus, Iran has demonstrated an increasing influence in this region, especially in the Republic of Dagestan. This strong influence on Muslim identity was confirmed by the author during fieldwork in Dagestan and through discussions with the local political elites in 2020. They confirmed that Dagestan has close relations with Iran even in comparison to the Gulf Cooperation Council (GCC) states. Moreover, during a visit to Derbent, the author also saw large banners displaying slogans about Imam Ali in many areas. Although arguably somewhat localized, these examples demonstrate close existing shared identities operating below the national level. For example, Iran has long imported huge quantities of mutton from Dagestan, and the import demand has become so large that prices rose by 80–100 percent in 2018 alone. Allegedly, Iran has begun re-exporting mutton to the Gulf countries. The trade comes with cultural influence in tow, and according to Ahmed Yarlykapov of the Moscow State Institute of International Relations (MGIMO), several hundred former Dagestani Sunnis have

---

[12]"Visit to Grozny Shows Iran's Interest in Regions of Northern Caucasus," Caucasian Knot, November 4, 2022, https://eng.kavkaz-uzel.eu/articles/61621/.
[13]"Suleimanov Reveals the Number of Shia Muslims in Russia," Shia Waves, January 12, 2021, https://shiawaves.com/english/news/72297-suleimanov-reveals-the-number-of-shia-muslims-in-russia/#:~:text=Russia%20Today%20quoted%20the%20editor,total%20number%20of%20Muslims%20there.
[14]"Russia: Muharram in Shia Cities of Dagestan," Shafaqna, August 22, 2021, https://en.shafaqna.com/227482/muharram-in-shia-cities-of-dagestan-russia-video/.

converted to Shiism.[15] They largely came to Shiism through the pan-Islamist political organization Hizb ut-Tahrir.

In neighboring Chechnya, Iranian influence has been regarded with suspicion (prior to the Ukraine crisis). The screening of Majid Majidi's film *Muhammad: Messenger of God* was promoted by Shia Dagestanis in the Muftiate despite very strong criticism from the Sunni side, accusing the film of being based only on Shiite sources. There was an aggressive reaction to Majidi's film from the Chechen Muftiate. On June 24, 2017, an online appeal was circulated by the Mufti of the Chechen Republic, Salakh-Hajji Mezhiyev, regarding the ban on the distribution of Shiite books. He said: "Under the guise of its culture, Iran is spreading Shiite religious literature, thereby disturbing the true path of Islam, Books such as 'Collection of Fatwas' by Aytollah Sayyid Ali Sistani, 'The personality of the prophet of Islam' by Hussein Sayyidi, 'The personality of Ali ibn Abi Talib' and many others confuse young people."[16] This "fatwa" was a direct reaction to the screening of a "Shiite" film in the neighboring region. But in terms of inter-Muftiate relations, the Chechen Mufti did not mention the Dagestani Muftiate and Majidi's film directly, blaming Shiite "propaganda" via books instead, drawing a connection to Iranian influence. In general, Chechnya has kept close ties with the GCC states, building closer ties with the UAE and Bahrain, especially in recent years.

However, following the Ukraine war, some dynamics have shifted Iran closer to Chechnya (this is not to suggest that Chechnya has cut its links with the GCC states, but rather, it has diversified its relations). Its leader, Ramzan Kadyrov, whose *Kadyrovtsy* fighters have supported the Kremlin course in the Ukraine crisis, has even been granted the top rank in Russia's army as army general[17] in October. A month later, his republic hosted the Russian-Iranian Intergovernmental Commission on Trade and Economic Cooperation in Grozny, at which it was agreed to develop collaboration in the fields of oil, gas, nuclear industry, finance, and logistics.[18] According

---

[15]Ahmed Yarlykapov, "'The North Caucasus' (Chechnya, Dagestan, Ingushetia) and the Islamic World," *Russia and the Muslim World: Through the Lens of Shared Islamic Identities*, March 18 and 19, 2021, https://www.oxcis.ac.uk/sites/default/files/inline-files/Conference_Programme_Russia-and-Muslim-World_18-19_March_2021_0.pdf.
[16]Yarlykapov, "'The North Caucasus.'"
[17]"Putin Makes Chechnya's Kadyrov an Army General," *The Moscow Times*, October 5, 2022, https://www.themoscowtimes.com/2022/10/05/putin-makes-chechnyas-kadyrov-an-army-general-a78992 (accessed January 14, 2023).
[18]Caucasian Knot, "Visit to Grozny."

to Lana Ravandi-Fadai, a senior researcher at the Institute of Oriental Studies of the Russian Academy of Sciences (RAS), as Iranians are known for their pragmatism, they try not to officially divide Muslims into Sunnis and Shiites and speak primarily of a single Muslim Ummah. Interestingly, Akhmet Yarlykapov noted the role of Kadyrov in this meeting as he could not both mediate the session and represent Russia's interests in Iran. "He mainly operates in the Arab counties of the Middle East, while Chechen authorities treated Iran with suspicion."[19] This visit might suggest that the Ukraine war is bringing Iran closer to Russia, with the regions housing the Muslim populations building cultural, religious, along with economic and financial collaborations. Moreover, even with mutual suspicion, relations are built based on the pragmatism of both sides.

The Role of Shared Muslim Identities

Not only is the aforementioned meeting arguably mostly symbolic, but it is also an example of Chechnya's diversification in the economic realm based on shared Muslim identities. As Adlan Margoev of the Institute for International Studies, Moscow State Institute of International Relations (MGIMO University), clarifies,[20] the

> shared identity of Russian and Iranian Muslims is an instrumental rather than a fundamental factor in the bilateral relationship and requires a nuanced discussion. Most Russian Muslims practice Sunni Islam, which makes Iranian religious sight no match to Mecca and Medina. However, the commonalities in culture and traditions may help some Muslim-populated regions in Russia establish deeper ties with their Iranian counterparts, especially in fields like halal food production and Islamic banking, a modest yet potentially promising area for exploration.

Indeed, the impact of the Russia-Ukraine conflict is illustrative in active engagements between the Sunni-majority Republic of Tatarstan and the Iranian officials. Due to the Western sanctions, the Republic of Tatarstan has been exploring options for Iran to act as a hub for entering

---

[19] Caucasian Knot, "Visit to Grozny."
[20] Adlan Margoev, interview with the author, December 12, 2023.

different markets. It should also be added that Tatarstan has built close links with the GCC states. However, due to the ongoing outcomes of the Ukraine war, Tatarstan has taken further steps to build collaborations with Iran. For example, in March 2022, the head of Tatarstan, Rustam Minnikhanov, met with the ambassador of Iran in Russia, Kazem Jalali.[21] They discussed the potential for collaborations in Islamic banking, the halal industry, and Islamic education. Despite long-term discussions on developing Islamic banking and finance in Russia, it was only in November 2022 that the Russian state bank Sberbank opened a branch in Kazan, the capital of Tatarstan. The latest pressure on the economic sector contributed to speeding up the process. A review of the development of Islamic banking was submitted to the State Duma, which negotiated the introduction of an experimental legal regime for partner financing in four regions of the Russian Federation with Muslim populations. If this is approved, it will start on February 1 and last for a period of two years.[22] This means challenges to build collaborations with Iran based on the Muslim factor are going to be limited. Furthermore, during fieldwork in one of the Muslim-populated republics, the author learned that the leadership of one of the special economic zones sent an unofficial delegation to Iran to learn more about how the state has operated under sanctions. This again illustrates a shift toward Iran based on the Muslim identity factor and also connects with Neumann's proposed "Eastern excursion," which suggests that states sharing a "strangers" status, at least toward the Western-dominated world, are learning and collaborating to overcome the limitations of economic and financial sanctions.

Finally, as Margoev correctly argues, "this Islamic awareness and bonding is not going to outcompete practical economic interests that other, mainly non-Muslim regions of Russia like Astrakhan have with regard to Iran."[23] The Astrakhan case is another interesting one for observation. The distinctive feature of Astrakhan is its 140 different nationalities, and there are representatives of different sects (Sunni and Shia) and different schools of jurisprudence (Hanafi, Shafi'i). This Muslim diversity complements its strategic location on the two banks

---

[21] "Rustam Minnikhanov Met with Iranian Ambassador to Russia Kazem Jalali," Russia-Islamic World, March 11, 2022, https://russia-islworld.ru/en/novosti/rustam-minnikhanov-met-with-iranian-ambassador-to-russia-kazem-jalali-2022-03-11-23181/.
[22] Diana Galeeva, "Moscow Shifts Its Focus to the Muslim World," *Arab News*, December 17, 2022, https://www.arabnews.com/node/2217786.
[23] Margoev, interview with the author.

of the Volga, 60 miles from the Caspian Sea, in geographic proximity to Iran. In July, it was reported that the government of the Astrakhan region and Iran's Mostazafan Foundation signed an agreement to build a shipping company to develop the International North-South Transport Corridor.[24] According to Bloomberg, in December of that same year, Russia and Iran spent US$20 billion to ease the passage of goods along waterways and railways by building a new transcontinental trade route stretching from the eastern edge of Europe to the Indian Ocean. Astrakhan is a nexus in these routes—the International North-South Transport Corridor.[25] Jonathan Tirone and Golnar Motevalli argue that "it is an example of how great-power competition is rapidly reshaping trade networks in a world economy that looks set to fragment into rival blocs."[26] The extensive presence of Muslim communities in Russia, from Astrakhan to the Urals, makes it possible to have geographic areas integrated in this process, which may link to further collaborations based on shared identities in the future. The role of shared Muslim identities can be seen at a geopolitical level, with perhaps the most illustrative example being the XVIII International Muslim Forum "Justice and Moderation: Divine Principles of World Order" (December 7–10), which was organized by the International Muslim Forum, Religious Board of Muslims of the Russian Federation, and the Moscow Islamic Institute, in addition to co-organizers such as the Turkish Directorate of Religious Affairs (Diyanet) and the Al-Mustafa International University (Iran). In his message to the participants of the forum, delivered by his advisor, Dr. Abul Qasim Dolabi, President Ebrahim Raisi's focus was that Islam in Russia was a platform for deepening relations with Iran. Beginning with Tolstoy's comments on the greatness of the Prophet of Islam, the address stated that Russia was considered to be one of the first remote places where Islam penetrated: "We, the Muslims of Iran, are proud that Derbent [as mentioned earlier, also the main home for

---

[24] "Russia's Astrakhan Region, Iran to Form Joint Shipping Co," Interfax, July 7, 2022, https://www.arabnews.com/node/2217786.
[25] Jonathan Torne and Golnar Motevalli, "Russia and Iran Are Building Trade Route that Defies Sanctions," Bloomberg, December 21, 2022, https://www.bloomberg.com/graphics/2022-russia-iran-trade-corridor/#xj4y7vzkg. Also, on the history and emergence of the North-South Transport Corridor, see Belov (Yurtaev) V. I., "India, Russia and Iran: A New Study on 'North-South' International Transport Corridor," *Information and Innovation* 16, no. 4, (2021), 20.
[26] Torne and Motevalli, "Russia and Iran Are Building Trade Route."

Shia Muslims in Russia], which became the centre of the intersection of Russian, Iranian and Islamic cultures, became the first Muslim home in this land." Today, the presence of Islam in Russia has made it the largest center of Muslims—both Shia and Sunni—among non-Islamic countries. Nonetheless, perhaps the most significant speeches were those of Dr. Mahmood Al Habbash, chief justice of Palestine; Dr. Aytollah Hamid Shahriyari, secretary-general of the World Assembly for the Convergence of Islamic Madhhabs (Iran); Sheikh Dr. Ahmed Hasan Taha Al-Samraei, chairman of the Iraqi Council of Scientists (Iraq); and Mahmood Hafiz Muhammad Tahir Ashrafi, chairman of the Ulema Council of Pakistan (Pakistan), whose key messages were behind the importance of having an alternative world order, and a great power that might unite the Muslim world under anti-colonial powers. There were repeated criticisms of the policies of the United States and its Western allies in intervening in the affairs of Iraq and Afghanistan, their ongoing support for Israel, and, in the case of Iran, the ongoing efforts to provoke a color revolution (referring to the ongoing protest sparked by the death of 22-year-old Mahsa Amini). In other words, Russian and Iranian collaboration at a geopolitical level using shared Muslim identity can be explained in its attempts to unite the Muslim world based on anti-colonialism and post–9/11 policies in the Muslim world. All these examples clearly show the role of the ethnographic path of consideration of self and other by Neumann and the extent to which the Ukraine war has brought both states closer in this dimension.

The Psychological Path: Shared "West-Toxification"

In her work, Ghoncheh Tazmini argues that Iranian and Russian development has revealed the tension between their overlapping cultural-civilizational identities and the drive to "catch up with the West."[27] The author also reminds us of historic resistance in both Iran and Russia to the adoption of Western institutions. For example, she states that Slavophiles believed that Russia was destined to preserve the purity of Christianity, to bring the various Christian churches together, and to usher in the

---

[27] Ghoncheh Tazmini, "Parallel Discursive Fields in Pre-Revolutionary Russia and Iran: The West as a Model or an Anti-Model," *British Journal of Middle Eastern Studies* 50 (2021), 1–21.

thousand-year global kingdom of God. This special sense of destiny was based on the "Russian idea" that openly espoused the rejection of Western culture, political systems, and the models of modernization. Tazmini concludes that the Russian idea, especially the notions of Russian uniqueness (*samobytnost'*), statehood (*gosudarstvennost*), and community (*sobornost*), forms the basis of Putin's discourse of the Russian state. She compares this Russian Slavophile position—which argues that Russia's future depends on a return to native principles on "overcoming the Western disease"—with the emergence in the 1960s of Third World postcolonial narratives introduced by Iranian intellectuals, such as Jalal al-Ahmad, who suggested the popular Gharbzadegi or "West-toxification" of the areas they dominated through imperialism.

The same "West-toxification" can arguably be seen in the current leadership view. In January 2022, in the shadow of the buildup of the Ukraine crisis, President Ebrahim Raisi visited Moscow and met with President Putin, calling for closer collaboration to counter pressure from the United States, stating that "Just like you, we have also stood up against US sanctions from 40 years ago." He continued: "Today's exceptional circumstances require significant synergy between our two countries against US unilateralism."[28] Furthermore, this "West-toxification" can also be seen in Raisi's view of the North Atlantic Treaty Organization (NATO), as he stressed during his address to the State Duma members that he expected Western states to continue to follow an expansionary policy. "NATO penetrates into different countries using various pretexts and covers. NATO's agenda includes [the] imposition of the Western model and opposition to independent democracies, rejection of identity of the nations, culture and traditions."[29] This somewhat reflects the view of the Russian leadership. As Ivo Daalder for Politico states, recalling Putin's words of the collapse of the USSR as "the greatest geopolitical disaster of the 20th century," "he was going to bring all of Ukraine back into Russia's fold; he was going to expand Russia's influence throughout Eastern and Central Europe; he was going to fracture, if not force, the collapse of NATO."[30] In his own words, in September 2022, Putin blasted

---

[28]"Raisi in Russia," The Iran Primer, January 21, 2022, https://iranprimer.usip.org/blog/2022/jan/21/raisi-russia.
[29]"Raisi in Russia."
[30]Ivo Daalder, "Putin's NATO Bungle," Politico, September 16, 2022, https://www.politico.eu/article/putins-nato-bungle/.

what he called the US attempts to preserve its worldwide domination, stating that "the objective development toward a multipolar world faces [the] resistance of those who try to preserve their hegemony in global affairs and control everything—Latin America, Europe, Asia and Africa." He continued, "The hegemon has succeeded in doing so for quite a long time, but it can't go on forever ... regardless of the developments in Ukraine."[31] The very similar discourses of both leaderships between Russia and Iran based on "West-toxification" can be seen as a united psychological path to building alliances based on shared identities.

Expert analyses also demonstrate this view, as Sanam Vakil of Chatham House shares with the author:[32]

> Despite historical tensions,[33] the shared experience of Western sanctions and isolation coupled with their paranoid worldview brings Russia and Iranian policy elites together in more determined anti-Western and security-based cooperation. Both states are deeply focused on pushing back against Western pressure and motivated by this shared concept of resistance. Their mutual experience affords Moscow and Tehran with an opportunity to deepen economic and security-based exchanges.

Giorgio Cafiero of Gulf State Analytics shared that "leaders in Tehran and Moscow see the Iran-Russia partnership as increasingly necessary to advance Iranian and Russian interests amid a period of accelerating East-West bifurcation."[34] In other words, stressing "West-toxification" by building this alternative view of the West against the East. He continues, "This year, two countries have invested efforts into strategizing ways to

---

[31] Vladimir Isachenkov, "Putin Blasts US Attempts to Preserve Global Domination," *AP*, September 20, 2022, https://apnews.com/article/russia-ukraine-putin-moscow-d52c18653 7841b574f3d8ceb2368e809.

[32] Sanam Vakil, interview with the author, December 3, 2022.

[33] Mark Katz in his article "Russia and Iran" reminds us that the list of Iranian historical grievances against Russia is long, including the loss of territory to the Russian empire in the early 19th century, Tsarist Russian military intervention against the Iranian Constitutional Revolution in the early 20th century, Soviet support for secessionist movements in northwestern Iran at the end of both world wars, the Soviet occupation of Iran during the Second World War, Moscow's support for the Tudeh (the Iranian Communist Party), and Soviet support for Baghdad during the Iraq-Iran War (1980-8). See Mark N. Katz, "Russia and Iran," *Middle East Policy* 19, no. 3 (Fall 2012), 54–64.

[34] Giorgio Cafiero, interview with the author, December 3, 2022.

circumvent US- and EU-imposed sanctions in a bilateral capacity while working to establish an anti-hegemonic geopolitical order in which the US is a far weaker country." These efforts can be seen particularly in the growing number of regular personal visits in 2022: Russian president Vladimir Putin met with his Iranian counterpart Ebrahim Raisi bilaterally in addition to their meeting on June 29 during the Sixth Caspian Summit in Ashgabat, while Putin visited Tehran on July 19 for trilateral talks with Raisi and Turkish president Recep Tayyip Erdogan.

The Continental Philosophical Path: Challenging the Liberal Order

The similarity of native cultural markers in both Russia and Iran suggests common ground for cooperation during the current era of geopolitical tensions. The impact of these shared anti-Western identities may be seen at both the global and bilateral levels. Prior to the Ukraine war, Ghoncheh Tazmini[35] explained the shared Russia-Iran view as both are "anti-hegemonic," opposing the idea of a single state or a constellation of states (an "order") being also to impose particular normative values and power structures as universal. Both Russia and Iran follow a broadly anti-Western agenda and pursue policies designed to undermine the US-led liberal world order by countering its components: democracy (versus autocracy), international organizations (countering Western-led organizations, such as NATO, with the SCO [Shanghai Cooperation Organization] and BRICS [Brazil, India, Russia, China, South Africa]), and economic interdependence (avoiding economic interdependence with the West).

The first agenda then is opposing democracy with autocracy, which can be seen in the context of sharp power. Christopher Walker and Jessica Ludwig proposed the notion of sharp power in 2017,[36] which in contrast to soft power refers to the ability to influence others to achieve

---

[35]Ghoncheh Tazmini, "Russian-Iranian Relations: Impact on Persian Gulf Interests," in *Russia's Relations with the GCC and Iran*, edited by Nikolay Kozhanov (London: Springer, 2021), 183.
[36]Christopher Walker and Jessica Ludwig, "The Meaning of Sharp Power: How Authoritarian States Project Influence," *Foreign Affairs*, November 16, 2017, https://www.foreignaffairs.com/articles/china/2017-11-16/meaning-sharp-power.

the desired outcomes, not through attraction, but via distraction and the manipulation of information. The distinctive feature of sharp power is that it is conducted by authoritarian states, with the authors specifically focusing on Russia (and China).

Jeffrey Mankoff and Mahsa Rouhi explain in a chapter in this volume that the hostility of these nations toward the US-led order is aimed at making the world safer for autocracy as well as irredentist and expansionary in seeking a world "safe for empire." Moreover, in her analyses of the myth of a Russia-China-Iran "axis," Nicole Grajewski argues that the development of an alternative world order for these three countries is based on the validity of ostensible "liberal" norms via "civilizational essentialisation" and "counter-norm entrepreneurship."[37] Scholars agree that among the components of Russia and Iran countering the US-led order is the promotion of autocracy versus democracy. This is also one of the key foundations of bilateral relations, which Abdolrasool Divsallar calls "standing back-to-back for regime security."[38] He explains that:

> Russia has no agenda for regime change in Iran, but like the Iranian leadership, it sees the expansion of Western values and political structure as a threat. Both states perceive Western values like freedom of speech and human rights as a security threat, endangering their state identity, civilizational narratives, and regime stability. In addition, elites on both sides view internal order as the state's top priority and share a similar view on means of fighting Western intervention.

Connecting with the psychological path mentioned earlier, this also ties to the elite's perception. As Divsallar notes, Khamenei and Putin have faced unprecedented domestic instabilities in 2022, so this domestic security cooperation based on shared values, which are contradictory to the Western traditional values of democracy and human rights, unites both actors at the global and bilateral levels.

---

[37] Nicole Grajewski, "An Illusory Entente: The Myth of a Russia-China-Iran Axis," *Asian Affairs* 53, no. 1 (2022), 167.
[38] Abdolrasool Divsallar, "Protective Integration and Rising Interdependency: Making Sense of Iranian Response to Russian Invasion of Ukraine," *Chinese Journal of International Politics* (CJIP), (forthcoming).

Second, among the key features of the liberal order is international organizations. In this regard, it seems the ongoing expansion of bloc-to-bloc cooperation among non-Western countries aims to counterweight the influence of the United States and well-established, powerful blocs such as NATO or the EU. Iran applied to join China and Russia in BRICS (in addition to India, South Africa, and Brazil) club in June 2022,[39] in addition to the SCO (Kazakhstan, China, Kyrgyzstan, Russia, Tajikistan, Uzbekistan, India, and Pakistan). In the last SCO summit in Samarkand, Iran—currently an observer state—signed a memorandum of obligation to join the organization. Nicole Grajewski explains, "Iran's full accession to the SCO—a process that could take up to two years once formally set in motion—should be viewed in the context of Tehran's efforts to expand its ties to both Russia and China rather than the realisation of an alliance."[40]

Finally, the most striking efforts to oppose the liberal world order are those linked with severing economic connections with the West. This can be discussed in the context of the "Eastern excursion," as two strangers to the West, or the most-sanctioned states, have had to overcome limitations, and the next section will discuss their attempts to overcome Western sanctions, in addition to challenging the established economic system based on independence, especially from US economic power.

Neumann's "the Eastern Excursion"

Russia and Iran have emerged as the two most-sanctioned states, which further leads to collaborations. Giorgio Cafiero of Gulf State Analytics shares his view:[41]

> Throughout 2022, Iran and Russia have become geopolitically oriented toward the West in increasingly similar ways. A decade ago, one factor that stoked an undeniable amount of suspicion between the two powers was a set of concerns that both had about the other striking a grand bargain with the US that would "sell out" the other. Because

---

[39]Parisa Hafezi and Guy Faulconbridge, "Iran Applies to Join China and Russia in BRICS Club," Reuters, June 28, 2022, https://www.reuters.com/world/middle-east/iran-appl ies-join-brics-group-emerging-countries-2022-06-27/.
[40]Grajewski, "An Illusory Entente," 175.
[41]Cafiero, interview.

of the prospects for a JCPOA revival fading with few experts having any sense of optimism about the 2015 nuclear deal being revived at any point in the foreseeable future and Russia becoming the most sanctioned country on earth as a result of the February 24 invasion of Ukraine, such concerns on the part of officials in Tehran and Moscow are very much assuaged by this point. Iran and Russia both expect their countries to remain heavily sanctioned by the West, at least while their current governments maintain power.

Having obtained the status of heavily sanctioned states, Iran and Russia developed the following initiatives and collaborations, sharing a very similar political fate. During Russian deputy prime minister Alexander Novak's visit to Tehran in May, Russian and Iranian officials signed memoranda of understanding to increase collaboration in the fields of banking and energy.[42] They agreed to use their national currencies for energy and trade payments between the two countries. In December, Russia's second-largest bank, VTB, was the first Russian bank to launch money transfers in Iranian rials.[43] The cross-border transfers would be possible for individuals and businesses that open a new rial account with the bank. According to Russia's *Kommersant* newspaper, the bank would charge a 1 percent commission for transfers of up to $300,000 (20 million rubles) to an Iranian bank account that would take place within one business day.

This move is not surprising as Russia had strategically deployed de-dollarization, or the movement away from using the US dollar as the primary medium for financial transactions, since 2014.[44] It began when Russia and China formed what some experts have called a "financial alliance," when Beijing and Moscow signed a three-year currency swap deal worth 150 billion yuan ($24.5 billion). In 2019, another milestone occurred when the two countries signed a deal to swap the dollar for their national currencies in any global settlements between them (ruble and

---

[42]"Iran, Russia Sign Energy, Banking MoUs," Tasnim News Agency, May 26, 2022, https://www.tasnimnews.com/en/news/2022/05/26/2717165/iran-russia-sign-energy-banking-mous.
[43]"Russia's VTB Bank Launches Transfer Services to Iran," Iran Chamber of Commerce, December 24, 2022, https://en.otaghiranonline.ir/news/44330.
[44]Dimitri Simes, "China and Russia Ditch Dollar in Move towards 'Financial Alliance,'" *Financial Times*, August 16, 2020, https://www.ft.com/content/8421b6a2-1dc6-4747-b2e9-1bbfb7277747.

yuan). Iran, as another heavily sanctioned state, also became instrumental in this process of de-dollarization, simply because it also needs to avoid sanctions introduced by the West. Prior to the Ukraine war, in 2021, Irina Khominich and Samira Alikhani of the Plekhanov Russian University of Economics stated that as both Iran and Russia were under sanctions, they could support growth and development by following strategies such as decreasing dependency on the US dollar, developing bilateral economic relations, and avoiding trade obstacles.[45]

Indeed, after more severe sanctions from the West, the sanctioned status of both states has contributed to collaborations in trade as well. Russian Foreign Minister Sergey Lavrov stated during his recent visit to Tehran that in 2021, trade between Russia and Iran grew by more than 80 percent, exceeding $4 billion, despite Western sanctions.[46] Carrying the title of "the world's most-sanctioned states" has pulled Russia and Iran together with a shared identity of weathering international sanctions. In fact, there are other initiatives in the plan, such as the integration of Iran's Shetab and Russia's MIR payment and banking systems for agreements on bilateral barter trade. The integration of the two systems would allow Moscow to import auto parts and gas turbines to prop up its ailing economy and war machine, and Iran would gain access to Russian steel. In addition to these immediate benefits, this structure provides Moscow and Tehran with an arrangement that challenges the established financial system and strikes a blow against economic interdependence with the West.

Conclusion

Given Neumann's well-introduced theoretical categorization of alliance formation between the countries, this chapter considered Russia-Iran relations in the age of geopolitical rivalry. The chapter presented two central areas of the role of shared identities in relations between both states, particularly how they were shaped by Russia's invasion of Ukraine.

---

[45]Irina P. Khominich and Samira Alikhani, "Russia and Iran in Conditions of Economic Sanctions: Anti-Sanction Policy and Resistance Economy," *Vestnik of the Plekhanov Russian University of Economics* 18, no. 2 (2021), 11.
[46]"Russia's Lavrov in Tehran as Iran Seeks Post-Ukraine Realignment," Iran International Newsroom, June 23, 2022, https://www.iranintl.com/en/202206234989.

The first part of the chapter focused on the role of shared Muslim identities that play a less important role in Russia-Iran relations but are increasingly important in the current realm to consider. Analysis for this is primarily based on observations during the author's fieldwork before and after February 24. The central observation is that Russia has further integrated its Muslim minorities into building ties, especially with Iran, due to the shift of Russia from the West toward the East. This shift is similar to Iran's "Look to the East" policy adopted earlier, which initially meant developing relations with China and India, but Iranian policymakers (especially by the Supreme Leader Ayatollah Ali Khamenei) also strategically included Russia.[47] Arguably, anti-Western views and Muslim identities were the foundation in building this joint "Look to the East" policy in both countries. Iran, on its side uses the Muslim factor pragmatically. While there are efforts to build links with the Shia population, at the same time, Tehran seeks to further collaborations with the rest of the Russian Muslim world, a largely Sunni population. Russia similarly integrated this factor pragmatically, with some security concerns. In other words, both states use pragmatism with a degree of concern in this direction.

An anti-Western agenda seems more trusted in bilateral relations, as both states' policies centralize this policy direction. Using the language of Iver Neumann, the chapter understood these dynamics through specific policies. The psychological path was seen in the shared "West-toxification" seen by the leaders of both states. The continental philosophical path was illustrated by efforts to challenge the existing Western-dominated liberal world order. Finally, Neumann's special category of "Eastern excursion" (as Russia and Iran are "the two most-sanctioned states") was demonstrated in the ever more close dynamics of overcoming existing Western sanctions by building alternative financial systems. To what extent these efforts will be successful depends on a variety of factors. However, what is clear while the war is still unfolding is that the identity factor plays a crucial role in bilateral engagements between the two states, and collaborations based on this shared view will continue in the future under the current leadership.

---

[47] See Clement Therme, "Iran and Russia in the Middle East: Toward a Regional Alliance?" *Middle East Journal* 72, no. 4 (2018), 559.

Bibliography

Abrams, Dominic, and Michael A. Hogg. *Social Identifications: A Social Psychology of Intergroup Relations and Group Processes*. Abingdon: Routledge, 1998.

Barth, Fredrik. *Ethic Groups and Boundaries*. Long Grove, IL: Waveland Press, 1969.

Belov, Yurtaev V. I. "India, Russia and Iran: A New Study on 'North-South' International Transport Corridor." *Information and Innovation* 16, no. 4 (2021): 18–25.

Caucasian Knot, "Visit to Grozny Shows Iran's Interest in Regions of Northern Caucasus." November 4, 2022. https://eng.kavkaz-uzel.eu/articles/61621/.

Daalder, Ivo. "Putin's NATO Bungle." POLITICO, September 16, 2022. https://www.politico.eu/article/putins-nato-bungle/.

Divsallar, Abdolrasool. "Protective Integration and Rising Interdependency: Making Sense of Iranian Response to Russian Invasion of Ukraine," *Chinese Journal of International Politics* (CJIP), (forthcoming).

Galeeva, Diana. "Moscow Shifts Its Focus to the Muslim World." *Arab News*, December 17, 2022, https://www.arabnews.com/node/2217786.

Grajewski, Nicole. "An Illusory Entente: The Myth of a Russia-China-Iran 'Axis.'" *Asian Affairs* 53, no. 1 (2022): 164–83.

Hafezi, Parisa, and Guy Faulconbridge. "Iran Applies to Join China and Russia in BRICS Club." Reuters, June 28, 2022, https://www.reuters.com/world/middle-east/iran-applies-join-brics-group-emerging-countries-2022-06-27/.

Hegel, Georg Wilhelm Friedrich. *Phenomenology of Spirit*. Delhi: Shri Jainendra Press, 1977.

Interfax. "Russia's Astrakhan Region, Iran to Form Joint Shipping Co." July 7, 2022, https://www.arabnews.com/node/2217786.

Iran Chamber of Commerce. "Russia's VTB Bank Launches Transfer Services to Iran." December 24, 2022, https://en.otaghiranonline.ir/news/44330.

Iran International Newsroom. "Russia's Lavrov in Tehran as Iran Seeks Post-Ukraine Realignment." June 23, 2022, https://www.iranintl.com/en/202206234989.

The Iran Primer. "Raisi in Russia." January 21, 2022. https://iranprimer.usip.org/blog/2022/jan/21/raisi-russia.

Isachenkov, Vladimir. "Putin Blasts US Attempts to Preserve Global Domination." *AP*, September 2020, https://apnews.com/article/russia-ukraine-putin-moscow-d52c186537841b574f3d8ceb2368e809.

Katz, Mark N. "Russia and Iran." *Middle East Policy* 19, no. 3 (Fall 2012): 54–64.

Khominich, Irina, and Samira Alikhani. "Russia and Iran in Conditions of Economic Sanctions: Anti-Sanction Policy and Resistance Economy." *Vestnik of the Plekhanov Russian University of Economics* 18, no. 2 (2021): 5–12

Marx, Karl. *Economic and Philosophic Manuscripts of 1844*. Moscow: Progress, 1959.

Middle East Institute. "The War in Ukraine and Its Impact on Russia-Iran Relations." May 26, 2022, https://www.mei.edu/events/war-ukraine-and-its-impact-russia-iran-relations.

The Moscow Times. "Putin Makes Chechnya's Kadyrov an Army General." October 5, 2022. https://www.themoscowtimes.com/2022/10/05/putin-makes-chechnyas-kadyrov-an-army-general-a78992.

Neumann, Iver B. *Uses of the Other: "The East" in European Identity Formation.* Manchester: Manchester University Press, 1999.

Russia-Islamic World. "Rustam Minnikhanov Met with Iranian Ambassador to Russia Kazem Jalali." March 11, 2022. https://russia-islworld.ru/en/novosti/rustam-minnikhanov-met-with-iranian-ambassador-to-russia-kazem-jalali-2022-03-11-23181/.

Shafaqna. "Russia: Muharram in Shia Cities of Dagestan." August 22, 2021. https://en.shafaqna.com/227482/muharram-in-shia-cities-of-dagestan-russia-video/.

Shia Waves. "Suleimanov Reveals the Number of Shia Muslims in Russia." January 12, 2021. https://shiawaves.com/english/news/72297-suleimanov-reveals-the-number-of-shia-muslims-in-russia/.

Simes, Dimitri. "China and Russia Ditch Dollar in Move towards 'Financial Alliance.'" *Financial Times*, August 16, 2020. https://www.ft.com/content/8421b6a2-1dc6-4747-b2e9-1bbfb7277747.

Tasnim News Agency. "Iran, Russia Sign Energy, Banking MoUs." May 26, 2022, https://www.tasnimnews.com/en/news/2022/05/26/2717165/iran-russia-sign-energy-banking-mous.

Taylor, Charles. *Sources of the Self: The Making of the Modern Identity.* Cambridge: Cambridge University Press, 1989.

Tazmini, Ghoncheh. "Parallel Discursive Fields in Pre-Revolutionary Russia and Iran: The West as a Model or an Anti-Model." *British Journal of Middle Eastern Studies* 50 (2021): 1–21.

Tazmini, Ghoncheh. "Russian-Iranian Relations: Impact on Persian Gulf Interests." In *Russia's Relations with the GCC and Iran*, edited by Nikolay Kozhanov, 177–203. London: Springer, 2021.

Therme, Clement. "Iran and Russia in the Middle East: Toward a Regional Alliance?" *Middle East Journal*, 72, no. 4 (2018): 549–62.

Thomas, Garth J., and D. M. Gash. "Differential Effects of Posterior Septal Lesions on Dispositional and Representational Memory." *Behavioural Neuroscience* 101, no. 1 (1986): 712–19.

Torne, Jonathan, and Golnar Motevalli. "Russia and Iran Are Building Trade Route that Defies Sanctions." Bloomberg, December 21, 2022. https://www.bloomberg.com/graphics/2022-russia-iran-trade-corridor/?leadSource=uverify%20wall.

Walker, Christopher, and Jessica Ludwig. "The Meaning of Sharp Power: How Authoritarian States Project Influence." *Foreign Affairs*, November 16,

2017, https://www.foreignaffairs.com/articles/china/2017-11-16/meaning-sharp-power.

Yarlykapov, Ahmed. "The North Caucasus (Chechnya, Dagestan, Ingushetia) and the Islamic World." *Russia and the Muslim World: Through the Lens of Shared Islamic Identities*, March 18 and 19, 2021. https://www.oxcis.ac.uk/sites/default/files/inline-files/Conference_Programme_Russia-and-Muslim-World_18-19_March_2021_0.pdf.

PART TWO

GEOSTRATEGIC FACTORS: CONSTRAINTS OR AN ENABLER?

4 THE UKRAINE WAR AND RUSSIAN POLICY IN THE MENA AND MEDITERRANEAN REGION: IMPLICATIONS FOR IRAN

Mark N. Katz

This chapter will examine how Russian policy toward the Middle East/North Africa (MENA) and the Mediterranean region has changed since the onset of Russia's war with Ukraine in February 2022, focusing on what this has meant for Iran and the Russian-Iranian relationship—especially in the context of Putin's long-standing efforts to build cooperative relations with all Middle Eastern governments—including those at odds with Iran. The chapter will also explore the different scenarios regarding how the outcome of the war in Ukraine might affect Russian policy toward MENA and the Mediterranean, and how this might impact Iran in particular. Something must first be said, though, about how Russian policy toward the MENA/Mediterranean region before its February 2022 invasion of Ukraine has affected Iran.

Russia's MENA/Mediterranean Policy before February 2022

Ever since the reign of Empress Catherine the Great in the late 18th century, Russia has gone through alternating periods of greater and lesser involvement in the Middle East. The periods of lesser involvement usually resulted from preoccupation with European wars and/or domestic political problems. But once these wars or domestic problems have ended or been overcome, Russia has resumed its efforts to expand its influence in the region. The Russian retreat from the Middle East in the 1990s after the breakup of the Soviet Union, then, was not the first such pullback. Similarly, Putin is not the first Russian leader to reassert an active role for Russia in the region after a Russian pullback from it.[1]

Putin, though, has asserted Russian influence very differently than his Soviet predecessors did during most of the Cold War. Under Khrushchev and Brezhnev, in particular, the Soviets supported anti-Western Arab Nationalist governments (as well as one lone Marxist-Leninist regime in South Yemen) against pro-Western governments in Israel, Turkey, the conservative Arab monarchies, and the Shah's Iran. Even when Moscow expressed friendship and support for various conservative Middle Eastern governments, it also welcomed (and sometimes helped bring about) their downfall and replacement with anti-Western governments. But while the Soviets experienced several wins in the region during the Cold War, they also experienced losses: Israel defeated Moscow's Arab allies in 1967 and 1973, Egypt and Somalia were defeated by the Western allies in the 1970s, and Iran's 1979 Revolution brought to power an Islamic revolutionary regime that was not just anti-Western but also anti-Soviet. In addition, the Soviet invasion and occupation of Afghanistan was opposed by most, though not all, Middle Eastern governments.[2]

After coming to power at the turn of the 21st century, Putin sought to rebuild Russia's moribund relations with Moscow's Soviet-era Arab partners: the Assad regime in Syria, Saddam Hussein in Iraq (until his

---

[1] Mark N. Katz, "Incessant Interest: Tsarist, Soviet and Putinist Mideast Strategies," *Middle East Policy* 27, no. 1 (2020): 141–52.
[2] Alexey Vasiliev, *Russia's Middle East Policy: From Lenin to Putin* (London: Routledge, 2018).

overthrow by a US-led invasion in 2003), Qaddafi in Libya, Saleh in Yemen (until their downfall in the Arab uprisings that began in 2011), Algeria, and Sudan. Putin, though, also improved Russian relations with all of America's partners in the Middle East, including Turkey, Jordan, Morocco, Egypt, the Arab monarchies of the Persian Gulf, and even Israel. Putin also improved Russia's relations with Iran. Unlike the Soviet Union, which had good relations with some Middle Eastern states and poor ones with others, Russia under Putin developed good relations with each and every government in the Middle East, plus Fatah, Hamas, and Hezbollah.[3]

Putin's policy toward the MENA/Mediterranean region has benefited Iran in numerous ways. Russia has sold arms to Iran, completed the nuclear reactor at Bushehr (albeit far more slowly than Tehran expected), expressed support for the Islamic Republic against the large-scale democratic opposition movement that arose in 2009 when Ahmadinejad was declared to have won reelection as president, and usually (though not always) supported Iran against the United States at the UN Security Council.[4] There have been numerous reports that Moscow helped smooth over differences between Iran and the Western states regarding the Iranian nuclear accord resulting in an agreement being reached in 2015.[5] And Russia—along with Britain, France, Germany, and China (the other signatories to the agreement)—continued to support the Joint Comprehensive Plan of Action (JCPOA; as the accord is officially titled), after the Trump administration unilaterally withdrew from it in 2018.[6] After the Biden administration came into office in January 2021 and signaled its willingness to rejoin the

---

[3] Vasiliev, *Russia's Middle East Policy*, 303–526.
[4] Mark N. Katz, "Russian-Iranian Relations in the Ahmadinejad Era," *Middle East Journal* 62 (2008): 203–4; Ghoncheh Tazmini, "Russia and Iran: Strategic Partners or Provisional Counterweights?" in *Russian Foreign Policy towards the Middle East: New Trends, Old Traditions*, edited by Nikolay Kozhanov (London: Hurst, 2022), 117–40.
[5] Jonas Bernstein, "Russia's Stake in Iran Nuclear Deal," Voice of America, July 18, 2015, https://www.voanews.com/a/russias-stake-in-iran-nuclear-deal/2867710.html; Anna Borshchevskaya, "Russia's Cooperation on the Iran Deal Is No Favor to Washington," Washington Institute for Near East Policy, July 7, 2016, https://www.washingtoninstitute.org/policy-analysis/russias-cooperation-iran-deal-no-favor-washington.
[6] Hamidreza Azizi, "Russia's Role in Brokering a Comprehensive Agreement between the United States and Iran," London School of Economics Middle East Centre, August 1, 2021, https://blogs.lse.ac.uk/mec/2021/08/01/russias-role-in-brokering-a-comprehensive-agreement-between-the-united-states-and-iran/.

JCPOA, Moscow initially pushed Tehran to come back into compliance with the terms of the agreement, but stopped doing so after the severe deterioration in Russian-Western relations that occurred when Russia invaded Ukraine in February 2022.[7]

One of the most spectacular examples of Russian-Iranian cooperation has been their joint support for the Assad regime in Syria against its many enemies since the start of the Arab uprisings in 2011. Iran, along with its Hezbollah and other Shi'a militia allies, took a more active role, and Russia played a more supporting role from 2011 to 2015, but in September 2015, Russian forces also intervened to prevent the Assad regime from falling. This Russian move not only helped the Assad regime survive and regain lost territory but also salvaged Iran's intervention in Syria, which had been at risk of foundering.[8] The continued presence of both Russian and Iranian forces in Syria helps both Moscow and Tehran retain influence in Syria.

There have been aspects of Putin's policy toward the MENA/Mediterranean region, though, which have not been beneficial to Iran. Under Putin, Moscow has developed close ties with the Arab monarchies of the Persian Gulf, including Saudi Arabia, the United Arab Emirates (UAE), and Bahrain, which all see Iran as an adversary. Saudi Arabia, the UAE, and Qatar (which does not have as hostile a relationship with Iran) are all petroleum-rich countries that Russia trades with and receives investments from.[9] The economic importance of the Arab monarchies of the Persian Gulf to Moscow has meant that Russia has not been willing to support Iran against them—something that the Saudis and Emiratis have very much been aware of. Indeed, Tehran has had to worry that there may be a line that triggers Russian criticism or even aid to these Gulf Arab monarchies if Iran crosses it.

Even more unpleasant for Iran has been the close relationship between Russia and Israel that has developed under Putin. While adversarial

---

[7]Hanna Notte, "Don't Expect Any More Russian Help on the Iran Nuclear Deal," War on the Rocks, November 3, 2022, https://warontherocks.com/2022/11/dont-expect-any-more-russian-help-on-the-iran-nuclear-deal/.
[8]Nicole Grajewski, "The Evolution of Russian and Iranian Cooperation in Syria," Center for Strategic and International Studies, November 17, 2021, https://www.csis.org/analysis/evolution-russian-and-iranian-cooperation-syria.
[9]Nikolay Kozhanov, "The Drivers of Russia-GCC Relations," in *Russian Foreign Policy towards the Middle East: New Trends, Old Traditions*, edited by Nikolay Kozhanov (London: Hurst, 2022), 141–63.

during much of the Cold War and not especially close during the 1990s after diplomatic ties severed at the time of the 1967 Arab-Israeli War were restored in 1990, a significant amount of economic, security, and cultural cooperation has developed between Russia and Israel under Putin. There has been much high-level interaction between the two governments, with Putin having made three visits to Israel and Israeli prime ministers (especially Netanyahu) making numerous visits to Russia.[10] Most concerning for Iran has been the never-officially acknowledged but well-publicized Russian-Israeli deconfliction agreement whereby Russian forces in Syria do not interfere with Israeli strikes on Hezbollah and Iranian targets. Not only does this limit the possibilities for Iran to undertake actions that Israel disapproves of (such as transferring Iranian missiles to Hezbollah), but it also limits Tehran's ability to compete with Russia for influence with the Assad regime (as they reportedly have been doing to some extent).[11]

There are other examples of differences between Russia and Iran over regional issues, including (1) Russia and Turkey being more willing to cooperate despite contention in Syria than Turkey and Iran have been there;[12] (2) Russian willingness to work with all sides in the ongoing Yemeni civil war compared to Iran just supporting the Houthis against their Saudi- and Emirati-backed opponents;[13] and (3) Russian support for the Sunni-minority–based government in Bahrain, suppressing the Shi'a majority there that Iran sympathizes with.[14]

---

[10]Mark N. Katz, "Russia and Israel: An Improbable Friendship," in *Russia Rising: Putin's Foreign Policy in the Middle East and North Africa*, edited by Dimitar Bechev, Nicu Popescu, and Stanislav Secrieru (London: I.B. Tauris, 2021), 123–9.

[11]Sergei Melkonian, "Russia-Israel Cooperation in Syria: Interests, Dynamics, and Impact of the War in Ukraine," Emirates Policy Council, August 22, 2022, https://epc.ae/en/details/featured/russia-israel-cooperation-in-syria-interests-dynamics-and-impact-of-the-war-in-ukraine.

[12]Daniel Brumberg, "Russian-Turkish-Iranian Cross-Purposes on Syria's Future," Arab Center Washington DC, September 8, 2020, https://arabcenterdc.org/resource/russian-turkish-iranian-cross-purposes-on-syrias-future/.

[13]Samuel Ramani, "Russia and the Yemeni Civil War," in *Russian Foreign Policy towards the Middle East: New Trends, Old Traditions*, edited by Nikolay Kozhanov (London: Hurst, 2022), 168–70.

[14]Giorgio Cafiero, "Can Bahrain Count on Moscow to Fill Washington's Shoes?" Al-Monitor, July 8, 2016, https://www.al-monitor.com/originals/2016/07/bahrain-russia-replace-washington-influence-iran.html#ixzz7mdZIlOoF; Hussein Ibish, "Iran's New Ploy to Disrupt the Mideast: Laying Claim to Bahrain," *Ibishblog*, September 21, 2022, https://ibishblog.com/2022/09/21/irans-new-ploy-to-disrupt-the-mideast-laying-claim-to-bahrain/.

Finally, Russia and Iran are both petroleum-exporting countries and so are the competitors in this market. Previously, Iranian interests were hurt by Russian unwillingness to cooperate with the OPEC (Organization of the Petroleum Exporting Countries) in reigning in production in order to bolster petroleum prices, but Iran—along with other producers—has benefited from Russia's increased willingness to do so via the OPEC+ format (despite the fact that Moscow and Riyadh dominate this forum).[15] Long before Russia's 2022 invasion of Ukraine, Moscow benefited from Washington's unwillingness to countenance Europeans importing gas from Iran as a substitute for the gas that the US government wanted them to buy less of from Russia.[16]

Thus, despite the significant degree of Russian-Iranian cooperation that developed during the Putin years, Putin has demonstrated a clear preference for balancing between Iran on the one hand and the MENA governments at odds with it on the other, instead of supporting Iran against its opponents. Further, Putin has been able to undertake policies in the MENA/Mediterranean region that Iran undoubtedly objects to without fearing a serious rupture in Russian-Iranian relations. This is because, with such strong Iran-US animosities, Moscow could be reasonably certain that the Islamic Republic was not going to turn toward Washington for protection against Moscow despite any differences there may have been between Russia and Iran. Iran's (and Russia's) differences with the United States have been far greater than Iran's differences with Russia over Russia's cooperation with Israel and the Arab monarchies of the Persian Gulf. Similarly, US-led sanctions on Iranian petroleum exports also benefited Russia before its invasion of Ukraine.

---

[15] In December 2022, Iranian Petroleum minister Javad Owji made statements supporting the OPEC+'s decision to reduce production by two million barrels per day effective November 2022. "Iran Believes an Excess of Supply in Oil Market Can Have a Negative Impact," Iran Press News Agency, December 4, 2022, https://iranpress.com/content/70349/iran-believes-excess-supply-oil-market-can-have-negative-impact.

[16] John Grady, "Panel: Russia Will Reap Benefits from Iranian Oil Crackdown," USNI News, May 1, 2019, https://news.usni.org/2019/05/01/panel-russia-will-reap-benefits-from-iranian-oil-crackdown.

Changes in Russia's MENA/ Mediterranean Policy since February 2022: Impact on Iran

Since the onset of the war in Ukraine in February 2022, Moscow has undertaken several specific policies with regard to Iran and the MENA/Mediterranean region, more broadly, that have benefited Tehran. Russian and Iranian cooperation has also increased since the start of the war. Indeed, Russia has even become dependent on Iran for armed drones, in particular. Despite this, Moscow has maintained its cooperative ties with other Middle Eastern governments, including Israel and the Arab monarchies of the Persian Gulf, which have long been at odds with Iran.

Since the outset of 2022, Putin has assiduously courted the Iranian leadership. He met with Iranian president Raisi in Moscow in January 2022, shortly before the onset of the war,[17] then at the 6th Caspian Summit in Turkmenistan in June 2022,[18] then again at the Astana Forum (the trilateral Russian-Iranian-Turkish summit meetings about Syria) in Tehran in July 2022,[19] and yet again at the Shanghai Cooperation Organization summit in Samarkand in September 2022.[20] While in Tehran, Putin also met with Iranian supreme leader Ali Khamenei, who expressed support for Russia's war against Ukraine.[21] At a time when the West in general and America in particular have been trying to isolate both the Russian and the Iranian leaders, their meeting together shows that they are not isolated from each other.

---

[17] Anton Troianovski, Farnaz Fassihi, and Steven Erlanger, "Russia and Iran Put on a Show of Unity—against the U.S.," *New York Times*, January 19, 2022, https://www.nytimes.com/2022/01/19/world/europe/russia-iran-unity-us.html.
[18] "Iranian President Wants Increased Trade with Russia to Bypass Western Financial Systems," Radio Free Europe/Radio Liberty, June 30, 2022, https://www.rferl.org/a/iran-russia-raisi-putin-meeting/31923231.html.
[19] Anton Troianovski and Farnaz Fassihi, "Putin Finds a New Ally in Iran, a Fellow Outcast," *New York Times*, July 19, 2022, https://www.nytimes.com/2022/07/19/world/europe/putin-ayatollah-erdogan-summit.html.
[20] Elena Teslova, "Russia's Putin Meets Iranian Counterpart Raisi on Sidelines of Regional SCO Summit," *Anadolu Agency*, September 15, 2022, https://www.aa.com.tr/en/asia-pacific/russias-putin-meets-iranian-counterpart-raisi-on-sidelines-of-regional-sco-summit/2686228#.
[21] Troianovski and Fassihi, "Putin Finds a New Ally."

The Russian reaction to the US-led sanctions effort aimed at reducing (if not eliminating) Russian petroleum exports after the onset of the Ukraine war definitely hurt Iran economically. Not only did the US not relent on its sanctions campaign against Iranian petroleum exports, but Russia itself undercut the export of sanctioned Iranian petroleum to China and India in particular.[22] Iran eventually responded by cutting even further the price at which it sold its already discounted oil.[23] This is an instance in which Russia has pursued its own interests at the expense of Iran's. Moscow, though, has also taken actions that have helped mitigate these problems. The announcement of a $40 billion Russian investment in the Iranian gas sector clearly benefits Iran, though it is uncertain how feasible all the planned projects are.[24] As Abdolrasool Divsallar observed, "Past business deals between Russia and Iran have always experienced delays and uncertainties."[25] In addition, the announced further work on building the Russian trade corridors through Iran to India will not only reduce shipment times between Russia and India but will also be beneficial to Iran by providing it with transit revenue.[26] These Russian-Indian trade corridors via Iran also incentivize New Delhi to resist American calls for India to distance itself from both Russia and Iran.

Ukraine and Russia have been important suppliers of wheat and other agricultural products to several MENA/Mediterranean countries. The Russian takeover of much of Ukraine's Black Sea coastline as well as the blockade of the port of Odessa resulted in a huge reduction in Ukrainian agricultural exports and increased agricultural prices in spring 2022 (though these subsequently subsided). Nor is it clear how much of a harvest Ukraine will be able to produce so long as the war

---

[22] MEE Correspondent, "Iran Sees No Benefit from Ukraine War as Russia Undercuts It on Steel and Oil," Middle East Eye, June 25, 2002, https://www.middleeasteye.net/news/iran-russia-ukraine-no-benefit-from-war-undercut-oil-steel.
[23] Andy Uhler, "Iran Is Following Russia's Lead and Selling Oil at a Discount," Marketplace, July 6, 2022, https://www.marketplace.org/2022/07/06/iran-is-following-russias-lead-and-selling-oil-at-a-discount/.
[24] Nikita Smagin, "Could a Russia-Iran Gas Partnership Bear Fruit?" Carnegie Politika, November 28, 2022, https://carnegieendowment.org/politika/88497.
[25] Abdolrasool Divsallar, "Rising Interdependency: How Russo-Iranian Relations Have Evolved with the War in Ukraine," Trends Research and Advisory, December 12, 2022, https://trendsresearch.org/insight/rising-interdependency-how-russo-iranian-relations-have-evolved-with-the-war-in-ukraine/.
[26] Charu Sudan Kasturi, "Is the INSTC Russia's New Economic Escape Route?" Al Jazeera, July 22, 2022, https://www.aljazeera.com/economy/2022/7/27/russias-new-economic-escape-route.

continues.[27] Russian agricultural production has continued strong, but Russian government export restrictions and the rise in insurance rates in the Black Sea have negatively impacted Russian agricultural exports.[28] The grain shortage and price rise negatively affected all importers of Black Sea agricultural produce, including Iran where this contributed to the rise of domestic unrest in spring 2022.[29] But as Divsallar pointed out to me in a private communication, the Black Sea export crisis was not the only factor that led to unrest over food prices in Iran; internal structural factors as well as Iranian government policies played a more important role.[30] Russia's cooperation with the Turkish/UN-negotiated agreements allowing freighters to move grain out of Ukrainian ports across the Black Sea, though, has benefited Iran and other Black Sea grain importers by increasing supplies and serving to lower prices. But just as Russian actions at the beginning of the war resulting in elevated grain prices may not have been the main cause of Iran's spring 2022 economic unrest, Russian cooperation with Turkey in allowing the export of Ukrainian grain resulting in lower grain prices did not serve to ameliorate economic conditions in Iran that contributed to the unrest there from late 2022.[31]

One spectacular way in which Moscow and Tehran have been cooperating since the beginning of the war is through the Russian purchase of Iranian drones for use in Ukraine. There have also been reports that Iranian advisers are helping Russian forces fire these Iranian drones against Ukrainian targets and that Iran is helping set up a production line for drones in Russia (though this project has not

---

[27]OECD, "The Impacts and Policy Implications of Russia's Aggression against Ukraine on Agricultural Markets," Organization for Economic Co-operation and Development, August 5, 2022, https://www.oecd.org/ukraine-hub/policy-responses/the-impacts-and-pol icy-implications-of-russia-s-aggression-against-ukraine-on-agricultural-markets-0030a 4cd/#figure-d1e360.
[28]OECD, "The Impacts and Policy Implications."
[29]Farnaz Fassihi, "Protests Triggered by Rising Food Prices Spread in Iran," *New York Times*, May 13, 2022, https://www.nytimes.com/2022/05/13/world/iran-protests-food-pri ces.html.
[30]See also "IMF: Rising Food Prices in Iran Have Nothing to Do with Ukraine War" [Google Translate title], VOA News, April 27, 2022, https://ir.voanews.com/a/us-iran-imf-outl ook-voa-inflation-food-shortage-ukraine/6547474.html.
[31]Babak Dehghanpisheh, "'Rage and a Lack of Hope': Iran's Economic Woes Add Fuel to Protests," *Washington Post*, January 10, 2023, https://www.washingtonpost.com/ world/2023/01/10/iran-protests-economy-mahsa-amini/.

yet come to fruition).[32] Mainly an exporter of weapons to developing countries in the past, the fact that Russia is importing weapons from Iran is an indication of how desperate Moscow is as well as that the Russian war effort is now dependent on cooperation with Iran to a certain extent. This Russian dependency on Iran could conceivably give Tehran some leverage over Moscow, but it is not yet clear how or whether this is happening.[33]

Moscow did yield, though, to Iranian interests after the war began regarding the negotiations over reinstating the JCPOA. After the war began and increased Western sanctions were imposed on Russia, Moscow demanded that these sanctions not apply to Russian economic interaction with Iran, which it claimed was necessary for Russia to carry out its duties as per the JCPOA. But when Tehran reportedly communicated its displeasure about this to Moscow, the Russian government backed down—a sign of Moscow's overwhelming desire to maintain good relations with Iran if not necessarily an indication that Tehran actually has leverage over Moscow.[34] Whether Moscow supports or opposes the resumption of the JCPOA, however, became increasingly moot as deteriorating Iranian-American relations since the onset of the war in Ukraine reduced the prospects of the Iranian nuclear accord being restored.

Some in the West and the Middle East anticipated that the exigencies of the war in Ukraine would result in Russia drawing down its military presence in Syria—leaving the burden of supporting the Assad regime against its many enemies more in the hands of Iran and its Hezbollah and other Shi'a militia allies as was the case between the outbreak of the Arab Spring uprising in Syria in 2011 and the beginning of the Russian intervention there in 2015. But while there have been reports that Russia has withdrawn some of its troops and air defense missiles from Syria to be redeployed in the Ukrainian theater, Putin appears determined that

---

[32]David Albright, Sarah Burkhard, and Spencer Faragasso, "Is Iran Contributing to Russian Drone Manufacturing in Yelabuga?" Institute for Science and International Security, February 24, 2023, https://isis-online.org/uploads/isis-reports/documents/Is_Iran_Contributing_to_Russian_Drone_Manufacturing_in_Yelabuga_February_24_2023.pdf.
[33]Mark N. Katz, "Despite Russian Reliance on Iranian Drones, Tehran's Leverage over Moscow Is Limited," Russia Matters, December 1, 2022, https://www.russiamatters.org/analysis/despite-russian-reliance-iranian-drones-tehrans-leverage-over-moscow-limited.
[34]Mark N. Katz, "Why Russia Upended the Iran Deal Talks, and Then Backed Down," National Interest, March 19, 2022, https://nationalinterest.org/blog/buzz/why-russia-upended-iran-deal-talks-and-then-backed-down-201323.

Russian forces remain there.[35] And so long as Russian armed forces remain in Syria, this relieves Iran and its militia allies of having to defend the Assad regime on their own against its various adversaries, which might well become emboldened if Russia's military presence declines further.

Russia's highly complex relations with Turkey's Erdogan have involved both cooperation and contention. Iran has not always benefited from this—but neither has Russia. Iran has obviously not benefited from Erdogan feeling emboldened to flex his muscles in Syria as a result of Russia's focus on the war in Ukraine. On the contrary, Iranian president Raisi was able to make common cause with Putin at the Tehran summit in opposing President Erdogan's attempt to gain Russian and Iranian approval for renewed Turkish intervention in Syria against Syrian Kurdish forces.[36] Iran (along with all other wheat-importing countries) also benefited from the lowered grain prices that resulted from Erodgan's role in arranging the deal that has allowed for the export of Ukrainian agricultural produce through ports that Russian naval forces had been blockading. The internal economic factors leading to unrest in Iran, after all, would hardly be ameliorated if grain prices had remained elevated.

Russia has also continued its pursuit of good relations with Iran's Arab adversaries in the Persian Gulf since the onset of the war in Ukraine. And these governments have continued their pursuit of good relations with Russia.[37] This may not be beneficial to Iranian interests, but there is little that the Islamic Republic can do about it—as Moscow is undoubtedly aware. There is one area, though, in which Russian cooperation with Tehran's Gulf Arab rivals has actually benefited Iran: the Saudi and Emirati refusal of the Biden administration's requests that they ramp up their oil production to make up for the sanctioned Russian oil that the West was no longer importing was intended to keep oil prices higher (or keep them from falling further) than they might

---

[35]Patrick Kingsley and Ronen Bergman, "Russia Shrinks Forces in Syria, a Factor in Israeli Strategy There," *New York Times*, October 19, 2022, https://www.nytimes.com/2022/10/19/world/middleeast/russia-syria-israel-ukraine.html.

[36]Fehim Tastekin, "Erdogan Returns Empty-Handed from Talks with Putin, Raisi," Al-Monitor, July 21, 2022, https://www.al-monitor.com/originals/2022/07/erdogan-returns-emptyhanded-talks-putin-raisi#ixzz7mt7kmKmj.

[37]Matthew Hedges, "The GCC Now Prefers Russia to the West," Fair Observer, October 21, 2022, https://www.fairobserver.com/politics/the-gcc-now-prefers-russia-to-the-west/.

have through their complying with US requests.[38] Oil prices, though, did decline after the October 2022 OPEC+ production cut, and so OPEC+ agreed to yet another production cut in April 2023, much to Western consternation.[39] If Saudi Arabia and the UAE did decide to cooperate with the United States, break their OPEC+ production agreement with Russia, and greatly increase their own oil production, then the result would be reduced oil prices that would negatively impact the amount of petroleum export income that Iran would receive. Tehran would clearly prefer, then, for Saudi Arabia and the UAE to continue cooperating more with Russia than with the United States on this issue.

After Russia invaded Ukraine in February 2022, the then-Israeli foreign minister Yair Lapid criticized Russian actions while the then-Israeli prime minister Naftali Bennet was reticent to do so. The latter's reluctance to criticize Russia's war on Ukraine was partly due to an Israeli desire to preserve the 2015 Russian-Israeli deconfliction agreement in Syria whereby Moscow has turned a blind eye to Israeli attacks on Iranian and Hezbollah targets.[40] But while this Russian-Israeli deconfliction agreement has continued, Moscow has become increasingly critical of Israeli attacks in Syria in an apparent effort to discourage them.[41] Russian-Israeli ties deteriorated further after the more anti-Russian Yair Lapid replaced Naftali Bennet as prime minister at the beginning of July 2022.[42] The return to power of the Putin-friendly but virulently anti-Iranian Benjamin Netanyahu, though, might reverse this trend. It may be difficult for Netanyahu, though, to fully restore his relationship with Putin at a time when Putin has moved closer to Iran.

---

[38] "OPEC+ Oil Cut Sparks Tremors in Washington, Ripples Round Iran," Iran International, October 8, 2022, https://www.iranintl.com/en/202210080221.
[39] Maha El Dahan and Ahmed Rasheed, "OPEC+ Announces Surprise Oil Output Cuts," Reuters, April 2, 2023, https://www.reuters.com/business/energy/sarabia-other-opec-producers-announce-voluntary-oil-output-cuts-2023-04-02/.
[40] Scott B. Lasensky and Vera Michlin-Shapir, "Avoiding Zero-Sum: Israel and Russia in an Evolving Middle East," in *The MENA Region: A Great Power Competition*, edited by Karim Mezran and Arturo Varvelli (Milan: ISPI, 2019), 148–50, https://www.ispionline.it/sites/default/files/pubblicazioni/ispi_report_mena_region_2019.pdf#page=141.
[41] Scott Lucas, "Shifting Its Position, Russia Criticizes 'Unacceptable' Israel Strikes Inside Syria," EA Worldview, July 5, 2022, https://eaworldview.com/2022/07/russia-israel-strikes-syria/.
[42] Rina Bassist, "Israel's Lapid Condemns Russian Attack on Kyiv," Al-Monitor, October 11, 2022, https://www.al-monitor.com/originals/2022/10/israels-lapid-condemns-russian-attack-kyiv.

Yet, despite the problems Tehran has experienced as a result of the war in Ukraine, Moscow's post-invasion policies toward Iran and the MENA/Mediterranean region have generally been favorable to Tehran's interests. The war in Ukraine appears to have made Iran more important to Russia than it was before. Still, even though Moscow has become dependent on Iran for armed drones and other weapons, the continued willingness of virtually all other Middle Eastern governments (including those such as Israel and the Arab monarchies) to cooperate with Moscow has enabled Putin to continue enjoying good relations with virtually all actors in the Middle East—even though all those actors (including Iran) would prefer that Moscow would be more supportive of them and less supportive of their adversaries.

Recently, however, there are signs that Russia is finding it more difficult to maintain its balancing act in the MENA/Mediterranean region. While Moscow continues to maintain its presence in Syria, it has withdrawn air defense missiles, Wagner mercenaries, and experienced Russian military commanders for redeployment to the Ukrainian theater. More significantly, Russians have pulled back from their positions in southwestern and far eastern Syria. This has resulted in Turkey, Iran, and Israel adopting more aggressive tactics in Syria (Turkey against the Kurds, and Israel and Iran against each other).[43] The more Russia redeploys its military assets from Syria to Ukraine, the less able Moscow will be to prevent conflict between or rein in these other actors.

In another dramatic development, Russian "peacekeepers" in the South Caucasus did not act to prevent renewed advances by Azerbaijan against Armenia—which is a member of the Russia-led Collective Security Treaty Organization (CSTO)—in late 2022 and early 2023. Turkish-backed Azeri forces prevailed in a 44-day war against Armenia in late 2020, but the Moscow-negotiated conflict resolution process ending the war resulted in 2,000 Russian peacekeepers being deployed to positions between the two sides designed to halt further Azeri advances. But apparently, due to its need to focus on the war in Ukraine, these Russian forces did not do so—much to the chagrin of Armenia.[44] Indeed, it has been Iran, and

---

[43] Mona Yacoubian, "Ukraine's Consequences Are Finally Spreading to Syria," War on the Rocks, January 10 2023, https://warontherocks.com/2023/01/ukraines-consequences-are-finally-spreading-to-syria/.
[44] Anton Troianovski, "Renewed Armenia-Azerbaijan Conflict Underlines Russia's Waning Influence," *New York Times*, January 17, 2023, https://www.nytimes.com/2023/01/17/world/europe/armenia-azerbaijan-russia-nagorno.html.

not Russia, that has been more supportive of Armenia against Azerbaijan (which Tehran sees as collaborating with Israel).[45]

The image of Russia becoming a less capable actor not just in Syria but even in the South Caucasus may serve to undermine its reputation as a steadfast ally even among Middle Eastern governments that very much want it to be. The longer the Ukraine war goes on, the less capable Moscow may be of maintaining balance among opposing actors in the Middle East. Even if Moscow grows closer to Tehran as a result of Russian dependence on Iranian drones and other weapons, decreased Russian ability to pay attention to the Middle East may result in Iran having to take on a more active role as its regional adversaries and others do so. The war in Ukraine, though, may not remain in its current state indefinitely.

Ukraine War Scenarios and Their Impact on Russia's MENA/Iran Policy

It is not at all clear at the time that this is being written how or when the war in Ukraine will come to an end or whether it will continue to drag on indefinitely. This uncertainty, of course, makes predicting what impact the future of the war in Ukraine will have on Moscow's MENA/Mediterranean policies as well as on Iran even more uncertain. It appears, though, that there are three possible scenarios for the future of the war in Ukraine: (1) "Russia wins," (2) "Russia loses," and (3) "prolonged conflict." Each of these scenarios will be discussed in terms of their possible impact on Russia's MENA/Mediterranean policy and on Iran in particular.

The *"Russia wins" scenario* can be defined as Russia militarily defeating Ukraine and the war ending on terms favorable to Russia (which would, at a minimum, include Kyiv accepting territorial losses to Russia and agreeing not to join NATO and, at a maximum, result in a Russian takeover of all of Ukraine). Russia winning its war with Ukraine could allow Moscow to return to playing a larger role in the MENA/Mediterranean region. Russia playing a stronger, and America presumably playing a weaker, role in the MENA/Mediterranean region could be good for Iran in general, especially with regard to Syria, where the question of Russia withdrawing

---

[45]Paul Iddon, "Iran, Azerbaijan Tensions Heighten Risks of Military Conflict," Middle East Eye, April 22, 2023, https://www.middleeasteye.net/news/prospect-military-conflict-between-iran-and-azerbaijan.

its forces would no longer be relevant. A Russia victorious in Ukraine, though, might be less dependent on Iran for drones or anything else than it was during the war. Indeed, if the United States becomes less of a factor in the Middle East, the international relations of the region may become a contest among the various governments there—Iran, Turkey, Arab states, and even Israel—for Moscow's favor. On the contrary, if a Russian win in Ukraine results in Putin focusing his attention on pushing NATO out of Eastern Europe (as he indicated he sought in one of the extraordinary "draft treaties" that the Russian foreign ministry published in December 2021),[46] then Russia will probably not be able to undertake increased military involvement in the Middle East. And the more threatened by Russia that European countries feel, the more willing they may be to drop sanctions against Iran in order to buy oil from it instead of Russia—irrespective of whether the United States approves of such a move or not. But whether Putin turns his attention to confronting NATO or quits while he's ahead, a Russian win in Ukraine would be a further step in the establishment of a post-American world order dominated by Russia and China. While Iran would not be on par with these two, this "Russia wins" scenario could help Iran escape from the American-imposed economic isolation that has depended on other nations following Washington's lead in enforcing it.

The *"Russia loses" scenario* can be defined at a minimum as Russia ceasing all military operations, withdrawing from some (if not all) Ukrainian territory, and the Ukrainian government remaining intact and aligned with (if not formally a member of) NATO. Under these circumstances, Russia may be unable, and even unwilling, to continue an active policy in the Middle East, including in Syria. In need of trade and investment, Moscow will want to have friendly relations with a variety of states capable of providing these, including the Arab monarchies of the Persian Gulf and Israel. Moscow will certainly want to export as much petroleum as it can at the highest price that it can, which would entail restoring relations with the West so that economic sanctions could be removed. Under these circumstances, supporting Iran against America and the West would not be a priority for Moscow (much as it wasn't in the early and mid-1990s when Yeltsin saw good relations with the West as a

---

[46]Andrew E. Kramer and Steven Erlanger, "Russia Lays Out Demands for a Sweeping New Security Deal with NATO," *New York Times*, December 17, 2021, https://www.nytimes.com/2021/12/17/world/europe/russia-nato-security-deal.html.

foreign policy priority for Russia).[47] All this would be bad for Iran, but it would be worse still if the end of the war in Ukraine occurred as a result of either leadership change or regime change in Russia that ushered in a new period of Russian retrenchment as occurred in the wake of the collapse of the USSR. A defeated Russia that withdraws from Syria would force Iran to make the stark choice between shouldering the burden of the war there against an Israel and Turkey unconstrained by Russia or Iran itself having to withdraw from Syria. In short, the "Russia loses" scenario, whatever its form, could indeed have a very negative impact on Iran.

The *"prolonged conflict" scenario* can be defined as a continuation of the present situation in which Russian forces still occupy a significant portion of Ukrainian territory (perhaps more or less than what they have now), but the fighting continues with neither Russia nor Ukraine being in a position to force or persuade the other to yield. The impact of this particular scenario on Iran is likely to be mixed. On the one hand, Russia would be highly likely to continue selling its sanctioned oil at a steep discount to China and India despite the continued negative impact of this on Iran's oil exports. But Russia may not be in a position to carry out the investments in the Iranian petroleum sector despite previous promises. On the other hand, Russian dependence on Iran for drones and perhaps other weaponry might increase as Russia's inventory of weapons is depleted through battlefield use and the inability of the Western-sanctioned Russian arms industry to import the technological components needed for it to manufacture advanced weapons. The longer the war goes on, the more Europe may be willing—even desperate—to import oil from Iran that it cannot or will not buy from Russia, provided that Europe does not feel threatened by Russian use of Iranian drones or other weapons against Ukraine. The United States may even tacitly approve of this if the situation grows desperate enough (indeed, at the onset of the war, the Biden administration seemed willing to drop sanctions against the Western purchases of Iranian oil after its hoped-for resumption of the JCPOA).[48] On the contrary, the longer the war continues, the more likely it becomes that Russia will have to redeploy even more men and weapons systems from Syria to Ukraine, thus putting a greater burden on Iran and

---

[47]Divsallar, "Rising Interdependency."
[48]"White House Does Not Rule Out Importing Iranian Oil," Iran International, March 5, 2022, https://www.iranintl.com/en/202203050288.

its Shi'a militia allies to defend the Assad regime against what are likely to be adversaries emboldened by Russia's drawdown. Finally, while the grain crisis caused by the war subsided in the summer of 2022 due to the agreement negotiated by Turkey and the UN whereby Russia allowed Ukrainian exports from the ports it had been blockading, a prolonged war could result in a significantly reduced Ukrainian harvest that could lead to renewed food shortages and price rises. If severe, this could in turn lead to unrest and instability throughout the MENA/Mediterranean region even if Iran's own agricultural production improves. And Russia may not be in a position to either ameliorate or suppress this problem. Thus, while prolonging the war may provide both opportunities and risks for Iran, the costs would appear more likely to outweigh the benefits for Iran the longer the war goes on—whether or not other Middle Eastern governments, including those at odds with Iran, continue to cooperate with Russia.

Conclusion

According to my analysis, Russia losing the war in Ukraine would be the worst outcome for Iran, its prolongation would present both opportunities and risks for Iran, but the risks would grow the longer the war continues, and Iran would gain through Russia winning the war in Ukraine—provided Moscow did not go on to fight a new war anywhere else in Eastern Europe. What Iran—and perhaps several other governments in the MENA/Mediterranean region—would prefer is if Russia would quickly win its war with Ukraine and then not attempt any further expansion (at least for now). Iran, though, is not in a position to bring about this outcome that would be the most favorable to Tehran.

Further, each of these scenarios would have a differing impact on Moscow's ability to continue its balancing act between Iran on one side and other Middle Eastern governments (including Iran's adversaries) on the other. The "Russia wins" in Ukraine scenario, followed by no further conflict in Europe, would result in Moscow being less dependent on Iran for drones and other weapons as well as more able to interact with Turkey, Israel, and the Arab monarchies of the Persian Gulf. Whatever leverage Iran may have gained from increased Russian dependence on Tehran during the war will be reduced or even lost if Russia wins in Ukraine. On the contrary, Russia is likely to continue cooperating with Iran despite any objections that its Middle Eastern adversaries might have. In the "Russia loses" scenario, by contrast, Moscow may simply no longer have the means to continue balancing among Middle Eastern governments as it has been so successful under the Putin administration so far. All Middle Eastern governments, including Iran, would have to adjust to a situation in which, despite its continued desire to do so, Moscow may simply not be able to play as active a role in the Middle East after losing in Ukraine. Iran and others seeking a counterbalance to the United States may then seek to engage China more in the region. China might not yet be ready to play this role, but just being invited to do so could help precipitate its further involvement (though it, like Moscow, could be expected to try to maintain good relations with opposing sides in the Middle East and not side with Iran against the others). Finally, the "prolonged conflict" scenario may result in even greater Russian dependence on and less ability to constrain Iran. But it may also result in less Russian ability to rein in opposing Middle Eastern actors, and hence increased conflict among them—which will not benefit Iran if the West aids Iran's regional adversaries while Iran cannot get similar support from Russia, China, or any other external actor.

In other words, while Iran has made some gains in terms of its relations with Russia as a result of the war in Ukraine, Iran may not be able to keep them or may even incur some degree of costs, no matter which scenario eventually unfolds.

Bibliography

Albright, David, Sarah Burkhard, and Spencer Faragasso. "Is Iran Contributing to Russian Drone Manufacturing in Yelabuga?" Institute for Science and International Security, February 24, 2023. https://isis-online.org/uplo ads/isis-reports/documents/Is_Iran_Contributing_to_Russian_Drone_ Manufacturing_in_Yelabuga_February_24_2023.pdf.

Azizi, Hamidrezah. "Russia's Role in Brokering a Comprehensive Agreement between the United States and Iran." London School of Economics Middle East Centre, August 1, 2021. https://blogs.lse.ac.uk/mec/2021/08/01/russ ias-role-in-brokering-a-comprehensive-agreement-between-the-united-sta tes-and-iran/.

Bassist, Rina. "Israel's Lapid Condemns Russian Attack on Kyiv." Al-Monitor, October 11, 2022. https://www.al-monitor.com/originals/2022/10/isra els-lapid-condemns-russian-attack-kyiv.

Bernstein, Jonas. "Russia's Stake in Iran Nuclear Deal." Voice of America, July 18, 2015. https://www.voanews.com/a/russias-stake-in-iran-nuclear-deal/2867710.html.

Borshchevskaya, Anna. "Russia's Cooperation on the Iran Deal Is No Favor to Washington." Washington Institute for Near East Policy, July 7, 2016. https://www.washingtoninstitute.org/policy-analysis/russias-cooperation-iran-deal-no-favor-washington.

Brumberg, Daniel. "Russian-Turkish-Iranian Cross-Purposes on Syria's Future." Arab Center Washington, DC, September 8, 2020. https://arabcenterdc.org/resource/russian-turkish-iranian-cross-purposes-on-syrias-future/.

Cafiero, Giorgio. "Can Bahrain Count on Moscow to Fill Washington's Shoes?" Al-Monitor, July 8, 2016. https://www.al-monitor.com/originals/2016/07/bahrain-russia-replace-washington-influence-iran.html#ixzz7mdZIlOoF.

Dehghanpisheh, Babak. "'Rage and a Lack of Hope': Iran's Economic Woes Add Fuel to Protests." *Washington Post*, January 10, 2023. https://www.washingtonpost.com/world/2023/01/10/iran-protests-economy-mahsa-amini/.

Divsallar, Abdolrasool. "Rising Interdependency: How Russo-Iranian Relations Have Evolved with the War in Ukraine." Trends Research and Advisory, December 12, 2022. https://trendsresearch.org/insight/rising-interdependency-how-russo-iranian-relations-have-evolved-with-the-war-in-ukraine/.

El Dahan, Maha, and Ahmed Rasheed. "OPEC+ Announces Surprise Oil Output Cuts." Reuters, April 2, 2023. https://www.reuters.com/business/energy/sarabia-other-opec-producers-announce-voluntary-oil-output-cuts-2023-04-02/.

Fassihi, Farnaz. "Protests Triggered by Rising Food Prices Spread in Iran." *New York Times*, May 13, 2022. https://www.nytimes.com/2022/05/13/world/iran-protests-food-prices.html.

Grady, John. "Panel: Russia Will Reap Benefits from Iranian Oil Crackdown." USNI News, May 1, 2019. https://news.usni.org/2019/05/01/panel-russia-will-reap-benefits-from-iranian-oil-crackdown.

Grajewski, Nicole. "The Evolution of Russian and Iranian Cooperation in Syria." Center for Strategic and International Studies, November 17, 2021. https://www.csis.org/analysis/evolution-russian-and-iranian-cooperation-syria.

Hedges, Matthew. "The GCC Now Prefers Russia to the West." Fair Observer, October 21, 2022. https://www.fairobserver.com/politics/the-gcc-now-prefers-russia-to-the-west/.

Ibish, Hussein. "Iran's New Ploy to Disrupt the Mideast: Laying Claim to Bahrain." *Ibishblog*, September 21, 2022. https://ibishblog.com/2022/09/21/irans-new-ploy-to-disrupt-the-mideast-laying-claim-to-bahrain/.

Iddon, Paul. "Iran, Azerbaijan Tensions Heighten Risks of Military Conflict." Middle East Eye, April 22, 2023. https://www.middleeasteye.net/news/prospect-military-conflict-between-iran-and-azerbaijan.

"Iran Believes an Excess of Supply in Oil Market Can Have a Negative Impact." Iran Press News Agency, December 4, 2022. https://iranpress.com/cont

ent/70349/iran-believes-excess-supply-oil-market-can-have-negative-impact.

"Iranian President Wants Increased Trade with Russia to Bypass Western Financial Systems." Radio Free Europe/Radio Liberty, June 30, 2022. https://www.rferl.org/a/iran-russia-raisi-putin-meeting/31923231.html.

Iran International. "OPEC+ Oil Cut Sparks Tremors in Washington, Ripples Round Iran." October 8, 2022. https://www.iranintl.com/en/202210080221.

Iran International. "White House Does Not Rule Out Importing Iranian Oil." March 5, 2022. https://www.iranintl.com/en/202203050288.

Kasturi, Charu Sudan. "Is the INSTC Russia's New Economic Escape Route?" Al Jazeera, July 22, 2022. https://www.aljazeera.com/economy/2022/7/27/russias-new-economic-escape-route.

Katz, Mark N. "Despite Russian Reliance on Iranian Drones, Tehran's Leverage over Moscow Is Limited." Russia Matters, December 1, 2022. https://www.russiamatters.org/analysis/despite-russian-reliance-iranian-drones-tehrans-leverage-over-moscow-limited.

Katz, Mark N. "Incessant Interest: Tsarist, Soviet and Putinist Mideast Strategies." *Middle East Policy* 27, no. 1 (2020): 141–52.

Katz, Mark N. "Russia and Israel: An Improbable Friendship." In *Russia Rising: Putin's Foreign Policy in the Middle East and North Africa*, edited by Dimitar Bechev, Nicu Popescu, and Stanislav Secrieru, 123–9. London: I.B. Tauris, 2021.

Katz, Mark N. "Russian-Iranian Relations in the Ahmadinejad Era." *Middle East Journal* 62 (2008): 202–16.

Katz, Mark N. "Why Russia Upended the Iran Deal Talks, and Then Backed Down." *National Interest*, March 19, 2022. https://nationalinterest.org/blog/buzz/why-russia-upended-iran-deal-talks-and-then-backed-down-201323.

Kingsley, Patrick, and Ronen Bergman. "Russia Shrinks Forces in Syria, a Factor in Israeli Strategy There." *New York Times*, October 19, 2022. https://www.nytimes.com/2022/10/19/world/middleeast/russia-syria-israel-ukraine.html.

Kozhanov, Nikolay. "The Drivers of Russia-GCC Relations." In *Russian Foreign Policy towards the Middle East: New Trends, Old Traditions*, edited by Nikolay Kozhanov, 141–63. London: Hurst, 2022.

Kramer, Andrew E., and Steven Erlanger. "Russia Lays Out Demands for a Sweeping New Security Deal with NATO." *New York Times*, December 17, 2021. https://www.nytimes.com/2021/12/17/world/europe/russia-nato-security-deal.html.

Lasensky, Scott B., and Vera Michlin-Shapir. "Avoiding Zero-Sum: Israel and Russia in an Evolving Middle East." In *The MENA Region: A Great Power Competition*, edited by Karim Mezran and Arturo Varvelli, 141–57. Milan: ISPI, 2019. https://www.ispionline.it/sites/default/files/pubblicazioni/ispi_report_mena_region_2019.pdf#page=141.

Lucas, Scott. "Shifting Its Position, Russia Criticizes 'Unacceptable' Israel Strikes Inside Syria." EA Worldview, July 5, 2022. https://eaworldview.com/2022/07/russia-israel-strikes-syria/.

MEE Correspondent. "Iran Sees No Benefit from Ukraine War as Russia Undercuts It on Steel and Oil." Middle East Eye, June 25, 2002. https://www.middleeasteye.net/news/iran-russia-ukraine-no-benefit-from-war-undercut-oil-steel.

Melkonian, Sergei. "Russia-Israel Cooperation in Syria: Interests, Dynamics, and Impact of the War in Ukraine." Emirates Policy Council, August 22, 2022. https://epc.ae/en/details/featured/russia-israel-cooperation-in-syria-interests-dynamics-and-impact-of-the-war-in-ukraine.

Notte, Hanna. "Don't Expect Any More Russian Help on the Iran Nuclear Deal." War on the Rocks, November 3, 2022. https://warontherocks.com/2022/11/dont-expect-any-more-russian-help-on-the-iran-nuclear-deal/.

OECD. "The Impacts and Policy Implications of Russia's Aggression against Ukraine on Agricultural Markets." Organization for Economic Co-operation and Development, August 5, 2022. https://www.oecd.org/ukraine-hub/policy-responses/the-impacts-and-policy-implications-of-russia-s-aggression-against-ukraine-on-agricultural-markets-0030a4cd/#figure-d1e360.

Ramani, Samuel. "Russia and the Yemeni Civil War." In *Russian Foreign Policy towards the Middle East: New Trends, Old Traditions*, edited by Nikolay Kozhanov, 165–90. London: Hurst, 2022.

Smagin, Nikita. "Could a Russia-Iran Gas Partnership Bear Fruit?" Carnegie Politika, November 28, 2022. https://carnegieendowment.org/politika/88497.

Tastekin, Fehim. "Erdogan Returns Empty-Handed from Talks with Putin, Raisi." Al-Monitor, July 21, 2022. https://www.al-monitor.com/originals/2022/07/erdogan-returns-emptyhanded-talks-putin-raisi#ixzz7mt7kmKmj.

Tazmini, Ghoncheh. "Russia and Iran: Strategic Partner or Provisional Counterweight?" In *Russian Foreign Policy towards the Middle East: New Trends, Old Traditions*, edited by Nikolay Kozhanov, 117–40. London: Hurst, 2022.

Teslova, Elena. "Russia's Putin Meets Iranian Counterpart Raisi on Sidelines of Regional SCO Summit." Anadolu Agency, September 15, 2022. https://www.aa.com.tr/en/asia-pacific/russias-putin-meets-iranian-counterpart-raisi-on-sidelines-of-regional-sco-summit/2686228#.

Troianovski, Anton. "Renewed Armenia-Azerbaijan Conflict Underlines Russia's Waning Influence." *New York Times*, January 17, 2023. https://www.nytimes.com/2023/01/17/world/europe/armenia-azerbaijan-russia-nagorno.html.

Troianovski, Anton, and Farnaz Fassihi. "Putin Finds a New Ally in Iran, a Fellow Outcast." *New York Times*, July 19, 2022. https://www.nytimes.com/2022/07/19/world/europe/putin-ayatollah-erdogan-summit.html.

Troianovski, Anton, Farnaz Fassihi, and Steven Erlanger. "Russia and Iran Put on a Show of Unity—against the U.S." *New York Times*, January 19, 2022. https://www.nytimes.com/2022/01/19/world/europe/russia-iran-unity-us.html.

Uhler, Andy. "Iran Is Following Russia's Lead and Selling Oil at a Discount." Marketplace, July 6, 2022. https://www.marketplace.org/2022/07/06/iran-is-following-russias-lead-and-selling-oil-at-a-discount/.

Vasiliev, Alexey. *Russia's Middle East Policy: From Lenin to Putin*. London: Routledge, 2018.

VOA News. "IMF: Afzayesh ghemat mavade ghazaei dar iran abti be jange ukrain nadarad [IMF: Rising Food Prices in Iran Have Nothing to Do with Ukraine War]." April 27, 2022. https://ir.voanews.com/a/us-iran-imf-outlook-voa-inflation-food-shortage-ukraine/6547474.html.

Yacoubian, Mona. "Ukraine's Consequences Are Finally Spreading to Syria." War on the Rocks, January 10, 2023. https://warontherocks.com/2023/01/ukraines-consequences-are-finally-spreading-to-syria/.

5 THE PRINCIPLE OF STRATEGIC STABILITY: HAS THE WAR CHANGED RUSSIA'S NUCLEAR POLICY TOWARD IRAN?

Anastasia Malygina

Before discussing the factors that framed the Russian approach to managing the Iranian nuclear crisis during Moscow's military campaign in Ukraine, we should acknowledge that any state would look at foreign policies more like a set of situational compromises than a logical application of explicit principles. Observing Russia-Iran relations in the nuclear sphere requires putting it in the context of the nuclear nonproliferation regime. Russian nuclear nonproliferation policy is a multifaceted affair, which involves many national stakeholders ranging from the Ministry of Foreign Affairs to the national atomic industries. In other words, the Russian nuclear policy toward Iran is a distilled compromise that encompasses internal debates to shape positions among different groups, including the Russian political and business elites. The decision-making process in Russia is not transparent, which makes it almost impossible to speculate on the share of each of the players. However, by analyzing the official Russian narrative, one can judge the basics of Russian foreign and security policy and its core principles that seem to remain unchanged. By observing the events of 2022 and comparing this dynamic with the previous stages of the Iranian nuclear crisis, which appeared in 2018 after US president Trump decided to withdraw from the nuclear deal with Iran, we can answer the following set of questions:

Did the post-February 2022 events affect the scope and dynamics of Russo-Iranian interactions regarding the Joint Comprehensive Plan of Action (JCPOA)? What are the possible consequences of the armed phase of the Ukrainian crisis for the long-term prospects of nuclear cooperation between Moscow and Tehran, including on nuclear power plants (NPPs) and international commitments? Is there any correlation between the dynamics of the US-Russia confrontation and the trends in Russo-Iranian economic cooperation in the nuclear sphere? Is there any chance that growing tensions between Russia and the West could alter Russia's nuclear nonproliferation principles?

The chapter starts with introducing the Russia-China concept of global strategic stability as a framework that can help answer the abovementioned questions and proceeds to review Russia's priorities regarding the global nuclear nonproliferation regime. An overview of the Russian foreign and security policy doctrine will be helpful in understanding the drivers of the Russian approach to disputes over the Iranian nuclear program. For Russia, the JCPOA is a local, albeit important, case that Russia attempts to address in the context of the overall situation in the field of arms control and nonproliferation. Extracting the JCPOA case from the Nuclear Non-Proliferation Treaty (NPT) context may lead to incorrect conclusions about Russia's motives and intentions. This chapter will challenge some of the beliefs about Russia-Iran relations in the nuclear sphere, which circulate in the expert community. It provides an interpretation of the post-February 2022 events around the JCPOA as they are seen from the point of view of Russia. Although many observers in the West believe that the Russian approach to restoring the JCPOA has radically shifted since February 2022, this chapter argues that the fluctuations of diplomatic interactions and the obvious slowdown in Vienna Talks cannot be qualified as a policy change or strategic shift in the Russian nuclear nonproliferation policy. Russia's understanding of its role and priorities with regard to settling the Iranian nuclear crisis remained unchanged in 2022 and beyond.

Global Strategic Stability: What's in a Name?

The Ukrainian crisis of 2014 disentangled Russia from its dream of an exclusive strategic partnership with the West. Russia's actions in the context of the Ukrainian crisis in 2014 aggravated the confrontation between Russia and NATO. However, over the next eight years, Russia continued collaborating with the West on many global security issues, including managing the Iranian nuclear crisis. Although economic sanctions introduced by the West in response to Russia's actions in Crimea and Eastern Ukraine in 2014 influenced the structure of the Russian international partnerships and forced Russian businesses to seek opportunities in non-Western markets, the scope and intensity of continued economic cooperation between Russia and the European Union (EU) were so large that it would be not an exaggeration to call the Russian economy in 2014–22 Western-oriented.

February 24, 2022, was a tipping point when Russia radically and symbolically opposed itself to the West and started its geopolitical turn to the East. Russia-China relations became the foundation for building the structure of Russia's relations with those whom, after February 2022, the Kremlin started calling "friendly countries." The unity of the Russo-European approach to settling the crisis caused by America's withdrawal from the JCPOA was gradually replaced by a tough and catch-all confrontation between Russia and the West. This confrontation impacted many sectors of international security, including the dynamic of negotiations aimed at restoring the JCPOA. To better understand these circumstances, Russia-China relations and the emerging contours of their common strategic vision appear to have a noteworthy significance.

The term "global strategic stability" appeared for the first time in a joint statement by the president of the Russian Federation and the president of the People's Republic of China at the end of June 2016[1] and was later detailed in the joint statements of the two presidents in June 2019,[2] early February

---

[1] "Joint Statement by the President of the Russian Federation and the President of the People's Republic of China on Strengthening Global Strategic Stability," *Kremlin*, June 25, 2016, http://kremlin.ru/supplement/5098.

[2] "Joint Statement of the Russian Federation and the People's Republic of China on Strengthening Global Strategic Stability in the Modern Era," *Kremlin*, June 5, 2019, http://www.kremlin.ru/supplement/5412.

2022,[3] and March 2023.[4] The concept of global strategic stability suggests an alternative to a Western unipolar world order. From Moscow's perspective, the concept strove to replace universal norms of international law.[5] In a nutshell, this concept can be reduced to three key principles: balance of interests in a polycentric world, peaceful coexistence, and fairness. In a close-up, these are the principles already stated in the UN Charter, but in the frame of the Russia-China strategic vision, they obtained additional meaning.

The principle of balance of interests opposes rules introduced by an exclusive club of Western states that realize policy of pressure, "bullying, unilateral sanctions and exterritorial implementation of jurisdiction," "misuse of export control policies," and inappropriate unjust trade competition.[6] Russia keeps criticizing the Western policy of "fragmentation of security of regions,"[7] which in the Russian view provokes a split and confrontation and is realized by means of narrow-format military alliances and coalitions of the willing built to promptly fix international crisis with hard power. To counterbalance this policy,

---

[3] "Joint Statement by the Russian Federation and the People's Republic of China on International Relations Entering a New Era and Global Sustainable Development," *Kremlin*, February 4, 2022, http://www.kremlin.ru/supplement/5770.

[4] "Joint Statement by the Russian Federation and the People's Republic of China on Deepening Comprehensive Partnership and Strategic Cooperation, Entering a New Era," *Kremlin*, March 21, 2023, http://www.kremlin.ru/supplement/5920.

[5] "Foreign Minister Sergey Lavrov's Remarks and Answers to Media Questions during Talks with Foreign Minister of the Islamic Republic of Iran Hossein Amir-Abdollahian," Ministry of Foreign Affairs of Russia, August 31, 2022, https://mid.ru/ru/foreign_policy/news/1827971/?lang=ru; "Welcome Remarks by the Minister of Defense of Russia at the Opening of the 10th Moscow Conference on International Security," Ministry of Defense of Russia, August 16, 2022, https://function.mil.ru/news_page/country/more.htm?id=12433 677@egNews; Sergey Ryabkov, "Mezhdunarodnaia Mozaika Dolzhna Skladivatsia Ne Iz Serogo I Ego Piatidesiati Ottenkov, Kotorie Naviazivaiutsia Zapadom, A Deistvitelno Bit Mnogograннoi I Monogokrasochnoi Kartinoi [International Life Should Be Constructed Not from Grey and Its Fifty Shadows Imposed by the West but Be Truly Multifaceted and Multicolor]," Interview by Armen Oganesian. *Mezhdunarodnaia Zhizn* no. 9 (2022), https://interaffairs.ru/jauthor/material/2713; Frolov, Piotr. "O Nekotorikh Vozmozhnikh Aspektakh Formiruiuschigosia Postneoliberalnogo Mira [On Some Possible Aspects of the Forming Post-Neoliberal World]," *Mezhdunarodnaia Zhizn* no. 6 (2022), https://interaffairs.ru/jauthor/material/2673.

[6] "Joint Statement on Entering a New Era and the Global Sustainable Development."

[7] "Briefing by Foreign Ministry Spokeswoman Maria Zakharova," Moscow, February 1, 2023, https://www.mid.ru/ru/press_service/spokesman/briefings/1851724/?lang=ru.

Russia and China agreed to strengthen BRICS[8] and the Shanghai Cooperation Organization (SCO) and to promote dialogue in these formats and regional integration associations and organizations of developing countries. Russia sees the careful and persistent search for a balance of interests through diplomatic dialogue as a key principle in a "polycentric world order based on the universally recognized principles of international law, multilateralism, and equal, joint, indivisible, integrated and sustainable security."[9] On the one hand, it sounds like a variation of the principle of indivisible security, and on the other hand, it refers to the concept of general and complete disarmament (the connection between global strategic stability and general and complete disarmament was explicitly pronounced in the 2016 joint statement).

The principle of peaceful coexistence counterbalances the policy of American-centric strategic alliances and coalitions of the willing. As it was said in the 2022 Russia-China joint statement, "The parties … confirm that Russian-Chinese interstate relations of a new type are superior to the military-political alliances of the Cold War era. … the strengthening of bilateral strategic cooperation is not directed against third countries, is not affected by the changing international environment and situational changes in third countries."[10] In early November 2022, Moscow made a statement that reassured its adherence to the tenet "a nuclear war cannot be won and must never be fought," which included among other ideas the following lines: "Russia continues to advocate for a revamped, more robust architecture of international security based on ensuring predictability and global strategic stability, as well as on the principles of equal rights, indivisible security and mutual account of core interests of the parties."[11]

Fairness, mentioned three times in the 2016 Concept of Foreign Policy of the Russian Federation, is seen by the Kremlin as a guarantee of peace, stability, and sustainable development and a cornerstone principle of a polycentric world order and one of the building bricks of "the common

---

[8] A group of big emerging economies initially comprising Brazil, Russia, India, China, and South Africa (BRICS). As of 2024, Iran, Saudi Arabia, Egypt, Argentina, the UAE, and Ethiopia have joined the group.
[9] "Joint Statement on Entering a New Era and the Global Sustainable Development."
[10] "Joint Statement on Entering a New Era and the Global Sustainable Development."
[11] "Statement of the Russian Federation on Preventing Nuclear War," Russian Ministry of Defense, November 2, 2022, https://mid.ru/ru/foreign_policy/news/1836575/?lang=en#sel=2:1:V,2:1:V.

spiritual and moral potential of the main world religions."[12] In the 2016 and 2019 Russia-China joint statements, the term "fair" appeared only once in the context of describing the appropriate nature of measures in the field of arms reduction and arms limitation as a guarantee of global strategic stability, while in the 2022 joint statement, the word "fair" was used eight times, and in the 2023 joint statement, it appeared nine times in different contexts. In the security realm, fairness means ensuring one's own security without compromising the security of others. In the economic domain, fairness is synonymous with the absence of discriminatory conditions for scientific and technological development. As the 2022 joint statement puts it, "Democracy is not built on stencils" and "The right to judge whether a state is democratic belongs only to its people." This implies that all states, regardless of their political regime and the achieved level of democratization, should have "equal access to the right to development."[13] Iran and other members of the Non-Aligned Movement have regularly raised this issue with regard to export control restrictions vis-à-vis nonproliferation.

The 2019 joint statement explicitly expressed appreciation of the NPT as "one of the foundations of the modern system of international security" and underlined its uniqueness, which rests on "a harmonious conjunction of solving non-proliferation issues, disarmament, and equal cooperation in peaceful uses of nuclear energy."[14] The 2022 statement, which was focused primarily on global sustainable development, characterized the NPT as an important element of the system of international security, which was formed after the Second World War. Russia and China called on the international community to guarantee "[the] authority, effectiveness and universal character" of the NPT as well as to contribute to "balanced implementation of the three fundamental elements of the Treaty" implying nonproliferation, disarmament, and peaceful uses of nuclear energy.

Despite the differences between the classical concept of strategic stability and the new concept of global strategic stability, it would be incorrect to conclude that these two concepts have no connections. Traditionally, the concept of strategic stability, as used in the Russian official discourse, addresses three aspects. First, the term "strategic

---

[12]"Joint Statement on Strengthening Global Strategic Stability."
[13]"Joint Statement on Entering a New Era and the Global Sustainable Development."
[14]"Joint Statement on Strengthening Global Strategic Stability."

stability" is a descriptive category that characterizes the strategic relationship between the major nuclear powers and identifies the preconditions for the absence of incentives for a first nuclear strike and, therefore, is a tool for preventing nuclear war. Second, this term refers to the set of criteria for assessing the various actions of nuclear weapon states, which may increase or decrease the risk of a nuclear war. Third, this term refers to the fundamental goal for strategic arms control and reflects a relatively structured scale for determining the possible scope and limits of Russo-American negotiations on reductions of nuclear arsenals.

The 2016 joint Russo-Chinese statement argued that "strategic stability as a purely military category in [the] field of nuclear weapons ... does not reflect the full scope and versatility of issues at the present stage." The statement introduces the concept of global strategic stability as a broader and more advanced view of strategic stability characterized by the following factors: in the political domain—strict observance by all states and associations of states of the principles and norms of international law and the provisions of the UN Charter governing the use of force and the adoption of coercive measures, respect for the legitimate interests of all states and peoples in solving urgent international and regional problems, and inadmissibility of interference in the domestic political affairs of other states; in the military domain—the maintenance by all states of their military potentials at the minimum level necessary for the needs of their national security, purposeful refraining from steps in military build-up, the creation and expansion of military-political alliances, which could be perceived by other members of the international community as threatening their national security and would force them to take retaliatory measures aimed at restoring the disturbed balance, resolving differences through positive and constructive dialogue, and strengthening mutual trust and cooperation.[15]

The New Russian Concept of Foreign Policy, published in March 2023,[16] introduced a renewed and expanded interpretation of the classical formula of strategic stability but did not include the term "global strategic stability." However, all ideas mentioned in the Russia-China joint

---

[15] "Joint Statement on Strengthening Global Strategic Stability."
[16] "Kontseptsia Vneshnei Polotiki Rossiiskoi Federatsii [The Concept of Foreign Policy of the Russian Federation]," Kremlin, March 31, 2023, http://kremlin.ru/events/president/news/70811.

statements referring to global strategic stability have been incorporated into the text of the new Concept of Foreign Policy.

Russia, Iran, China, and the West in the Context of the Nuclear Nonproliferation Regime

Russia views the nuclear nonproliferation policy in conjunction with other global security issues.[17] Observing Russia-Iran relations in the nuclear sphere requires putting it in the context of the nuclear nonproliferation regime. Russia, as a state successor to the USSR, together with the United States and the UK are state depositories to the NPT. Iran is traditionally active within the NPT review cycle as a member of the Non-Aligned Movement. The adoption of the JCPOA in 2015 was seen in Russia as a significant step toward strengthening the NPT. And vice versa, the US's withdrawal from the nuclear deal with Iran in 2018 was seen by Moscow as a disruptive act against the NPT regime.

Within the first two decades of the 21st century, Russian NPT-related diplomacy has evolved from balancing confrontation and cooperation with the West to demonstrative withdrawal from the US-led initiatives and blocking the adoption of the August 2022 NPT Review Conference's final document. Russia's confrontation with the West and its attempts to build an anti-American coalition do not mean that Russia will encourage anyone to breach the NPT. To prove this argument, we need to have a closer look at thirty years of Russia's policy in the NPT regime.

In the 1990s, Russian president Boris Yeltsin supported all the initiatives proposed by the United States and their allies in the context of the NPT. A good example is the decision to extend the NPT for an indefinite period of time, adopted by the state parties to the NPT in 1995. The expert community in Russia provided strong arguments against the idea of an indefinite extension, explaining that this decision would devalue the power of the nonnuclear states in the NPT, catalyze their dissatisfaction about the progress of nuclear disarmament in the context

---

[17]Anastasia Malygina, "Russia in Nuclear Nonproliferation Regime," in *Nuclear Russia: International and Domestic Agendas*, edited by Andrey Pavlov and Larisa Deriglazova (Tomsk: Tomsk University Press, 2020), 67–110.

of Article VI, and, as a consequence, undermine the whole stability of the nuclear nonproliferation regime. Contrary to expert advice, Yeltsin promised the then US president Bill Clinton to support the American approach and kept his word. For the sake of partnership with the West, the Russian leader was ready to risk the NPT regime's stability.

In the 2000s, oil and gas price dynamics played in favor of the Russian economy, which enabled the Russian Ministry of Foreign Affairs to start converting Russia's profound intellectual and technical capacity in the nuclear field into political influence within the NPT regime. The Russian Ministry of Foreign Affairs tested innovative approaches in cooperation with NGOs,[18] extensively utilized the format of Track II diplomacy, and coordinated its International Atomic Energy Agency (IAEA)–related policy with the Russian nuclear energy corporation (Rosatom).

The construction of the first operational unit of the Bushehr Nuclear Power Plant (NPP) in Iran was conducted under the agreement signed by Moscow and Tehran in 1992. This was the first overseas contract that Russian nuclear engineers got after the dissolution of the USSR. The construction of the Bushehr NPP, which started in 1998 and finished in 2010, helped to maintain Russian atomic technological and construction capability during the years of a systemic crisis in Russia precipitated by the dissolution of the USSR. The successful realization of this project moved Rosatom forward in the search for new customers in the Middle East and other segments of the global nuclear energy market. Since then, Rosatom's business aspirations in the Middle East, Asia, and Latin America have been considered among the decisive factors for Russian policy in the NPT regime. It is important for Russia to maintain its status as a high-tech nuclear supplier. The export of nuclear technologies is not only the pride of the Russian leadership but also a guarantee of income and jobs for Russian citizens. After 2014 and beyond, defending

---

[18]Sergey Ryabkov, "Venskie Dogovorennosti Po Iranskoi Iadernoi Programme: Rol Rossii I Perspektivi Realizatsii [Vienna Agreements on Iranian Nuclear Program: The Role of Russia and the Prospects for Realization]," transcript of the remarks by D. N. Konukhov, I. V. Nasteka, and A. M. Tiutiunnikov, Center for Security and Energy Studies, August 14, 2015, http://ceness-russia.org/index.php?id=1490; Anton Khlopkov, "One Year of JCPOA Implementation: Achievements and Prospects for Sustainability," Remarks at the side-event co-organized by the Permanent Mission of the Russian Federation to the United Nations and the Center for Energy and Security Studies at the 71st Session of the UN General Assembly, Center for Energy and Security Studies, January 16, 2017, http://ceness-russia.org/index.php?id=1499.

Rosatom's right to continue commercial activities in the field of peaceful uses of nuclear energy under Western sanctions caused by the Ukraine crisis was an important task for Russian diplomacy.

In the early 2000s, the tendency for coercive counterproliferation in US policy was not as strong as it later became, and Russia was an integral part of several US-led arrangements such as the Proliferation Security Initiative, the Global Nuclear Energy Partnership, and the Global Initiative to Combat Nuclear Terrorism. At the beginning of the second decade of the 21st century, the United States was still stuck in Iraq and Afghanistan, Europe was busy solving its domestic problems aggravated by the 2008 global economic recession, while China and India, together with other developing economies, continued to demonstrate increasing independence in their behavior, and countries like Cuba, North Korea, Iran, and Venezuela were openly challenging the liberal Euro-Atlantic community in different domains.

Since 2008, Russia has been extending its partnerships with the countries of Latin America, the Middle East, and Southeast Asia. The US-led coalition operation in Libya in 2011 strengthened Russia's conviction that to secure its national interests in a turbulent strategic environment, Russia must take responsibility for sustaining international order based on the principles of international law and the UN's leading role. In terms of the NPT regime, Russia aimed to strengthen traditional elements such as the IAEA safeguards system, the nuclear export control regulations, the nuclear security arrangements, and the zones free of nuclear weapons. At that time, Moscow's economic resources and political influence were not enough to build a solid international coalition to counterbalance Washington's policy based on unilateralism and departure from cooperative diplomacy. However, putting pressure on Iran and supporting the United States in its policy of building exclusive clubs of like-minded states did not correspond to how Russia saw its mission within the NPT regime. Russia saw its role as a mediator who did not take sides but ensured that general principles were respected by all involved actors.

A good example is the case of Nuclear Security Summits and Russia's endeavor to resist attempts at the diplomatic isolation of Iran. The then Russian president Dmitry Medvedev took part in the Nuclear Security Summit hosted by US president Barack Obama in April 2010. This summit convened shortly before the NPT Review Conference scheduled for May 2010. One of the implicit goals pursued by the United States at the summit was to get additional space for informal consultations with China and other major players regarding the crisis around the Iranian nuclear program and agree on strengthening sanctions pressure on Tehran. Iran was not invited to participate in the 2010 Nuclear Security Summit in Washington, denounced the summit and all decisions taken by its participants, and arranged a two-day Tehran International Conference on Disarmament and Non-Proliferation just four days after the end of the US-hosted Nuclear Security Summit. A group of countries, including Russia[19] and China, sent their delegates to the conference in Iran.

The Nuclear Security Summit, initially envisioned as a one-time event, seemed for its participants to be such an attractive multipurpose format that the follow-on biennial iterations occurred in 2012 in South Korea, in 2014 in the Netherlands, and the final one in 2016 back in the United States. Up until the end, these meetings held at the head-of-state level were sort of a private elite club for technologically advanced states with nuclear technologies.[20] Although in 2010 and 2012 Russia participated actively in the Nuclear Security Summits, the summits in 2014 and 2016 were held without Russia's participation due to the deterioration of relations between Russia and the West in the context of the Ukrainian crisis starting in 2014.

During this period, Russia started playing a more proactive role in resolving the crisis around the Iranian nuclear program with the tools of classical diplomacy in Geneva and Vienna as well as by means of Track II diplomacy. In 2010–15, Moscow-based NGO, the Center for Energy and Security Studies, hosted twenty-three meetings in Moscow and five meetings in Tehran.[21] Russian and American experts were also jointly searching for a solution to the security problems on the Korean peninsula. Later on, the accumulated experience, reputation, and partnership among the Iranian, American, and European expert communities made

---

[19] Sergey Ryabkov, "Tegeranskaia Konferentsia Stala Uspeshnoi [The Tehran Conference Was a Success]." Transcript of the interview by the Russian Service of the Voice of Islamic Republic of Iran Radio, *Atominfo*, April 21, 2010, http://www.atominfo.ru/news/air9 985.htm.

[20] Anton Khlopkov, ed. "Perspektivi Razvitiia Atomnoi Energetiki Na Blizhnem Vostoke [Prospects for the Development of Atomic Energy in the Middle East: Russia's Interests]." Report. International discussion club Valdai, 2016, 13, https://ru.valdaiclub.com/files/10669/.

[21] Ryabkov, "Vienna Agreements on Iranian Nuclear Program."

Russian Track II diplomacy an important tool for facilitating dialogue on restoring the JCPOA.

Russia's experience of participating in the Nuclear Security Summits and the P5 Conferences, which were held regularly beginning in 2009, showed that in cases of fundamental disagreements between Russia and the West regarding the architecture of the global nuclear nonproliferation regime, China was behaving independently and pragmatically, not demonstrating a readiness to support any Russian initiative by default. So, synchronizing the nuclear nonproliferation policies of Moscow and Beijing in the framework of an emerging Russia-China strategic partnership was a significant step forward. However, in 2022, when increased confrontation between Russia and the West resulted in a stalemate in the process of restoring the JCPOA, China did not publicly demonstrate any solidarity with the Russian position regarding the JCPOA. In 2023, China started playing a more visible role in managing the security crisis in the Middle East. This factor had an indirect but positive impact on the dynamics of diplomacy regarding the restoration of the JCPOA.

Between 2014 and 2022, Russian policy was focused on balancing confrontation and cooperation with the West. As it was seen from Moscow, the US withdrawal from the JCPOA in 2018 was evidenced by how American inconsistency in its nuclear nonproliferation policy may put Russian national interests at risk. Pursuing its own policy in the areas of disagreement, Russia demonstrated a willingness to cooperate in the fields where it was still possible. Within the NPT regime, cooperation between Russia and the US prevailed up until 2022.

The fluctuations in the US policy toward Iran and the waves of follow-up sanctions made Russia conclude that Rosatom's technical cooperation with Iran in the framework of the JCPOA was connected with high financial risks. In 2020, Russian independent experts expressed concerns that the interests of the Russian atomic industry were at serious risk as the US presidential administration constructed a basis for introducing secondary sanctions against Rosatom, its subsidiaries, as well as against other Russian legal entities and individuals for the implementation of projects provided under the JCPOA. Such possible risks and barriers were established with regard to the construction of the Bushehr NPP as well as technical projects in Fordow and Arak. For instance, the Russian nuclear industry found itself in a kind of a trap when one US administration asked Moscow to accept fuel blanks for the Tehran Research Reactor for temporary storage in Russia, but the subsequent American administration adopted legislation providing for the introduction of sanctions if Russia returns them to Iran.[22] Reviewing this experience, Russian experts came to the conclusion that Russia's possible participation in the technical projects under the JCPOA in case it would be brought back to realization requires high-level consultations between Washington and Moscow. Rosatom, its subsidiaries, and other Russian legal entities and individuals involved in the JCPOA-related projects needed assurances that they would not be subject to unilateral US sanctions. Moreover, in a policy paper published in December 2020, Russian experts recommended the introduction of a mechanism guaranteeing that if the United States withdraws again, the materials of the Iranian nuclear industry, which were transported to Russia for temporal storage, would not get stuck in Russia because of new sanctions. All these recommendations were broadly presented through different channels of communication both for Russian and for American expert communities as well as to the Russian Ministry of Foreign Affairs in December 2020.[23] All the conditions for restoring the effectiveness of the JCPOA, which affected the interests of Russia, were designed and included in the draft agreement before February 2022. It is in this context that Russia demanded guarantees in March 2022, and thus, demands for guarantees were not linked to the developments in Ukraine. Let us review this case in more detail.

On March 4, 2022, Russia requested written assurances from the United States that sanctions imposed on Russia due to its military actions in Ukraine would not affect the restored economic and trade cooperation between Moscow and Tehran after all parties of the JCPOA got back to implementing the agreement. First and foremost, it was important for further Bushehr NPP construction, transportation of nuclear fuel for the Bushehr NPP's operating nuclear reactor, and export of spent nuclear fuel back to Russia. On March 11, 2022, the high representative of the EU for Foreign Affairs and Security Policy, Josep Borrell, wrote on Twitter: "A pause in #ViennaTalks is needed, due to external factors," which became

---

[22]Sergey Batsanov, Anton Khlopkov, and Vladislav Chernavskikh. "Vosstanovlenie Deistvennosti SVPD: Printsipi I Podkhodi. Vzgliad Iz Rossii [Restoring the Effectiveness of the JCPOA: Principles and Approaches View from Russia]," *Rossiia v Globalnoi Politike*, December 7, 2020, https://globalaffairs.ru/articles/vosstanovlenie-svpd/#_ftnref17.
[23]Batsanov, Khlopkov, and Chernavskikh, "Restoring the Effectiveness of the JCPOA."

an informal announcement that the negotiations were temporally suspended.[24] Although some high-ranking Iranian diplomats expressed disappointment off the record about the Russian request, which slowed down the Vienna Talks, Tehran refrained from publicly expressing its frustration.

On March 15, 2022, Russian foreign minister Sergey Lavrov made a statement that Russia "received written guarantees" and that it was being "actually included in the text of the agreement" on the resumption of the JCPOA. These guarantees protect "all projects and areas of activity envisaged by the JCPOA ... including the direct involvement of Russian companies and specialists in the cooperation on the Bushehr Nuclear Power Plant ... and in the context of all existing plans associated with it." Lavrov also stated that Russia's "rights in cooperation with Iran on the JCPOA projects are reliably protected" and that it was not Russia who was obstructing the restoration of the JCPOA: "Speculations that we are delaying the process of JCPOA restoration are a lie. The text of the agreement hasn't been approved by some of the Vienna Talks participants, and Moscow is not one of them."[25] Obviously, Russia's demand for extra guarantees that Russo-Iranian nuclear cooperation would not fall under the Western sanctions launched in response to Russian military actions in Ukraine was not a ploy to delay Vienna Talks, but a need to protect sensitive commercial interests.

The second half of 2022 and the first part of 2023 were when Russia behaved reactively and showed the minimum necessary activity in the negotiating process on restoring the JCPOA. The Tenth NPT Review Conference held in August 2022 suffered from tensions between Russia and the West, which made the conference extremely politicized. The United States and its allies were trying to connect almost every agenda item of the conference to the Ukrainian crisis, and the safety of the Zaporizhzhia NPP was one issue among other topical issues that the United States put in the context of the Ukrainian crisis. The Russian delegation fought back and reciprocated. Despite that, the participants

---

[24]John Irish, Parisa Hafezi, and Francois Murphy, "Russia Demands Leave Iran Talks in Limbo Negotiations Pause," Reuters News Agency, March 11, 2022, https://www.reuters.com/world/eus-borrell-pause-needed-iran-nuclear-talks-final-text-ready-2022-03-11/.

[25]Sergey Lavrov, "Remarks and Answers to Media Questions Following Talks with Foreign Minister of the Islamic Republic of Iran Hossein Amir-Abdollahian," Ministry of Foreign Affairs of Russia, March 15, 2022, https://mid.ru/ru/foreign_policy/news/1804343/?lang=en.

in the JCPOA negotiations were cautious not to give any negative signals about the Vienna Talks during the NPT Review Conference. Even after the end of the NPT Review Conference, Russian officials refrained from any criticism of the European parties to the Iranian nuclear deal and continued explicitly appreciating the EU's attempts to facilitate the deal's restoration. The slowdown in Vienna Talks was painfully received in Iran, but it did not give Iran reasons to say that Russia was departing from its fundamental principles of nuclear nonproliferation.

In the last quarter of 2022, as it was seen from the Kremlin, the West was playing in the risky vicinity of Russia's "red lines" and was waging a "total hybrid war" aimed at a "strategic defeat" of Russia;[26] Moscow started signaling to Washington that "business as usual" mode in nuclear arms control was no longer possible, implying that before talking about the technical issues and practicalities of arms control, more fundamental principles of international security should be discussed and agreed upon. In January 2023, deputy foreign minister Sergei Ryabkov stated in his interview with a Russian newspaper that

> as a result of Washington's actions, arms control has become a hostage to the overall deep degradation of our bilateral relations ... This, of course, does not mean that we are giving up arms control as such. But this sphere cannot exist in isolation from the military-political and geostrategic realities. To ensure long-term and truly viable solutions in this area, it will be necessary to come to an understanding with the West about the parameters and principles of coexistence that would ensure the minimization of conflict potential.[27]

By spring 2023, it became obvious that sustaining a global balance of power, minimizing conflict potential, as well as contouring the parameters of coexistence with the West were seen in Russia as a precondition for further cooperation with the West in the NPT regime. In late March 2023, Russia announced withdrawal from the Proliferation Security Initiative,[28]

---

[26]Sergey Ryabkov, "V SSHA Prekrasno Ponimaiut, Kakikh Shagov Po Deeskalatsii Mi Ot Nikh Zhdem [The United States Is Well Aware of What De-escalation Steps We Expect from Them]," interview by Elena Chernenko, *Kommersant*, January 26, 2023, https://www.kommersant.ru/doc/5785723.
[27]Ryabkov, interview, January 26, 2023.
[28]"Vneshnepoliticheskaia I iplomaticheskaia Deiatelnost Rossiiskoi Federatsii V 2022 Godu [Foreign Policy and Diplomatic Activities of the Russian Federation in 2022]," review by the

which became another signal that business as usual with the United States in the NPT regime was no longer possible. However, confrontation with the West does not mean that Russia has any intention to break the NPT regime. The new Concept of Foreign Policy of the Russian Federation published at the end of March 2023 showed that Russia still takes the sustainability of the NPT regime seriously and intends to provide security assurances to the state parties. Among such assurances are supporting regional treaties on nuclear weapon–free zones, commitment to the prevention of a nuclear war, and strengthening the nuclear export control and nuclear security mechanisms.[29] In general, principles of Russia's nuclear nonproliferation policy remained unchanged after the crisis in Ukraine. But the parts dedicated to the practical realization of these principles have been changed.

Global Strategic Stability and the Nuclear Deal with Iran

The full-scope implementation of the JCPOA started on January 16, 2016, and lasted till US president Donald Trump's administration withdrew from the deal in May 2018. After the United States suspended the realization of its part of the agreement and introduced new sanctions against Iran, the other parties of the agreement, including Russia, China, the EU, and Iran, tried to sustain routine realization of the JCPOA for some time. But when Washington continued to impose unilateral economic sanctions, further fulfillment of obligations by the EU became difficult. China and Russia also began to face certain difficulties due to the risks of American secondary sanctions. This situation prompted Tehran to phase out some of the terms of the deal. As long as it was possible, Russia continued to have dialogues with European states and Iran aimed at restoring the implementation of the JCPOA. Russia's approach to restoring the JCPOA can be explained through several considerations.

First, from the Russian perspective, the JCPOA was not just a bilateral Washington-Tehran affair but a result of persistent efforts by all five

---

Ministry of Foreign Affairs of Russia, Ministry of Foreign Affairs of Russia, March 29, 2023, https://www.mid.ru/ru/detail-material-page/1860242/#_Toc130229924.
[29]"The Concept of Foreign Policy of the Russian Federation."

permanent members of the UN Security Council, Germany, and Iran. The deal was approved unanimously by the UN Security Council in Resolution 2231. Formally, the JCPOA does not provide any withdrawal procedure, and therefore, the actions of the United States or possible similar actions of any of the participants to revise the terms of the deal or leave it may be qualified if not as a breach of the UN Security Council Resolution 2231, then at least as another challenge to the UN Security Council's central role in resolving global and regional crises and sustaining peace and stability. That's what Russian experts warned their American counterparts in 2016[30] and Russian officials continued to repeat in 2023.[31] However, Russia recognizes that the chances of restoring the full implementation of the JCPOA depend on the political will of the United States and Iran. If Tehran and Washington do not have the appetite to reach a compromise, then the efforts of mediators, facilitators, and coordinators from Russia, China, or the EU will remain useless. Russia's experience of dealing with Iran proves that if Iran is pressured, it fights back. Russia had no motives to pressure Iran neither before nor after February 2022.

Second, restoring effective implementation of the JCPOA was and remains critical for Russia in terms of preventing the weakening of the nuclear nonproliferation regime, including impartiality of the IAEA and adherence to the spirit of the NPT. Russia views the JCPOA as essential to safeguarding the NTP and the IAEA's central role in managing any crisis within the global nuclear nonproliferation regime. In 2016, a Russian expert who was actively involved in Track II diplomacy with both Iran and the Democratic People's Republic of Korea warned that North Korean diplomats were carefully monitoring the progress of the talks on the Iranian nuclear program: "Attempts at revising the Vienna agreements would significantly strengthen Pyongyang's doubts about the

---

[30] Anton Khlopkov, "Renegotiating the JCPOA: Potential Consequences," Center for Energy and Security Studies, December 1, 2016, http://ceness-russia.org/data/doc/Khlopkov_Renegotiating_the_JCPOA_Potential_Consequences_Final.pdf.

[31] Mikhail Ulyanov, "Interviu Postoiannogo Predstavitelia Rossiiskoi Federatsii Pri Mezhdunarodnikh Organizatsiaiakh V Vene M.I. Ulianova Informatsionnomu Agentsvu Sputnki Iran [Interview of the Permanent Representative of Russia to the International Organizations in Vienna for the News Agency Sputnik Iran]," Permanent Mission of the Russian Federation to the International Organizations in Vienna, January 31, 2023, https://viennamission.mid.ru/-/interv-u-postoannogo-predstavitela-rossijskoj-federacii-pri-mezdunarodnyh-organizaciah-v-vene-m-i-ul-anova-informacionnomu-agentstvu-sputnik-iran-.

possibility of achieving a sustainable long-term agreement on reducing tensions on the Korean peninsula and, at some point in the future, its complete denuclearization."[32]

Russian officials have constantly been referring to the absence of evidence that Iran was going to review its membership in the NPT and insisted on preserving a technically justified and depoliticized approach to dealing with Iran: "the West likes to speculate on the break-out capability of the Iranian nuclear program ... but the IAEA has never applied such criterion in its assessments of nuclear weapons proliferation concerns as there are many other countries, including in Europe who possess the advanced technologies of nuclear fuel cycle and stand much closer to the threshold than Iran."[33] Russia proposed that the United States and Iran make a series of reciprocal steps that would unfreeze Iran's previously halted voluntary obligations on limiting its nuclear program. As it is seen from Moscow, the proliferation risks, as well as any concerns about hidden or unaccounted stockpiles of nuclear material in Iran, might be mitigated within the framework of the Comprehensive Safeguards Agreement (CSA) with the IAEA in combination with the Additional Protocol (AP). Iran was ready to bring its relations with the IAEA back with this legal framework as soon as the JCPOA came back into force. In this regard, the Russian position remains unchanged in 2022 and beyond: the overall aim of the JCPOA was to normalize the situation around the Iranian nuclear program so that in the long run, all the restrictions voluntarily assumed by Tehran would be lifted, and Iran could exercise its sovereign right for peaceful uses of nuclear energy guaranteed by the NPT.

In fact, Russia's attitude toward the JCPOA has remained unchanged since 2015. The nuclear deal with Iran is seen as "a major breakthrough not only with regard to the Iranian nuclear program but also in what concerns the strengthening of the nonproliferation regime" as the JCPOA "made it possible to remove the IAEA's questions to Tehran, create maximum transparency in its nuclear program, and reaffirm its lawful right to master and develop civilian nuclear technology under the IAEA

---

[32]Khlopkov, "Renegotiating the JCPOA."
[33]Vladimir Ermakov, "Interviu Direktora Departamenta Po Voprosam Nerasprostranenia I Kontrolia and Vooruzheniiami MID Rossii V.I. Ermakova MIA Rossiia Segondia [Interview of the Director of the Nonproliferation and Arms Control Department at MFA of Russia to Rossiia Segodnya News Agency]," Ministry of Foreign Affairs of Russia, November 30, 2022, https://www.mid.ru/ru/foreign_policy/international_safety/disarmament/1841047/.

control."[34] As Russian officials keep repeating, when the JCPOA was in force, together with the UN Security Council Resolution 2231, they made Iran "the most verified country in the world." In his interview in November 2022, Vladimir Ermakov, the director of the Nonproliferation and Arms Control Department at the Russian Ministry of Foreign Affairs, underscored that "Iran has been and remains a conscientious party to the NPT" and reminded that the IAEA identified no cases of Iranian violations through the duration of the JCPOA. The diplomat also mentioned that Russia and Iran make no secret of their nuclear energy cooperation, which "completely corresponds to nonproliferation obligations and contributes to realization of the JCPOA and the UN Security Council Resolution 2231."[35] He added: "The IAEA has never expressed any discontent about this cooperation either to Moscow or to Tehran."[36]

Although Iran, in response to America's withdrawal from the JCPOA, began to gradually move away from fulfilling its part of the deal, its nuclear activities remained within the limits of its obligations under the NPT and the nuclear safeguards agreement with the IAEA. In 2022, four years after the US's withdrawal from the JCPOA, the Iranian nuclear program grew far beyond what it was in 2015, and Iran exceeded almost all limitations set up by the JCPOA. However, as Russia continually repeated, all Iranian actions remained under the IAEA safeguards and were reversible.[37]

While some Russian experts on Iran or on the nuclear issue continued expressing concerns about Iran's intentions to covertly expand technological potential for the development of nuclear weapons, leading Russian experts who advise the Russian Foreign Ministry and are directly involved in Track II diplomacy with Washington, the Europeans, and Iran stand on the assumption that in 2003, Iran renounced any intention to continue experimenting with components significant for the development

---

[34]Sergey Lavrov, "Foreign Policy Priorities of the Russian Federation in Arms Control and Nonproliferation in the Context of Changes in the Global Security Architecture. Foreign Minister's Remarks at the Moscow Nonproliferation Conference," Ministry of Foreign Affairs of Russia, November 8, 2019, https://www.mid.ru/ru/press_service/minister_speeches/1475160/?lang=en.
[35]Ermakov, interview.
[36]Ermakov, interview.
[37]Ulyanov, interview.

of nuclear weapons.[38] Moscow's official position is that Russia had no issues with Iran concerning its compliance with the nuclear deal after the JCPOA entered into force. It was so in 2019–21 during the Vienna Talks on restoring the deal, and it stayed unchanged in 2022.

In early February 2023, the IAEA publicly shared its report to member states which was formally not subject to disclosure. The Iranian Atomic Energy Organization spokesman said that the IAEA report was based on outdated information and that all problems had already been solved with the IAEA Technical Secretariat. The IAEA stated that undeclared changes to Iran's configuration of centrifuges enriching to 60 percent purity found during an unannounced IAEA inspection at Iran's underground Fordow enrichment facility posed proliferation concerns: "This is inconsistent with Iran's obligations under its Safeguards Agreement and undermines the Agency's ability to adjust the safeguards approach for Fordow Fuel Enrichment Plant and implement effective safeguards measures at this facility." Russia in response accused the West of politicizing the work of the IAEA,[39] killing the chances of restoring the JCPOA and opting for "aggressive actions, including using military force, instead of implementing the decisions of the highest body of the UN."[40]

The hypothetical possibility that Iran will accumulate a nuclear weapons arsenal is not assessed by Russian experts as an existential threat. However, as the analysis of the Russian Foreign Policy Concept 2023 shows, such a scenario, in case of its realization, will be qualified as a factor that undermines strategic stability. A violation of the NPT undertaken by Iran, or any country, will be assessed by Russia as a destabilization of global security.

Third, Russia strives to prove to hardliners in Washington, Tehran, and other capitals that constructive dialogue is not only possible but is the only reasonable way of managing this type of crisis. Negotiations on restoring the Iranian nuclear deal started in Vienna in April 2021, with the eighth round of the so-called Vienna Talks launched on December 27,

---

[38] "SSHA: Iran Prekratil Razrabotku Iadernogo Oruzhiia V 2003 [The USA: Iran Stopped Developing Nuclear Weapons in 2003]," RBK, December 3, 2007, https://www.rbc.ru/politics/03/12/2007/5703ca279a79470eaf768200.

[39] "Ryabkov Said that the IAEA Should Not Make Documents on Iran Public," TASS, February 6, 2023, https://tass.ru/politika/16970155.

[40] Marianna Belenkaia, "Iran Sbivaiut S Iadernogo Kursa [Iran Is Being Thrown Off the Nuclear Course]," *Kommersant*, February 2, 2023, https://www.kommersant.ru/doc/5799140.

2021. During this period, Moscow continued dialogue with North Korea and South Korea and continuously insisted that responsible behavior by Tehran and Pyongyang and their consistency in the implementation of previously reached agreements should be respected and rewarded through different measures, including the easing of sanctions. Prior to February 24, 2022, Russia complied with the corresponding UN Security Council resolutions but was exploring opportunities for humanitarian and trade cooperation with both Iran and North Korea. This kind of cooperation was seen as a tool for sustaining dialogue and counterbalancing the Western policy of maximum pressure that Russia considers counterproductive.

Moscow had no intention to make the JCPOA a victim of the intensified confrontation between Russia and the West. Even against the backdrop of warfighting in Ukraine, Russian diplomats continued paying tribute to the EU's constructive role and refrained from criticizing their European counterparts at the Vienna Talks. For instance, as the chief Russian negotiator at the Vienna Talks explained to the Iranian public at the end of January 2023, "The JCPOA is the product of many years of difficult but successful diplomatic efforts within the current membership of the process. ... Both the United States and the European External Action Service, and individual European countries have made their positive contribution to the development of the 'package' of the agreement."[41] That's why, when in early 2023 the Iranians showed a lack of trust to the EU negotiators and wanted to see new faces at the negotiation table, Russia as a facilitator who safeguards the structure and the procedure of the negotiations warned that such demands for change would be counterproductive.

Fourth, in its confrontation with the United States, Russia promoted the concept of balance of interests as an opposition to the American policy of maximum pressure. Moscow criticized the United States for its policy of compelling the states to join the American side in a conflict, calling this practice a "coercion to solidarity."[42] As it is seen from the Kremlin, Washington used such tactics in the situation around the Iranian nuclear program intimidating states with secondary sanctions and applied the

---

[41] Ulyanov, interview.
[42] Maria Zakharova, "Briefing by Foreign Ministry Spokeswoman Maria Zakharova," Ministry of Foreign Affairs of Russia, February 1, 2023, https://www.mid.ru/ru/press_serv ice/spokesman/briefings/1851724/?lang=ru.

same practice against Russia in the context of the Ukrainian crisis. At all stages of the crisis around the JCPOA, Russia insisted on the resumption of a full implementation of the JCPOA and argued that the restoration of its effectiveness was possible only on the basis of "the balance of interests which initially was the foundation of the JCPOA" and "in compliance with the parameters and conditions agreed upon in 2015."[43] So, both Russia and Iran were thinking not about concluding a new deal to replace the comprehensive agreements, but about restoring the implementation of what was agreed in 2015 and set down in the UN Security Council Resolution 2231.

Fifth, as it is seen in Moscow, Russia's mission in settling the crisis around the Iranian nuclear program was to facilitate the search for sustainable solutions and provide technical support for the implementation of the later agreed JCPOA. Russian ideas and diplomatic efforts played an important role during the development of the JCPOA. Russia's contribution included designing basic concepts such as the idea of a "phased step-by-step approach" and "the principle of reciprocity," as well as purely technical proposals on how to ease up some of the contradictions (e.g., conversion of the uranium enrichment plant in Fordow). The assistance from the Russian state corporation Rosatom, together with the coordinating role of the Russian Ministry of Foreign Affairs, were critical factors in bringing Tehran's nuclear program into compliance with the JCPOA. From Moscow's perspective, previous attempts to squeeze Russia out of the Vienna Talks intensified after February 2022. Until the fall of 2022, there was hope that the parties could construct a firewall between the negotiations on restoring the JCPOA and the general confrontation between Russia and NATO. However, by the end of the year, it was obvious that interaction on the issue of restoring the JCPOA was overshadowed by more pressing issues related to the dynamics of the armed conflict in Ukraine. Both Russia and the West could not separate their interactions on tackling the crisis around the Iranian nuclear program from their positions on the Ukrainian crisis. Staying involved in diplomatic interactions in the format of the Vienna Talks was a matter of geopolitical prestige and, therefore, had a symbolic meaning for the Russian leaders. While the West expected that Russia and

---

[43]Maria Zakharova, "Briefing by Foreign Ministry Spokeswoman Maria Zakharova," Ministry of Foreign Affairs of Russia, December 30, 2021, https://www.mid.ru/ru/foreign_policy/news/1792974/?lang=en.

China would pressure Iran to agree to the drafted agreement proposed by the EU in the fall of 2022, Moscow and Beijing were reluctant to push Tehran forward to make another step in restoring the JCPOA. In 2022, Russia neither urged nor intentionally slowed down the progress of the negotiations, admitting that there were two players in that ping pong game (Tehran and Washington) and that China and Russia were only facilitators who sometimes were able to mitigate some of the shocks that arose from tensions between Iran and the West.

Sixth and lastly, avoiding further development of the political crisis around the Iranian nuclear program into a military escalation in the Middle East has been a constant interest for Moscow. The Biden administration became quite passive on the diplomatic track with Iran in 2022, bringing the negotiations on restoring the JCPOA to a successful end shifted down in the list of President Biden's political priorities. The EU's increased dependence on the alliance with the United States weakened the EU's maneuverability as a coordinator of the negotiation process. As a result, Iran's motivation to look for a compromise solution weakened.

Meanwhile, Israel intensified its interactions with the United States to prove that Iran should not be trusted and there could be no deal with Tehran.[44] Israel also intensified its efforts to prevent Germany, France, the UK, and the EU from restoring the JCPOA. Tel Aviv continued increasing its pressure on Iran by carrying out special operations on Iranian soil and against pro-Iranian forces in Syria. At the beginning of 2023, the United States and Israel conducted unprecedentedly large joint military exercises, Juniper Oak, and Israel carried out a symbolic drone attack on a munitions factory in Iran's central city of Isfahan, which the *Wall Street Journal*, citing US officials and "people familiar with the operation," described as another US-Israeli step "to contain Tehran's nuclear and military ambitions."[45] Under these circumstances, the regional players' efforts intensified, and Egypt and Qatar undertook a series of diplomatic

---

[44]Daniel Brumberg, "No Plan B for the US as Geostrategic Shifts Threaten to Scuttle Iran Nuclear Deal," Arab Center Washington DC, September 20, 2022, https://arabcenterdc.org/resource/no-plan-b-for-the-us-as-geostrategic-shifts-threaten-to-scuttle-iran-nuclear-deal/.

[45]Dion Nissenbaum, Benoit Faucon, and Gordon Lubold, "Israel Strikes Iran Amid International Push to Contain Tehran," *Wall Street Journal*, January 29, 2023, https://www.wsj.com/articles/israel-strikes-iran-amid-new-international-push-to-contain-tehran-11675004979?mod=mhp.

efforts to build bridges between Washington and Tehran. At the same time, Iran was continuing its direct consultations with the IAEA, and Russia, China, and Iran were confirmed to have the political will to conclude the process of restoring the JCPOA.[46]

By the beginning of February 2023, the hope for restoring the JCPOA grew even more fragile than it was a year ago. When both Tehran and Washington showed poor interest in overcoming the stalemate in the Vienna Talks and Iran and the EU continued exercising confrontational rhetoric, the facilitators from Russia, China, and the regional players from the Middle East had very limited tools to revive the diplomatic process. Fears of a wider military conflict in the Middle East remained quite strong. From Moscow's perspective, another round of escalation of the Iranian nuclear crisis may provoke an Israeli military operation against Iran. Such a scenario of uncontrolled escalation does not correspond to Russia's security needs and strategic interests in the Middle East.

Conclusion

The dynamic of the Ukrainian crisis in 2022–3 has not altered Russia's assessments of the Iranian nuclear program in terms of nuclear proliferation risks. In its assessments, Russia proceeds from the fact that in 2005, Iran renounced any intention to continue experimenting with components critical for the development of nuclear weapons. Although by 2023, Iran exceeded almost all limitations set up by the JCPOA, Russia argues that all changes remain under the IAEA safeguards and have reversible character. The adoption of the JCPOA and further efforts to restore its effective implementation had a symbolic meaning for Russia in the context of global strategic stability. Avoiding further development of the political crisis around the Iranian nuclear program into a military escalation in the Middle East has been a constant and direct interest of Moscow. While facilitating the negotiations on restoring the implementation of the JCPOA, Russia kept reminding about the voluntary nature of limitations agreed to by Iran and the uselessness of the policy of intimidation and sanctions. As it is seen from Moscow, the proliferation risks, as well as any concerns about the hidden or

---

[46] "The Diplomat Called a Situation around JCPOA a Stalemate," RIA Novosti, January 31, 2023, https://ria.ru/20230131/svpd-1848647024.html.

unaccounted stockpiles of nuclear material in Iran, might be mitigated within the framework of the Comprehensive Safeguards Agreement with the IAEA in combination with the Additional Protocol. In this regard, the Russian position remained unchanged: the overall aim of the JCPOA was to normalize the situation around the Iranian nuclear program so that, in the long run, all the restrictions voluntarily assumed by Tehran would be lifted, and Iran could exercise its sovereign right for peaceful uses of nuclear energy guaranteed by the NPT.

In 2022, Moscow seemed to have no intention of making the JCPOA a victim of the intensified confrontation between Russia and the West. During 2022, Russia neither urged nor intentionally slowed down the progress of the negotiations. However, it should be acknowledged that the deterioration of relations between the United States and Russia was one among other factors that made it difficult to reach an agreement on restoring the JCPOA. In 2022 and beyond, Moscow's understanding of its role in restoring the JCPOA, as well as the driving motives of its policy in the NPT regime, remained unchanged. Russia sees its mission in settling the crisis around the Iranian nuclear program as a facilitator who assists Tehran and Washington in the search for a sustainable solution and provides technical support for the implementation of what has been agreed. Sustaining the structure and the procedures of the Vienna Talks is critical for Russia in terms of performing its role as a facilitator since being involved in the diplomatic interactions at the Vienna Talks is a matter of geopolitical prestige for Russian leadership.

Cooperation between Iran and Russia in the field of nuclear energy has its own inertia. This cooperation was established long before the start of the Ukrainian crisis in 2014. While the sanction pressure slowed down this cooperation, it did not stop the Russia-Iran cooperation in the sphere of peaceful uses of nuclear energy. The principles of nuclear nonproliferation remain an integral part of Russian foreign and security policy. Since Russia is building nuclear power plants not only in Iran, but in other countries of the Middle East as well as in other regions of the world, it is important for Russia to observe consistency and unfailing adherence to the norms and principles of the NPT. Although the confrontation between Russia and the West strengthened the Russo-Iranian political partnership, this cohesion did not make Russia tolerant of the nuclear proliferation risks that may come from Iran or any other country. In fact, the Kremlin has no incentive to encourage any attempts of diversion of peaceful uses of nuclear energy to the purpose of developing nuclear weapons in any of the countries, where Russia exports nuclear technologies.

Bibliography

Batsanov, Sergey, Anton Khlopkov, and Vladislav Chernavskikh. "Vosstanovlenie Deistvennosti SVPD: Printsipi I Podkhodi. Vzgliad Iz Rossii [Restoring the Effectiveness of the JCPOA: Principles and Approaches View from Russia]." *Rossiia v Globalnoi Politike*, December 7, 2020. https://global affairs.ru/articles/vosstanovlenie-svpd/#_ftnref17.

Belenkaia, Marianna. "Iran Sbivaiut S Iadernogo Kursa [Iran Is Being Thrown Off the Nuclear Course]." *Kommersant*, February 2, 2023. https://www.kom mersant.ru/doc/5799140.

Brumberg, Daniel. "No Plan B for the US as Geostrategic Shifts Threaten to Scuttle Iran Nuclear Deal." Arab Center Washington, DC, September 20, 2022. https://arabcenterdc.org/resource/no-plan-b-for-the-us-as-geostrate gic-shifts-threaten-to-scuttle-iran-nuclear-deal/.

Ermakov, Vladimir. "Interviu Direktora Departamenta Po Voprosam Nerasprostranenia I Kontrolia and Voorozheniiami MID Rossii V.I. Ermakova MIA Rossiia Segondia [Interview of the Director of the Nonproliferation and Arms Control Department at MFA of Russia to Rossiia Segodnya News Agency]." Ministry of Foreign Affairs of Russia, November 30, 2022. https://www.mid.ru/ru/foreign_policy/international_safety/disa rmament/1841047/.

Frolov, Piotr. "O Nekotorikh Vozmozhnikh Aspektakh Formiruiuschigosia Postneoloberalnogo Mira [On Some Possible Aspects of the Forming Post-Neoliberal World]." *Mezhdunarodnaia Zhizn* 6 (2022). https://interaffairs.ru/jauthor/material/2673.

Irish, John, Parisa Hafezi, and Francois Murphy. "Russia Demands Leave Iran Talks in Limbo Negotiations Pause." Reuters, March 11, 2022. https://www.reuters.com/world/eus-borrell-pause-needed-iran-nuclear-talks-final-tex t-ready-2022-03-11/.

Kremlin. "Joint Statement by the President of the Russian Federation and the President of the People's Republic of China on Strengthening Global Strategic Stability." June 25, 2016. http://kremlin.ru/supplement/5098.

Kremlin. "Joint Statement of the Russian Federation and the People's Republic of China on Strengthening Global Strategic Stability in the Modern Era." June 5, 2019. http://www.kremlin.ru/supplement/5412.

Kremlin. "Joint Statement by the Russian Federation and the People's Republic of China on International Relations Entering a New Era and Global Sustainable Development." February 4, 2022. http://www.kremlin.ru/sup plement/5770.

Kremlin. "Joint Statement by the Russian Federation and the People's Republic of China on Deepening Comprehensive Partnership and Strategic

Cooperation, Entering a New Era." March 21, 2023. http://www.kremlin.ru/supplement/5920.

Kremlin. "Kontseptsia Vneshnei Polotiki Rossiiskoi Federatsii [The Concept of Foreign Policy of the Russian Federation]." March 31, 2023. http://kremlin.ru/events/president/news/70811.

Khlopkov, Anton. "One Year of JCPOA Implementation: Achievements and Prospects for Sustainability." Remarks at the side-event co-organized by the Permanent Mission of the Russian Federation to the United Nations and the Center for Energy and Security Studies at the 71st Session of the UN General Assembly, New York, January 16, 2017. http://ceness-russia.org/index.php?id=1499.

Khlopkov, Anton, ed. "Perspektivi Razvitiia Atomnoi Energetiki Na Blizhnem Vostoke [Prospects for the Development of Atomic Energy in the Middle East: Russia's Interests]." Valdai International Discussion Club, 2016, 13, https://ru.valdaiclub.com/files/10669/.

Khlopkov, Anton. "Renegotiating the JCPOA: Potential Consequences." Center for Energy and Security Studies, December 1, 2016. http://ceness-russia.org/data/doc/Khlopkov_Renegotiating_the_JCPOA_Potential_Consequences_Final.pdf.

Lavrov, Sergey. "Foreign Policy Priorities of the Russian Federation in Arms Control and Nonproliferation in the Context of Changes in the Global Security Architecture. Foreign Minister's Remarks at the Moscow Nonproliferation Conference." Ministry of Foreign Affairs of Russia, November 8, 2019. https://www.mid.ru/ru/press_service/minister_speeches/1475160/?lang=en.

Lavrov, Sergey. "Remarks and Answers to Media Questions Following Talks with Foreign Minister of the Islamic Republic of Iran Hossein Amir-Abdollahian." Ministry of Foreign Affairs of Russia, March 15, 2022. https://mid.ru/ru/foreign_policy/news/1804343/?lang=en.

Malygina, Anastasia. "Russia in Nuclear Nonproliferation Regime." In *Nuclear Russia: International and Domestic Agendas*, edited by Andrey Pavlov and Larisa Deriglazova, 67–110. Tomsk: Tomsk University Press, 2020.

Ministry of Foreign Affairs of Russia. "Foreign Minister Sergey Lavrov's Remarks and Answers to Media Questions during Talks with Foreign Minister of the Islamic Republic of Iran Hossein Amir-Abdollahian." August 31, 2022. https://mid.ru/ru/foreign_policy/news/1827971/?lang=ru.

Ministry of Foreign Affairs of Russia. "Statement of the Russian Federation on Preventing Nuclear War." November 2, 2022. https://mid.ru/ru/foreign_policy/news/1836575/?lang=en#sel=2:1:V,2:1:V.

Ministry of Foreign Affairs of Russia. "Vneshnepoliticheskaia I iplomaticheskaia Deiatelnost Rossiiskoi Federatsii V 2022 Godu [Foreign Policy and Diplomatic Activities of the Russian Federation in 2022]." March 29, 2023. https://www.mid.ru/ru/detail-material-page/1860242/#_Toc130229924.

Ministry of Defense of Russia. "Welcome Remarks by the Minister of Defense of Russia at the Opening of the 10th Moscow Conference on International

Security." August 16, 2022. https://function.mil.ru/news_page/country/more.htm?id=12433677@egNews.

Nissenbaum, Dion, Benoit Faucon, and Gordon Lubold. "Israel Strikes Iran amid International Push to Contain Tehran." *Wall Street Journal*, January 29, 2023. https://www.wsj.com/articles/israel-strikes-iran-amid-new-international-push-to-contain-tehran-11675004979?mod=mhp.

RBK. "SSHA: Iran Prekratil Razrabotku Iadernogo Oruzhiia V 2003 [The USA: Iran Stopped Developing Nuclear Weapons in 2003]." December 3, 2007, https://www.rbc.ru/politics/03/12/2007/5703ca279a79470eaf768200.

RIA Novosti. "The Diplomat Called a Situation around JCPOA a Stalemate." January 31, 2023. https://ria.ru/20230131/svpd-1848647024.html.

Ryabkov, Sergey. "Mezhdunarodnaia Mozaika Dolzhna Skladivatsia Ne Iz Serogo I Ego Piatidesiati Ottenkov, Kotorie Naviazivaiutsia Zapadom, A Deistvitelno Bit Mnogogrannoi I Monogokrasochnoi Kartinoi [International Life Should Be Constructed Not from Grey and Its Fifty Shadows Imposed by the West but Be Truly Multifaceted and Multicolor]." Interview by Armen Oganesian. *Mezhdunarodnaia Zhizn* 9 (2022). https://interaffairs.ru/jauthor/material/2713.

Ryabkov, Sergey. "Tegeranskaia Konferentsia Stala Uspeshnoi [The Tehran Conference Was a Success]." Transcript of the interview by the Russian Service of the Voice of Islamic Republic of Iran Radio. *Atominfo*, April 21, 2010. http://www.atominfo.ru/news/air9985.htm.

Ryabkov, Sergey. "Venskie Dogovorennosti Po Iranskoi Iadernoi Programme: Rol Rossii I Perspektivi Realizatsii [Vienna Agreements on Iranian Nuclear Program: The Role of Russia and the Prospects for Realization]." Transcript of the remarks by Konukhov Dmitri N., I. V. Nasteka, and A. M. Tiutiunnikov. Center for Security and Energy Studies, August 14, 2015. http://ceness-russia.org/index.php?id=1490.

Ryabkov, Sergey. "V SSHA Prekrasno Ponimaiut, Kakikh Shagov Po Deeskalatsii Mi Ot Nikh Zhdem [The United States Is Well Aware of What De-escalation Steps We Expect from Them]." Interview by Elena Chernenko. *Kommersant*, January 26, 2023. https://www.kommersant.ru/doc/5785723.

"Ryabkov Said that the IAEA Should Not Make Documents on Iran Public." TASS, February 6, 2023. https://tass.ru/politika/16970155.

Ulyanov, Mikhail. "Interviu Postoiannogo Predstavitelia Rossiiskoi Federatsii Pri Mezhdunarodnikh Organizatsiaiakh V Vene M.I. Ulianova Informatsionnomu Agentsvu Sputnki Iran [Interview of the Permanent Representative of Russia to the International Organizations in Vienna M.I. Ulyanov for the News Agency Sputnik Iran]." Permanent Mission of the Russian Federation to the International Organizations in Vienna, January 31, 2023. https://viennamission.mid.ru/-/interv-u-postoannogo-predstavitela-rossijskoj-federacii-pri-mezhdunarodnyh-organizaciah-v-vene-m-i-ul-anova-informacionnomu-agentstvu-sputnik-iran-.

Zakharova, Maria. "Briefing by Foreign Ministry Spokeswoman Maria Zakharova." Ministry of Foreign Affairs of Russia, December 30, 2021. https://www.mid.ru/ru/foreign_policy/news/1792974/?lang=en.

Zakharova, Maria. "Briefing by Foreign Ministry Spokeswoman Maria Zakharova." Ministry of Foreign Affairs of Russia, February 1, 2023. https://www.mid.ru/ru/press_service/spokesman/briefings/1851724/?lang=ru.

6 AN AUTHORITARIAN ALLIANCE: SYSTEMIC FACTORS THAT BRING RUSSIA AND IRAN TOGETHER

Abdolrasool Divsallar

The war in Ukraine might be at a critical juncture to facilitate a gradual growth in the Russia-Iran partnership. At the time of writing this chapter, and notwithstanding the cautiousness and constraints that tide the relations, it can be speculated that the top leadership in Moscow and Tehran have shown a strong political will to boost ties. This chapter attempts to answer the following questions: What strategic logic has convinced the leaders of the two countries to improve relations after the war in Ukraine? Can economic logic or a quest to improve their position in the international order explain the leadership's decisions? How do the two states tackle the limits and disputes they face?

I argue in this chapter that Russian and Iranian leaders are motivated to build stronger ties because of the benefits of their partnerships in guaranteeing the regime's security. The political systems in both the countries are challenged by hybrid threats, comprised of war and internal instability, that have endangered state security. Working

---

The views expressed in this chapter are those of the author and are not an official policy or position of the UNIDIR or the United Nations.

together has a "protective function" against such threats and thus shapes a strategic logic for the relations that outmaneuvers the limits and obstacles ahead. As Roy Allison defines, such a protective integration among authoritarian regimes refers to forming a collective political solidarity against international processes or agendas interpreted as challenging politically incumbent regimes and their leaders.[1] That's why the two states have continuously improved relations, despite various challenges and conflicts of interest over the last decade. Through the war in Ukraine, protective integration between Russia and Iran manifested itself in four domains: strategic sympathy and political solidarity, shielding each other against international punishments, policy learning and knowledge exchange, and finally, the provision of mutual security assistance—all with the goal to strengthen regime stability and security.

The chapter argues that the two states are experiencing a greater level of interdependence, both as a consequence of their protective logic and as a context that strengthens protectionism. Indeed, immediate interests and opportunity costs encourage this process of interdependence. The two capitals view the war as an opportunity for decoupling from the West by forming a club of states outside the US-led liberal order. This thinking is based on an unfolding understanding that neither country's relationship with the West will be normalized soon. Besides, the conditions after the invasion of Ukraine have created wartime urgencies for the Kremlin that have only facilitated this process. In this situation, the classic definition of interdependence prevails. Each participant sees its path to attain valued outcomes as dependent to some important degree on the choices made by the other participant.[2] The chapter then looks at the limits that are impacting these processes. A combination of limitations effectively imposes cautiousness on both sides and constrains the speed of a comprehensive partnership. Yet, they might be ineffective in eroding the leaders' willingness to work together because the security benefits behind this convergence are stronger than the limits.

---

[1] Roy Allison, "Virtual Regionalism, Regional Structures and Regime Security in Central Asia," Central Asian *Survey* 27, no. 2 (2008), 186, https://doi.org/10.1080/0263493080 2355121.

[2] Robert Axelrod and Robert Keohane, "Achieving Cooperation under Anarchy: Strategies and Institutions," *World Politics* 38, no. 1 (1985), 226–54; T. C. Schelling, *The Strategy of Conflict* (Oxford: Oxford University Press, 1960).

I conclude by proposing that the study of Russo-Iranian relations through the lens of protective integration and interdependence can better explain the strategic thinking behind the leadership's decisions. The chapter makes a concluding claim that the war in Ukraine has accelerated a gradual process that can potentially give a strategic character to the Russo-Iranian relations. However, the limits and the states' vulnerability to external pressures and domestic considerations should not be fully ignored. These factors seem strong enough to derail the partnership too. That means the extent to which the war in Ukraine can eventually elevate relations remains unclear and should be assessed only after the end of the military phase of the conflict in Ukraine.

The Logic for Cooperation

Notwithstanding the abundance of limits and constraints, Russo-Iranian relations have grown recently. What brings Moscow and Tehran together? The literature on Russia-Iran relations highlights several explanations. Experts have extensively written about Russia and Iran as two dissatisfied states with the status-quo order that have common prospects for revisioning the international order, and their strategic hedging brings them together.[3] According to this view, these countries share anti-Western policies and hopes of strengthening multipolarity with parallel orders through which they can exert regional hegemony and gain prestige. Mutual gains from cooperating on regional security issues are the natural products of this revisionist stand, often mentioned as a separate factor when explaining Russo-Iranian ties.[4] The two states' interlinked interests and threats and a history of cooperation in Syria, Afghanistan, and elsewhere in the South Caucasus and Central Asia make the regional level of ties critical. But probably a dominant view is an argument that a combination of sporadic economic, security, and political opportunities helps to converge the interests of the two sides and feed transactional cooperation. Many of the two sides' important initiatives fall under this category, such as Russia's participation in the

---

[3] Samir Puri, "The Strategic Hedging of Iran, Russia, and China: Juxtaposing Participation in the Global System with Regional Revisionism," *Journal of Global Security Studies* 2, no. 4 (2017), 307–23 https://doi.org/10.1093/jogss/ogx015.
[4] See Gary James Schmitt, ed., *Rise of the Revisionists: Russia, China, and Iran* (Washington, DC: AEI Press, 2018).

construction of the Bushehr Nuclear Power Plant, the joint economic projects, and political support of each other on the international stage.[5]

However, less has been discussed about the leadership's perception of cooperation as a way to improve the resiliency and stability of their political systems. The political systems in Moscow and Tehran are challenged by hybrid threats comprising domestic discontent and international pressures. In this situation, the strategic logic behind the two capitals' overtures toward each other is an understanding that even if closer ties fail to contribute significantly to economic cooperation or to resolve the other's pressing needs, it can be instrumental in increasing the resiliency of the system and insulating it from hybrid threats.[6] As Whitehead shows, insecure governments and vulnerable regimes can be expected to devote extra attention to their coordination in an integrated defensive posture.[7] Alexander Libman and Anastassia Obydenkova have identified a similar trend that cooperation among regional nondemocratic states can fail to contribute significantly to economic causes among their members. Yet, they greatly help in stabilizing authoritarian rules.[8] In this way, the departure point for protective integration is the state's attempt to thwart threats and guarantee survival rather than hegemonic aspirations, the quest for prestige, or economic advancements. There is growing evidence to conclude that Moscow and Tehran are resorting to a similar logic and assessing greater values in mutually supporting each other to combat threats against the state.

With the events of 2022, which deepened the perception of threat in the two capitals, this trend has gained new momentum for Russian and Iranian leaders. Closure of social space, widespread corruption, governments' malfunctions in maintaining public service, and difficulties in providing developmental needs have increased the perception of state vulnerability in Russia and Iran. In 2022, the Islamic Republic faced what could probably be its worst nationwide protest since 1979,

---

[5] See Ariane Tabatabai and Dina Esfandiary, *Triple Axis: Iran's Relations with Russia and China* (London: I.B. Tauris, 2021).
[6] Abdolrasool Divsallar, "Protective Integration and Rising Interdependency: Making Sense of Iranian Response to Russian Invasion of Ukraine," *Chinese Journal of International Politics* (forthcoming).
[7] Laurence Whitehead, "Three Angles on the Alliance Options of Authoritarian Regimes," *Taiwan Journal of Democracy* 14, no. 1 (2018), 7.
[8] Alexander Libman and Anastassia V. Obydenkova, "Understanding Authoritarian Regionalism," *Journal of Democracy* 29, no. 4 (2018), 153-8.

sparked by the killing of Mahsa Amini while in police custody. Indeed, the protests manifested widespread public dissatisfaction with the regime. On the Russian side, the social pains of the military campaign in Ukraine manifested itself in a national mobilization order, economic deterioration, and an oppressive atmosphere, which have generated domestic dissatisfaction and elite fear. To crush the dissidents, Putin has introduced severe punishments of up to fifteen years for antiwar protests and ten years in prison and fines for evading mobilization.[9] Some reports claimed 1,300 arrests of people across Russian cities after the mobilization order.[10] The public discontent contributed to the fear of the medium-term consequences of war, at least among pragmatic Russian elites. The elites—from the *siloviki* to big businesses—were united in seeing defeat as a threat that could bring sociopolitical destabilization.[11]

At the same time, the external security environment continued to deteriorate for both countries in the era after the outbreak of war in Ukraine. Iran remained under the threat of Israeli and US military strikes in the name of countering Iran's nuclear program. The Islamic Republic's brutal crackdown on protests, military assistance to Russia, and the Iranian diaspora's intensive international campaigns against the government in Tehran massively raised external pressures on the Islamic Republic throughout 2022 and 2023. On the contrary, Russia's war plans were shattered by extensive Western military assistance to Ukraine. Moscow even encountered a geostrategic defeat in the Baltic by Finland and Sweden's accession to the NATO (North Atlantic Treaty Organization). This plethora of threats has squeezed top leadership in Moscow and Tehran and has contributed to the perception of insecurity and a feeling of being under siege among the elites. While similar shared threat perceptions have contributed to Moscow and Tehran's

---

[9]Mikhail Rodionov, "Avtory zakonoproekta o nakazanii uklonistov ot mobilizazii zayavili, chto on utratil svoyu aktualnost [The Authors of the Bill to Punish Evaders from Mobilization Said That It Has Its Relevance]," Gazeta.ru, November 1, 2022, https://www.gazeta.ru/army/2022/11/01/15716725.shtml.
[10]Kelly Kasulis Cho, "Over 1300 Arrests Reported as Russians Protest Military Mobilization," *Washington Post*, September 22, 2022, https://www.washingtonpost.com/world/2022/09/22/russia-protests-arrests-putin-war-mobilization/.
[11]Tatiana Stanovaya, "Divided in the Face of Defeat: The Schism Forming in the Russian Elite," Carnegie Endowment for International Peace, December 13, 2022, https://carnegieendowment.org/politika/88630.

security convergence in the past,[12] this time, radical shifts in the security environment have made a close partnership a strategic necessity for regime survival.

Strong evidence from the Middle East and Central Asia suggests that regional intrastate linkage reduces the likelihood of an autocratic regime breakdown.[13] For example, Russia actively sought to intervene to bolster the position of incumbent autocrats who were threatened by public mobilization during the so-called color revolutions in Central and Eastern Europe—not least due to a fear of democratizing contagion.[14] Saudi Arabia's policy during the Arab Spring is another case in which the kingdom "positioned itself as the chief architect of a counterrevolution to contain, and perhaps even to reverse, the Arab Spring as much as possible."[15] Saudi Arabia successfully defended Bahrain, helped Egyptian autocrats, and initiated a war to protect the Yemeni government. Also, the Syrian example is illustrative in this regard. Tehran and Moscow quickly joined forces and managed to save Bashar Assad's regime from collapse. Russia and Iran's partnership in Syria was a demonstration of their commitment to the regime security of a fellow authoritarian friend. In a nutshell, as Tansey et al. find, "When authoritarian regimes are confronted with an immediate challenge to their stability, we would expect external autocratic allies to intervene in support in cases of high linkage density, but not in cases in which linkages are weak."[16] This view explains why Moscow and Tehran have renewed interest in working together after February 24, 2022, when both have faced diverse threats.

In the case of Iran and Russia, institutional elements and factional politics seem to accommodate protective integration. The dominance of the security-military sector in foreign policy decision-making of both states played a significant role in such decisions. As Grajevski argues in her chapter, Russian decisions toward Iran originate in the security sector,

---

[12]Abdolrasool Divsallar, "The Pillars of Iranian-Russian Security Convergence," *The International Spectator* 54, no. 3 (2019), https://doi.org/10.1080/03932729.2019.1586147.
[13]Alexander Schmotz and Oisín Tansey, "Regional Autocratic Linkage and Regime Survival," *European Journal of Political Research* 57 (2018), 670-2.
[14]Schmotz and Tansey, "Regional Autocratic Linkage," 667.
[15]Mehran Kamrava, "The Arab Spring and the Saudi-Led Counterrevolution," *Orbis* 56, no. 1 (2012), 96–104.
[16]Oisín Tansey, Kevin Koehler, and Alexander Schmotz, "Ties to the Rest: Autocratic Linkages and Regime Survival," *Comparative Political Studies* 50, no. 9 (2017), 1221, https://doi-org.ezproxy.unicatt.it/10.1177/0010414016666859.

while the foreign ministry is mostly sidelined on the matter. Interestingly, a similar pattern can be traced on the Iranian side, where decisions about Russia are taken in a closed military-security circle, which has been able to sideline the popular social mistrust toward Russia.[17] The greater role of the military-security sector in decisions strengthens pragmatism while contributing to the centrality of security logic and survival concerns as the foundations of relations. That is in line with these sectors' organizational culture and tradition of focusing on repelling threats.[18] These elites recognize a vast domain of shared threats originating from "systemic" US hostility against their regimes. This shared understanding has just been reinforced after the Ukraine war by the united Western support of Kyiv, thus playing into their vision of a more significant role in their long-term confrontation with threats.

As scholars have argued, even under intense external pressure, foreign alliance strategies are shaped by political contingencies as well as by the direct calculus of payoffs.[19] In this context, factional politics and domestic power rivalries also become meaningful in the Russia-Iran case of protective integration. At least on the Iranian side, the conservatives and military-security sector that promote a closer tie with Moscow count on Russian support for their grip on power. Domestic autocrats searching for an international sponsor and seeking assistance from external actors to hold power is nothing new.[20] In this case, Russia emerges as a sponsor for part of the political elites in Iran. A grand battle in the Iranian political landscape is expected to take place to select the future supreme leader, and having foreign support can be a major plus.[21] Russia is the candidate of choice for conservative forces in Tehran.

---

[17] Abdolrasool Divsallar, "The Foreign Policy Establishment in Iran," in *The Sacred Republic: Power and Institutions in Iran*, edited by Mehran Kamrava, 227 (London: Hurst, 2023).

[18] Abdolrasool Divsallar, "Shifting Threats and Strategic Adjustment in Iran's Foreign Policy: The Case of Strait of Hormuz," *British Journal of Middle Eastern Studies* 49, no. 5 (2022), 873–95, https://doi.org/10.1080/13530194.2021.1874873; Timofei Bordachev, "Russia's Turn to the East: Between Choice and Necessity," Valdai Discussion Club, September 1, 2022, https://valdaiclub.com/a/highlights/russia-s-turn-to-the-east-between-choice/.

[19] Whitehead, "Three Angles on the Alliance Options," 10.

[20] Thomas Ambrosio, "Democratic States and Authoritarian Firewalls: America as a Black Knight in the Uprising in Bahrain," *Contemporary Politics* 20, no. 3 (2014), 331–46.

[21] See , Alex Vatankha, *The Battle of the Ayatollahs in Iran: The United States, Foreign Policy, and Political Rivalry since 1979* (London: I.B. Tauris, 2021).

Besides, these groups see a deeper tie with Moscow as helpful in solving the challenges they face in governance and proving the functionality of their political ideology. In this way, they can better counterweight democratic reformist groups inside the country that may tilt toward the West. Thus, in addition to seeking protection against international pressures, a substate level of analysis can be distinguished in which part of the elites find payoffs from getting closer to Russia. Ebrahim Raisi's administration stands for promoting closer ties with Moscow, which should be seen from this lens. It is exactly for this internal factional dimension that if the Ukrainian war had happened during the Rouhani administration, the Iranian response could have been different and probably less focused on the security benefits of assisting Russia as the core factor in its calculus.

Strategies for Protective Integration

Analyzing the events after the outbreak of the war in Ukraine unfolds at least four protective strategies adopted by Moscow and Tehran,[22] contributing to the formation of an authoritarian alliance.

The first strategy deals with providing political solidarity and strategic sympathy. The two capitals politically supported and reinforced each other's narratives while adopting a more coordinated and supportive public policy. The conservative elites and security establishments in Tehran—who play a dominant role in Iranian politics—view Moscow as a fellow victim of Western hegemonic actions and feel an ideological duty to help Putin fight back against the so-called US malign behaviors. Iran's supreme leader, Ayatollah Ali Khamenei, clearly sympathized with Russia in this regard and said, "The US started the Ukraine war … . US created the grounds for this war to expand NATO in the east."[23] Khamenei had even told Vladimir Putin during a trip to Tehran in July 2022 that the NATO would have started the war if the Russian president had "not taken the initiative."[24] Later, Ali Akbar Velayati, an influential figure and chief foreign policy advisor to the supreme leader, expanded

---

[22]Divsallar, "Protective Integration."
[23]Maziar Motamedi, "Iran's Khamenei Says US Wants to Keep Ukraine War Going," *Al Jazeera*, March 21, 2023, https://www.aljazeera.com/news/2023/3/21/irans-khamenei-says-us-wants-to-keep-ukraine-war.
[24]Motamedi, "Iran's Khamenei," 2023.

Khamenei's view and said, "NATO broke its post-Cold War commitment to Russia for keeping former Soviet Republics as a buffer zone and avoided NATO expansion to these areas. Russia has announced its red lines several times."[25]

In Moscow, a Kremlin under sanction and direct collision with the West is better at perceiving the difficulties the Islamic Republic faced in its decades of confrontation with the West. Indeed, a general sense of respect seems to be emerging among the Russian elites for Iran's decades of resisting Western sanctions. These views are aligned with Russia's Concept of Foreign Policy (CFP) published in March 2023, which is moving further toward a blueprint for resisting external pressures and counter-hegemony in international relations. The CFP states, "A number of countries [the West] refuse to recognize the realities of a multipolar world and to agree on the parameters and principles of the world order ... they use the logic of global dominance and neocolonialism."[26] The document proposes, "A logical response to the crisis of the world order is the strengthening of cooperation between the states that are subject to external pressure."[27] As Elena Dunaeva comments, "While before the war in Ukraine, Russia may not have been willing to confront the West, now Russian view of the West is getting closer to Iranian style of anti-Americanism."[28] For example, the Russian stand on Iran's nuclear file after the outbreak of the war leaned toward Tehran's line of argument. Russia, along with Iran, portrays the United States as the main obstacle to the revival of Iran's nuclear deal, known as the Joint Comprehensive Plan of Action (JCPOA). Mikhail Ulyanov, the Russian ambassador to international organizations in Vienna, reflects Tehran's view when he said, "US maximum pressure policy against Iran has no credible, peaceful

---

[25]"Iran, russie va chin; se ghodrate mohem dar moghabele tosetalabi amrica va gharb [Iran, Russia, and China: Three Important Power against US and West Hegemony]," Khamenei.ir, June 22, 2022, https://farsi.khamenei.ir/others-dialog?id=50652.
[26]"The Concept of the Foreign Policy of the Russian Federation," The Ministry of Foreign Affairs of Russian Federation, March 31, 2023, https://mid.ru/en/foreign_policy/fundam ental_documents/1860586/?TSPD_101_R0=08765fb817ab2000f238fe4073d30bdd359c cb6094a7bf5eba80bd0bf21140a480b7b58271504b8208dabff6be143000ff6b52db228cea bd8c992a54f78849c24b7a7f7006ecb76cf83fbf957112a615fe52518c343463705c59203d5 b58fda4.
[27]"The Concept of the Foreign Policy of the Russian Federation," 2023.
[28]Elena Dunaeva (senior research fellow with the Russian Academy of Sciences Institute of Oriental Studies), in discussion with the author, May 1, 2023.

purpose. It was the main reason which compelled Iran to start 60 percent uranium enrichment."[29]

Sympathy and mirroring each other's political positions are reflected in the two countries' media and public policy too. Both sides frequently vowed to fight against the so-called Western propaganda, which has led to cooperation and coordination in disseminating their preferred narratives of global developments. Putting aside the public discussions about the impact of the war in Ukraine on Iran, which Mahmood Shoori elaborated on in his chapter, few open discussions took place in Iran about the war itself. Those few public debates were also often dominated by narrating Russian perspectives. Indeed, the Islamic Republic discouraged any critical discussion about the Russian invasion of Ukraine, a full-fledged shift of policy compared to a similar situation when the United States invaded Iraq and Afghanistan. To formalize this cooperation, new partnership agreements were signed in October 2022 between the Russian News Agency and Radio Sputnik with the State Television and Radio of Iran. As one Sputnik official, Vasily Pushkov, claimed, "The agreement is a sign for unity of goals and objectives to respond to common challenges for Russian and Iranian media in the era of information wars."[30]

Political solidarity and strategic sympathy are followed by a second strategy of shielding each other from isolation and international punishment. A well-noticed collaboration among authoritarians that aims at lowering the costs of their actions.[31] Annoyed by the international condemnation of its attack on Ukraine, Moscow sees ties with Tehran as a step toward breaking out of isolation. The relations showcase that Moscow has remained valuable for regional powers in the Global South and has the ability to work with them collectively despite Western pressures. Putin's travel to Tehran in July 2022 in the context of the Astana peace process and just a few days after Biden's Middle East tour was one such occasion to convey this message and prove a Western failure in isolating Russia.[32]

---

[29]Mikhail Ulyanov (@Amb_Ulyanov), "Let's Don't Forget that the #US Maximum Pressure Policy against #Iran Has No Credible Peaceful Purpose," November 16, 2022, https://twitter.com/Amb_Ulyanov/status/1592932630148046849.
[30]"Sputnik Expands Cooperation with Iranian Media," Sputnik, October 31, 2022, https://ria.ru/20221031/sputnik-1828051200.html.
[31]See Oisín Tansey, *The International Politics of Authoritarian Rule* (Oxford: Oxford University Press, 2016).
[32]Nima Khorrami, "Putin's Visit to the Islamic Republic: Bringing Iran Closer to Russia while Building Long-Term Leverage over Tehran," Middle East Institute, August 1, 2022,

Iran's voting in the UN General Assembly (UNGA) on the issue of Ukraine was another part of the mutual counter-isolation attempt. In March and October 2022, and later February 2023, the UNGA voted on whether to condemn Russia's annexation of the Ukrainian territory and end the war. Iran abstained in the first and last votes while refusing to participate in the October voting. But in November 2022, Tehran voted against a resolution stating that Russia must bear the legal consequences of the war, including by making reparations.

Similarly, Tehran considers close ties with Moscow as a sort of security umbrella that can prevent or at least complicate international consensus against it. Especially, Russia's veto power is regarded as a critical instrument in neutralizing Western attempts to legalize any punitive measures against the Islamic Republic. Moscow had previously shown a willingness to use its heavy weight in international organizations in favor of Tehran when the political linkage between the two countries was strong enough. In the last noticeable case in November 2022, Moscow voted against the censure resolution in the International Atomic Energy Agency (IAEA) Board of Governors that condemned Iran for failing to meet its commitments under the safeguards agreement. In addition, by mutually supporting each other's discourses, Moscow and Tehran hope to build a unified legitimizing discourse that constructs their ideational counterattack, while questioning the credibility and legitimacy of any international punishment for their actions.

The third strategy of protection is about exchanging knowledge, intelligence, and successful policies that can improve the regime's survivability. This aspect has been extensively explored under the rubric of authoritarian learning.[33] These learning processes facilitate convergence in the states' tactics and strategies to guarantee security. For example, American sources accused Moscow of transferring some of its "best practices" in punitive measures and suppression techniques to Tehran in a sort of support to the Islamic Republic's ability to crack

---

https://www.mei.edu/publications/putins-visit-islamic-republic-bringing-iran-closer-russia-while-building-long-term.

[33]Stephen G. F. Hall and Thomas Ambrosio, "Authoritarian Learning: A Conceptual Overview," *East European Politics* 33, no. 2 (2017), 143–61, https://doi.org/10.1080/21599 165.2017.1307826; André Bank and Mirjam Edel, "Authoritarian Regime Learning: Comparative Insights from the Arab Uprisings." *GIGA Working Papers*, German Institute of Global and Area Studies, no. 274, 2015.

down on the protesters.[34] The reports hinted similar anti-riot training of the Islamic Revolutionary Guards Corps (IRGC) forces by Russia at least since 2013.[35] Since September 2022, and by the expansion of protests across Iran, observers reported Russian provision of training courses for the IRGC paramilitary Basij forces.[36] This cooperation was later formalized when Brigadier General Ahmadreza Radan, Iran's police commander, signed a long-term memorandum of understanding (MoU) with General Viktor Zolotov, commander in chief of the National Guard Troops of the Russian Federation, to strengthen security and law enforcement cooperation.[37] An important part of the agreement covers the exchange of experiences to combat the factors that create domestic insecurity.

In another case, on April 25, 2022, the Iranian government approved an information security agreement with Russia, initially signed in January 2021 under the Rouhani administration. The agreement complements an existing linkage between intelligence services and expands areas of cooperation in the cybersecurity domain. It paves the way for establishing a joint coordination mechanism in the information domain, exchanging cybersecurity data, monitoring cybersecurity threats, combined training, and mutual provision of technical assistance.[38] The agreement covers a wide range of cybercrimes defined by the national law in both countries, most importantly political actions against the state that originates on social media platforms. Russia's provision of advanced cyber-surveillance technologies, facial recognition systems, and other digital control technologies have assisted Tehran in improving its ability to suppress popular uprisings.

---

[34]Maegan Vazquez, "White House Claims US Is Seeing Signs Russia MAY Be Advising Iran on How to Crack Down on Protests," CNN, October 26, 2022, https://edition.cnn.com/2022/10/26/politics/white-house-russia-iran-protests/index.html.

[35]"Amozesh Mamoran Sepah dar Rusiye [Training of IRGC Forces in Russia]," Diplomacy Irani, February 16, 2013, http://www.irdiplomacy.ir/fa/news/1912860/آموزش-نیروهای-سپاه-در-روسیه-.

[36]Unanimous Russian expert, in discussion with the author, April 6, 2023.

[37]"Iran, Russia Officials Sign MoU to Enhance Security Cooperation," Mehr News Agency, June 28, 2023, https://en.mehrnews.com/news/202586/Iran-Russia-officials-sign-MoU-to-enhance-security-coop.

[38]IRNA News Agency, "layehe movafeghatname amkari iran va rusiye dar hoze amniyat etelat tasvib shod [The Law for Agreement on Information Security between Iran and Russia Passed]," December 10, 2023, https://www.irna.ir/news/85317194/لایحه-موافقت‌نامه-همکاری-ایران-و-روسیه-در-حوزه-امنیت-اطلاعات-تصویب (accessed January 30, 2024).

On the non-security front, learning and sharing best practices include economic and trade issues. Iran's experiences and knowledge of circumventing sanctions have become a priority for Moscow across a number of topics, from banking solutions to sanction-busting trading techniques and even sanction-resistant industrial policies. According to one Iranian official, "after the War in Ukraine, Russian companies have approached our mining and industrial companies to learn how Iranian businesses have managed to maintain operation in sectors [in] which technologies and procedures are mostly Western. Russians were surprised by [the] diversity of our engineering solutions and supply chains to counter US sanctions."[39] As one *Kommersant* commentator writes, "Iran can teach Russia the art of parallel import and gray zone operations."[40] After the war, this area has occupied ample space in the two countries' state-level transactions as Moscow can learn techniques that Iran used during decades of evading sanctions. As one Iranian official argued,

> It is surprising to see Russian state agencies of various sectors, from oil and gas to mining and agriculture, rush to Tehran after the war in order to hear our story of sanction evasion. For example, they are interested to know how Iran managed to overcome specific technological and engineering challenges caused by sanctions in the mining section and other industrial sectors. We provide them with this information.[41]

Finally, in their fourth strategy and at the military level, the war has accelerated the provision of mutual security assistance to reinforce the two sides' ability to resist military threats. Tehran cannot afford for Putin to lose in Ukraine;[42] such a defeat would damage the Islamic Republic's interests. Russian loss may result in either leadership and regime change in Moscow or a substantially weaker Russia, all heralding new political dynamics that can risk Russian support of Iran across their various files of cooperation. Tehran's decision to deliver drones to Russia manifested its willingness to prevent such a damaging outcome. Also, the provision

---

[39] Unanimous Iranian official in the Ministry of Industry, Mine and Trade in discussion with the author, September 4, 2023.
[40] "Moskva i Tegeran uglublyaut svyazi [Moscow and Tehran Deepen Ties]," *Kommersant*, October 2, 2022, https://www.kommersant.ru/doc/5646418.
[41] Unanimous Iranian official, in discussion with the author, April 18, 2023.
[42] Mark N. Katz, "Iran Can't Afford for Russia to Lose in Ukraine," *Barron's*, July 22, 2022, https://www.barrons.com/articles/iran-russia-ukraine-putin-51658516904.

of weapons in a time of war may have been Tehran's signaling to push for a full-term defensive pact, demanding a similar request in the case of future Iranian needs. This fact does not mean that Tehran does not expect Moscow to pay back its favor in the short term, yet also highlights Tehran's considerations to protect Russian security interests.

Russia, in return, seems to be adopting a similar policy and fully supports Iran's deterrence strategy. Moscow has traditionally avoided criticizing the core aspects of Iran's military strategy and has not joined any international pressure campaign against Iran's missile program and regional proxies known as the "axis of resistance." Instead, even Moscow assisted Tehran in building some of these programs in their early stages.[43] The news of the SU-35 fighter jet's delivery to Tehran aligns with this Russian policy. But given the attritional nature of the war in Ukraine, Moscow's method of delivering security assistance to Iran seems to be uncertain. A closer look at Russian defense industries and challenges stemming from the war in Ukraine casts doubts on the Russian ability to deliver major arms to Tehran while the war in Ukraine continues. There is a huge pressure on Russian weapons manufacturers to address wartime demands and resupply Russian army deposits. At the same time, Western sanctions have created obstacles for the Russian defense industry to maintain the production of advanced weapons. By March 2023, these logistical challenges led to the cancelation of a major Russian arms delivery to the Indian Air Force. In addition, Russia did not intend to upset the balance of force in the Persian Gulf by exporting sensitive capabilities that could substantially improve Iran's conventional power vis-à-vis its regional rivals. Such a decision can have consequences for Moscow's relations with the UAE and Saudi Arabia at a time when Moscow is seeking to expand its partnership with these countries. Already, Israel held discussions with Moscow to cancel such arms transfer to Tehran.

A combination of these considerations may lead Moscow to choose a less sensitive alternative to support Tehran, one that would not provoke a reaction from the regional actors and upset Russia's Middle East policy. Such a solution may look like a renewed version of the late 1990s and early 2000s model based on transferring military know-how, technology, and

---

[43]See Michael Eisenstadt, "Russian Arms and Technology Transfers to Iran: Policy Challenges for the United States," *Arms Control Today*, March 1, 2001, https://www.arms control.org/act/2001-03/iran-nuclear-briefs/russian-arms-technology-transfers-iranpol icy-challenges-united.

services to Iran. Areas with critical defensive roles, such as Anti-Access/Area Denial (A2/AD) capabilities, radar and detection technologies, space technology, and passive defense, may receive the most attention this time. For example, on August 9, 2022, a Russian Soyuz put an Iranian telemetry satellite in orbit that was expected to boost Iran's early warning capabilities and monitoring of military targets. A few months later, in December 2022, the two sides signed an MoU for space cooperation that is expected to be critical for the realization of Iran's ten-year space program. This model seems to be a win-win for Moscow and Tehran. It fits with an Iranian approach that prioritizes the substitution of arms imports with technology transfer and investment in domestic defense industries while accommodating Moscow's regional concerns and logistical limits.

Greater Degrees of Interdependence

The authoritarian alliance between Russia and Iran has one main distinctive feature from similar Russian-centric attempts to support authoritarian regimes. It is marked by greater interdependence that originates from Russia's growing need for Iranian support after the war in Ukraine. Unusually, in this case, the two sides' interdependence does not follow the standard European model in which self-sustaining development is pushed forward by interests from within the region.[44] Quite the contrary, Moscow and Tehran's interdependence is an unprecedented and necessary process for dividing tasks and sharing resources in resisting Western pressure. Mutual benefits in strengthening ties, as well as shared opportunity costs in disrupting the relationship, are rising as vital factors in the strategic calculation of Tehran and Moscow. Previous researchers have contended that an increase in linkage intensity between authoritarian systems improves the chances of receiving assistance for regime survival.[45] In this way, Russo-Iranian interdependence is a logical prerequisite for realizing a full-fledged authoritarian alliance between the two states.

---

[44]Sebastian Krapohl and Johannes Muntschick, "Two Logics of Regionalism: The Importance of Interdependence and External Support for Regional Integration in Southern Africa," *Bamberger Online Papers on Integration Research* 3 (2008), https://nbn-resolving.org/urn:nbn:de:0168-ssoar-130518.
[45]Tansey et al., "Ties to the Rest," 1243

In practice, rising interdependence is seen most clearly in security affairs characterized by the reciprocal actions of both sides. The Vienna Talks for reviving the JCPOA were the first to be impacted by Moscow's decision. The Kremlin demanded guarantees that Russian benefits from the JCPOA would be protected from US sanctions. This demand highlighted that though the United States and Iran are the principal players in the JCPOA revival, Tehran's desired outcome is somehow dependent on Moscow's satisfaction and support. As the introduction to this book reveals, the demand initially caused dissatisfaction in Tehran but later was replaced by a more coordinated approach when Moscow's support of the Iranian stand began to grow. On the military front, Russia became dependent on Iran's security assistance. Tehran's decision to deliver thousands of drones to Moscow became critical in sustaining Russian long-range strike capability and effectively depleting Ukraine's missile defense stockpiles. On regional issues, Moscow's dependency on security cooperation with Iran seems to be growing too. This development has led to a new division of labor between Tehran and Moscow, according to which the Iranian forces became in charge of confronting the revival of radical armed groups and maintaining pro-Assad positions in eastern and central Syria, while Russian forces continued to provide air power and concentrate at the western areas where their vital interests, that is, Mediterranean bases, are located.[46]

The war also accelerated the economic interlinkage. But, based on the work by Tansey et al., authoritarian regimes increase trade with one another as part of a purposeful decision tied to a survival strategy since such linkages "foster preferences for status quo politics both among international partners and domestic constituencies."[47] This fact means that the parties are aware of the limitation of their economic cooperation in boosting their economies and development indexes. Yet, they proceed with this policy as a necessary step to mitigate the damages of international pressures and impede its negative effects. For this reason, understanding the economic ties between Russia and Iran's relations will be incomplete if the protective logic behind these economic decisions is not considered.

---

[46]Hamidreza Azizi, "The Impact of Ukrainian War in Iran-Russia Relations in Syria," Al-Sharq Strategic Forum, June 17, 2022, https://research.sharqforum.org/2022/06/17/iran-russia-relations-in-syria/.

[47]Tansey et al., "Ties to the Rest," 1250.

On this basis, the two countries' leadership discussed initiatives to offset Western sanctions and the de-dollarization of trade. They signed an agreement on monetary transactions and memorandums on interbank cooperation in July 2022, which enabled payments in the Iranian rial and the Russian ruble.[48] The two sides also signed a $40 billion MoU between Gazprom and the National Iranian Oil Company. In their sixteenth Joint Economic Commission held in Moscow on October 31, 2022, officials said that they would move forward with concrete steps for activating bilateral logistical routes, establishing free trade zones, coordinating the standardization of industrial and agricultural products, and ensuring state export credit guarantees. In addition, new efforts were initiated to promote bilateral grassroots trade and tourism at the provincial levels.

The North-South Transit Corridor (NSTC) and Iran's signature on the free trade agreement (FTA) with the Eurasian Economic Union (EAEU) were at the top of the list of efforts that could potentially raise the economic linkages between the two countries. The NSTC is a logistical corridor with a strategic value, which has increasingly gained significance for the Kremlin after the war, when sanctions interrupted Russia's westward trade routes. Transit through NSTC doubled in the first quarter of 2023 and is expected to increase sharply when it becomes fully operational. Moscow agreed to invest $500 million in the Astra-Rasht railway project, which is the most important unfinished segment of the NSTC. Russian presidential aide Igor Levitin's several rounds of travel to Tehran and visits to the project advancements show the importance of the NSTC for the Kremlin. The year 2022 also witnessed an expansion of the sea-based segment of the NSTC, which links Iran and Russia directly through the Caspian Sea. Finally, by September 2023, the EAEU and Iran had implemented a newly negotiated FTA agreement that included 8,000 products, which could hugely facilitate trade between Iran and Russia. As research shows, an earlier Iranian Preferential Trade Agreement with the EAEU had a major impact on mutual trade.[49] This far more comprehensive FTA is expected to mitigate, to some extent, the adverse macroeconomic effects of Western sanctions.

---

[48] "Tehran Stock Exchange Launches Ruble-Rial Pair Trades," Tass News Agency, July 19, 2022, https://tass.com/economy/1481927.
[49] See Amat Adarov and Mahdi Ghodsi, "The Impact of the Eurasian Economic Union–Iran Preferential Trade Agreement on Mutual Trade at Aggregate and Sectoral Levels," *Eurasian Economic Review* 11 (2021), https://doi.org/10.1007/s40822-020-00161-2.

The Changing Face of Limits

Can the limits stop the protective integration between Moscow and Tehran? This section argues that limits have an impact on both the depth and the speed of integration and have often defined the threshold for bilateral ties. But so far, they have not been able to alter a general trend of deepening relations. The limits in the Russo-Iranian relations refer to networks of obstacles and considerations that originate from social, strategic, institutional, and international issues. They go beyond the leaders' individual aspirations and "restrict the range of alternatives."[50] However, these limits are not static. The war in Ukraine and the domestic political environment in Moscow and Tehran have imposed changes on the structure of such limits.

Mutual mistrust and a lack of public support due to negative historical memories is often cited as one of the biggest limits in Russo-Iranian ties.[51] The history of territorial losses in the Treaties of Golestan (1813) and Turkmenchay (1828) and the Soviets' meddling in Iran's domestic affairs are taught in every school and university in Iran and have thus remained fresh in the Iranian psyche. Shoori identifies in his chapter that the sensitivities of public perception toward Russia act as a factor that defines the extent to which the Islamic Republic can proceed with a sort of formal alliance with Russia. This fact, for example, explains why, despite close political ties, Iran has not yet permitted Russian cultural centers to operate inside the country while its own cultural activities inside Russia have expanded in recent years.[52] A similar societal gap exists on the Russian side. Opinion polls of the Center for Strategy and Technology Analysis (CAST) demonstrate a lack of knowledge and interest in Iran among the Russian population. The polls reveal that 42 percent of Russians consider Iran friendly, only 15 percent hold the

---

[50]Thomas J. Price, "Constraints on Foreign Policy Decision Making: Stability and Flexibility in Three Crises," *International Studies Quarterly* 22, no. 3 (September, 1978), 357–60.
[51]Vladimir Sazhin and Jahangir Karami, "Iran-Russia Strategic Partnership at the New Stage: What Could We Propose to Each Other?" in *RIAC Report 29: Russia-Iran Partnership: an Overview and Prospects for Future* (Moscow: Russian International Affairs Council, 2016).
[52]Elahe Karimi Riabi and Mahnaz Norouzi, "Iran-Russia Cultural Relations," *Central Asia and Caucuses Journal* 115 (2021), 123–4.

opposite opinion, and 43 percent find it difficult to answer.[53] As Robert Keohane and Joseph Nye argue, social mistrust can prevent the formation of a complex interdependence.[54] But, a lack of trust exists at the state level too, mainly because of possible rapid changes in partnerships when realpolitik necessitates. For example, the Russian elite fear that Iran can at any time change its position in favor of the West,[55] while there is a diffused belief among a part of the elite in Tehran that Iran is a political card in the Russian hand in its struggles with the West. For example, if Moscow fails to publicly pay back Tehran's assistance to the Russian military operation in Ukraine, then it is not hard to imagine that both elite and public debates in Iran will shift against Russia, accusing Moscow of being a non-reliable partner who only imposes costs on Tehran.

However, it is important to avoid an overstatement here. It is a mistake to exaggerate the role of mistrust in the current political atmosphere between the two countries. Neither Russia nor Iran is a democracy, and given their current state-society rift, the societal views are not necessarily represented in the policy domains. As discussed earlier in this chapter, the key decisions regarding relations are taken in closed security circles and their views, in many cases, contradict public opinion. Also, the level of mutual trust among the various foreign policy institutions involved in decision-making varies. For example, while Iranian reformists, technocrats, and civilian agencies trust Moscow less, the high-ranking military-security officers have a substantially higher trust in Moscow, given their decade of having close working relations with their Russian counterparts.

Conflicts of interest and differences in the national security objectives create another set of limits in the Russo-Iranian relations. The divergence of objectives, methods, and interests in Syria, energy competition, disagreements over the legal status of the Caspian Sea, and inconsistencies of two sides' objectives in the nuclear field are often

---

[53] "Rossia i Iran: Otnosheniya Rossii i Irana. Sravnenie dvukh stran [Russia and Iran: Relations between Russia and Iran: Comparison of Two Countries]," FOM, August 16, 2022, https://fom.ru/Mir/14764.
[54] Robert O. Keohane and Joseph S. Nye, Jr., "Power and Interdependence Revisited," *International Organization* 41, no. 4 (1987), 731 https://doi.org/10.1017/S0020818300027661.
[55] Marianna Belenkaya (journalist at the Kommersant) in discussion with the author, April 6, 2023.

raised as examples that have constrained relations.[56] This has led to a situation in which neither side can be supportive of every policy of the other party as interests might collide at some point. The war in Ukraine has highlighted several cases of conflicts of interest. The first case relates to Iran's position of not recognizing the annexed Ukrainian territories. From Moscow's perspective, the Iranian position means that Tehran does not look at the war through the Russian lens and thus does not fully support Russian policy.[57] Tehran's position, however, is linked to its own national security concerns and territorial integrity. Tehran faces ethnic-separatist movements in the Kurdistan and Baluchistan provinces, and thus, supporting separatists in Ukraine is seen as legitimizing similar movements inside. In another case, Moscow joined the Arab League and the Gulf Cooperation Council (GCC) in supporting the UAE's claims about Iranian islands in the Persian Gulf. Russian actions are directly linked to Moscow's goal of boosting trade and partnership with the UAE and the GCC as part of its strategy to adapt to Western sanctions. Russian interests, in this case, clash with Iran's territorial integrity—raising concerns in Tehran about the depth of the partnership with Moscow. A similar case of conflict of interest can be spotted on the economic front, where Tehran and Moscow compete for the market. As Batmanghelidj and Godzimirski argue in their respective chapters, the structure of the two countries' economies and hydrocarbon dependency makes them natural rivals. The war, indeed, has expanded the levels of competition in these areas.

Intense political-military dialogues at various levels, from the Ministry of Foreign Affairs to the armed forces and the offices of presidents, which were further reinforced after February 2022, are working as a strong dispute-resolution mechanism. The Syrian issue, the dispute over the islands, and the legal status of the Caspian Sea are examples showing how high-level and multilayered political-military contacts helped to minimize the negative effects of these disagreements and conflicts of interest. In the Syrian case, General Qasem Soleimani, the former commander in chief of Quds Forces, became a regular point of contact

---

[56] Igor Matveev and Yeghia Tashijian, "Russia and Iran in Syria: A Competitive Partnership?" Russian International Affairs Council, July 19, 2022, https://russiancouncil.ru/en/analytics-and-comments/analytics/russia-and-iran-in-syria-a-competitive-partnership/.

[57] Dunaeva, discussion with the author; Andrey Kortunov (former director of Russian International Affairs Council), in discussion with the author, April 7, 2023.

to resolve operational disagreements between Moscow and Tehran after 2015, until his assassination in January 2022. This military channel was complemented by steady political contacts at the president and foreign minister levels and regional contacts through the trilateral Astana Process. These channels of communication and coordination helped both sides to establish critical dialogues, clarify redlines, adjust agendas, and avoid direct collision.

Ali Akbar Velayati, advisor to Iran's supreme leader, confirms this fact when he said, "In some occasions we had different positions [on Syria], but with talks our positions became clear and synchronized. The strategic military-security cooperation of Iran and Russia is a new thing and coordination takes time."[58] A similar pattern can be seen in the Caspian Sea case. While differences in Russian and Iranian views over the Caspian Sea were often portrayed as a major point of division, the shared principle of preventing a military presence of non-littoral states, a decade-long political discussion, and finally, a surge in the transit value of the Caspian route contributed to the transformation of the Caspian Sea to one of the hot spots of cooperation between Moscow and Tehran. Again, in this case, the intensity of multilayer political contacts and the opportunity costs of confrontation worked in favor of containing the disagreements.

The next group of limits relates to the fact that a full-term pact that formalizes partnership and creates commitments bears risks and costs for both sides. For Moscow, having close ties may have consequences for its Middle East policies, while Tehran may bear costs at the international level from fully tilting toward Moscow. The GCC's "positive neutrality" and reluctance to adopt an anti-Russian position is not just a political gain for Putin, but it also provides an important economic lifeline for Moscow.[59] From energy cooperation under the OPEC+ format to the Arab investment in Russia and being the hub of Russian financial activates to a venue for circumventing sanctions, the Arab-Russian relations are too valuable for Moscow to be negatively impacted because of its ties with Iran. As Mark Katz argues, it is hard to imagine Russia leaving behind its

---

[58]"Velayati: Assad khate ghrmeze mast [Velayati: Assad Is Our Red Line]," BBC Persian, December 6, 2015, https://www.bbc.com/persian/iran/2015/12/151206_l30_iran_syria_velayati_asad.

[59]Nourhan ElSheikh, "Arabs and the Silent Support for Russia," Valdai Club, January 31, 2023, https://valdaiclub.com/a/highlights/arabs-and-the-silent-support-for-russia/.

balanced Middle East policy after the Ukraine war.[60] This fact naturally bounds Russian willingness to go too far with Tehran.

On the Iranian side, however, getting close to Moscow has provoked Western reactions. The European and US economic sanctions and political pressures due to arms exports to Russia have hurt Iran. It is not hard to imagine that concerns over stronger Western pressures for future Iranian arms export to Moscow have become a part of Tehran's calculus now. In fact, these costs have spurred a crisis management mode in Tehran so as not to escalate tensions with Europe to new heights—Tehran seems not to be in favor of a full breakup of ties with Europe because of Russia. Thus, it is increasingly difficult for Tehran to give commitments to Moscow, which might lead to new external pressures, especially at a time when fulfilling Russian demands is becoming more costly.

Notwithstanding these facts, the actual implications of this group of limits on Russo-Iranian relations are relative and will change over time. For example, the Saudi-Iran agreement that led to the restoration of diplomatic ties between Riyadh and Tehran and substantially reduced open hostilities between Iran and the GCC has an impact on Russian balancing capabilities. Moscow has a substantially easier job and bears less political pressure to maintain a close relationship with all sides if the Arab-Iranian de-escalations become a sustained process. On the other side, new US and EU sanctions on several Iranian companies and assets involved in trade with Russia seem to be insignificant for Tehran while a larger umbrella of sanctions is already in place. Almost every key segment of the Iranian defense industry has already been under Western sanctions, which, as a result, makes new sanctions bearable with minimum tangible costs.

The final group of limits is caused by the fact that Russo-Iranian ties are not guided and governed by a firm and formal foundation and, thus, remain constrained by external fluctuations and institutional limits. The lack of strategic vision for relations has resulted in an increased role of external actors and has made the relationship situational in nature.[61]

---

[60] "The War in Ukraine and Its Impact on Russia-Iran Relations," panel discussion, Middle East Institute, May 26, 2023, https://www.youtube.com/watch?v=lWE0Rn145TA.
[61] Pyotr Topychkanov and Mohammad Kazem Sajjadpour, "Iranian and Russian Perspectives on the Global System," in *RIAC Report 29: Russia-Iran Partnership: An Overview and Prospects for Future* (Moscow: Russian International Affairs Council, 2016), 29–33.

The two countries' state of relations with the United States acts as an important variable while China becomes more important for both the sides; gradually, Beijing's view of Russo-Iranian ties is also rising as a new determining external factor. These challenges are complemented by underdeveloped legislative bases and implementation mechanisms.[62]

At the institutional level, the state bureaucracies have shown great inefficiencies in implementing political agreements. Sometimes, even mid-level bureaucrats resist and delay the implementation of political agreements as they see little value in them, highlighting a lack of trust in the importance of the relationship. Inconsistencies between the political and the technical-bureaucratic levels are often the case on the Iranian side, given the country's unique structure of foreign policy decision-making.[63] In addition, both sides lack the ability and willingness to fully respond to mutual needs and make a commitment. Vladimir Putin's comments after Washington's withdrawal from the JCPOA in May 2018 is one of those occasions that elaborated this limit. Putin said, "Russia is not a fire brigade …We cannot rescue everything that does not fully depend on us. We've played our part."[64] These limits are expected to be mostly continued despite the two states' measures to resolve them. The signing of a long-term strategic cooperation agreement is one such step that may help the ties find a solid vision.

In a nutshell, the changing structure of limits and the rising importance of the relationship's security benefits have helped decision-makers to show more flexibility in giving concessions and overcoming obstacles. For example, this is best seen in the Iranian official's stand to replace competition in the energy sector with cooperation,[65] and Tehran's mild reaction to the Russian support of the UAE's claims in the Persian Gulf. Thus, the limits on relations seem manageable as long as the strategic

---

[62]See Andrey Kortunov, "Russia and Iran: How Far from a Strategic Partnership?," Russian International Affairs Council, May 6, 2021, https://russiancouncil.ru/en/analytics-and-comments/analytics/russia-and-iran-how-far-from-a-strategic-partnership/.
[63]Divsallar, "The Foreign Policy Establishment in Iran."
[64]"Russia Not a 'Fire Brigade' to Save Disintegrating Iran Deal, Says Putin," *Times of Israel*, May 16, 2019, https://www.timesofisrael.com/russia-not-fire-brigade-to-save-disintegrating-iran-deal-says-putin/.
[65]Alex Vatanka and Abdolrasool Divsallar, "Can the West Stop Russian-Iranian Convergence?," Middle East Institute, April 3, 2023, https://www.mei.edu/publications/can-west-stop-russian-iranian-convergence.

logic of protecting the regime's survival drives the bilateral relations. This fact is facilitated by constant shifts in the nature of some limits and the two countries' intense political dialogue that has effectively worked as a dispute-resolution mechanism.

Conclusion

As long as normalization with the West remains elusive for Moscow and Tehran and the current threat structure endures, Russian and Iranian interests and policies will continue to converge. In other words, the events of 2022 accelerated a gradual process in which Moscow and Tehran raised their interdependence and improved strategies to mutually protect each other. In the eyes of both Supreme Leader Ali Khamenei and Russian president Vladimir Putin, similar threats make them natural allies who must pool their resources. Thus, any problems and conflicts of interest that might stand in the way are deemed minor and will be resolved for the sake of one strategic objective: ensuring state security and regime survival. This approach explains why bilateral relations remain stable and growing despite the conflicts of interest at the regional and economic levels. Although the outcome of the war in Ukraine, US-Iran nuclear talks, and EU-Iran relations will broadly impact future directions, a gradual process has already been reinforced, which may contribute to the emergence of a strategic partnership in the future. This analysis does not alter the possibility that changing the dynamics of limits and the cautiousness that they cause may turn out to be a game changer and disrupt the aforementioned process.

At the same time, it should be remembered that the war's substantive impact on Russo-Iranian relations indicates the situational nature of the two countries' ties. Under different political circumstances and with different leaders in power, Tehran and Moscow may well have continued to diverge. Besides, it is becoming increasingly difficult for both sides to balance the commitments they can give with their other complicated relations at the international level. These facts, coupled with the reality that breaking with Iran doesn't disrupt Russia's interests in a strategic way, remain the most important factors explaining why a full strategic pact between the two states is yet a far-fetched reality.

Bibliography

Adarov, Amat, and Mahdi Ghodsi. "The Impact of the Eurasian Economic Union–Iran Preferential Trade Agreement on Mutual Trade at Aggregate and Sectoral Levels." *Eurasian Economic Review* 11 (2021): 125–57. https://doi.org/10.1007/s40822-020-00161-2.

Allison, Roy. "Virtual Regionalism, Regional Structures and Regime Security in Central Asia," *Central Asian Survey* 27, no. 2 (2008): 185–202. https://doi.org/10.1080/02634930802355121.

Ambrosio, Thomas. "Democratic States and Authoritarian Firewalls: America as a Black Knight in the Uprising in Bahrain." *Contemporary Politics* 20, no. 3 (2014): 331–46.

Axelrod, Robert, and Robert Keohane. "Achieving Cooperation under Anarchy: Strategies and Institutions." *World Politics* 38, no. 1 (1985): 226–54.

Azizi, Hamidreza. "The Impact of Ukrainian War in Iran-Russia Relations in Syria." Al-Sharq Strategic Forum, June 17, 2022. https://research.sharqforum.org/2022/06/17/iran-russia-relations-in-syria/.

Bank, André, and Mirjam Edel. "Authoritarian Regime Learning: Comparative Insights from the Arab Uprisings." *GIGA Working Papers*, German Institute of Global and Area Studies, no. 274, 2015.

BBC Persian. "Velayati: Assad khate ghrmeze mast [Velayati: Assad Is Our Red Line]." December 6, 2015. https://www.bbc.com/persian/iran/2015/12/151206_l30_iran_syria_velayati_asad.

Bordachev, Timofei. "Russia's Turn to the East: Between Choice and Necessity." Valdai Club, September 1, 2022. https://valdaiclub.com/a/highlights/russia-s-turn-to-the-east-between-choice/.

Cho, Kelly Kasulis. "Over 1300 Arrests Reported as Russians Protest Military Mobilization." *Washington Post*. September 22, 2022. https://www.washingtonpost.com/world/2022/09/22/russia-protests-arrests-putin-war-mobilization/.

Diplomacy Irani. "Amozesh Mamoran Sepah dar Rusiye [Training of IRGC Forces in Russia]," February 16, 2013. http://www.irdiplomacy.ir/fa/news/1912860/آموزش-ماموران-سپاه-در-روسیه-.

Divsallar, Abdolrasool. "The Foreign Policy Establishment in Iran." In *The Sacred Republic: Power and Institutions in Iran*, edited by Mehran Kamrava, 221–57. London: Hurst, 2023.

Divsallar, Abdolrasool. "The Pillars of Iranian-Russian Security Convergence." *The International Spectator* 54, no. 3 (2019): 107–22. https://doi.org/10.1080/03932729.2019.1586147.

Divsallar, Abdolrasool. "Protective Integration and Rising Interdependency: Making Sense of Iranian Response to Russian Invasion of Ukraine." *Chinese Journal of International Politics* (forthcoming).

Divsallar, Abdolrasool. "Shifting Threats and Strategic Adjustment in Iran's Foreign Policy: The Case of Strait of Hormuz." *British Journal of Middle*

Eastern Studies 49, no. 5 (2022): 873–95. https://doi.org/10.1080/13530 194.2021.1874873.

Eisenstadt, Michael. "Russian Arms and Technology Transfers to Iran: Policy Challenges for the United States." *Arms Control Today*, March 1, 2001. https://www.armscontrol.org/act/2001-03/iran-nuclear-briefs/russian-arms-technology-transfers-iranpolicy-challenges-united.

ElSheikh, Nourhan. "Arabs and the Silent Support for Russia." Valdai Club, January 31, 2023. https://valdaiclub.com/a/highlights/arabs-and-the-silent-support-for-russia/.

FOM. "Rossia i Iran: Otnosheniya Rossii i Irana. Sravnenie dvukh stran [Russia and Iran: Relations between Russia and Iran: Comparison of Two Countries]." August 16, 2022. https://fom.ru/Mir/14764.

Hall, Stephen G. F., and Thomas Ambrosio. "Authoritarian Learning: A Conceptual Overview." *East European Politics* 33, no. 2 (2017): 143–61. https://doi.org/10.1080/21599165.2017.1307826.

IRNA News Agency. "layehe movafeghatname amkari iran va rusiye dar hoze amniyat etelat tasvib shod [The Law for Agreement on Information Security between Iran and Russia Passed]." December 10, 2023. https://www.irna.ir/news/85317194/لایحه-موافقتنامه-همکاری-ایران-و-روسیه-در-حوزه-امنیت-اطلاعات-تصویب (accessed January 30, 2024).

Kamrava, Mehran. "The Arab Spring and the Saudi-Led Counterrevolution." *Orbis* 56, no. 1 (2012): 96–104.

Karimi Riabi, Elahe, and Mahnaz Norouzi. "Iran-Russia Cultural Relations." *Central Asia and Caucuses Journal* 115 (2021): 123–42.

Katz, Mark N. "Iran Can't Afford for Russia to Lose in Ukraine." *Barron's*, July 22, 2022. https://www.barrons.com/articles/iran-russia-ukraine-putin-5165 8516904.

Keohane, Robert O., and Joseph S. Nye, Jr. "Power and Interdependence Revisited." *International Organization* 41, no. 4 (1987): 725–53. https://doi.org/10.1017/S0020818300027661.

Khamenei.ir. "Iran, russie va chin; se ghodrate mohem dar moghabele tosetalabi amrica va gharb [Iran, Russia, and China: Three Important Power against US and West Hegemony]." June 22, 2022. https://farsi.khamenei.ir/others-dia log?id=50652.

Khorrami, Nima. "Putin's Visit to the Islamic Republic: Bringing Iran Closer to Russia while Building Long-Term Leverage over Tehran." Middle East Institute. August 1, 2022. https://www.mei.edu/publications/putins-visit-isla mic-republic-bringing-iran-closer-russia-while-building-long-term.

Kommersant. "Moskva i Tegeran uglublyaut svyazi [Moscow and Tehran Deepen Ties]." October 2, 2022. https://www.kommersant.ru/doc/5646418.

Kortunov, Andrey. "Russia and Iran: How Far from a Strategic Partnership?" Russian International Affairs Council, May 6, 2021, https://russiancouncil.ru/en/analytics-and-comments/analytics/russia-and-iran-how-far-from-a-strategic-partnership/.

Krapohl, Sebastian, and Johannes Muntschick. "Two Logics of Regionalism: The Importance of Interdependence and External Support for Regional Integration in Southern Africa." *Bamberger Online Papers on Integration Research* 3 (2008). https://nbn-resolving.org/urn:nbn:de:0168-ssoar-130518.

Libman, Alexander, and Anastassia V. Obydenkova. "Understanding Authoritarian Regionalism." *Journal of Democracy* 29, no. 4 (2018): 151–65.

Matveev, Igor, and Yeghia Tashjian. "Russia and Iran in Syria: A Competitive Partnership?" Russian International Affairs Council, July 19, 2022. https://russiancouncil.ru/en/analytics-and-comments/analytics/russia-and-iran-in-syria-a-competitive-partnership/.

Mehr News Agency. "Iran, Russia Officials Sign MoU to Enhance Security Cooperation." June 28, 2023. https://en.mehrnews.com/news/202586/Iran-Russia-officials-sign-MoU-to-enhance-security-coop.

Middle East Institute. "The War in Ukraine and Its Impact on Russia-Iran Relations." May 26, 2023. https://www.youtube.com/watch?v=lWE0Rn145TA.

Mikhail Rodionov. "Avtory zakonoproekta o nakazanii uklonistov ot mobilizazii zayavili, chto on utratil svoyu aktualnost [The Authors of the Bill to Punish Evaders from Mobilization Said That It Has Its Relevance]." Gazeta.ru, November 1, 2022. https://www.gazeta.ru/army/2022/11/01/15716725.shtml.

The Ministry of Foreign Affairs of Russian Federation. "The Concept of the Foreign Policy of the Russian Federation." March 31, 2023. https://mid.ru/en/foreign_policy/fundamental_documents/1860586/?TSPD_101_R0=08765fb817ab2000f238fe4073d30bdd359ccb6094a7bf5eba80bd0bf21140a480b7b58271504b8208dabff6be143000ff6b52db228ceabd8c992a54f78849c24b7a7f7006ecb76cf83fbf957112a615fe52518c343463705c59203d5b58fda4.

Motamedi, Maziar. "Iran's Khamenei Says US Wants to Keep Ukraine War Going." Al Jazeera, March 21, 2023. https://www.aljazeera.com/news/2023/3/21/irans-khamenei-says-us-wants-to-keep-ukraine-war.

Price, Thomas J. "Constraints on Foreign Policy Decision Making: Stability and Flexibility in Three Crises." *International Studies Quarterly* 22, no. 3 (1978): 357–76.

Puri, Samir. "The Strategic Hedging of Iran, Russia, and China: Juxtaposing Participation in the Global System with Regional Revisionism." *Journal of Global Security Studies* 2, no. 4 (2017): 307–23. https://doi.org/10.1093/jogss/ogx015.

Sazhin, Vladimir, and Jahangir Karami, "Iran-Russia Strategic Partnership at the New Stage: What Could We Propose to Each Other?" In *RIAC Report 29: Russia-Iran Partnership: An Overview and Prospects for Future*, 9–28. Moscow: Russian International Affairs Council, 2016.

Schelling, Thomas C. *The Strategy of Conflict*. Oxford: Oxford University Press, 1960.

Schmitt, Gary James, ed. *Rise of the Revisionists: Russia, China, and Iran*. Washington, DC: AEI Press, 2018.

Schmotz, Alexander, and Oisín Tansey. "Regional Autocratic Linkage and Regime Survival." *European Journal of Political Research* 57 (2018): 662–86.

Sputnik. "Sputnik Expands Cooperation with Iranian Media." October 31, 2022. https://ria.ru/20221031/sputnik-1828051200.html.

Stanovaya, Tatiana. "Divided in the Face of Defeat: The Schism Forming in the Russian Elite." Carnegie Endowment for International Peace, December 13, 2022. https://carnegieendowment.org/politika/88630.

Tabatabai, Ariane, and Dina Esfandiary. *Triple Axis: Iran's Relations with Russia and China*. London: I.B. Tauris, 2021.

Tansey, Oisín. *The International Politics of Authoritarian Rule*. Oxford: Oxford University Press, 2016.

Tansey, Oisín, Kevin Koehler, and Alexander Schmotz. "Ties to the Rest: Autocratic Linkages and Regime Survival." *Comparative Political Studies* 50, no. 9, (2017): 1242–54. https://doi-org.ezproxy.unicatt.it/10.1177/0010414016666859.

Tass News Agency. "Tehran Stock Exchange Launches Ruble-Rial Pair Trades." July 19, 2022. https://tass.com/economy/1481927.

Topychkanov, Pyotr, and Mohammad Kazem Sajjadpour. "Iranian and Russian Perspectives on the Global System." In *RIAC Report 29: Russia-Iran Partnership: An Overview and Prospects for Future*. Moscow: Russian International Affairs Council, 2016.

Ulyanov Mikhail. (@Amb_Ulyanov). "Let's Don't Forget that the #US Maximum Pressure Policy against #Iran Has No Credible Peaceful Purpose." November 16, 2022. https://twitter.com/Amb_Ulyanov/status/1592932630148046849.

Vatankha, Alex. *The Battle of the Ayatollahs in Iran: The United States, Foreign Policy, and Political Rivalry since 1979*. London: I.B. Tauris, 2021.

Vazquez, Maegan. "White House Claims US Is Seeing Signs Russia May Be Advising Iran on How to Crack Down on Protests," CNN, October 26, 2022. https://edition.cnn.com/2022/10/26/politics/white-house-russia-iran-protests/index.html.

Whitehead, Laurence. "Three Angles on the Alliance Options of Authoritarian Regimes." *Taiwan Journal of Democracy* 14, no. 1 (2018): 1–24.

PART THREE

A HYBRID STATUS: COMPETITION AMID COOPERATION

7 ANTI-AMERICANISM AND THE DREAM OF A NON-WESTERN ORDER

Jeffrey Mankoff and Mahsa Rouhi

A deepening cooperation between Moscow and Tehran has been a prominent by-product of Russia's war in Ukraine. Notwithstanding a long history of antagonism; the ongoing geopolitical competition in the Middle East, the Caucasus, and Central Asia; as well as the multifaceted nature of their respective relationships with Western powers, the war has helped align Russian and Iranian critiques of the existing international system and encouraged them to coordinate their respective challenges to it. Opposition to US domination of the global order, as well as to the liberal ideology underpinning many US-led global institutions, was among the strongest forces pulling Moscow and Tehran together even before Russia's full-scale invasion of Ukraine in February 2022 and the outbreak of massive anti-regime protests in Iran. The war and the protests have helped cement Russo-Iranian cooperation while elevating Moscow and Tehran as the two most ambitious opponents of the US-led order.

The views expressed in this chapter are those of the authors and are not an official policy or position of the National Defense University, the Defense Department, or the US government.

Russian officials and commentators have long criticized the rules and institutions of the US-led order, but until the invasion of Ukraine in February 2022, Moscow remained happy to take advantage of its benefits. Russia was an important pillar of multilateral arrangements on arms control, nonproliferation, and energy security, among other global issues—even as the United States suggested that Moscow sought to "play a disruptive role on the world stage" by sowing chaos and challenging US global leadership.[1] While Russia has faced Western sanctions of one sort or another since its 2014 annexation of Crimea and the invasion of eastern Ukraine, it remained, until February 2022, deeply enmeshed with the global economy and an important actor in global and regional governance mechanisms. It was only with the full-scale invasion of Ukraine that Russia embraced an almost wholly antagonistic stance toward the rules and institutions of a post–Cold War system against which it had long chafed.

Russia's shift to open revisionism aligned it more closely with the Islamic Republic of Iran, which has placed rejection of the US-led order at the center of its foreign policy since the 1979 Revolution.[2] Tehran sits at the nucleus of what it calls the "Axis of Resistance" against the domination of the international system by the "Arrogant Powers," among which the United States (the "Great Satan") is primary.[3] Its international behavior challenges the norms and institutions of that system on multiple fronts. Iran has faced economic sanctions of one kind or another ever since the Islamic Revolution.[4] In recent years, these sanctions have not only focused on Iran's nuclear program but have also been directed at its

---

[1] "Interim National Security Strategic Guidance," The White House, March 2021, https://www.whitehouse.gov/wp-content/uploads/2021/03/NSC-1v2.pdf.
[2] See, for instance, Farideh Farhi and Saideh Lotifan, "Iran's Post-Revolution Foreign Policy Puzzle," in *Worldviews of Aspiring Powers: Domestic Foreign Policy Debates in China, India, Iran, Japan, and Russia*, edited by Henry R. Nau and Deepa M. Ollapally (Oxford: Oxford University Press, 2012), 114–45;. Houman A. Sadri, "Trends in the Foreign Policy of Revolutionary Iran," *Journal of Third World Studies* 15, no. 1 (1998), 13–37; Christin Marschall, *Iran's Persian Gulf Policy: From Khomeini to Khatami* (London: Routledge Curzon, 2003), 179–82.
[3] Ali Khamenei, "Role of Arrogant Powers' Policies in Recent Bitter Events in Iran Is Obvious," Office of the Supreme Leader, October 3, 2022, https://english.khamenei.ir/news/9189/Role-of-Arrogant-Powers-policies-in-recent-bitter-events-in.
[4] Ashish Kumar Sen, "A Brief History of Sanctions on Iran," Atlantic Council, May 8, 2018, https://www.atlanticcouncil.org/blogs/new-atlanticist/a-brief-history-of-sanctions-on-iran/.

support for terrorism, violations of human rights internally, and foreign military interventions.[5]

We argue that this parallel alienation of Moscow and Tehran from the US-led international order has accelerated their mutual rapprochement, which is likely to result in the emergence of an overlapping critique of the liberal order and more coordinated steps to challenge it, sometimes in collaboration with other authoritarian powers like China. The durability of their entente remains questionable; however, Russia and Iran remain wary partners, limiting their threat to the existing world order. Western sanctions coupled with military setbacks on the ground are raising the pressure on an increasingly isolated Vladimir Putin even as the Islamic Republic faced some of the most intense public protests in its history following the death of Jina Mahsa Amini, a young Kurdish woman, in the custody of the so-called morality police and the competition over the succession to the elderly supreme leader Ayatollah Ali Khamenei accelerates.[6] Significant political change in either or both countries could undercut the pillars of their current alignment, based above all on their shared alienation from the West. Short of such epochal change, however, this parallel alienation is likely to continue, and with it, efforts by both Moscow and Tehran to whittle away the existing international system.

Russia and Iran against the "Liberal International Order"

Deepening Russo-Iranian cooperation rests on the two countries' converging perceptions of the international order. The governments in both Moscow and Tehran see important pillars of that order as

---

[5]Esfandyar Batmanghelidj and Mahsa Rouhi, "The Iran Nuclear Deal and Sanctions Relief: Implications for US Policy," *Survival* 63, no. 4 (2021), 183–98, doi: 10.1080/00396338.2021.1956192.

[6]Steven Pifer, "The Russia-Ukraine War and Its Ramifications for Russia," Brookings, December 8, 2022, https://www.brookings.edu/articles/the-russia-ukraine-war-and-its-ramifications-for-russia/; Christina Lu, "Putin Faces Military Debacle," *Foreign Policy*, October 5, 2022, https://foreignpolicy.com/2022/10/05/russia-military-ukraine-retreat-counteroffensiveputin/; Mahsa Rouhi, "Woman, Life, Freedom in Iran," *Survival* 64, no. 6 (December 2022), 189–96, doi: 10.1080/00396338.2022.2150441; Niels de Hoog and Elena Morresi, "Mapping Iran's Unrest: How Mahsa Amini's Death Led to Nationwide Protests," *The Guardian*, October 31, 2022, https://www.theguardian.com/world/ng-interactive/2022/oct/31/mapping-irans-unrest-how-mahsa-aminis-death-led-to-nationwide-protests.

fundamentally illegitimate, even as they, like many self-identified "rising" powers, seek to preserve at least some aspects of the international status quo for their benefit.[7] Both Russia and Iran question the legitimacy of an order they had little role in creating. An order that, in their view, reflects the norms and priorities of a US-led West that they regard as alien—a frustration they share with many states in the Global South.[8] Their shared critique focuses on the role of the United States as the main driver and source of ideological legitimation within the international system. Russia and Iran also criticize the existing order for the way in which the United States and its allies maintain a normative preference for liberalism and democracy that not only casts their own respective political systems as flawed, but also openly imperils them.

While the two countries oppose both the centrality of the United States to the international order and the normative preference for liberalism and democracy that constitutes the "software" of that order, their respective critiques are not identical, reflecting their different geopolitical and ideological outlooks. Key to the Russian critique is the belief that US hegemony represents the greatest threat to international stability, and that a more stable, just international order requires buy-in from all of the major powers—one reason that Russia often looks to the UN Security Council (where it is a veto-wielding permanent member) as the basis of international law and legitimacy. Iran, conversely, is guided by its grand strategy and ideological underpinnings toward nonalignment with world powers and resistance against dominance-seeking states in general, forming an "Axis of Resistance" in an effort to counter the US-led order—above all in the Middle East. The Iranian critique, therefore, has traditionally had more of a regional dimension. The combination of the war in Ukraine and the apparent collapse of efforts to revive the Iranian nuclear deal (the so-called Joint Comprehensive Plan of Action or JCPOA) is now giving Moscow and Tehran an incentive to align their critiques and collaborate in seeking changes to the international status quo.

---

[7] Thomas Biersteker and Erica Moret, "Rising Powers and Reform of International Security Institutions," in *Rising Powers, Global Governance and Global Ethics*, edited by Jamie Gaskarth(London: Routledge, 2015), 57–73.

[8] Shivshankar Menon, "Nobody Wants the Current World Order," *Foreign Affairs*, August 3, 2022, https://www.foreignaffairs.com/world/nobody-wants-current-world-order.

Central to Russia and Iran's shared aspiration to reshape global order is the belief that US-promoted norms cannot be divorced from the projection of US power. They criticize the United States for weaponizing its domination of the international system to impose its own interpretation of liberalism and democracy on other countries whose civilizational identity, they claim, inclines them to different political models. In that sense, both Moscow and Tehran would like to see a world order that is more "democratic" and "pluralistic," in the sense of making space for non-Western and non-liberal states to elaborate their own behavioral norms.[9] Iranian supreme leader Ayatollah Ali Khamenei demanded that "this new order should be based on the participation of all nations and equal rights for all of them," while Russian president Putin has called for an order that upholds "the principles of equality, justice, and respect" for all states.[10]

Just as the Kremlin portrays the "color revolutions" across much of the former Soviet Union and the anti-Putin uprisings that broke out in 2011–12 as part of a deliberate Western strategy to bring about regime change, so too Iran's ruling clerics see the 2009 Green Movement and the ongoing (2022–3) anti-regime uprisings as what Supreme Leader Ali Khamenei called "not normal acts [that were] designed by the U.S., fake Zionist regime, their mercenaries, and some treasonous Iranians abroad who helped them."[11] This shared perception that the United States, and by extension, the global order that the United States helms, is dedicated to the replacement of their regimes "solidified the shared normative basis for Iran [and] Russia ... against the West's democratization agenda," and

---

[9] On Russian views, see Konstantin Kosachev, "Rossiya mozhet stat' initsiatorom reformy mezhdunarodnogo prava [Russia May Become the Initiator of Reform of International Law]," Russian International Affairs Council, December 6, 2022, https://russiancouncil.ru/analytics-and-comments/comments/rossiya-mozhet-stat-initsiatorom-reformy-mezhdunarodnogo-prava; Sergey A. Karaganov, "Budushchii miroporyadok [Future World Order]," Council of the President of the Russian Federation in Human Rights, September 11, 2017, http://www.president-sovet.ru/members/blogs/post/budushchiy_miroporyadok.

[10] "Supreme Leader's Inaugural Speech at the 16th Non-Aligned Summit," Office of the Supreme Leader, August 30, 2012, https://www.leader.ir/en/content/9708/Supreme-Leader%E2%80%99s-Inaugural-Speech-at-the-16th-Non-Aligned-Summit; "Uchastniki 'BRIKS plyus'vystupili za mnogopolyarnyi poryadok, zayavil Putin [Participants in the 'BRICS+' Called for a Multipolar Order, Putin Announced]," RIA Novosti, June 24, 2022, https://ria.ru/20220624/putin-1797912967.html.

[11] Ali Khamenei, "Recent Riots in Iran Were Designed," Office of the Supreme Leader, October 3, 2022, https://english.khamenei.ir/news/9183/Recent-riots-in-Iran-were-designed.

is today perhaps the strongest force driving the Islamic Republic and Putin's Russia together.[12]

Both Russia and Iran suggest that the norms underpinning the "liberal international order" reflect not just US policy preferences, but also the United States' (and other Western countries') historical experiences and are, therefore, not relevant for states whose rulers self-identify as non-Western. This critique rests on the portrayal of both Russia and Iran as not only non-Western, but also as "civilizational states" with their own distinctive traditions that predate Western liberalism and, allegedly, predispose them, along with other such states, to regard Western models as alien.[13] As social constructivists have long recognized, ideas and norms can be an element of power and a way in which Tehran, Moscow, Beijing, and others actively exercise a challenge to the existing liberal international order through "civilizational essentialization" and counter-norm entrepreneurship. Civilizational essentialization is the "articulation of particular types of domestic and regional identities, constituted by a set of cultural and normative features, which are presented as 'other' to and mobilized to contest the universal validity of liberal norms and identities."[14] The "other" facet of civilization essentialization results in the creation of a set of values that Iran, Russia, and China employ to counter the normative foundations of the West and as an "integrative power political maneuver."[15]

Another unifying element at play is Russia and Iran's common civilizational threat perception of the West and their desire to counter the dominance of the liberal culture of the current world order as a means of protection.[16] By providing an alternative to the West, any political or

---

[12]Nicole Grajewski, "An Illusory Entente: The Myth of a Russia-China-Iran 'Axis,'" *Asian Affairs* 53 (2022), 175.
[13]On "civilizational states," see Christopher P. Coker, *The Rise of the Civilizational State* (Cambridge: Polity, 2019). On the use of the "civilizational state" idea as a basis for challenging the liberal international order, see Amitav Acharya, "The Myth of the 'Civilizational State': Rising Powers and the Cultural Challenge to World Order," *Ethics and International Affairs* 34, no. 2 (2020), 139–56. On Russia, see Henry Hale and Marlene Laruelle, "Rethinking Civilizational Identity from the Bottom Up: A Case Study of Russia and a Research Agenda," *Nationalities Papers* 48, no. 3 (May 2020), 585–602.
[14]Gregorio Bettiza and David Lewis, "Authoritarian Powers and Norm Contestation in the Liberal International Order: Theorizing the Power Politics of Ideas and Identity," *Journal of Global Security Studies* 5, no. 4 (2020), 568.
[15]Bettiza and Lewis, "Authoritarian Powers and Norm Contestation," 569.
[16]Abdolrasool Divsallar, "The Pillars of Iranian-Russian Security Convergence," *The International Spectator* 54, no. 3 (2019), 107–22, https://doi.org/10.1080/03932729.2019.1586147.

economic decision becomes indicative not just of state interest, but a force beyond that: an expression of a values-based civilization identity. Through regular contestation of liberal norms, Iran, Russia, and China can increasingly position liberal norms as products of and for the West, not universal truths.

Russia, Iran, and China also promote their own alternative norms—notably, those favoring the concepts of "traditional values," authoritarianism or illiberal "strongman" democracy, anti-globalization, and an emphasis on state-led development.[17] This counter-norm entrepreneurship can erode the liberal values underpinning the current international order, and the values put forth can transcend national borders, influencing domestic political dynamics even among Western countries themselves. Ultimately, the power of counter-norm entrepreneurship lies in its ability to provide Russia, Iran, and China with greater agency and the ability to mobilize within and across nations in the international system.[18] Moscow and Tehran (not to mention Beijing) do not necessarily draw the same conclusions from this emphasis on their own civilizational essence—but their common opposition to the centrality of the United States to the existing order and their desire to legitimize their own political models are leading them to develop an overlapping critique and to deepen their cooperation around the challenging key elements of the existing order.

Russia: For Stability and Authoritarianism?

Drawing on the Cold War legacy of bipolarity as well as its own history as a great imperial power, Russia's vision emphasizes the primacy within the international system of a small number of great powers that bear primary responsibility for global stability and regional order.[19] Russia's

---

[17]Liu Han, "The Beijing Consensus? How China Has Changed Western Ideas of Law and Economic Development," *International Journal of Constitutional Law* 17, no. 1 (January 2019); Irina du Quenoy and Dmitry Dubrovskiy, "Violence and the Defense of 'Traditional Values' in the Russian Federation," in *Religion and Violence in Russia: Context, Manifestations, and Policies*, edited by Olga Oliker (Washington, DC: CSIS, 2018), 93–117, https://csis-website-prod.s3.amazonaws.com/s3fs-public/publication/180530_Oliker_ReligionandViolenceinRussia_Web.pdf.
[18]Bettiza and Lewis, "Authoritarian Powers and Norm Contestation," 571.
[19]Jeffrey Mankoff, *Russian Foreign Policy: The Return of Great Power Politics*, 2nd edn (Lanham, MD: Rowman & Littlefield, 2012).

elite, which is drawn largely from the security services and has undergone comparatively little turnover since the Soviet collapse, looks to Cold War–era bipolarity as the paradigmatic example of a stable international system that also gave Moscow's great power aspirations free rein.[20] These elites consequently seek to reshape or replace the existing international order in ways that would recognize Moscow's status as a great power in a multipolar system and confer on Russia (and other major powers) the right to maintain a sphere of influence in its immediate neighborhood.[21]

Roger Kanet suggests that what Russia seeks is a global order "based on a multipolar system in which a Westphalian sense of absolute sovereignty prevails; the rules for international economic intercourse cannot continue to preference the West, and legitimacy must be based on a system that empowers Russia and other emerging state actors."[22] According to Andrey Sushentsov, dean of the Moscow State Institute of International Relations (MGIMO), Russia believes that a more legitimate international order "should rest on common rules of conduct fixed in international law that is supported by a balance of forces between the participants in the system. If Russia's vision of international relations is expressed as a metaphor, it would be the image of Atlases who carry the heavens on their shoulders with each Atlas representing a separate great power."[23]

Of course, Russia's occupation of several neighboring states' territories and its near-genocidal campaign against Ukraine suggest that Russia's view of Westphalian sovereignty is not universal. Moscow's claim, rather, is that a handful of major powers (Russia included) enjoy a right to full sovereignty (including the right to limit the activity of foreign corporations, NGOs, and other nonstate actors) on their territory, but that the smaller states, especially those carved out of the geobody of former empires, retain a sovereignty that is more limited and conditional on the consent of their larger neighbors. This view of two-tiered sovereignty is

---

[20] On the Russian elite, see Maria Snegovaya and Kirill Petrov, "Long Soviet Shadows: The Nomenklatura Ties of Putin Elites," *Post-Soviet Affairs* 38, no. 4 (2022), 329–48, https://doi.org/10.1080/1060586X.2022.2062657.
[21] See especially Andrew Radin and Clint Reach, *Russian Views of the International Order* (Santa Monica, CA: RAND Corporation, 2017).
[22] Roger E. Kanet, "Russia and Global Governance: The Challenge to the Existing Liberal Order," *International Politics* 55 (2018), 178, https://doi.org/10.1057/s41311-017-0075-3.
[23] Andrey Sushentsov, "Russia—A Global Revisionist?" Valdai Discussion Club, June 12, 2019, https://valdaiclub.com/a/highlights/russia-a-global-revisionist/.

one that Russia shares with many post-imperial states—including Iran. It also informs Russia's critique of the United States' alliances in Europe and Asia. Moscow suggests that Washington's allies are effectively under military occupation and have sacrificed their sovereignty to perpetuate US global domination, questioning why the United States should object to Russia's own efforts at regional domination.[24]

According to Russian officials and analysts, a genuinely multipolar system would be more stable than the existing, essentially unipolar model that emerged after the Soviet collapse, when the United States grew increasingly willing to bypass the UN Security Council and when Russia (and others) found themselves unable to prevent Washington from military intervention in the Balkans, Iraq, or elsewhere. Moscow argues that the United States' post–Cold War unilateralism has become the biggest threat to global order and stability: even as the United States and its allies condemn Russia as a "revisionist actor" seeking to overturn the rules-based international order, Russian officials and analysts reject this charge. They claim that the United States itself is the most dangerous global revisionist.[25] In his notorious speech at the 2007 Munich Security Conference, Putin argued that because of unchecked US power, "no one feels secure" in the current international system, where "one state and, of course, first and foremost the United States, has overstepped its national borders in every sphere."[26]

More recently, the declaration on "International Relations Entering a New Era and Global Sustainable Development" signed by Putin and Chinese president Xi Jinping a few weeks before the invasion of Ukraine claims that "Some forces, representing a minority on the international stage, continue to advocate unilateral approaches to

---

[24]"SShA po suti okkupiruyut Germaniyu, Koreyu i Yaponiyu, no govoryat o ravnopravii s nimi—Putin [The USA Effectively Occupies Germany, Korea and Japan, but Speaks of Equality with Them—Putin]," RIA Novosti, September 30, 2022, https://ria.ru/20220930/ssha-1820624233.html.
[25]Anne L. Clunan, "Russia and the Liberal World Order," *Ethics and International Affairs* 32, no. 1 (2018), 45–59. On Russia as a "revisionist actor," see "Interview with Jake Sullivan," in *A Kennan for Our Times: Revisiting America's Greatest 20th Century Diplomat in the 21st Century*, edited by Michael Kimmage and Matthew Rojanksy (Washington, DC: Woodrow Wilson Center, 2018), https://www.wilsoncenter.org/sites/default/files/media/uploads/documents/Sullivan%20Kennan%20Legacy%20Chapter.pdf.
[26]Vladimir Putin, "Vystuplenie i diskussiya na Myunkhenskoi konferentsii po voprosam politiki bezopasnosti [Address and Discussion at the Munich Security Conference]," The Kremlin, February 10, 2007, http://kremlin.ru/events/president/transcripts/copy/24034.

resolving international problems and resort to the politics of force; they interfere in the internal affairs of other states, promoting contradictions, divisions, and confrontation, preventing the development and progress of humankind, in the face of disapproval on the part of the international community."[27] Or as Putin argued at the 2022 St. Petersburg Economic Forum, the United States at the end of the Cold War "proclaimed itself the emissary of God on earth, with no obligations but only interests, which, by the way, are declared sacred."[28]

According to this view, the idea of a "rules-based" international order is little more than an attempt by the United States and its allies to dictate the norms of international behavior to the rest of the world, bypassing the UN Security Council and other multilateral constraints while imposing its own norms on others. As Foreign Minister Sergey Lavrov wrote in 2021,

> The beauty of these Western "rules" lies precisely in the fact that they lack any specific content. When someone acts against the West's will, it immediately responds with a groundless claim that "the rules have been broken" (without bothering to present any evidence) and declares its "right to hold the perpetrators accountable."[29]

Moscow therefore portrays Washington's commitment to democracy promotion as something akin to the early Soviet Union's aspiration to spread Communism, an ideological obsession that risks global disruption.[30] This concern with democracy promotion as a tool of US geopolitics dates to the first "color revolutions" that broke out in Georgia (2003) and Ukraine (2004), which saw the replacement of post-Soviet

---

[27]"Sovmestnoe zayavlenie Rossiiskoi Federatsii i Kitaiskoi Narodnoi Respubliki o mezhdunarodnykh otnosheniyakh, vstupayushchikh v novuyu epokhu, i global'nom ustoichivom razvitii [Joint Declaration of the Russian Federation and the People's Republic of China on International Relations Entering a New Era and Global Sustainable Development]," The Kremlin, February 4, 2022, http://kremlin.ru/supplement/5770.
[28]Vladimir Putin, "Plenarnoe zasedanie Peterburgskogo mezhdunarodnogo ekonomicheskogo foruma [Plenary Session of the St. Petersburg International Economic Forum]," June 17, 2022, http://kremlin.ru/events/president/news/68669.
[29]Sergey V. Lavrov, "On Law, Rights and Rules," *Russia in Global Affairs*, 19, no. 3 (2021), 228–40, https://eng.globalaffairs.ru/articles/the-law-the-rights-and-the-rules/.
[30]Sergey Lavrov, "Vystuplenie na XXIX Assamblee SVOP [Address at the XXIX Assembly of SVOP]," Russian International Affairs Council, October 4, 2021, https://russiancouncil.ru/analytics-and-comments/comments/vystuplenie-na-xxix-assamblee-svop/.

kleptocracies by Western-leaning governments that sought to promote their democratic credentials as an argument for winning admission to NATO. Coming in the wake of the US invasion of Iraq and the proclamation of the Bush administration's "Freedom Agenda," the color revolutions cemented a widespread Russian perception that the United States had become a revolutionary power, intent on remaking other countries in its own image using whatever tools were available—including military force and also support for political parties, nongovernmental organizations, media outlets, and other elements of civil society.[31] In response, Kremlin adviser Vladislav Surkov in 2006 coined the term "sovereign democracy [*суверенная демократия*]," implying that, as a fully sovereign state, Russia did not need to rely on Western ideas about the meaning of democracy.[32] The description of Russia's political system as a "sovereign democracy" was an important step in the Kremlin's campaign to challenge the "normative hegemony" of Western-style liberalism, with its implication that the West had a monopoly on defining the meaning of political legitimacy for others.[33]

The view of the United States as a revolutionary power intent on forcibly democratizing the rest of the world provides much of the intellectual foundation for contemporary Russian foreign policy, including its alignment with other authoritarian states (notably China), as well as its military interventions and support for embattled authoritarian regimes in the Middle East, Africa, and elsewhere. It also underpins Russia's internal targeting of civil society organizations labeled "foreign agents," as well as efforts to intervene in the political and informational environments of other states. Russian general staff chairman Valery

---

[31]On the Freedom Agenda, see "Institutionalizing the Freedom Agenda: President Bush Calls on Future Presidents and Congresses to Continue Leading the Cause of Freedom Worldwide," U.S. Department of State, October 9, 2008, https://2001-2009.state.gov/r/pa/prs/ps/2008/oct/110871.htm.
[32]On the meaning of this term, see, for instance, "Vladislav Surkov razvel demokratiyu na suverennuyu i upravlyaemuyu [Vladislav Surkov Divided Democracy into Sovereign and Managed]," June 29, 2006, https://www.kommersant.ru/doc/686274; "Suverennaya filologiya 'Suverennaya demokratiya' okazalas' ne natsional'noi ideei, a predmetom diskussii [Sovereign Philology: 'Sovereign Democracy' Turns Out to Be Not a National Idea, but a Topic of Discussion]," Lenta.ru, September 13, 2006, https://lenta.ru/articles/2006/09/13/surkov/.
[33]Igor A. Istomin, "The Logic of Counterpoint: Aspirations of Liberal Hegemony and Counter-Ideological Alignment," *Russia in Global Affairs*, 2 (April/June 2019), 8–34, https://doi.10.31278/1810-6374-2019-17-2-8-34.

Gerasimov's notorious writings on what Western analysts often term "hybrid" warfare reflect a belief that the United States has mastered the art of political interference and that Russia needs to catch up if it is to compete effectively.[34] As Gerasimov observed in 2019, "The emergence of new spheres of confrontation in modern conflicts and methods of warfare increasingly shift towards the integrated application of political, economic, informational, and other non-military measures, realized with reliance on military force."[35]

If Russian elites and officials are generally consistent in arguing that the Western-led order must be changed in fundamental ways, they are less specific about how they would like to overhaul that order. Specific proposals for revamping international architecture are few and generally unrealistic; the two treaties on European security that Moscow proposed to the United States and NATO in the months before its full-scale invasion of Ukraine were described by knowledgeable US observers as "intended to fail."[36] The February 2022 Sino-Russian declaration on International Relations Entering a New Era rehashed vague references to "the central coordinating role of the United Nations … the world order based on international law, … multipolarity and promoting the democratization of international relations."[37] Moscow recognizes that the United States and its allies are unlikely to accept its ideas, but believes (at least until the start of its full-scale war in Ukraine) that time was on its side. According to the well-connected analysts Sergey Karaganov and Dmitry Suslov,

---

[34]Much has been written on Gerasimov and his alleged "doctrine." See especially, V. V. Gerasimov, "Tsennost' nauki v predvidenii [The Value of Science Is in Foresight]," *Voenno-promyshlennyi kur'yer*, February 26, 2013, https://vpk-news.ru/articles/14632; Roger N. McDermott, "Does Russia Have a Gerasimov Doctrine?" *Parameters* 46, no. 1 (2016), https://doi.10.55540/0031-1723.2827; Mark Galleotti, "I'm Sorry for Creating the 'Gerasimov Doctrine,'" *Foreign Policy*, March 5, 2018, https://foreignpolicy.com/2018/03/05/im-sorry-for-creating-the-gerasimov-doctrine/.

[35]Quoted in Michael Kofman, Anya Fink, Dmitry Gorenburg, Mary Chesnut, Jeffrey Edmonds, and Julian Waller, "Russian Military Strategy: Core Tenets and Operational Concepts," Center for Naval Analyses, August 2021, 27, https://www.cna.org/archive/CNA_Files/pdf/russian-military-strategy-core-tenets-and-operational-concepts.pdf.

[36]Steven Pifer, "Russia's Draft Agreements with NATO and the United States: Intended for Rejection?" Brookings Institution, December 21, 2022, https://www.brookings.edu/blog/order-from-chaos/2021/12/21/russias-draft-agreements-with-nato-and-the-united-states-intended-for-rejection/.

[37]"Sovmestnoe zayavlenie Rossiiskoi Federatsii i Kitaiskoi Narodnoi Respubliki [Joint Declaration of the Russian Federation and the People's Republic of China]."

Russia's policy, therefore, is to remain tactically flexible, prepared for every eventuality, but also to be more strategic than ever in building a world order that is stable, peaceful, and comfortable for Russia. As the U.S. and Europe are not ready to engage in order-building with Russia and other major non-Western actors ... a new international order's emergence is more likely to occur in the 2030s or 2040s than in the 2020s, after the inevitable rotation of elites in the U.S. and the E.U.[38]

Iran: Nonalignment and Resistance

Like Russia, Iran criticizes the existing international order for being excessively beholden to the United States and calls for a multipolar alternative. From Tehran's view, such a multipolar system would provide "more opportunities at the regional and international level since the distribution of power along multiple regional poles renders the imposition of a single dominant power untenable."[39] Practically speaking, Tehran envisions a multipolar international system where the United States would not wield such substantial power that it could unilaterally pressure Iran through sanctions or military threats. To that end, Iran will continue to develop and implement policies that accelerate the erosion of US power through several strategies—especially support for the "Axis of Resistance," which includes Syrian president Bashar al-Assad, Palestinian militant groups like Hamas, as well as Iranian-sponsored Shi'a militias in Lebanon, Iraq, Yemen, and elsewhere. Partnerships with outside powers such as Russia and China also support Iran's challenge to US unilateralism and perceived US hegemony—both within the Middle East and globally.[40]

Challenging the US-led international order has been a cornerstone of Iranian grand strategy since the 1979 Islamic Revolution. The 1979 Revolution promised a rejection of Iran's previous dependence on Western

---

[38] Sergei A. Karaganov and Dmitry V. Suslov, "A New World Order: A View from Russia," Russia in International Affairs, October 4, 2018, https://eng.globalaffairs.ru/articles/a-new-world-order-a-view-from-russia/.
[39] Grajewski, "Illusory Entente," 167.
[40] "Chinese TV Says Iran-China Cooperation Major Challenge to U.S. Unilateralism," Islamic Republic News Agency, December 18, 2022, https://en.irna.ir/news/83859280/Chinese-TV-says-Iran-China-cooperation-major-challenge-to-U.S.

allies, even as Tehran remained cool to the officially atheist Soviet Union. For much of the post-revolutionary era, Tehran emphasized the idea of nonalignment as a rejection of Iran's history of foreign domination. Today, Iran perceives an exceptional opportunity to upend the current existing liberal international order by capitalizing on the decline of US hegemony, while also pursuing policies that further erode US power and influence in the regional and international systems. As relations with the United States have again worsened in recent years, Tehran has utilized nonalignment as a vehicle for confronting the United States, including through closer cooperation with other US rivals such as China and Russia.

Within months of the revolution, Iran formally became a member of the Non-Aligned Movement, espousing the shared principles of anti-colonialism, independence, and nonalignment with the United States or USSR in the midst of the Cold War.[41] Nonalignment and resistance to powers as a strategy in post-revolutionary Iran had basis in Shi'a religious ideology, enshrined in the Islamic Republic's constitution, and based on political grievances against the perceived injustices carried out by great powers.[42] Revolutionary leader Ayatollah Ruhollah Khomeini himself often underscored the value of nonalignment, proclaiming "neither East nor West, only an Islamic Republic." In a March 1980 speech, Khomeini encouraged Iranians, especially intellectuals, to "free" themselves of the East or West, to instead "stand on your own feet and refrain from relying on foreigners."[43] From Tehran's perspective, nonalignment today continues to embody many of the same basic principles of the Non-Alignment Movement of the Cold War era: namely anti-colonialism, political and economic independence (rejection of dependency), self-reliance, as well as nonalignment with global superpowers.[44] Rather than

---

[41]"History of NAM and Its Relations with Iran," Islamic Republic News Agency, August 13, 2012, https://en.irna.ir/news/80274417/History-of-NAM-and-its-relations-with-Iran.
[42]For more on those origins, see Houman Sadri, "An Islamic Perspective on Non-alignment: Iranian Foreign Policy in Theory and Practice," *Journal of Third World Studies* 16, no. 2 (1999), 29–46.
[43]"Khomeini, 'We Shall Confront the World with Our Ideology,'" Middle East Report 88 (June 1980), https://merip.org/1980/06/khomeini-we-shall-confront-the-world-with-our-ideology/.
[44]Ali Khamenei, "Supreme Leader's Inaugural Speech at the 16th Non-aligned Summit," Office of the Supreme Leader, August 30, 2012, https://www.leader.ir/en/content/9708/Supreme-Leader%E2%80%99s-Inaugural-Speech-at-the-16th-Non-Aligned-Summit.

two superpowers exercising hegemonic tendencies,[45] in the post–Cold War era, the United States is perceived as one superpower dominating the international system, with a liberal political and economic order it defined.

This emphasis on nonalignment remains central to Tehran's position vis-à-vis the US-led global order, though Iranian assessments of how to implement a nonalignment strategy have varied over time. More dovish presidential administrations, such as those of Mohammad Khatami (1997–2005) or Hassan Rouhani (2013–21), believed that diplomatic rapprochement with the United States would serve Iran's interests. This would not signify an alignment with the West. Rather, resolving the animosity would translate into greater opportunities for Iran to deter security threats and cement its power in the region. In contrast, more hawkish administrations believed that there is no reliable or sustainable option for rapprochement and, consequently, that Iran and other states should bind together in opposition to the West to challenge and eventually change elements of the world order. President Mahmoud Ahmadinejad (2005–13), for instance, forged closer alliances in Latin America after his election in 2005, developing strategic partnerships with Venezuela and later Bolivia and Ecuador, all of which shared similar anti-Western sentiments.[46] Ahmadinejad leveraged these relationships to relieve some economic pressure due to sanctions and to cultivate an extra-regional base of operations for Iran's network of nonstate actors, notably Hezbollah.[47]

Iranian leaders believe that the current liberal international order is a vehicle for US domination in political, military, and economic spheres. The institutions, norms, and values that shape interactions within the international community are all perceived by Tehran as the United States exerting its influence to pursue its interest with such substantial power that the United States can compel states to behave accordingly or face serious consequences. In a 2012 speech at the Non-Aligned Movement Summit hosted by Iran, supreme leader Ayatollah Ali Khamenei directly critiqued the international liberal order and its primary architect, the

---

[45]Fouad Ajami, "The Fate of Nonalignment," *Foreign Affairs* 59, no. 2 (Winter 1980–1), https://www.foreignaffairs.com/world/fate-nonalignment.

[46]Joseph M. Humire and Ilan Berman, eds. *Iran's Strategic Penetration of Latin America*, Lanham, MD: Lexington Books, 2014, 15.

[47]Humire and Berman, *Iran's Strategic Penetration*.

United States, characterizing the UN Security Council as an "improper mechanism" exploited by the United States to protect and advance its own interests, or "to disguise their bullying as noble concepts and impose them on the world."[48] He expanded:

> They protect the interests of the West in the name of "human rights." They interfere militarily in other countries in the name of "democracy." They target defenseless people in villages and cities with their bombs and weapons in the name of "fighting terrorism" … They impose their interests on the nations of the world in the name of "international law" … They impose their domineering and illegal words in the name of "international community."[49]

President Ebrahim Raisi reiterated these sentiments in his 2022 speech at the UN General Assembly, describing how "America has pursued their interests at the expense of other countries and cannot accept the fact that certain countries have the right to stand on their own two feet."[50] Simply put, Tehran views Western dominance as a threat to its own national interests and prefers/advocates for an international order that would afford it the freedom to grow its power and influence in the region and globally.

The US withdrawal from the JCPOA underscored Tehran's concerns, especially among hardliners who were the weariest of its engagement with the West. Iran has paid a hefty price, facing decades of comprehensive and severe economic sanctions that, at a minimum, contributed greatly to Iran's economic woes.[51] Despite its efforts to build a "resistance economy," Iran's economy is still very much impacted by US influence and policies, with growth being more dependent on integration into the international community than Iran's own industries.[52] As sanctions were

---

[48]"Supreme Leader's Inaugural Speech at the 16th Non-Aligned Summit."
[49]"Supreme Leader's Inaugural Speech."
[50]Aya Batrawy, "Watch: Iranian President Ebrahim Raisi Addresses the 2022 United Nations General Assembly," PBS, September 21, 2022, https://www.pbs.org/newshour/world/watch-iranian-president-ebrahim-raisi-addresses-the-2022-united-nations-general-assembly.
[51]Djavad Salehi-Isfahani, "The Simple Reason Iran's Economy Stopped Growing," Bourse and Bazaar Foundation, August 25, 2022, https://www.bourseandbazaar.com/tyranny-of-numbers/2022/5/3/the-simple-reason-irans-economy-stopped-growing.
[52]Ray Takeyh, "Iran's 'Resistance Economy' Debate," Council on Foreign Relations, April 7, 2016, https://www.cfr.org/expert-brief/irans-resistance-economy-debate.

lifted as a result of the JCPOA, Tehran realized a 20 percent increase in its GDP, which immediately declined after the US withdrawal from the agreement. The remaining parties to the JCPOA were unable to effectively circumvent US sanctions to provide Iran the sanctions relief promised in exchange for its compliance.[53] The mere fact that the withdrawal of the single most powerful party of a multilateral deal effectively killed the deal (and with it, the hopes of economic relief) has reinforced Tehran's perceptions and interests in creating a multipolar order.

From Dreams to Realities: Russo-Iranian Cooperation against the Liberal Order

In practical terms, their common antipathy to the US-led global order provides a basis for Russia and Iran to collaborate on advancing a normative critique of the international status quo, sharing strategies and tools for more effective authoritarian rule, pursuing the construction of multilateral cooperation frameworks outside the "liberal international order," and cooperating bilaterally to check US objectives—including now in Ukraine. Such cooperation is helping cement a more durable Russo-Iranian partnership, even as Moscow and Tehran remain at odds over a range of issues in their shared periphery—including the Middle East and the South Caucasus. This partnership rests on reducing the centrality of the United States in the global system, excluding the United States and other outside powers from the Middle East, and legitimating both nondemocratic forms of rule and the rights of major states to intervene in the affairs of their smaller neighbors—while jealously guarding their own sovereignty.

Authoritarian Solidarity and Learning

According to Hal Brands, Russia, Iran, and other modern authoritarian powers increasingly see the world as ideologically divided, with

---

[53] Djavad Salehi-Isfahani, "The Road to Iran's 'Resistance Economy' Passes through a Revived JCPOA," *Responsible Statecraft*, July 13, 2022, https://responsiblestatecraft.org/2022/07/13/the-road-to-the-irans-resistance-economy-passes-through-a-revived-jcpoa/.

their respective forms of authoritarianism serving as "more than an approach to governing or a means of enriching a corrupt ruling class," and also as "a distinctive way of looking at the world" that they share and seek to legitimate at the global level.[54] As popular mobilization has increasingly challenged their existing regimes, Russia and Iran—along with other authoritarian states—have moved ideologically to assert the legitimacy not only of their own systems but also of nondemocratic rule in general.

Russia and Iran have been at the forefront of efforts by authoritarian states to share "best practices" around the preservation of autocratic rule. They are among the authoritarian regimes whose growing resilience is enhanced by learning from the success and failures of counterparts and opportunities to cooperate to advance their self and mutual interests.[55] This learning process can accelerate a regime's consolidation of power, strengthen its durability in the face of domestic uprising or external threat, or foster an alternative model of governance.[56] Mechanisms of policy transfer and diffusion via authoritarian learning foster the development of an authoritarian political model less dependent on a particular form of government, but instead centered on principles of "blunting" democracy promotion in favor of state sovereignty.[57]

This emphasis on refining authoritarian rule's tools and techniques is consistent with Russia and Iran's shared history of seeking modernization without Westernization—or "modernization without modernity."[58] In practical terms, Russo-Iranian cooperation in making the world "safe for authoritarianism" encompasses converging approaches to the operation of security services, control over the information environment, controlling civil society, surveilling political opponents, and promoting economic development under Western sanctions. Since the start of Russia's war in

---

[54] Hal Brands, "Democracy vs. Authoritarianism: How Ideology Shape Great Power Competition," *Survival* 60 (2018), 66.

[55] Stephen G. F. Hall and Thomas Ambrosio, "Authoritarian Learning: A Conceptual Overview," *East European Politics* 33, no. 2 (2017), 144–5.

[56] Adam Hug, ed., "Sharing Worst Practice: How Countries and Institutions in the Former Soviet Union Help Create Legal Tools of Repression," https://fpc.org.uk/wp-content/uploads/2016/05/1749.pdf

[57] Thomas Ambrosio, "Constructing a Framework of Authoritarian Diffusion: Concepts, Dynamics, and Future Research," *International Studies Perspective* 11 (2010), 376–7.

[58] Ghoncheh Tazmini, "'To Be or Not to Be' (Like the West): Modernisation in Russia and Iran," *Third World Quarterly* 39 (2018), 1998–2015.

Ukraine, that cooperation has expanded to include agreement for the coproduction of weapons systems not reliant on Western technologies.[59]

Internet Control

In the information space, Iran and Russia are among the handful of authoritarian states seeking to develop domestic "splinternets" independent of, and separable from, the global internet. While China and other authoritarian states employ various forms of online censorship, Russia and Iran have adopted a distinct approach emphasizing physical control of infrastructure and separate Domain Name Systems (DNSs). In contrast to, for instance, China's "Great Firewall," which can be pierced using a virtual private network (VPN), the Russo-Iranian model could be wholly isolated from the global internet.[60]

First raised in the aftermath of the Crimea annexation, the idea of physically walling off the Russian internet, or RUnet, from the global internet reflects the Kremlin's concern with maintaining sovereignty over the information environment. Russia's 2016 Information Security Concept criticizes "the desire of individual states to use their technological superiority to dominate the information space" and calls for the "development of a national system for administering the Russian segment of the Internet."[61] Work on developing the capacity to isolate the RUnet accelerated around 2019, with the adoption of a draft law and the announcement of plans for a separate DNS and the domestic hosting of almost all web traffic.[62]

---

[59] Joby Warrick, Souad Mekhennet, and Ellen Nakashima, "Iran Will Help Russia Build Drones for Ukraine War, Western Officials Say," *Washington Post*, November 19, 2022, https://www.washingtonpost.com/national-security/2022/11/19/russia-iran-drones-secret-deal/.
[60] Justin Sherman, "Russia and Iran Plan to Fundamentally Isolate the Internet," *Wired*, June 6, 2019, https://www.wired.com/story/russia-and-iran-plan-to-fundamentally-isolate-the-internet/.
[61] "Doktrina informatsionnoi bezopasnosti Rossiiskoi Federatsii [Doctrine of Information Security of the Russian Federation]," Security Council of the Russian Federation, December 5, 2016, http://www.scrf.gov.ru/security/information/document5/.
[62] For an overview of the RUnet's development, see Robert Morgus and Justin Sherman, "Analysis: Russia's Plan for a National Internet," New America, February 19, 2019, https://www.newamerica.org/cybersecurity-initiative/c2b/c2b-log/russias-plans-for-a-national-internet/.

Though the idea had already been circulating since 2005, the then Iranian president Rouhani (under pressure from conservative clerics) announced similar plans for a separate Iran-based "halal internet" in 2016. Iran invested heavily in what was officially termed the "Iranian National Information Network (NIN)" and, by the 2019 protests, when Iran shut down the internet, "it was clear that the NIN could function independently," though not totally without issue.[63] According to the 2022 Freedom on the Net report by Freedom House, Iran's Supreme Council for Cyberspace (SCC) began meetings focused on expanding the NIN within the next five years, indicating a strong commitment on Iran's part to strengthen the network.[64]

Economic Decoupling

Financial transactions are another area where Russian and Iranian efforts to blunt the effects of US influence have promoted both convergence and cooperation. The two countries explored wider adoption of a Russian alternative to the globally dominant SWIFT payments messaging system after the United States compelled SWIFT to cut off Iranian banks in 2012.[65] Chinese and Russian stakeholders, as part of their support for the Iran nuclear deal, praised the EU's Instrument in Support of Trade Exchanges (INSTEX) project adopted as a workaround when the Trump administration withdrew from the JCPOA in 2018, suggesting that it could be expanded to include their participation.[66] A fully functional INSTEX would be a significant step toward advancing the objective, shared by Russia, Iran, and many other authoritarian states, of reducing the centrality of the US dollar to the global financial architecture.

---

[63] Ryan Grace, "Shatter the Web: Internet Fragmentation in Iran," Middle East Institute, February 1, 2023, https://www.mei.edu/publications/shatter-web-internet-fragmentation-iran.

[64] "Iran: Freedom on the Net 2022 Country Report," Freedom House, 2022, https://freedomhouse.org/country/iran/freedom-net/2022; Sophie Bushwick, "How Iran Is Using the Protests to Block More Open Internet Access," *Scientific American*, October 13, 2022, https://www.scientificamerican.com/article/how-iran-is-using-the-protests-to-block-more-open-internet-access/.

[65] "Russia Weighs Local Alternative to Swift Payment System—Agencies," Reuters, August 27, 2014, https://www.reuters.com/article/russia-banks-swift/russia-weighs-local-alternative-to-swift-payment-system-agencies-idUSL5N0QX33W20140827.

[66] "Russia Welcomes INSTEX Progress," *Tehran Times*, April 3, 2020, https://www.tehrantimes.com/news/446430/Russia-welcomes-INSTEX-progress.

With Russia's own financial system facing the prospect of being cut off from SWIFT after the annexation of Crimea, Moscow moved to create its own domestically based alternative known as the SPFS (Система передачи финансовых сообщений, System for Transfer of Financial Messages) as well as the Mir (Мир) payment card system as an alternative to the US-based MasterCard and Visa.[67] With the sanctions imposed over Russia's 2022 war in Ukraine, Moscow pivoted a larger share of its foreign transactions to these networks. Because of US and EU pressure on allies and partner states to sever financial links with Moscow, fellow "pariah" states like Iran and China stand to be the major users of such alternatives. Tehran has indicated an interest in using currency swaps and Russian (or Russo-Chinese) payment mechanisms to bypass sanctions, and from the spring of 2022, press reports indicated that Iran's Central Bank was in negotiations to join Mir.[68] While these protocols have yet to gain widespread acceptance, they provided a proof of concept for bypassing the US-led global financial architecture that could become more important should large-scale sanctions on both Russia and Iran endure.

Non-Western Multilateralism

Among the most lasting products of Russo-Iranian cooperation is the proliferation of multilateral frameworks and institutions—many with a regional focus on Eurasia—outside the boundaries of the US-led order. Both informal groupings, like the Astana Framework for Syria, and more formal institutions, such as the Shanghai Cooperation Organization (SCO), help consolidate multilateral cooperation outside Western-dominated frameworks while also providing institutional ballast for relations among authoritarian powers. They represent a kind of "illiberal

---

[67] Polina Smorodskaya, "SWIFT dlya malen'kikh [SWIFT for the Small]," *Kommersant*, May 19, 2020, https://www.kommersant.ru/doc/4348494.
[68] Steven Terner, "A China-Russia SWIFT Alternative Will Not Undermine Iran Sanctions," Washington Institute for Near East Policy, February 25, 2022, https://www.washingtoninstitute.org/policy-analysis/china-russia-swift-alternative-will-not-undermine-iran-sanctions; Tatyana Akinshina, "Rossiya i Iran obsuzhdayut priznanie 'Mira' i peredachu finsoobshchenii v obkhod SWIFT [Russia and Iran Discuss Recognition of 'Mir' and Transmission of Financial Data Bypassing SWIFT]," *Kommersant*, March 24, 2022, https://www.kommersant.ru/doc/5272074.

internationalism," where states seek cooperation on areas of common interest without committing to respect liberal values.[69]

Russia has been at the forefront of efforts to construct non-Western, non-liberal multilateral bodies on the territory of the former Soviet Union since the 1990s. For long something of an international pariah, Iran has had more limited opportunities for joining, much less creating new regional bodies. With growing challenges to US hegemony and the erosion of the US-led order, both Moscow and Tehran have taken advantage of opportunities to forge new frameworks for multilateral cooperation. What most of these frameworks share is a regional focus, an emphasis on noninterference in members' internal affairs, agnosticism (at best) about liberal norms, and a commitment to regime security. This emphasis is best captured in the SCO's commitment to fighting the "three evils" of extremism, separatism, and terrorism.[70] Likewise, Moscow and Tehran's growing emphasis on internet sovereignty is in keeping with, and legitimated by reference to, the commitment to "ensuring international information security" adopted by the SCO's member states at the organization's June 2009 summit in Yekaterinburg, Russia.[71]

While some Russian thinkers and analysts have long promoted Eurasian regionalism as the crucible for a new non-Western international order, for much of the post-Soviet period, Moscow pursued regional integration as a strategy for managing the breakup of the USSR and slowing, if not reversing, the drift of the smaller post-Soviet states out of Moscow's strategic orbit.[72] With the collapse of hopes for Russia's integration with the Euro-Atlantic West and the growth of strategic competition between Moscow and Washington, the Kremlin pivoted to

---

[69]Philippa Hetherington and Glenda Sluga, "Liberal and Illiberal Internationalisms," *Journal of World History* 31, no. 1 (2020), 1–9, https://doi.org/10.1353/jwh.2020.0000.
[70]On the commitment to fighting the "three evils," see "Общие сведения," Shanghai Cooperation Organization, https://rus.sectsco.org (accessed January 30, 2024). Also see "Shankhaiskaya konventsiya o bor'be s terrorizmom, separatizmom i ekstremizmom [Shanghai Convention on the Struggle against Terrorism, Separatism and Extremism]," The Kremlin, June 14, 2001, http://www.kremlin.ru/supplement/3405.
[71]"Soglashenie mezhdu pravitel'stvami gosudarstv-chlenov ShOS o sotrudnichestve v oblasti obespecheniya mezhdunarodnoi informatsionnoi bezopasnosti [Agreement between Member State Governments of the SCO on Cooperation in the Field of Securing International Information Security]," Shanghai Cooperation Organization, June 16, 2009, https://ccdcoe.org/uploads/2018/11/SCO-090616-IISAgreementRussian-1.pdf.
[72]On competing ideas of Eurasian regionalism, see Alexander Libman and Evgeny Vinokurov, *Eurasian Integration: Challenges of Trans-Continental Regionalism* (Basingstoke: Palgrave Macmillan, 2012).

a more geopolitical (and ideological) vision of Eurasian regionalism. The construction of organizations like the Eurasian Economic Union and the Collective Security Treaty Organization are part of a deliberate strategy of consolidating a Russo-centric Eurasia as what Putin termed "one of the poles in the modern world and ... an efficient bridge between Europe and the dynamic Asia-Pacific region," and a rejection of the idea that Russia can integrate itself into a globalized world dominated by the West.[73]

More recently, Russian attempts to build a "Greater Eurasia Partnership" linked to China's Belt and Road Initiative suggest an ambition to extend this attempt at consolidating a Eurasia-based alternative to the Western-led order beyond the borders of the former Soviet Union.[74] Iran too has a role in this vision, signing a preferential trade agreement with the Eurasian Economic Union in 2019 and agreements for membership in the SCO in late 2022.[75] The international North-South Transit Corridor (NSTC), a multimodal transit project connecting Russia to South Asia via Iranian ports, could also become an important platform for Russo-Iranian cooperation (and sanctions evasion) following the inaugural shipment of goods along the route in July 2022.[76]

---

[73]Vladimir Putin, "A New Integration Project for Eurasia: The Future in the Making," Russian Embassy to the United Kingdom, October 4, 2011, https://www.rusemb.org.uk/press/246; Dmitri Trenin, *The End of Eurasia: Russia on the Border between Geopolitics and Globalization* (Washington, DC: Carnegie Endowment, 2002); Marcin Kaczmarski, "Non-Western Visions of Regionalism: China's New Silk Road and Russia's Eurasian Economic Union," *International Affairs* 93, no. 6 (November 2017), 1357–76, https://doi.org/10.1093/ia/iix182; David Lewis, "Geopolitical Imaginaries in Russian Foreign Policy: The Evolution of Greater Eurasia," *Europe-Asia Studies* 70, no. 10 (2018), 1612–37, https://doi.org/10.1080/09668136.2018.1515348.

[74]"K velikomu okeanu: Ot povorota na vostok k Bol'shoi Yevrazii [Toward the Great Ocean: From the Pivot to the East to Greater Eurasia]," *K velikomu okeanu: khronika povorota na vostok* [Toward the Great Ocean: A Chronicle of the Pivot to the East], edited by S. A. Karaganov and T. V. Bordachev (Moscow: Valdai, 2017), 242–303; Sergey Luzyanin, "Bol'shaya Yevraziya: obshchie zadachi dlya Kitaya i Rossii [Greater Eurasia: Common Tasks for China and Russia]," Valdai Discussion Club, April 16, 2018, https://ru.valdaiclub.com/a/highlights/bolshaya-evraziya-zadachi.

[75]Vali Kaleji, "Iran and Eurasian Economic Union Negotiations: Upgrading EAEU-Iran Preferential Trade Agreement into a Free Trade Agreement," Russian International Affairs Council, January 24, 2022, https://russiancouncil.ru/en/analytics-and-comments/columns/middle-east-policy/iran-and-eurasian-economic-union-negotiations-upgrading-eaeu-iran-preferential-trade-agreement-into-/; Umud Shokri, "Iran and the Shanghai Cooperation Organization," Carnegie Endowment, November 16, 2022, https://carnegieendowment.org/sada/88427.

[76]Jonathan Tirone and Golnar Motevalli, "Russia and Iran Are Building a Trade Route That Defies Sanctions," Bloomberg, December 21, 2022, https://www.bloomberg.com/graphics/2022-russia-iran-trade-corridor/.

From Tehran's view, participation in regional or international organizations, especially non-Western oriented ones, further contributes toward a power shift away from the West. In 2005, Iran secured observer status in the SCO and in 2021 signed a memorandum to begin the accession process for full membership status. Membership provides Tehran a boost to its international prestige and legitimacy, a consolidation of its regional partnerships, and, most importantly, a direct challenge to hegemony, insofar as it views the SCO as an "anti-Western" organization and building block for creating a multipolar international system.[77] Even as the SCO faces difficulty in accomplishing the ambitious cooperation goals it seeks, it serves as an important symbolic development in the role of power and non-Western norms in the international system.

Russo-Iranian (and Turkish) cooperation in Syria through the Astana Framework represents a less institutionalized example of this pursuit of multilateralism outside the framework of the US-led order. Despite the long history of rivalry between Iran and Russia in the Middle East, Washington's efforts to contain Iran (including the imposition of sanctions over its nuclear program) prompted Tehran to adopt a "Look to the East" policy in the mid-2000s that encompassed Russia as a potential bulwark against American pressure. Tehran views today's shift to the East as an opportunity, not just to circumvent its international isolation, but more importantly, as an opportunity to consolidate power to establish an alternative world order, starting with Iran's immediate neighborhood.[78]

Though both Moscow and Tehran supported Syrian president Bashar al-Assad against the foreign-backed rebels and Sunni Islamists seeking to oust his Alawite-led regime, their collaboration in Syria remains limited and wary.[79] Russia opposes Tehran's sectarian approach and its efforts to

---

[77]Nicole Grajewski, "Iranian Membership in the Shanghai Cooperation Organization: Motivations and Implications," Washington Institute for Near Eastern Policy, September 15, 2021, https://www.washingtoninstitute.org/policy-analysis/iranian-membership-shanghai-cooperation-organization-motivations-and-implications.

[78]Annalisa Perteghella, ed. *Iran Looking East: An Alternative to the EU?* (Milan: ISPI), 7, https://www.ispionline.it/sites/default/files/pubblicazioni/ispi_iran_looking_web.pdf.

[79]Charles Lister, "Russia, Iran, and the Competition to Shape Syria's Future," Middle East Institute, September 12, 2019, https://www.mei.edu/publications/russia-iran-and-competition-shape-syrias-future. On Russian objectives in Syria, see Anna Borchevskaya, *Putin's War in Syria: Russian Foreign Policy and the Price of America's Absence* (London: I.B. Tauris, 2022), 69–126. On Iran, see Hassan Ahmadian and Payam Mohseni, "Iran's Syria Strategy: The Evolution of Deterrence," *International Affairs* 95, no. 2 (2019), 341–64, https://doi.10.1093/ia/iiy271.

consolidate Shi'ite power in both Syria and its neighbors. Russia seeks to work not just with many of Iran's regional rivals (including Israel, the United Arab Emirates, and Saudi Arabia, along with Turkey), but has also developed a de-confliction mechanism allowing Israel to carry out strikes on Iranian and Hezbollah targets in Syria using Russian-controlled airspace.[80] Iran, meanwhile, is wary of Russia's long-term military deployments to the region; although the two have cooperated to an extent in Syria, it remains an "uneasy alliance."[81]

The Astana Format, named for the Kazakh capital where the first meeting was held, emerged in early 2017, following the failure of Moscow's efforts to work with the United States on a plan for ending the conflict bilaterally.[82] The Astana Framework operated parallel to UN-mediated talks in Geneva, which the United States and other Western powers continued to prioritize. Unlike the Geneva talks, the Astana Framework brought together actors from the region who had a direct stake in the outcome of the Syrian conflict. Russia, Iran, and Turkey had each intervened with their own forces in the conflict, seeking economic and strategic gain. As shown by Hamidreza Azizi in his chapter, though all three participants backed different proxies and had different visions for Syria's ideal end-state, they were able to work together pragmatically, recognizing the legitimacy of one another's interests and the need for mutual accommodation—even amid the kind of coercive bargaining tactics usually lacking from interactions within US-led institutions.[83]

Though the Astana Framework resolved neither the litany of disputes between Ankara, Moscow, and Tehran nor the wider conflict in Syria, it did provide an important demonstration that non-Western, illiberal, and

---

[80] Giorgio Cafiero, "Israel's Working Relationship with Russia Inside Syria," *Inside Arabia*, November 16, 2021, https://insidearabia.com/israels-working-relationship-with-russia-inside-syria/.

[81] Jon Alterman and Hanna Notte, "Russia in the Middle East after Ukraine," Center for Strategic and International Studies, January 24, 2023, https://www.csis.org/analysis/russia-middle-east-after-ukraine.

[82] Andrey Kortunov, "The Astana Model: Methods and Ambitions of Russian Political Action," in *The MENA Region: A Great Power Competition*, edited by Karim Mezran and Arturo Varvelli (Washington, DC: Atlantic Council, 2021), 53–63.

[83] "Turkey, Syria, Russia to Hold New Talks on Civil War, Terrorism," Bloomberg, January 1, 2023, https://www.bloomberg.com/news/articles/2023-01-01/turkey-syria-russia-to-hold-new-talks-on-civil-war-terrorism; Sam Heller, "Turkey's Russian Red Light in Syria," War on the Rocks, December 30, 2022, https://warontherocks.com/2022/12/turkeys-russian-red-light-in-syria/.

post-imperialist powers can manage regional conflicts without relying on US-led institutions. In that sense, it will likely serve as a model for conflict management involving these states elsewhere (indeed, Russia and Turkey have developed similar patterns of cooperation to manage their conflicts in Libya and the South Caucasus).[84] It remains an open question whether Moscow and Tehran will be able to extend this kind of cooperation to the wider Middle East, where Russia's reemergence as a power broker has complicated the calculations of all regional players, including Iran—even if setbacks in Ukraine have called into question the durability of Russia's newfound Middle Eastern influence.[85] Though Tehran officially welcomed Russia's call for the creation of an "inclusive" regional security system for the Persian Gulf modeled on the Conference on Security and Cooperation in Europe (CSCE), the involvement of Israel and possibly insurmountable differences over nuclear weapons are likely to limit Tehran's enthusiasm in practice.[86]

Bilateral Cooperation and the War in Ukraine

Iran's support for the Russian war effort in Ukraine hints at the emergence of a more durable Russo-Iranian axis, united by the shared opposition to US leadership of the global order and the threat to regime security each perceives from it. While Iran's initial attitude to the war in Ukraine was cautious, as the conflict has dragged on, it has emerged as Russia's most important source of military support (other Russian partners—notably

---

[84] Jeffrey Mankoff, "Regional Competition and the Future of Russia-Turkey Relations: A World Safe for Empire?" Center for Strategic and International Studies, January 2022, https://www.csis.org/analysis/regional-competition-and-future-russia-turkey-relations.
[85] Pavel K. Baev, "Russian Influence Fades in the Middle East," Jamestown Foundation Eurasia Daily Monitor, November 28, 2022, https://jamestown.org/program/russian-influence-fades-in-the-middle-east/.
[86] "Lavrov: kontesptsiya RF po Persidskomu zalivu podtazumyvaet voenno-politicheskuyu koordinatsiyu [Lavrov: RF Convention on the Persian Gulf Implies Military-Political Coordination]," TASS, February 21, 2022, https://tass.ru/politika/13779363. For the text of the Russian proposal, see "Rossiiskaya Kontseptsiya kollektivnoi bezopasnosti v zone Persidskogo zaliva [The Russian Collective Security Concept in the Persian Gulf zone]," Russian Ministry of Foreign Affairs, August 24, 2021, https://archive.mid.ru/ru/foreign_policy/international_safety/conflicts/-/asset_publisher/xIEMTQ3OvzcA/content/id/3733575. On Iranian skepticism, see Hanna Notte and Hamidreza Azizi, "Will Iran Accept Russia's Idea for a Middle East Regional Security Process?" Valdai Discussion Club, April 8, 2022, https://valdaiclub.com/a/highlights/will-iran-accept-russia-s-ideas-for-a-middle-east/.

China—have been cautious precisely because of their dependence on the US-led financial system and other global institutions). Both Moscow and Tehran perceive the war through the lens of their strategic and systemic confrontation with the United States. While Iran has few concrete interests at stake in Ukraine, it is providing Moscow military support out of a calculation that a Russian victory will strike a blow at the wider US-led order that Iran too opposes.

The months since the outbreak of the war have seen an intensification of Russo-Iranian diplomatic contacts. Iranian leaders have publicly embraced Russia's portrayal of the invasion as a response to NATO expansion and US efforts at containment.[87] With sanctions imposing increasing costs on Russia's military-industrial complex, Iran has emerged as a major supplier of weapons and training for Russian forces, in the process cementing its own isolation from the United States and the EU as hopes for a return to the JCPOA fade.

Russian and Iranian leaders held a record number of meetings among senior officials in 2022, focusing on economic and investment agreements as well as lessons on building a model of a resistance economy; Putin made his first trip outside the former USSR after the start of the war to Tehran and met with Raisi twice more before the end of the year.[88] Like China, Iran has largely echoed Russian talking points about responsibility for the war lying with the West. In a call with Putin on the first day of the war, Raisi stated, "NATO's expansion eastward creates tension and is a serious threat to the stability and security of independent states in various areas. I hope what is happening will benefit people and the entire region."[89]

This tacit support was counter to Iran's position of objecting to "imperialism," for long a source of Iranian grievance (notably, Iran itself has been a target of Russian imperial expansion on numerous occasions until the aftermath of the Second World War). Iranian officials specifically linked their support for Moscow to efforts at consolidating a more

---

[87]"Iran Blames NATO 'Provocation' for Russian War on Ukraine," Al-Monitor, February 24, 2022, https://www.al-monitor.com/originals/2022/02/iran-blames-nato-provocation-russian-war-ukraine.
[88]Nikita Smagin, "Comrades-in-Sanctions: Can Iran Help Russia Weather the Economic Storm?" Carnegie Endowment, November 4, 2022, https://carnegieendowment.org/politika/88318.
[89]"Iranian President Tells Putin That NATO's Expansion Is 'Serious Threat' to Region's Security and Stability," Reuters, February 24, 2022, https://www.reuters.com/world/iranian-president-tells-putin-that-natos-expansion-is-serious-threat-regions-2022-02-24/.

multipolar order. In an April 2022 meeting, Ayatollah Khamenei argued that "the issues of the recent war in Ukraine should be seen more deeply and in context of the formation of a new world order."[90] Similarly, Putin suggested that the crisis touched off by Russia's invasion had created new opportunities for "all civilizations, states, and their integration institutions … [to develop] their own, democratic, and original development path."[91]

Beyond rhetorical support, Iran has increasingly provided weapons to Russia, which has rapidly depleted its own stocks and struggled to produce new systems in the face of US/European sanctions and export controls. Particularly noteworthy has been Iran's provision of drones and loitering munitions that have been used in deadly attacks across Ukraine. The provision of Iranian weapons to Russia represents a twist on Tehran's long-standing efforts to acquire Russian weapons, one that could cement a mutual dependence between two of the most prominent antagonists of the current international order and which find themselves increasingly shut out from deals with Western arms manufacturers.

Iran has provided Russia hundreds of *Shahed* loitering munitions, mainly employed for attacks on Ukrainian infrastructure—though claiming that deliveries were made before the outbreak of the war in February 2022.[92] US officials have confirmed Iranian involvement on the ground, and some Western commentators have even called for strikes against Iranian targets involved in producing or shipping weapons to Russia.[93] In late November 2022, Ukrainian missile strike reportedly

---

[90] Supreme Leader Khamenei cited in Javad Heiran-Nia, "How Iran's Interpretation of the World Order Affects Its Foreign Policy," Atlantic Council, May 11, 2022, https://www.atla nticcouncil.org/blogs/iransource/how-irans-interpretation-of-the-world-order-affects-its-foreign-policy/.

[91] Vladimir Putin, "Zasedanie Mezhdunarodnogo diskussionogo kluba 'Valdai' [Meeting of the Valdai Discussion Club]," The Kremlin, October 27, 2022, http://kremlin.ru/events/president/news/69695.

[92] Cassandra Vinograd, "Iran's Foreign Minister Acknowledges That Drones Were Sent to Russia, but Says It Happened before the War," *New York Times*, November 5, 2022, https://www.nytimes.com/2022/11/05/world/europe/irans-foreign-minister-acknowledges-that-drones-were-sent-to-russia-but-says-it-happened-before-the-war.html.

[93] John Hardie and Benham Ben Talebu, "Iran Is Now at War with Ukraine," *Foreign Policy*, October 26, 2022, https://foreignpolicy.com/2022/10/26/iran-ukraine-russia-war-drones-missiles-military-advisors-middle-east-nuclear/; David E. Sanger, "United States Enters a New Era of Direct Confrontation with Iran," *New York Times*, November 24, 2022, https://www.nytimes.com/2022/11/24/us/politics/iran-protests-ukraine-nuclear-enrichm ent.html.

killed several Iranian troops deployed to Crimea to train Russians on Iranian drones.[94]

The decision to acquire Iranian weapons is at once a consequence of international sanctions and export controls that have dramatically impacted Russia's ability to produce drones and other modern weapons domestically. Meanwhile, Tehran stands to gain access to advanced Russian capabilities. In late 2022, Israeli sources reported that Russia was prepared to sell dozens of SU-35 fighter jets to Tehran, potentially upending the local power balance between Iran and Israel, complicating Israeli strategy in Syria, and threatening to undermine the *modus vivendi* between Jerusalem and Moscow.[95] In that sense, this emerging Russo-Iranian defense partnership could further complicate US objectives in both Europe and the Middle East, while reinforcing the two states' shared challenge to the US-led order.

Conclusion

The more the United States and its allies succeed in isolating Russia and Iran, the more likely they are to focus their cooperation on challenging the legitimacy of the US-led order. Expanding efforts to isolate and contain them, along with recognition among elites in both states about the fragility of their respective regimes, have conspired to simultaneously push Moscow and Tehran in the direction of open revisionism. It is consequently not surprising that the war in Ukraine has become a pivotal moment in the convergence of Russo-Iranian critiques of the global order and a catalyst for deepening Russo-Iranian pragmatic cooperation.

Iran and Russia, of course, are not the only states worried about the implications of a global order dominated by the United States and that—in principle, if not always in practice—regards liberal democracy as the only legitimate form of rule. Along with Xi Jinping's China and perhaps a few others, though, they are unique by virtue of not merely seeking to vindicate authoritarian rule but also asserting special privileges for

---

[94] Julian Borger, "Iranian Advisers Killed Aiding Russians in Crimea, Says Kyiv," *The Guardian*, November 24, 2022, https://www.theguardian.com/world/2022/nov/24/iranian-military-advisers-killed-aiding-moscow-in-crimea-kyiv.
[95] "Report: Russia to Supply Iran with Dozens of Sukhoi SU-35 Fighter Jets," *Times of Israel*, December 25, 2022, https://www.timesofisrael.com/report-russia-to-supply-with-iran-with-dozens-of-sukhoi-su-35-fighter-jets/.

themselves by virtue of their historical-cultural status. In their current incarnations, Iran and Russia portray themselves as heirs to long imperial traditions that they use to legitimate claims to a sphere of influence in their respective regions and—particularly in Russia's case—to seize territory from their smaller, weaker neighbors. Their opposition to the US-led order is, consequently, both ideological, in the sense of seeking to make the world "safe for autocracy," and irredentist and expansionary in seeking a world "safe for empire."[96]

At the same time, the durability of the current Russo-Iranian alignment remains uncertain. Despite their parallel critiques of the US-led international order and efforts to insulate themselves from Western influence, Russia and Iran remain ambitious powers with competing objectives in key regions. Though both have been instrumental to the survival of the Assad regime in Syria and would like to see a reduced US presence in the region, their long-term goals diverge. Russia's interest in maintaining its inherited status as a regional power broker in the South Caucasus and its cultivation of Azerbaijan, meanwhile, pose a challenge for Iran, which accuses Baku of promoting separatism among the large ethnic Azeri population in northern Iran and providing military assistance to archfoe Israel.[97] Tehran is also wary of a possible peace deal between Armenia and Azerbaijan, which would open new transit corridors and reduce Tehran's leverage over both Baku and Yerevan.[98]

As argued by Jakub M. Godzimirski and Esfandyar Batmanghelidj in their chapters, Iran and Russia also find themselves navigating competition and cooperation in the energy sector. With the imposition of sanctions on Russian energy companies, Tehran and Moscow are struggling for market share in China and the limited number of other states willing to buy their oil and gas at a discount—even as Russian

---

[96]Jeffrey Mankoff, *Empires of Eurasia: How Imperial Legacies Shape International Security* (New Haven, CT: Yale University Press, 2022), 1–15; Jessica Chen Weiss, "A World Safe for Autocracy? China's Rise and the Future of Global Politics," *Foreign Affairs* 98, no. 4 (July/August 2019), 92–102.

[97]"'Iranskii lev' poteryaet golovu. Yuzhnyi Azerbaidzhan stremitsya k nezavisimosti! [The 'Iranian Lion' Loses Its Head: Southern Azerbaijan Strives for Independence!]," *Haqqin.az*, August 22, 2022, https://haqqin.az/democracy/258047.

[98]Nikola Mikovic, "How an Armenia-Azerbaijan Peace Deal Upsets Iran," EurActiv, November 8, 2022, https://www.euractiv.com/section/global-europe/opinion/how-an-armenia-azerbaijan-peace-deal-upsets-iran/; Emil Avdaliani, "Iran and Turkey Are Squaring Off in the South Caucasus," *World Politics Review*, December 20, 2022, https://www.worldpoliticsreview.com/turkey-iran-relations-caucasus-war-nagorno-karabakh/.

energy companies have committed to investing in Iran now that they find themselves already sanctioned because of the war in Ukraine.[99] Simultaneously, the degree of their competition has been blunted by two realities: a failing JCPOA, which means Iran is likely to continue to face sanctions and severe limitations on its energy trade, and Russia's dwindling presence in European energy markets, which means neither will compete for those shares soon.

To the extent leaders in Moscow and Tehran perceive US centrality to the global order as a threat to their core interests—notably regime survival—they are likely to remain revisionist powers vis-à-vis that order, subordinating their regional disputes to the larger objective of creating a more "democratic" order. That aspiration is shared not just with other authoritarian powers advocating for civilization essentialism (like China), but also to varying degrees by many "rising" or "middle" powers that do not see the existing order as consonant with their own status. What distinguishes Russia and Iran from these other revisionists, even China, is the extent to which they have positioned themselves as complete outsiders seeking change that is more revolutionary than incremental. The extent of their revisionism and willingness to countenance large-scale violence and disorder makes them dangerous to US-led order. Yet, both Iran and Russia are deeply troubled at home, with aging leaders, growing volatility, rapidly weakening economies, and uncertain futures. By themselves, they are not in a position to threaten the fundamentals of the US-centric global order, even as their bilateral relationship deepens.

The challenge for the United States and other defenders of the status quo then lies in ensuring that other partial revisionists like China, India, and Turkey remain committed to at least the basic outlines of the current international system rather than follow Tehran and Moscow into outright revisionism tinged with nihilism. Existing institutions have to adapt to ensure these states have a greater say in the international system, notwithstanding their less-than-perfect commitment (or, in the case of China, noncommitment) to liberal principles. They need, in other words, to contest Moscow and Tehran's contention that the post–Cold War order is an order of, by, and for the West. Accepting limited

---

[99] "Iran and Russia's Gazprom Sign Primary Deal for Energy Cooperation," Reuters, July 19, 2022, https://www.reuters.com/business/energy/iran-russias-gazprom-sign-primary-deal-energy-cooperation-2022-07-19/.

change is the best way for the United States and other supporters of the status quo to limit Moscow and Tehran's calls for more far-reaching changes.

At the same time, the further weakening of Putinist Russia and the Islamic Republic of Iran will further their isolation at the international and regional levels. The maintenance of sanctions and support for vulnerable neighbors like Ukraine and Iraq can also reduce the attractiveness of Russo-Iranian alternatives and put pressure on the Russo-Iranian axis. Already, Russia's setbacks in Ukraine have thrown cold water on the plans by Iranian proxy Hezbollah to intervene in the conflict.[100] The prospect of Western retaliation has also limited Russia's appetite for Iranian ballistic missiles.[101]

The failure of the Russian invasion and further Iranian difficulties in its neighborhood can also help the United States challenge a narrative long pressed by Moscow and Tehran that the US-led order (and the West in general) are in decline and ripe for being displaced from the perch they have occupied since the end of the Cold War. The 2008 financial crisis, the rise of populism, the failure to grapple with the consequences of the Covid-19 pandemic, and geopolitical failings (notably the chaotic US withdrawal from Afghanistan) have all fed into a perception shared by many authoritarian leaders that the West's best days are in the past and that the time is ripe for the reemergence of state and civilizations shunted aside by the rise of the West.

Belief in Western senescence has been a frequent theme in the rhetoric of both Putin and Khamenei over the past decade. As early as 2012, Putin claimed that "domestic socio-economic problems that have become worse in industrialized countries as a result of the (economic) crisis are weakening the dominant role of the so-called historical West."[102] Putin and other Russian officials and analysts often link this perceived decline

---

[100] "'I Know How They Think': A Hezbollah Official-Turned-Critic Explains the Group's Relationship with Moscow and How Russia's Failures in Ukraine Likely Derailed a Real Partnership," Meduza, December 19, 2022, https://meduza.io/en/feature/2022/12/29/i-know-how-they-think.

[101] "Russia and Iran Hesitate over Co-operation as West Warns of Costs," Financial Times, March 6, 2023, https://www.ft.com/content/b9361eae-5b05-4c17-8c59-7fb11e2579fe.

[102] Thomas Grove, "Russia's Putin Says the West Is on the Decline," Reuters, July 9, 2012, https://www.reuters.com/article/us-russia-putin-west/russias-putin-says-the-west-is-on-the-decline-idU.S.BRE86818020120709.

to the West's embrace of multiculturalism and "denying moral principles and all traditional identities."[103] Likewise, in 2019, Khamenei spoke of the "termite-like decline" of the United States in the political, social, and economic fronts. Three years later, Khamenei told students, "Today, the world is on the threshold of a new international order, which, after the era of bipolar world order and the theory of unipolar world order, is taking shape. In the current period, of course, the U.S. has become weaker day by day."[104]

As long as the United States and the order it upholds appear to be eroding from within, Russia and Iran (not to mention China and others) will remain emboldened to push back from without. Strengthening that order, and the states and institutions that comprise it, even as the problems facing Russia and Iran mount, could help the United States secure the future of the order it leads. Reinforcing democracy at home and the ability of current institutions to maintain security and stability abroad will also help discourage others from joining the Russo-Iranian challenge.

Should that challenge fail, the Russo-Iranian relationship will also face a reckoning, as the geopolitical and geo-economic tensions that have long characterized relations between Moscow and Tehran again come to the fore. Without a common foe, Russia and Iran will likely revert to their historical pattern of rivalry and mistrust, while the domestic legitimation strategies adopted by their respective regimes will become more difficult to maintain.

Bibliography

Acharya, Amitav. "The Myth of the 'Civilizational State': Rising Powers and the Cultural Challenge to World Order." *Ethics and International Affairs* 34, no. 2 (2020): 139–56. https://doi.org/10.1017/S0892679420000192.

Ahmadian, Hassan, and Payam Mohseni. "Iran's Syria Strategy: The Evolution of Deterrence." *International Affairs* 95, no. 2 (2019): 341–64. https://doi.10.1093/ia/iiy271.

---

[103] Vladimir Putin, "Zasedanie mezhdunarodnogo diskussionogo kluba 'Valdai' [Meeting of the Valdai Discussion Club]," The Kremlin, September 19, 2013, http://kremlin.ru/events/president/news/19243.

[104] Heiran-Nia, "How Iran's Interpretation of the World Order Affects Its Foreign Policy."

Ajami, Fouad. "The Fate of Nonalignment," *Foreign Affairs* 59, no. 2 (Winter 1980–1). https://www.foreignaffairs.com/world/fate-nonalignment.

Akinshina, Tatyana. "Rossiya i Iran obsuzhdayut priznanie 'Mira' i peredachu finsoobshchenii v obkhod SWIFT [Russia and Iran Discuss Recognition of 'Mir' and Transmission of Financial Data Bypassing SWIFT]." *Kommersant*, March 24, 2022. https://www.kommersant.ru/doc/5272074.

Al-Monitor. "Iran Blames NATO 'Provocation' for Russian War on Ukraine." February 24, 2022. https://www.al-monitor.com/originals/2022/02/iran-blames-nato-provocation-russian-war-ukraine.

Alterman, Jon, and Hanna Notte. "Russia in the Middle East after Ukraine." Center for Strategic and International Studies, January 24, 2023. https://www.csis.org/analysis/russia-middle-east-after-ukraine.

Ambrosio, Thomas. "Constructing a Framework of Authoritarian Diffusion: Concepts, Dynamics, and Future Research." *International Studies Perspective* 11 (2010): 375–92. https://doi.org/10.1111/j.1528-3585.2010.00411.x.

Avdaliani, Emil. "Iran and Turkey Are Squaring Off in the South Caucasus." *World Politics Review*, December 20, 2022. https://www.worldpoliticsreview.com/turkey-iran-relations-caucasus-war-nagorno-karabakh/.

Baev, Pavel K. "Russian Influence Fades in the Middle East." Jamestown Foundation Eurasia Daily Monitor, November 28, 2022. https://jamestown.org/program/russian-influence-fades-in-the-middle-east/.

Batmanghelidj, Esfandyar, and Mahsa Rouhi. "The Iran Nuclear Deal and Sanctions Relief: Implications for US Policy." *Survival* 63, no. 4 (2021): 183–98. https://doi.org/10.1080/00396338.2021.1956192.

Batrawy, Aya. "Watch: Iranian President Ebrahim Raisi Addresses the 2022 United Nations General Assembly." PBS, September 21, 2022. https://www.pbs.org/newshour/world/watch-iranian-president-ebrahim-raisi-addresses-the-2022-united-nations-general-assembly.

Bettiza, Gregorio, and David Lewis, "Authoritarian Powers and Norm Contestation in the Liberal International Order: Theorizing the Power Politics of Ideas and Identity." *Journal of Global Security Studies* 5, no. 4 (2020): 559–77. https://doi.org/10.1093/jogss/ogz075.

Biersteker, Thomas, and Erica Moret, "Rising Powers and Reform of International Security Institutions." In *Rising Powers, Global Governance and Global Ethics*, edited by Jamie Gaskarth, 57–73. London: Routledge, 2015.

Bloomberg. "Turkey, Syria, Russia to Hold New Talks on Civil War, Terrorism." January 1, 2023. https://www.bloomberg.com/news/articles/2023-01-01/turkey-syria-russia-to-hold-new-talks-on-civil-war-terrorism.

Borchevskaya, Anna. *Putin's War in Syria: Russian Foreign Policy and the Price of America's Absence*. London: I.B. Tauris, 2022.

Borger, Julian. "Iranian Advisers Killed Aiding Russians in Crimea, Says Kyiv." *The Guardian*, November 24, 2022. https://www.theguardian.com/world/2022/nov/24/iranian-military-advisers-killed-aiding-moscow-in-crimea-kyiv.

Brands, Hal. "Democracy vs. Authoritarianism: How Ideology Shape Great Power Competition." *Survival* 60 (2018): 61–114. https://doi.org/10.1080/00396338.2018.1518371.

Bushwick, Sophie. "How Iran Is Using the Protests to Block More Open Internet Access." *Scientific American*, October 13, 2022. https://www.scientificamerican.com/article/how-iran-is-using-the-protests-to-block-more-open-internet-access/.

Cafiero, Giorgio. "Israel's Working Relationship with Russia inside Syria." *Inside Arabia*, November 16, 2021. https://insidearabia.com/israels-working-relationship-with-russia-inside-syria/.

Clunan, Anne L. "Russia and the Liberal World Order." *Ethics and International Affairs* 32, no. 1 (2018): 45–59. https://doi.org/10.1017/S0892679418000096.

Coker, Christopher P. *The Rise of the Civilizational State*. Cambridge: Polity, 2019.

De Hoog, Niels, and Elena Morresi. "Mapping Iran's Unrest: How Mahsa Amini's Death Led to Nationwide Protests." *The Guardian*, October 31, 2022. https://www.theguardian.com/world/ng-interactive/2022/oct/31/mapping-irans-unrest-how-mahsa-aminis-death-led-to-nationwide-protests.

Divsallar, Abdolrasool. "The Pillars of Iranian-Russian Security Convergence." *The International Spectator* 54, no. 3 (2019): 107–22. https://doi.org/10.1080/03932729.2019.1586147.

Du Quenoy, Irina, and Dmitry Dubrovskiy. "Violence and the Defense of 'Traditional Values' in the Russian Federation." In *Religion and Violence in Russia: Context, Manifestations, and Policies*, edited by Olga Oliker, 93–117. Washington, DC: CSIS, 2018. https://csis-website-prod.s3.amazonaws.com/s3fs-public/publication/180530_Oliker_ReligionandViolenceinRussia_Web.pdf.

Farhi, Farideh, and Saideh Lotifan. "Iran's Post-Revolution Foreign Policy Puzzle." In *Worldviews of Aspiring Powers: Domestic Foreign Policy Debates in China, India, Iran, Japan, and Russia*, edited by Henry R. Nau and Deepa M. Ollapally, 114–45. Oxford: Oxford University Press, 2012.

Financial Times. "Russia and Iran Hesitate over Co-operation as West Warns of Costs." March 6, 2023. https://www.ft.com/content/b9361eae-5b05-4c17-8c59-7fb11e2579fe.

Freedom House. "Iran: Freedom on the Net: 2022 Country Report." 2022. https://freedomhouse.org/country/iran/freedom-net/2022.

Galleotti, Mark. "I'm Sorry for Creating the 'Gerasimov Doctrine.'" *Foreign Policy*, March 5, 2018. https://foreignpolicy.com/2018/03/05/im-sorry-for-creating-the-gerasimov-doctrine/.

Gerasimov, V. V. "Tsennost nauki v predvidenii [The Value of Science Is in Foresight]." *Voenno-promyshlennyi kur'yer*, February 26, 2013. https://vpk-news.ru/articles/14632.

Grace, Ryan. "Shatter the Web: Internet Fragmentation in Iran." Middle East Institute, February 1, 2023. https://www.mei.edu/publications/shatter-web-internet-fragmentation-iran.

Grajewski, Nicole. "An Illusory Entente: The Myth of a Russia-China-Iran 'Axis.'" *Asian Affairs* 53 (2022): 164–83. https://doi.org/10.1080/03068 374.2022.2029076.

Grajewski, Nicole. "Iranian Membership in the Shanghai Cooperation Organization: Motivations and Implications." Washington Institute for Near Eastern Policy, September 15, 2021. https://www.washingtoninstitute.org/pol icy-analysis/iranian-membership-shanghai-cooperation-organization-moti vations-and-implications.

Grove, Thomas. "Russia's Putin Says the West Is on the Decline." Reuters, July 9, 2012. https://www.reuters.com/article/us-russia-putin-west/russias-puti n-says-the-west-is-on-the-decline-idU.S.BRE86818020120709.

Hale, Henry, and Marlene Laruelle, "Rethinking Civilizational Identity from the Bottom Up: A Case Study of Russia and a Research Agenda." *Nationalities Papers* 48, no. 3 (May 2020): 585–602. https://doi.org/10.1017/nps.2019.125.

Hall, Stephen G. F., and Thomas Ambrosio, "Authoritarian Learning: A Conceptual Overview." *East European Politics* 33, no. 2 (2017): 143–61. https://doi.org/10.1080/21599165.2017.1307826.

Han Liu. "The Beijing Consensus? How China Has Changed Western Ideas of Law and Economic Development." Review of *The Beijing Consensus? How China Has Changed Western Ideas of Law and Economic Development*, edited by Weitseng Chen, *International Journal of Constitutional Law* 17, no. 1 (January 2019): 375–8. https://doi.org/10.1093/icon/moz016.

Haqqin.az. "'Iranskii lev' poteryaet golovu. Yuzhnyi Azerbaidzhan stremitsya k nezavisimosti! [The 'Iranian Lion' Loses Its Head: Southern Azerbaijan Strives for Independence!]." August 22, 2022. https://haqqin.az/democr acy/258047.

Hardie, John, and Benham Ben Talebu. "Iran Is Now at War with Ukraine." *Foreign Policy*, October 26, 2022. https://foreignpolicy.com/2022/10/26/iran-ukraine-russia-war-drones-missiles-military-advisors-middle-east-nuclear/.

Heiran-Nia, Javad. "How Iran's Interpretation of the World Order Affects Its Foreign Policy." Atlantic Council, May 11, 2022. https://www.atlanticcoun cil.org/blogs/iransource/how-irans-interpretation-of-the-world-order-affe cts-its-foreign-policy/.

Heller, Sam. "Turkey's Russian Red Light in Syria." War on the Rocks, December 30, 2022. https://warontherocks.com/2022/12/turkeys-russ ian-red-light-in-syria/.

Hetherington, Philippa, and Glenda Sluga. "Liberal and Illiberal Internationalisms." *Journal of World History* 31, no. 1 (2020): 1–9. https://doi.org/10.1353/jwh.2020.0000.

Hug, Adam, ed. "Sharing Worst Practice: How Countries and Institutions in the Former Soviet Union Help Create Legal Tools of Repression." Foreign Policy Centre, May 2016. https://fpc.org.uk/wp-content/uploads/2016/05/1749.pdf.

Humire, Joseph M., and Ilan Berman, eds. *Iran's Strategic Penetration of Latin America*. Lanham, MD: Lexington Books, 2014.

Islamic Republic News Agency. "Chinese TV Says Iran-China Cooperation Major Challenge to U.S. Unilateralism." December 18, 2022. https://en.irna.ir/news/83859280/Chinese-TV-says-Iran-China-cooperation-major-challenge-to-U.S.

Islamic Republic News Agency. "History of NAM and Its Relations with Iran." August 13, 2012. https://en.irna.ir/news/80274417/History-of-NAM-and-its-relations-with-Iran.

Istomin, Igor A. "The Logic of Counterpoint: Aspirations of Liberal Hegemony and Counter-Ideological Alignment." *Russia in Global Affairs* 2 (April/June 2019): 8–34. https://doi.10.31278/1810-6374-2019-17-2-8-34.

"K velikomu okeanu: Ot povorota na Vostok k Bol'shoi Yevrazii [Toward the Great Ocean: From the Pivot to the East to Greater Eurasia]." In *K velikomu okeanu: khronika povorota na Vostok [Toward the Great Ocean: Chronicle of the Pivot to the East]*, edited by S. A. Karaganov and T. V. Bordachev, 242–303. Moscow: Valdai, 2017.

Kaczmarski, Marcin. "Non-Western Visions of Regionalism: China's New Silk Road and Russia's Eurasian Economic Union." *International Affairs* 93, no. 6 (November 2017): 1357–76. https://doi.org/10.1093/ia/iix182.

Kaleji, Vali. "Iran and Eurasian Economic Union Negotiations: Upgrading EAEU-Iran Preferential Trade Agreement into a Free Trade Agreement." Russian International Affairs Council, January 24, 2022. https://russiancouncil.ru/en/analytics-and-comments/columns/middle-east-policy/iran-and-eurasian-economic-union-negotiations-upgrading-eaeu-iran-preferential-trade-agreement-into-/.

Kanet, Roger E. "Russia and Global Governance: The Challenge to the Existing Liberal Order." *International Politics* 55 (2018): 177–88. https://doi.org/10.1057/s41311-017-0075-3.

Karaganov, Sergei A., and Dmitry V. Suslov. "A New World Order: A View from Russia." Russia in International Affairs, October 4, 2018. https://eng.globalaffairs.ru/articles/a-new-world-order-a-view-from-russia/.

Karaganov, Sergey A. "Budushchii miroporyadok [Future World Order]." Council of the President of the Russian Federation in Human Rights, September 11, 2017. http://www.president-sovet.ru/members/blogs/post/budushchiy_miroporyadok.

Khamenei, Ali. "Recent Riots in Iran Were Designed." Office of the Supreme Leader. October 3, 2022. https://english.khamenei.ir/news/9183/Recent-riots-in-Iran-were-designed.

Khamenei, Ali. "Role of Arrogant Powers' Policies in Recent Bitter Events in Iran Is Obvious." Office of the Supreme Leader, October 3, 2022. https://english.khamenei.ir/news/9189/Role-of-Arrogant-Powers-policies-in-recent-bitter-events-in.

Khamenei, Ali. "Supreme Leader's Inaugural Speech at the 16th Non-Aligned Summit." Office of the Supreme Leader, August 30, 2012. https://www.leader.ir/en/content/9708/Supreme-Leader%E2%80%99s-Inaugural-Speech-at-the-16th-Non-Aligned-Summit.

Kofman, Michael, Anya Fink, Dmitry Gorenburg, Mary Chesnut, Jeffrey Edmonds, and Julian Waller. "Russian Military Strategy: Core Tenets and Operational Concepts." Center for Naval Analyses, August 2021. https://www.cna.org/archive/CNA_Files/pdf/russian-military-strategy-core-tenets-and-operational-concepts.pdf.

Kommersant. "Vladislav Surkov razvel demokratiyu na suverennuyu i upravlyaemuyu [Vladislav Surkov Separated Democracy into Sovereign and Managed]." June 29, 2006. https://www.kommersant.ru/doc/686274.

Kortunov, Andrey. "The Astana Model: Methods and Ambitions of Russian Political Action." In *The MENA Region: A Great Power Competition*, edited by Karim Mezran and Arturo Varvelli, 53–63. Washington, DC: Atlantic Council, 2021.

Kosachev, Konstantin. "Rossiya mozhet stat' initsiatorom reformy mezhdunarodnogo prava [Russia May Become the Initiator of Reforms of International Law]." Russian International Affairs Council, December 6, 2022. https://russiancouncil.ru/analytics-and-comments/comments/rossiya-mozhet-stat-initsiatorom-reformy-mezhdunarodnogo-prava.

Kremlin. "Shankhaiskaya konventsiya o bor'be s terrorizmom, separatizmom i ekstremizmom [Shanghai Convention on the Struggle against Terrorism, Separatism and Extremism]." June 14, 2001. http://www.kremlin.ru/supplement/3405.

Kremlin. "Sovmestnoe zayavlenie Rossiiskoi Federatsii i Kitaiskoi Narodnoi Respubliki o mezhdunarodnykh otnosheniyakh, vstupayushchikh v novuyu epokhu, i global'nom ustoichivom razvitii [Joint Statement of the Russian Federation and the People's Republic of China on International Relations Entering a New Era and Global Sustainable Development]." February 4, 2022. http://kremlin.ru/supplement/5770.

Lavrov, Sergey V. "On Law, Rights and Rules." *Russia in Global Affairs* 19, no. 3 (2021): 228–40. https://eng.globalaffairs.ru/articles/the-law-the-rights-and-the-rules/.

Lavrov, Sergey V. "Vystuplenie na XXIX Assamblee SVOP [Address at the XXIX Assembly of SVOP]." Russian International Affairs Council, October 4, 2021. https://russiancouncil.ru/analytics-and-comments/comments/vystuplenie-na-xxix-assamblee-svop/.

Lenta.ru. "Suverennaya filologiya 'Suverennaya demokratiya' okazalas' ne natsional'noi ideei, a predmetom diskussii [Sovereign Philology: 'Sovereign Democracy' Turns Out to Be Not a National Idea but a Topic of Discussion]." September 13, 2006. https://lenta.ru/articles/2006/09/13/surkov/.

Lewis, David. "Geopolitical Imaginaries in Russian Foreign Policy: The Evolution of Greater Eurasia." *Europe-Asia Studies* 70, no. 10 (2018): 1612–37. https://doi.org/10.1080/09668136.2018.1515348.

Libman, Alexander, and Evgeny Vinokurov. *Eurasian Integration: Challenges of Trans-Continental Regionalism.* Basingstoke: Palgrave Macmillan, 2012.

Lister, Charles. "Russia, Iran, and the Competition to Shape Syria's Future." Middle East Institute, September 12, 2019. https://www.mei.edu/publications/russia-iran-and-competition-shape-syrias-future.

Lu, Christina. "Putin Faces Military Debacle." *Foreign Policy*, October 5, 2022. https://foreignpolicy.com/2022/10/05/russia-military-ukraine-retreat-counteroffensiveputin.

Luzyanin, Sergey. "Bol'shaya Yevraziya: obshchie zadachi dlya Kitaya i Rossii [Greater Eurasia: Common Tasks for China and Russia]." Valdai Discussion Club, April 16, 2018. https://ru.valdaiclub.com/a/highlights/bolshaya-evraziya-zadachi.

Mankoff, Jeffrey. *Empires of Eurasia: How Imperial Legacies Shape International Security*. New Haven, CT: Yale University Press, 2022.

Mankoff, Jeffrey. "Regional Competition and the Future of Russia-Turkey Relations: A World Safe for Empire?" Center for Strategic and International Studies, January 2022. https://www.csis.org/analysis/regional-competition-and-future-russia-turkey-relations.

Mankoff, Jeffrey. *Russian Foreign Policy: The Return of Great Power Politics*, 2nd edn. Lanham, MD: Rowman & Littlefield, 2012.

Marschall, Christin. *Iran's Persian Gulf Policy: From Khomeini to Khatami*. London: Routledge Curzon, 2003.

McDermott, Roger N. "Does Russia Have a Gerasimov Doctrine?" *Parameters* 46, no. 1 (2016). https://doi.10.55540/0031-1723.2827.

Meduza. "'I Know How They Think': A Hezbollah Official-Turned-Critic Explains the Group's Relationship with Moscow and How Russia's Failures in Ukraine Likely Derailed a Real Partnership." December 19, 2022. https://meduza.io/en/feature/2022/12/29/i-know-how-they-think.

Menon, Shivshankar. "Nobody Wants the Current World Order." *Foreign Affairs*, August 3, 2022. https://www.foreignaffairs.com/world/nobody-wants-current-world-order.

Middle East Report. "Khomeini: 'We Shall Confront the World with Our Ideology.'" No. 88 (June 1980). https://merip.org/1980/06/khomeini-we-shall-confront-the-world-with-our-ideology/.

Mikovic, Nikola. "How an Armenia-Azerbaijan Peace Deal Upsets Iran." EurActiv, November 8, 2022. https://www.euractiv.com/section/global-europe/opinion/how-an-armenia-azerbaijan-peace-deal-upsets-iran/.

Morgus, Robert, and Justin Sherman. "Analysis: Russia's Plan for a National Internet." New America, February 19, 2019. https://www.newamerica.org/cybersecurity-initiative/c2b/c2b-log/russias-plans-for-a-national-internet/.

Notte, Hanna, and Hamidreza Azizi. "Will Iran Accept Russia's Idea for a Middle East Regional Security Process?" Valdai Discussion Club, April 8, 2022. https://valdaiclub.com/a/highlights/will-iran-accept-russia-s-ideas-for-a-middle-east/.

Perteghella, Annalisa, ed. *Iran Looking East: An Alternative to the EU?* Milan: ISPI, 2019. https://www.ispionline.it/sites/default/files/pubblicazioni/ispi_iran_looking_web.pdf.

Pifer, Steven. "Russia's Draft Agreements with NATO and the United States: Intended for Rejection?" Brookings Institution, December 21, 2022. https://www.brookings.edu/blog/order-from-chaos/2021/12/21/russias-draft-agreements-with-nato-and-the-united-states-intended-for-rejection/.

Pifer, Steven. "The Russia-Ukraine War and Its Ramifications for Russia." Brookings Institution, December 8, 2022. https://www.brookings.edu/articles/the-russia-ukraine-war-and-its-ramifications-for-russia/.

Putin, Vladimir. "A New Integration Project for Eurasia: The Future in the Making." Russian Embassy to the United Kingdom, October 4, 2011. https://www.rusemb.org.uk/press/246.

Putin, Vladimir. "Plenarnoe zasedanie Peterburgskogo mezhdunarodnogo ekonomicheskogo foruma [Plenary Session of the St. Petersburg International Economic Forum]." The Kremlin, June 17, 2022. http://kremlin.ru/events/president/news/68669.

Putin, Vladimir. "Vystuplenie i diskussiya na Myunkhenskoi konferentsii po voprosam politiki bezopasnosti [Address and Discussion at the Munich Security Conference]." The Kremlin, February 10, 2007. http://kremlin.ru/events/president/transcripts/copy/24034.

Putin, Vladimir. "Zasedanie mezhdunarodnogo diskussionogo kluba 'Valdai' [Meeting of the Valdai International Discussion Club]." The Kremlin, September 19, 2013. http://kremlin.ru/events/president/news/19243.

Putin, Vladimir. "Zasedanie mezhdunarodnogo diskussionogo kluba 'Valdai' [Meeting of the Valdai International Discussion Club]." The Kremlin, October 27, 2022. http://kremlin.ru/events/president/news/69695.

Radin, Andrew, and Clint Reach. *Russian Views of the International Order*. Santa Monica, CA: RAND Corporation, 2017.

Reuters. "Iran and Russia's Gazprom Sign Primary Deal for Energy Cooperation." July 19, 2022. https://www.reuters.com/business/energy/iran-russias-gazprom-sign-primary-deal-energy-cooperation-2022-07-19/.

Reuters. "Iranian President Tells Putin That NATO's Expansion Is 'Serious Threat' to Region's Security and Stability." February 24, 2022. https://www.reuters.com/world/iranian-president-tells-putin-that-natos-expansion-is-serious-threat-regions-2022-02-24/.

Reuters. "Russia Weighs Local Alternative to Swift Payment System—Agencies." August 27, 2014. https://www.reuters.com/article/russia-banks-swift/russia-weighs-local-alternative-to-swift-payment-system-agencies-idUSL5N0QX33W20140827.

RIA Novosti. "SShA po suti okkupiruyut Germaniyu, Koreyu i Yaponiyu, no govoryat o ravnopravii s nimi—Putin [The USA Effectively Occupies Germany, Korea and Japan, but Speaks of Equality with Them—Putin]." September 30, 2022. https://ria.ru/20220930/ssha-1820624233.html.

RIA Novosti. "Uchastniki 'BRIKS plyus' vystupili za mnogopolyarnyi poryadok, zayavil Putin [Participants in the 'BRICS+' Called for a Multipolar Order,

Putin Announced]." June 24, 2022. https://ria.ru/20220624/putin-1797912 967.html (accessed January 26, 2004).

Rouhi, Mahsa. "Woman, Life, Freedom in Iran." *Survival* 64, no. 6 (December 2022): 189–96. https://doi.org/10.1080/00396338.2022.2150441.

Russian Ministry of Foreign Affairs. "Rossiiskaya Kontseptsiya kollektivnoi bezopasnosti v zone Persidskogo zaliva [The Russian Collective Security Concept in the Persian Gulf Zone]." August 24, 2021. https://archive.mid.ru/ru/foreign_policy/international_safety/conflicts/-/asset_publisher/xIEMTQ3OvzcA/content/id/3733575.

Sadri, Houman. "An Islamic Perspective on Non-Alignment: Iranian Foreign Policy in Theory and Practice." *Journal of Third World Studies* 16, no. 2 (1999): 29–46.

Sadri, Houman A. "Trends in the Foreign Policy of Revolutionary Iran." *Journal of Third World Studies* 15, no. 1 (1998): 13–37.

Salehi-Isfahani, Djavad. "The Road to Iran's 'Resistance Economy' Passes through a Revived JCPOA." *Responsible Statecraft*, July 13, 2022. https://responsiblestatecraft.org/2022/07/13/the-road-to-the-irans-resistance-economy-passes-through-a-revived-jcpoa/.

Salehi-Isfahani, Djavad. "The Simple Reason Iran's Economy Stopped Growing." Bourse and Bazaar Foundation, August 25, 2022. https://www.bourseandbazaar.com/tyranny-of-numbers/2022/5/3/the-simple-reason-irans-economy-stopped-growing.

Sanger, David E. "United States Enters a New Era of Direct Confrontation with Iran." *New York Times*, November 24, 2022. https://www.nytimes.com/2022/11/24/us/politics/iran-protests-ukraine-nuclear-enrichment.html.

Security Council of the Russian Federation. "Doktrina informatsionnoi bezopasnosti Rossiiskoi Federatsii [Doctrine of Information Security of the Russian Federation]." December 5, 2016. http://www.scrf.gov.ru/security/information/document5/.

Sen, Ashish Kumar. "A Brief History of Sanctions on Iran." Atlantic Council. Last modified May 8, 2018. https://www.atlanticcouncil.org/blogs/new-atlanticist/a-brief-history-of-sanctions-on-iran/.

Shanghai Cooperation Organization. "Obshchie svedeniya [General Information]." Shanghai Cooperation Organization, July 5, 2023. https://rus.sectsco.org (accessed January 30, 2024).

Shanghai Cooperation Organization. "Soglashenie mezhdu pravistel'stvami gosudarstv-chlenov ShOS o sotrudnichestve v oblasti obespecheniya mezhdunarodnoi informatsionnoi bezopasnosti [Agreement between Member State Governments of the SCO on Cooperation in the Field of Securing International Information Security]." June 16, 2009. https://ccdcoe.org/uploads/2018/11/SCO-090616-IISAgreementRussian-1.pdf.

Sherman, Justin. "Russia and Iran Plan to Fundamentally Isolate the Internet." *Wired*, June 6, 2019. https://www.wired.com/story/russia-and-iran-plan-to-fundamentally-isolate-the-internet/.

Shokri, Umud. "Iran and the Shanghai Cooperation Organization." Carnegie Endowment, November 16, 2022. https://carnegieendowment.org/sada/88427.

Smagin, Nikita. "Comrades-in-Sanctions: Can Iran Help Russia Weather the Economic Storm?" Carnegie Endowment, November 4, 2022. https://carnegieendowment.org/politika/88318.

Smorodskaya, Polina. "SWIFT dlya malen'kikh [SWIFT for the Small]." *Kommersant*, May 19, 2020. https://www.kommersant.ru/doc/4348494.

Snegovaya, Maria, and Kirill Petrov. "Long Soviet Shadows: The Nomenklatura Ties of Putin Elites." *Post-Soviet Affairs* 38, no. 4 (2022): 329–48. https://doi.org/10.1080/1060586X.2022.2062657.

Sullivan, Jake. "Interview with Jake Sullivan." In *A Kennan for Our Times: Revisiting America's Greatest 20th Century Diplomat in the 21st Century*, edited by Michael Kimmage and Matthew Rojanksy. Washington, DC: Woodrow Wilson Center, 2018. https://www.wilsoncenter.org/sites/default/files/media/uploads/documents/Sullivan%20Kennan%20Legacy%20Chapter.pdf.

Sushentsov, Andrey. "Russia—A Global Revisionist?" Valdai Discussion Club, June 12, 2019. https://valdaiclub.com/a/highlights/russia-a-global-revisionist/.

Takeyh, Ray. "Iran's 'Resistance Economy' Debate." Council on Foreign Relations, April 7, 2016. https://www.cfr.org/expert-brief/irans-resistance-economy-debate.

TASS. "Lavrov: kontseptsiya RF po Persidskomu zalivu podrazumyvaet voenno-politicheskuyu koordinatsiyu [Lavrov: RF Concept on the Persian Gulf Implies Military-Political Coordination]." February 21, 2022. https://tass.ru/politika/13779363.

Tazmini, Ghoncheh. "'To Be or Not to Be' (Like the West): Modernisation in Russia and Iran." *Third World Quarterly* 39 (2018): 1998–2015. https://doi.org/10.1080/01436597.2018.1447375.

Tehran Times. "Russia Welcomes INSTEX Progress." April 3, 2020. https://www.tehrantimes.com/news/446430/Russia-welcomes-INSTEX-progress.

Terner, Steven. "A China-Russia SWIFT Alternative Will Not Undermine Iran Sanctions." Washington Institute for Near East Policy, February 25, 2022. https://www.washingtoninstitute.org/policy-analysis/china-russia-swift-alternative-will-not-undermine-iran-sanctions.

Times of Israel. "Report: Russia to Supply Iran with Dozens of Sukhoi Su-35 Fighter Jets." December 25, 2022. https://www.timesofisrael.com/report-russia-to-supply-with-iran-with-dozens-of-sukhoi-su-35-fighter-jets/.

Tirone, Jonathan, and Golnar Motevalli. "Russia and Iran Are Building a Trade Route That Defies Sanctions." Bloomberg, December 21, 2022. https://www.bloomberg.com/graphics/2022-russia-iran-trade-corridor/.

Trenin, Dmitri. *The End of Eurasia: Russia on the Border between Geopolitics and Globalization*. Washington, DC: Carnegie Endowment, 2002.

US Department of State. "Institutionalizing the Freedom Agenda: President Bush Calls on Future Presidents and Congresses to Continue Leading the Cause of Freedom Worldwide." October 9, 2008, https://2001-2009.state.gov/r/pa/prs/ps/2008/oct/110871.htm.

Vinograd, Cassandra. "Iran's Foreign Minister Acknowledges That Drones Were Sent to Russia, but Says It Happened before the War." *New York Times*, November 5, 2022. https://www.nytimes.com/2022/11/05/world/europe/irans-foreign-minister-acknowledges-that-drones-were-sent-to-russia-but-says-it-happened-before-the-war.html.

Warrick, Joby, Souad Mekhennet, and Ellen Nakashima, "Iran Will Help Russia Build Drones for Ukraine War, Western Officials Say." *Washington Post*, November 19, 2022. https://www.washingtonpost.com/national-security/2022/11/19/russia-iran-drones-secret-deal/.

Weiss, Jessica Chen. "A World Safe for Autocracy? China's Rise and the Future of Global Politics." *Foreign Affairs* 98, no. 4 (July/August 2019): 92–102.

White House. "Interim National Security Strategic Guidance." March 2021. https://www.whitehouse.gov/wp-content/uploads/2021/03/NSC-1v2.pdf.

8 PROSPECTS FOR RUSSO-IRANIAN ECONOMIC RELATIONS: COMPETITION OVER COOPERATION

Esfandyar Batmanghelidj

In January 2022, Iranian president Ebrahim Raisi made a two-day state visit to Moscow, his first trip abroad as president. During the trip, he announced that Iran had "no limits for expanding ties with Russia."[1] As multiple packages of Western sanctions were levied against Russia after its invasion of Ukraine, and as the floundering of the nuclear negotiations made clear that Iran would likely remain under US secondary sanctions, it appeared only natural that Russia and Iran would respond to their respective economic isolation by deepening their economic partnership. Indeed, back in January 2022, Raisi and Putin targeted an increase in bilateral trade to $10 billion within the framework of a new twenty-year strategic partnership—an ambitious

---

[1] Brett Cohen and Garrett Nada, "Raisi in Russia," Iran Primer, January 21, 2022, https://iranprimer.usip.org/blog/2022/jan/21/raisi-russia.

target given that bilateral trade had totaled just $4 billion in the prior year.[2] In the subsequent months, Russian and Iranian officials became more vocal about the prospects for greater trade and investment.[3] State enterprises such as energy giant Gazprom promised to invest billions of dollars in Iran.[4] The Iran Chamber of Commerce welcomed a delegation of Russian executives to Tehran for a bilateral business forum in December 2022.[5]

But the prospect of greater economic cooperation has obscured another consequence of Russia's invasion of Ukraine and Iran's failure to restore the nuclear deal. In many respects, the invasion has also increased prospects for intensified competition between Russia and Iran. Henry Rome has noted that while "Iran and Russia have a history of tepid cooperation in developing Iran's energy sector ... Russia's invasion of Ukraine and Western sanctions on Russian energy have shifted the relationship toward outright competition." Rome explains how Russia's need to shift energy exports away from Western customers has come at the expense of Iran's market share in China, its last remaining crude oil customer.[6] Nicole Grajewski has argued that while "the Russia-Iran relationship is growing stronger ... Russia's ties with Iran remain complex, characterized by areas of cooperation, stalled plans and competition across various domains."[7] Similarly, while many observers have assumed that Iran's arms sales to Russia have granted "Tehran a greater degree of leverage over Moscow than it had before," in his chapter, in this volume, Mark Katz has argued that Russia's need to maintain strong relations with Israel, Turkey, Saudi Arabia, and the United Arab Emirates could

---

[2]Henry Rome, "Iran and Russia: Growing Economic Competition," Iran Primer, July 18, 2022, https://iranprimer.usip.org/blog/2022/jul/18/iran-russia-growing-economic-competition.
[3]"Russia, Iran Tighten Trade Ties amid US Sanctions," Bloomberg, May 22, 2022, https://www.bloomberg.com/news/articles/2022-05-25/russia-iran-tighten-trade-ties-amid-us-sanctions-interfax-says.
[4]"Iran and Russia's Gazprom Sign Primary Deal for Energy Cooperation," Reuters, July 19, 2022, https://www.reuters.com/business/energy/iran-russias-gazprom-sign-primary-deal-energy-cooperation-2022-07-19/.
[5]"Russia Says $40 Billion Trade with Iran Achievable," Iran Chamber of Commerce Newsroom, December 5, 2022, https://en.otaghiranonline.ir/news/44279.
[6]Rome, "Iran and Russia."
[7]Nicole Grajewski, "Russia and Iran Get Closer While Still Competing, amid Balancing Act with Turkey," *Russia Matters*, August 5, 2022, https://www.russiamatters.org/analysis/russia-and-iran-get-closer-while-still-competing-amid-balancing-act-turkey.

limit its support for Iran. These perceptive analyses suggest that to fully understand the new dimensions in Russia-Iran economic relations, it is vital to look beyond areas of cooperation and also consider how political and economic forces may be pushing the two countries toward greater competition.

The chapter will examine the prospects for Russia-Iran economic cooperation. Russian and Iranian policymakers and economic actors clearly intend to foster greater bilateral trade and investment—their intentions are not in question, and there has been growing scholarly attention to the talk of partnership among Russian and Iranian stakeholders. Maria Shagina has noted how Russia sees Iran and other regional markets playing an important role in its adaptation to Western sanctions.[8] Nikolay Kozhanov has examined Iran's faltering efforts to increase cooperation with Russia over the last decade, likewise a response to sanctions pressure.[9] However, most discussions of the prospect for a deeper partnership focus on geopolitical drivers rather than economic realities. The geopolitical drivers for a partnership may be compelling, but whether greater trade and investment will occur as part of any such partnership depends on two factors. First, cooperation between Russia and Iran must alleviate three kinds of constraints that have long dogged economic ties—banking constraints, logistical constraints, and institutional constraints. Second, cooperation between Russia and Iran must not be derailed by increased competition in other areas. Either the competition must remain minimal or it must be compartmentalized.

Awareness of Hurdles

Iranian business leaders have been vocal about the limitations facing bilateral economic relations, even as they seek to increase trade and investment with Russian counterparts. Speaking during a Russia-Iran

---

[8] Maria Shagina, "Own Goods, New Markets: Russia's Adjustment to Western Sanctions," *Zeitschrift Osteuropa* 71, no. 10–12 (2021), 221–34, https://doi.org/10.35998/oe-2021-0089.
[9] Nikolay Kozhanov, "Iran and Russia: Between Pragmatism and Possibilities of a Strategic Alliance," in *Foreign Policy of Iran under President Hassan Rouhani's First Term (2013–2017)*, edited by Luciano Zaccara (Singapore: Springer Singapore, 2020), 131–56, https://doi.org/10.1007/978-981-15-3924-4_7.

business conference in November 2022, Gholamhossein Shafei, chairman of the Iran Chamber of Commerce, an influential private-sector body, noted that despite the opportunities for increased trade, significant hurdles remain, especially in the areas of banking and logistics. "Unfortunately, the current infrastructure is not developed enough and lags behind the financial, commercial, and production capacities in Iran and Russia as well as regional countries," he said.[10] On the one hand, these frank assessments are intended to spur policymakers to act, especially by making long-overdue investments to support trade across the Caspian. On the other hand, complaints about the lack of existing banking and logistics infrastructure belie a considerable skepticism that a Russia-Iran economic partnership can emerge. As Grajewski observes about efforts to forge such a partnership, "Progress has been modest due to incompatible import-export structures, bureaucratic delays, and limited ties between their business communities."[11]

Russian and Iranian policymakers are aware of the need to upgrade banking and logistics infrastructure, and various initiatives are underway to address constraints on trade. But those initiatives are themselves subject to a third kind of constraint—institutional constraints. To direct bilateral economic policy, Russian and Iranian officials are reliant on a set of bilateral governmental commissions and private-sector trade groups. Moreover, even if the focus on bilateral trade has only intensified recently, many of these bodies have been active for years, working to support Russia-Iran trade within the multilateral vision set out by the Eurasian Economic Union (EAEU). These bodies have been peripheral to the trade policy of both Russia and Iran. Their institutional capacity will need to expand if policymakers and business leaders are to turn political aspirations into practical actions. The hurdles are obvious—the solutions are not.

---

[10] "Se Galogâh-e Tijârat-e Iran-Rusiyye [Three Chock Point of Russia-Iran Trade]," *Donya-E Eqtesad*, November 16, 2022, https://donya-e-eqtesad.com/ بخش-صنعت-معدن-3/3917517-س-گولگ اه-تراجت-ناریا-روسیه.

[11] Nicole Grajewski, "As the World Shuns Russia over Its Invasion of Ukraine, Iran Strengthens Its Ties with Moscow," Atlantic Council, March 7, 2022, https://www.atlanticcouncil.org/blogs/iransource/as-the-world-shuns-russia-over-its-invasion-of-ukraine-iran-strengthens-its-ties-with-moscow%ef%bf%bc/.

Banking Constraints

The lack of Russia-Iran banking relations primarily reflects Iran's long isolation from global banking networks. The imposition of financial sanctions on Iran in 2012 was a decisive blow to Iran's correspondent banking relationships. In 2006, Iran boasted over 600 correspondent banking relationships. By 2014, that number had fallen to around fifty.[12] Even during the brief period of sanctions relief that followed the implementation of the Joint Comprehensive Plan of Action (JCPOA), Iranian banks struggled to conduct basic cross-border financial transactions. The limited extent of Russia-Iran trade prior to 2012 has meant that today, as Russian and Iranian authorities seek to foster greater commerce, they must develop wholly new banking channels. This requires eliminating the use of the US dollar and euro in bilateral trade, which in turn requires increasing liquidity of the ruble and rial in both countries' foreign exchange markets. These efforts are not entirely new. A shared desire to develop resilience in the face of Western sanctions and a strategic interest in Eurasian trade has motivated Russian and Iranian authorities to explore financial cooperation for several years. Getting a clear picture of how financial transactions to support Russia-Iran trade are being conducted is difficult—it requires parsing statements from officials—but there appears to have been minimal progress to date. In 2019, Iran's then central bank governor Abdolnasser Hemmati announced that the dollar had been eliminated from Russia-Iran trade.[13] In August 2022, Iran's ambassador to Moscow, Kazem Jalali, announced that a ruble-rial exchange had been conducted in support of bilateral trade for the first time.[14] This suggests that while Russian and Iranian traders may now invoice trade in national currencies, a conversion through

---

[12]Chady Adel El Khoury, "Impediments to Correspondent Banking in Iran," International Monetary Fund, February 27, 2017, https://www.elibrary.imf.org/downloadpdf/journals/002/2017/063/article-A001-en.xml.
[13]"US Dollar Ditched in Iran's Trade with Russia, Turkey: CBI Chief," Tasnim, September 25, 2019, https://www.tasnimnews.com/en/news/2019/09/25/2104766/us-dollar-ditched-in-iran-s-trade-with-russia-turkey-cbi-chief.
[14]"Iran, Russia Exchange Rial, Rouble for the First Time to Trade," IRNA English, August 24, 2022, https://en.irna.ir/news/84864149/Iran-Russia-exchange-rial-rouble-for-the-first-time-to-trade.

a third currency such as the euro may be necessary given the limited liquidity in the foreign exchange markets of the two countries for ruble-rial trades. Ruble-rial trades were introduced in Iran's NIMA foreign exchange market, used by importers and exporters, in the summer of 2022.[15] However, transaction volumes remain low.

Alongside efforts to conduct trade using the national currencies, Russian and Iranian authorities have also sought to establish the technical infrastructures to ease payments. Iranian banks remain subject to secondary sanctions, and Russian banks have themselves been barred from key banking platforms, such as SWIFT, a global bank messaging service. Therefore, increasing cross-border financial transactions requires the development of a new financial infrastructure. Russia has sought to provide Iranian banks access to its SWIFT alternative, the System for Transfer of Financial Messages, known by its Russian acronym SPFS. Russia has also sought to allow Iranian banks to issue cards connected to the MIR payments system and to connect the MIR system with Iran's domestic equivalent, Shetab. MIR is an alternative to payment processors such as Visa and MasterCard, which have never done business in Iran and which withdrew from Russia following the Ukraine invasion. Against this backdrop, individual banks have also sought to establish correspondent banking links. In December 2022, Russia's second largest bank, VTB, began processing rial-denominated payments to Iranian banks on behalf of its clients.[16]

While there are signs of increased financial cooperation that might alleviate banking constraints, neither the SPFS nor MIR systems are widely used by Iranian banks, and the increased utilization of these infrastructures remains a priority for Russian and Iranian authorities alongside the increased settlement of trade in national currencies. In May 2022, Russian prime minister Alexander Novak noted the importance of greater banking cooperation within the agenda of the Russia-Iran

---

[15] "Tabdil-e Arz-e Saderat-i Ruble Dar Bazar-e Moteşakkel-e Nazdik-b-e Nerkh-e Bazar-e Azad [The Exchange of Ruble in State Market Is Close to Free Market Price]," IRNA, December 13, 2022, https://www.irna.ir/news/84973305/ تبدیل-ارز-صادراتی-روبل-در-بازار-متشکل-نزدیک-به-نرخ-بازار-آزاد.
[16] "Russia's VTB Bank Defies US Sanctions on Iran with Cross-Border Iranian Rials Transfers," Bne Intellinews, December 19, 2020, https://www.intellinews.com/russia-s-vtb-bank-defies-us-sanction-on-iran-with-cross-border-iranian-rials-transfers-265582/.

intergovernmental commission. Speaking to journalists after a meeting of the commission, Novak noted that among the

> key subjects were the creation of conditions for mutual settlements and processing of payments between our legal entities and organizations. Importantly, we agreed to move to the highest possible level of settlements in national currencies. We discussed together with central banks the spread and operation of the financial messaging system, as well as the connection of MIR and Shetab payment cards.[17]

Six months later, during a major bilateral business conference held in Tehran, Soren Vardanian, vice-chairman of the Moscow Chamber of Commerce, highlighted the importance of financial cooperation in an interview with an Iranian newspaper. Describing financial cooperation as the "lifeblood of bilateral relations," Vardanian warned that if Russia and Iran "do not have significant financial relations, their engagement will be difficult."[18]

Logistical Constraints

Aside from the significant constraints in banking infrastructure, Russia-Iran trade is also limited by physical bottlenecks owing to underdeveloped ports and limited merchant fleets in the Caspian Sea. The Russian seaport freight turnover totaled 835 million tons in 2021.[19] Of that total, just 7 million tons passed through Russia's Caspian ports.[20] Similarly, Iran's ports processed 153 million tons of goods in the Iranian calendar year ending March 2022.[21] But the annual throughput at Iran's

---

[17]"Russia, Iran Discussing Connection of Shetab, Mir Payment Systems, Says Deputy PM Novak," TASS, May 25, 2022, https://tass.com/economy/1455687.
[18]"aghaz be kare shoryae tejari irav va russiye [Iran-Russia Trade Council Starts to Work]," *Donyaye Eghtesad News Paper*, December 5, 2022, https://donya-e-eqtesad.com/بخش-هژیو-همان-63/3923371-زاغآ-هب-راک-یاروش-یراجت-ناریا-روسیه
[19]Sea Trade Ports Association via CEIC.
[20]Ibid.
[21]"Iranian Ports Show 17% Rise in Throughput in Fiscal 2021–22," *Financial Tribune*, April 4, 2022, https://financialtribune.com/articles/112991/iranian-ports-show-17-rise-in-throughput-in-fiscal-2021-22.

Caspian ports is around 7 million tons per year.[22] The lack of Russian and Iranian investment in the Caspian port infrastructure reflects the marginal importance of these ports for the overall trade flows of the two countries in recent decades. The recent attention toward the Caspian reflects the fact that Russia and Iran have been forced to think about trade in more regional terms as Western sanctions limit opportunities to trade with the global market. To this end, the discussion over the increased utilization of the Caspian ports reflects a desire to shift trade from ports like Novorossiysk on the Black Sea or Shahid Rajaee on the Persian Gulf. However, even if Russian and Iranian ports in the Caspian basin have significant unused capacity—a claim often made by authorities—shifting even a small fraction of the overall trade of each country to the Caspian would require a doubling or tripling of freight turnover in the basin. The bottlenecks in Caspian ports have led Iranian traders to doubt that the ambitious targets for Russia-Iran trade are possible. Speaking to a journalist, one Iranian trader asked, "Considering the capacity of the northern ports of our country, with what logic and basis are [authorities] talking about increasing the transportation of goods from the northern ports?."[23]

The constraints also extend to the merchant fleets in the Caspian. Russia's merchant fleet in the Caspian includes over 1,600 vessels, split evenly between cargo vessels and tankers.[24] By comparison, there are just 100 Iranian cargo vessels and tankers operating in the Caspian. Iranian traders believe that their cargo fleet would need to double in size to allow trade volumes to rise in line with targets.[25] For now, the lack of Iranian vessels forces Iranians to work with Russian charterers. According to a board member of an Iranian transport industry group, "The pricing in the Caspian Sea is in the hands of the Russians, because

---

[22]"Iran's Caspian Sea Ports Record 52% Rise in Container Throughput," *Financial Tribune*, November 26, 2022, https://financialtribune.com/articles/domestic-economy/116145/iran-s-caspian-sea-ports-record-52-rise-in-container-throughput.
[23]"Rusiyye Ejaze-Ye Afzayesh-e Navagan-e Daryai-Ye Iran Dar Khazar Ra Namidahad [Russia Does Not Allow Increase in Iran's Shipping Fleet in Caspian Sea]," Etemad Online, March 25, 2022, https://www.etemadonline.com/دهد-یمن-ار-رزخ-رد-ناریا-ییایرد-ناگوان-شیازفا-هزاجا-هیسور-22/564913-یداصتقا-شخب.
[24]"Fleets of the Caspian amid Emerging Profitable Trends," Azer News, March 15, 2019, https://www.azernews.az/nation/147380.html.
[25]"Jang-e Qeymat-Ha; Navgan-e Daryai-Ye Khazar Nakar-Amad Ast? [Price War: Caspian Fleet Is Non Efficient]," Moroor, November 24, 2022, https://www.iranchamber.com/calendar/converter/iranian_calendar_converter.php.

the majority of ships operating in the region belong to the Russians, and in estimating the prices, they determine the costs and round-trip times." These estimates have led to Iranian traders being charged a freight cost of $45 per ton, when Iranian traders believe that the real price is $17 per ton. Despite this apparent price gouging, Iranian traders "have no possibility to protest" given the shortage of Iranian vessels.[26] Moreover, Iranian sources frequently claim that Russian authorities make it difficult for additional Iranian vessels to enter the Caspian basin through the Volga-Don canal—an example of what Iranian media refers to as Russia's "self-interested policies."[27]

Institutional Constraints

Taken together, these constraints in logistics and infrastructure pose a major challenge to Russian and Iranian ambitions to grow bilateral trade. Authorities in both countries have identified these challenges and have suggested that bilateral and multilateral institutions work to identify solutions. For example, a long-awaited free trade agreement between Iran and the EAEU might offer the prospect of greater cooperation within the bloc to ease bottlenecks in the Caspian.[28] The Russia-backed Eurasian Development Bank (EDB) has also pointed to the importance of Russia and Iran within the International North-South Transport Corridor (INSTC). The bank estimates that full utilization of the corridor will require $12.9 billion of infrastructure investment in Iran and $13.2 billion of investment in Russia. But alongside physical barriers, the bank's research also points to "tariff, administrative, financial, technical, and cross-border barriers" that limit freight traffic. "Those barriers are of different origin, are not always exclusively related to the transport sector, and may have deeper macroeconomic or institutional roots."[29] In other

---

[26] "Russia Does Not Allow Increase in Iran's Shipping Fleet."
[27] "Amalkard-e Banadar-e Tijar-i Shamali-e Iran Dar Haft Mahe-Ye Separi-Shode Az Sal-e 1401 [The Performance of Northern Ports in the First 7 Months Passed from 1401]," TINN, December 22, 2022,https://www.tinn.ir/خبر-ش/الطاع-رامآت-77/250260-ع-کملـ-درکـب-ردان- یـراج-یـلامش-یناریا-نـرد-هفـت-هام-س-یـر-هدش-از-لاس) (accessed January 30, 2024).
[28] "Iran, Eurasian Economic Union to Sign FTA on January 18," Iran Chamber of Commerce Newsroom, December 26, 2022, https://en.otaghiranonline.ir/news/44343.
[29] "International North–South Transport Corridor: Investments and Soft Infrastructure," Eurasian Development Bank, 2022, https://eabr.org/en/analytics/special-reports/intern

words, macroeconomic factors, insofar as they push Russia and Iran as competitors, disincentivize the kind of cooperation that would end up addressing the nonphysical barriers to trade and investment.

The formation of a Russia-Iran business council in November 2022 suggests that Russian and Iranian firms may jointly lobby authorities to revise policies and rules in ways that address these nonphysical barriers to efficient logistics. At the launch of the business council, the head of the Iran Trade Promotion Organization heralded the new body as "a means to jointly address existing problems."[30] But to engage in such lobbying, Russian and Iranian firms need to see aligned incentives.

Rebalancing Trade

The notion that the Russian and Iranian economies would pursue integration to compensate for their isolation from the global economy is a sensible one. But it overlooks the ways in which differences in how Russia and Iran have been isolated from the global economy impact the scope for integration. Today, the two countries find themselves in a small club of nations that have been fully cut off from Western trade and finance—they are by far the most significant economies in this club. Countries targeted by sanctions typically rebalance their trade relations in response. Through the process of "export deflection," sanctioned countries seek new markets for their exports, shifting the balance of trade away from the states that have imposed sanctions.[31] Typically, this means shifting trade away from the West and toward the East. Through the parallel process of "import reflection," sanctioned countries seek new suppliers for imports, particularly capital goods such as machinery and vehicles that are necessary to maintain industrial output.[32] But even when adopting these tactics in pursuit of resilience, sanctioned countries remain subject to a simple macroeconomic condition. To afford imports,

---

ational-north-south-transport-corridor-investments-and-soft-infrastructure/ (accessed January 30, 2024).
[30]"Iran-Russia Trade Council Starts to Work."
[31]Jamal Ibrahim Haidar, "Sanctions and Export Deflection: Evidence from Iran," *Economic Policy (CEPR)* 32, no. 90 (2017), 319–55.
[32]Esfandyar Batmanghelidj, "The Ins and Outs of Iranian Industrial Resilience under Sanctions," *The Muslim World* 111, no. 1 (February 2021), 96–112, https://doi.org/10.1111/muwo.12374.

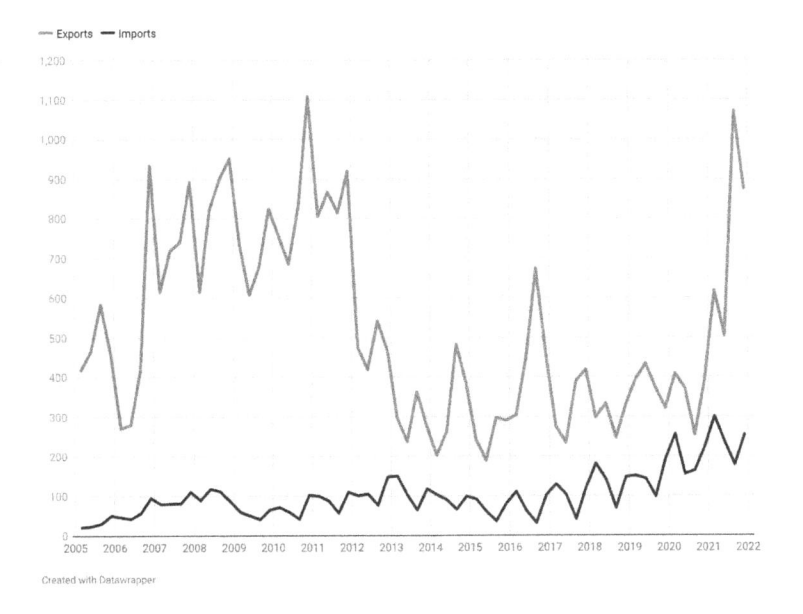

Figure 8.1 Russian trade with Iran (US$ millions). Federal Customs Service of Russia via CEIC.

a sanctioned country must sustain exports. The extent to which two sanctioned countries can develop bilateral trade depends on whether they are likelier to satisfy this macroeconomic condition for resilience through cooperation or competition.

Several observations about the developments in Russian and Iranian trade relationships suggest that competition is likelier than cooperation. Russia-Iran bilateral trade has remained low because other markets mattered more for both countries (Figure 8.1). Both countries are energy exporters, and so their most important trade partnerships need to be formed with buyers of their energy supplies. This is perhaps best exemplified by the significance of the European Union (EU) as a trade partner for both countries prior to the imposition of sectoral sanctions. Russia exported natural gas to Europe and imported industrial goods. Iran exported crude oil to Europe and imported industrial goods. Given the limited importance of the bilateral trade relationship, Russian trade with Iran collapsed after the imposition of financial sanctions on Iran in early 2012 and did not recover even after Russia faced its first Western sanctions following the annexation of Crimea in 2014. Since 2020, there has been an increase in Russia-Iran trade, which has again approached the peak in bilateral trade achieved in 2010. But underlying this increase is a trade in foodstuffs. In recent years, Russia has become a major supplier of wheat to Iran, while Iran has increased exports of fruits, vegetables, and nuts.[33] These goods are exempt from US secondary sanctions, meaning that the rise in trade is not actually indicative of success in resisting sanctions. Even with the recent growth, bilateral trade totaled just $1.1 billion in the second quarter of 2021. By comparison, Russian trade with the EU in the final quarter of 2021 totaled $78 billion. Even if Russia can expand trade with Iran many times over, it would not be enough to compensate for the impact of sanctions on trade with Europe.

The Federal Customs Service of Russia ceased publication of country-level trade data in March 2023, making it difficult to follow post-invasion trends in the Russia-Iran trade. However, data on vessel movements in the Caspian offer a proxy for trade volumes. Looking at the number of calls made by vessels at Iran's four major Caspian ports (Amirabad, Anzali, Astara, and Nowshahr) provides evidence of a modest rise in Russia-Iran trade since 2022 (Figure 8.2). In June 2023, the most recent month for which data are available, there was a combined average of 32.6 calls per week across the four Caspian ports, a 32 percent year-on-year increase. Information on port calls depends in part on automatic identification system (AIS) data, a global satellite tracking system that vessels can switch off to obscure their journeys.[34] The small vessels operating in the Caspian may not use AIS transponders reliably, and the true number of port calls may be higher than what is reflected in the data. But given the capacity constraints outlined earlier, the modest rise in calls is consistent with the expected increase in bilateral trade, which is rising from a low base.

The notion that Russia and Iran will further increase their economic cooperation is based on the view that the two countries have become more important to one another in the aftermath of being sanctioned.

---

[33]Esfandyar Batmanghelidj, "There Is No Russia-Iran Partnership," Bourse and Bazaar Foundation, July 17, 2022, https://www.bourseandbazaar.com/articles/2022/7/17/there-is-no-russia-iran-partnership.

[34]Lauren Kent and Salma Abdelaziz, 'Iran Has a Direct Route to Send Russia Weapons—and Western Powers Can Do Little to Stop the Shipments." CNN, May 26, 2023, https://edition.cnn.com/2023/05/26/europe/iran-russia-shipments-caspian-sea-intl-cmd/index.html.

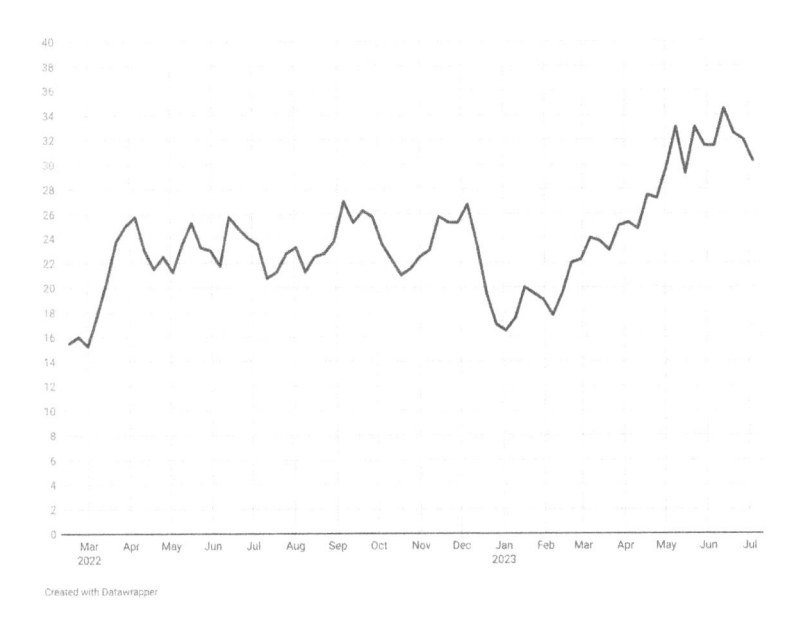

Figure 8.2 Weekly calls at Iran's Caspian ports. MarineTraffic via CEIC.

This is also sensible—sanctioned countries tend to pursue deeper trade relations with large regional economies, which can leverage geographic proximity and less formal banking channels, to overcome the financial and logistical barriers to trade created by sanctions. The expansion of Iran's trade with Iraq since 2012 is a good example of this phenomenon.[35] Trade between Iraq and Iran was negligible until Iran came under major sanctions. Shut out from markets further afield, Iranian manufacturers began to export their goods to Iran, aided by wholesalers who could trade goods for cash or on a barter basis at border checkpoints. But an examination of the composition of Russian and Iranian trade suggests that the two countries may lack an underlying compatibility for trade because the two countries boast similar economies and produce similar goods.

---

[35]Tamer Badawi, "Iran's Economic Leverage in Iraq," *Carnegie Endowment for International Piece*, *Sada* (blog), May 13, 2018, https://carnegieendowment.org/sada/76436.

Lack of Compatibility

When ranking the top fifteen goods exported by Russia and Iran, categorized according to the harmonized system of 2-digit classification, nine of the goods categories are shared by the two countries, reflecting the significant similarities in the complexity of Russian and Iranian economic production (Table 8.1). The same analysis for imports makes clear that Russia and Iran have similar needs from global trade. Among the top fifteen import categories, ten are shared (Table 8.2). While the United Nations Conference on Trade and Development (UNCTAD) data presented in this analysis may not fully capture the composition of Iranian trade owing to data completeness issues, such as Iran's obfuscation of mineral fuel exports under sanctions, this analysis nonetheless makes clear why Russia and Iran are likely to target the same trade partners.

The analysis also reveals the limited scope for bilateral trade. Of the top fifteen Russian import categories, only two correspond to the top categories of Iranian exports—plastics and fruits and nuts. The prospects for increased Iranian imports from Russia are a bit better, with five of the top fifteen import categories corresponding to the top Russian exports. Some of these compatibilities are reflected in the recent increase in bilateral trade, such as Iran's rising imports of Russian cereals. Other compatibilities, such as Iran's potential importation of Russian industrial and electrical machinery, remain largely untapped. There are indications that Russian and Iranian stakeholders are aiming to break out of old trade patterns. Iranian automakers have discussed entering the Russian market. Russian and Iranian industrial firms have also explored cooperation in the production of industrial machinery, such as turbines.[36] It is certainly possible, given the strong political support for expanded industrial cooperation between the two countries. But this cooperation faces a problem of scale. Taken together, Russia and Iran imported nearly $44 billion worth of industrial machinery in 2020. Even if significant industrial cooperation begins, it will not change the overall composition of the two economies, meaning that the potential for bilateral trade remains limited—Russia and Iran will continue to rely on other countries more than one another, a fact that contributes to a competitive dynamic.

---

[36]Anastasia Lyrchikova, "Russia Wants to Cooperate with Iran on Gas Turbines," Reuters, December 20, 2022, https://www.reuters.com/world/russia-wants-cooperate-with-iran-gas-turbines-2022-12-20/.

Table 8.1 Top Fifteen Categories of Russian and Iranian Goods Exports, 2020 (US$)

Iran		Russia	
Plastics†*	$3,954,287,348	Mineral fuels, oils, and waxes†	$145,974,516,909
Mineral fuels, oils, and waxes†	$2,759,772,478	Precious metals and stones	$31,151,630,008
Organic chemicals	$1,993,882,094	Iron and steel†	$16,801,272,006
Fruits and nuts*	$1,521,721,499	Cereals*	$8,963,975,074
Iron and steel†	$1,386,399,996	Wood	$8,138,485,252
Ores, slag, and ash†	$511,216,293	Fertilizers†	$7,247,961,080
Salt, sulfur, lime, cement, etc.	$475,711,581	Industrial machinery*	$6,622,448,564
Copper†	$446,502,506	Aluminum†	$5,988,337,587
Vegetables	$223,297,804	Copper†	$5,513,039,382
Fertilizers†	$222,251,705	Ores, slag, and ash†	$4,945,466,467
Fish†	$152,217,823	Fish†	$4,348,813,320
Zinc	$143,979,691	Inorganic chemicals†	$3,898,268,829
Aluminum†	$135,252,931	Electrical machinery and equipment*	$3,819,702,097
Inorganic chemicals†	$130,682,952	Plastics†	$3,683,209,117
Coffee, tea, and spices	$127,071,817	Animal or vegetable fats, oils, or waxes	$3,585,311,376

UNCTAD via Harvard University Atlas of Economic Complexity.
†Indicates a good that both countries export.
*Indicates a good in the country's top fifteen exports, which is in the other country's top fifteen imports.

Table 8.2 Top Fifteen Categories of Russian and Iranian Goods Imports, 2020 (US$)

Iran		Russia	
Electrical machinery and equipment†*	$4,039,284,520	Industrial machinery†	$39,084,000,000
Industrial machinery†*	$3,919,898,340	Electrical machinery and equipment†	$25,195,000,000
Cereals*	$2,400,683,611	Vehicles†	$18,962,000,000
Vehicles†	$1,166,219,286	Pharmaceutical products†	$9,802,045,868
Apparatuses (optical, medical, etc.)†	$1,140,599,350	Plastics†*	$8,177,735,983
Organic chemicals†	$901,438,665	Apparatuses (optical, medical, etc.)†	$7,872,212,618
Pharmaceutical products†	$849,552,011	Articles of iron or steel†	$4,693,674,345
Oil seeds and oleaginous fruits	$805,335,900	Fruits and nuts†*	$4,138,664,695
Plastics†*	$785,205,496	Apparel, not knit	$4,105,463,719
Paper and paperboard	$482,485,429	Organic chemicals†	$3,752,995,180
Tobacco	$475,335,417	Iron and steel	$3,402,995,868
Miscellaneous chemical products†	$473,397,736	Apparel, knit	$3,348,693,974
Articles of iron or steel†	$467,231,892	Furniture	$3,276,020,768
Fruits and nuts†	$463,428,518	Miscellaneous chemical products†	$3,018,143,829
Sugar and candy	$447,130,842	Rubber	$3,008,334,852

UNCTAD via Harvard University Atlas of Economic Complexity.
†Indicates a good that both countries import.
*Indicates a good in the country's top fifteen imports, which is in the other country's top fifteen exports.

Moreover, the viability of bilateral trade in manufactured goods remains in question as sanctions rattle Russian industrial supply chains, which were heavily dependent on European suppliers.[37]

As Russia and Iran seek to export mineral fuels, plastics, and iron and steel while under sanctions, one market is of preeminent importance. Greater dependence on China is a trademark of trade rebalancing by sanctioned countries. China is the only major economy willing to maintain significant volumes of trade, particularly energy trade, with countries subject to major sanctions programs. Notably, however, Russia and Iran are not equally encumbered by sanctions. So far, the Western sanctions imposed on Russia do not include secondary sanctions. This means Russia enjoys an inherent advantage as it seeks to shift trade to regional markets, some of which count among Iran's few major trade partners. Likewise, Russia will be aiming to consolidate trade with China, Iran's last major oil customer. When it comes to sanctions on Russia's energy sector, measures such as the oil price cap are less restrictive than the US secondary sanctions on energy trade with Iran.

Intensified Competition

For these reasons, Russia and Iran are poised for greater economic competition, and an examination of recent trade data suggests that this is a battle that Iran is already losing. The competition is clearly illustrated by trade data from Turkey and China, available for the period between January 2013 and June 2022. China is the largest trade partner for both Russia and Iran and the buyer of last resort for their respective energy exports. Turkey is the largest economy in West Asia and a major trade partner for both countries. Notably, Iran shares a border with Turkey, while Russia shares a border with China. Iran primarily relies on maritime transport to trade with China, while Russia relies on maritime transport across the Black Sea as part of its trade with Turkey.

One market in which Iran appears to be losing out to Russia is China. Iranian trade with China has languished under sanctions, while Russian trade with China has managed to grow, perhaps because Russian economic

---

[37] Anna Gross and Max Seddon, "'Everything Is Gone': Russian Business Hit Hard by Tech Sanctions," *Financial Times*, June 2, 2022, https://www.ft.com/content/caf2c d3c-1f42-4e4a-b24b-c0ed803a6245.

sectors are not yet subject to secondary sanctions. Iranian exports to China fell dramatically after May 2019, when the Trump administration revoked a series of waivers permitting Iranian oil exports (Figure 8.2). This made Iran's oil exports subject to secondary sanctions. A small number of Chinese refiners continued to purchase Iranian oil, especially after 2020. These Iranian imports are not reflected in the customs data as the trade is intermediated by the UAE and Malaysia. But while the true value of Iranian exports to China is higher than the customs data suggest, the level of Iranian imports from China remains depressed (Figure 8.3). This indicates that whatever revenues Iran is earning from its oil exports to China are not entirely accessible. Given the role of intermediaries, some of these revenues may be accruing outside of China.

By contrast, Russian trade with China has shown strong growth despite the specter of sanctions. Not only did trade continue to rise after the sanctions imposed following the Russian annexation of Crimea, but trade has also surged in the immediate aftermath of the Russian invasion of Ukraine and the imposition of much more significant

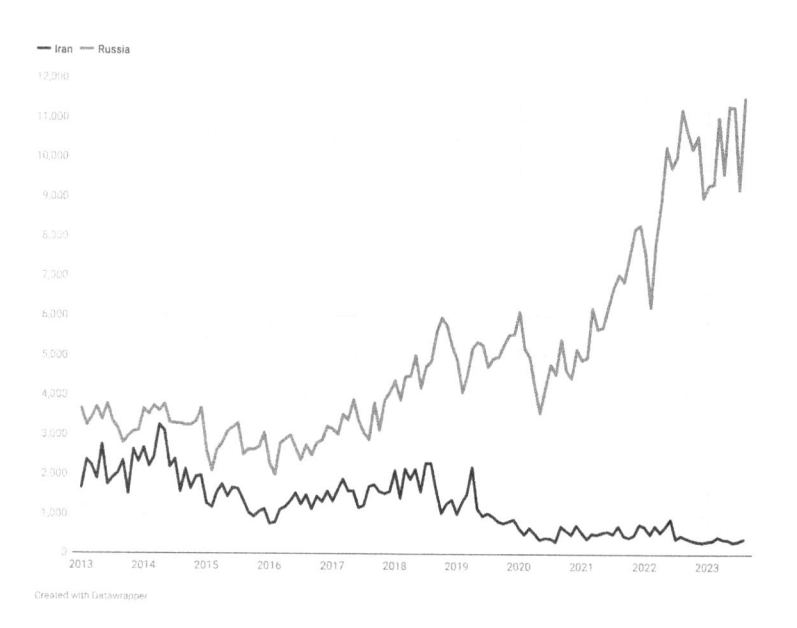

Figure 8.3 Russian and Iranian exports to China (US$ millions). General Administration of Customs of China via CEIC.

Western sanctions on the Russian economy in the first months of 2022. Buoyed by sales of crude oil, Russian exports to China are at historic highs, reaching $10.6 billion in September 2022 (Figure 8.2). Russian imports from China did fall in the aftermath of the 2014 sanctions, but this is likely due to the impact of the sanctions on business and consumer sentiment in Russia. The strong growth in Russian imports since 2014 suggests that the sanctions are not throttling trade with China. Russian imports from China totaled $1.1 billion in September 2022 (Figure 8.3). The growth in Russian exports to China may be explained in part by the fact that the imposition of sanctions on Iran led many Chinese buyers to seek new suppliers—energy is a major component of this trade. But more importantly, the Russian effort to deepen political and economic links with China accelerated following the increase in tensions with the West in the wake of the annexation of Crimea. Increasing bilateral trade was the low-hanging fruit. Considering the size of the economies and the shared border, the value of bilateral trade between Russia and China remains surprisingly low (see Figure 8.4).

Similar trends can be seen in Russian and Iranian trade with Turkey. Iranian trade with Turkey expanded beginning in 2012, reflecting Turkey's importance as a conduit for imports to Iran, including imports of gold, while the country remained under US and EU sanctions.[38] But growing geopolitical tensions between Iran and Turkey and the reimposition of US secondary sanctions in 2018 halted efforts to grow bilateral trade. Iranian trade with Turkey has languished since. Today, bilateral trade rarely exceeds $500 million per month. By contrast, Russian trade with Turkey has trended upward since 2016, when the two countries normalized relations after a 2015 incident in which Turkey shot down a Russian warplane. Bilateral trade has grown at a faster pace since the Russian invasion of Ukraine as Turkish firms took on the role of middlemen in critical Russian supply chains, funneling European technology to Russia that was no longer being directly exported from the EU owing to sanctions.[39] In the first three quarters

---

[38] Ivan Watson and Gul Tuysuz, "Iran Importing Gold to Evade Economic Sanctions, Turkish Official Says," CNN, November 29, 2012, https://edition.cnn.com/2012/11/29/world/meast/turkey-iran-gold-for-oil/index.html.

[39] Steve Stecklow, David Gauthtier-Villars, and Maurice Tamman, "The Supply Chain That Keeps Tech Flowing to Russia," Reuters, December 13, 2022, https://www.reuters.com/investigates/special-report/ukraine-crisis-russia-tech-middlemen/.

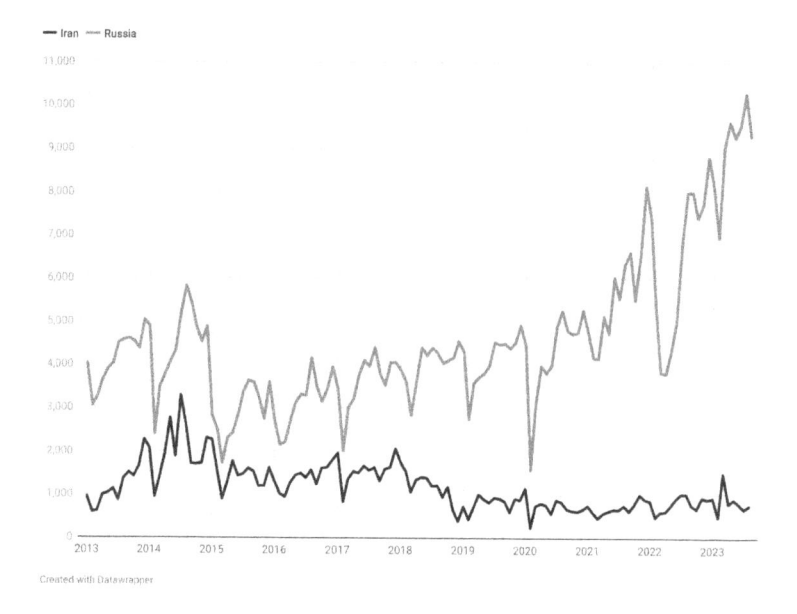

Figure 8.4 Russian and Iranian imports from China (US$ millions). General Administration of Customs of China via CEIC.

of 2022, Russia-Turkey bilateral trade averaged $5.6 billion per month, roughly ten times the value of the Turkey-Iran trade (see Figures 8.5 and 8.6).

Despite being more politically and economically isolated than ever before, Russia has managed to rebalance its trade relations more successfully than Iran. The surge in Russian trade with China and Turkey over the past year demonstrates that Russia is successfully consolidating trade with its key energy customers while also bolstering supply chains through a greater reliance on regional trade networks. While Iran attempted a similar rebalancing with both China and Turkey in the aftermath of the 2012 and 2018 imposition of US secondary sanctions, bilateral trade still fell. Today, with Iran poised to remain under secondary sanctions due to continued tensions over its nuclear program, its provision of drones to Russia, and ongoing human rights violations, the prospects for the Iranian economy are darkening. Long-term resilience to sanctions will require Iran to find new ways to grow, including by increasing trade with both regional economies and China.

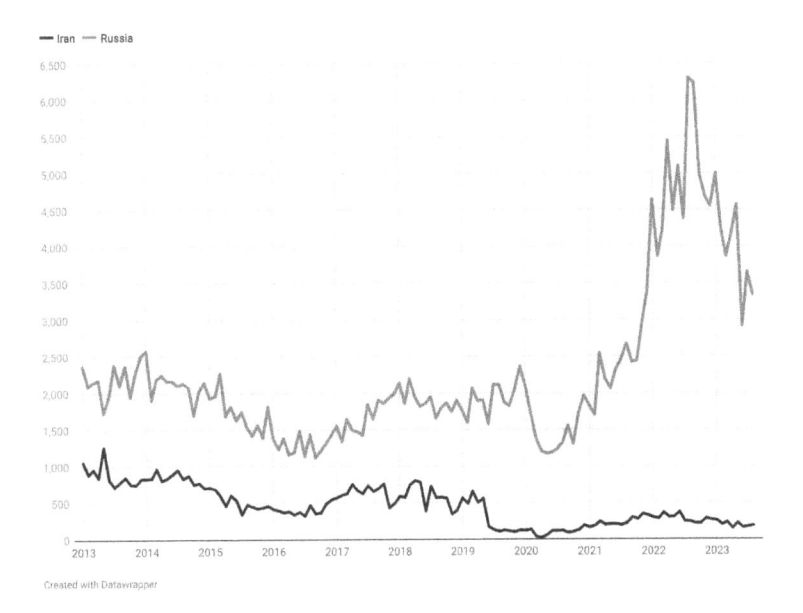

Figure 8.5 Russian and Iranian exports to Turkey (US$ millions). Turkish Statistical Institute via CEIC.

But the sudden surge in Russian trade with China and Turkey has made Iran's job much harder. By virtue of their economic isolation, Russia and Iran are forced to compete to win business among the limited number of firms in countries such as China and Turkey that remain willing to transact with sanctioned entities, or with companies whose operations are encumbered by sanctions. If the market for sanctions-proof trade is limited, and if Russian firms appear to be capturing a larger share of that market, then Iran will be increasingly vulnerable to Russian economic coercion. In this regard, economic competition in markets such as China and Turkey gives Russia the means to dictate the terms of bilateral trade in ways that may be more advantageous than what cooperation can achieve.

Three factors explain why Russia has proven more successful than Iran—at least so far—in rebalancing its trade in the face of sanctions. These factors make clear that any nascent economic partnership between Russia and Iran will be an unequal one. First, Russia boasts a larger economy than Iran and a more powerful geopolitical position, even

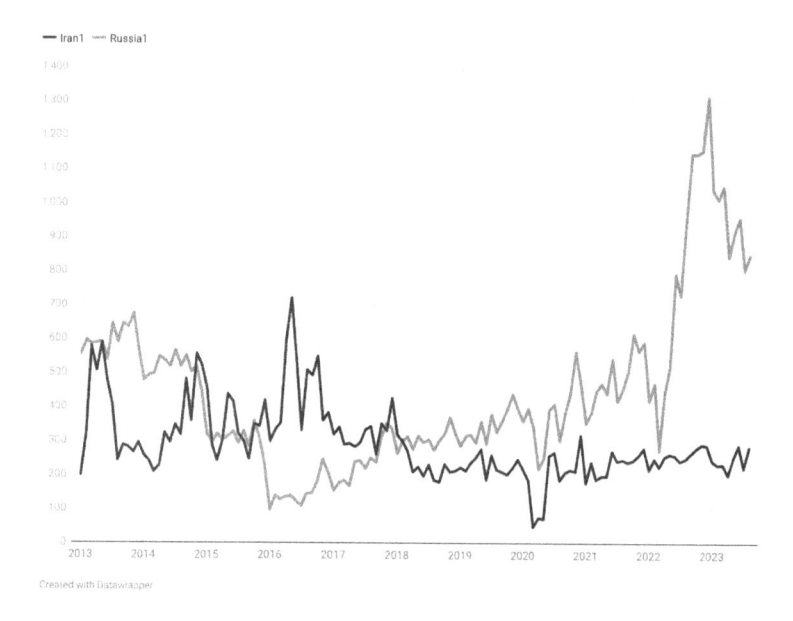

Figure 8.6 Russian and Iranian imports from Turkey (US$ millions). Turkish Statistical Institute via CEIC.

in the aftermath of the ill-fated invasion of Ukraine. Second, Russia remains less encumbered by sanctions than Iran, making it easier for commercial entities in countries like China and Turkey to transact with Russian firms. Even if Russia does end up facing secondary sanctions, the likely pullback from Chinese and Turkish enterprises will occur from a higher level, and there will be greater incentives to try and find the means to circumvent the sanctions. Finally, the Russian economy was more globalized at the time the sanctions were imposed, meaning that while the pain of sanctions may have been even more significant, Russian government bodies and firms had a greater understanding of how to devise and operate supply chains and financial channels. Despite facing significant economic headwinds, Russian officials appear encouraged by their early success in shifting trade relations. In December 2022, President Vladimir Putin stated "that by introducing sanctions, Western countries were trying to push Russia to the periphery of world development." He declared that Russia would "never take the route of self-isolation" and would instead increase "cooperation with all who have an interest in that."[40] In Iran, debates around how to resist sanctions continue to center on the concept of a "resistance economy," which posits that Iran should respond to isolation by achieving greater self-sufficiency.[41] While there is a growing awareness in Iran that self-isolation is a losing strategy, the fact that these debates remain unresolved speaks to Iran's position as a laggard in globalization, even before the imposition of Western sanctions a decade ago.

Conclusion

Russia will no doubt continue to use economic inducements as part of its diplomatic relations with Iran. In January 2023, Vyacheslav Volodin, speaker of the lower house of the Russian parliament, announced that bilateral trade with Iran totaled $4.6 billion in 2022. Speaking to Iranian counterparts, Volodin described the push to increase mutual trade as "extremely important given the conditions of sanctions pressure on our countries."[42] But Iranian policymakers are becoming aware that Russian promises of cooperation are only part of the story. Iranian politician Heshmatollah Falahatpisheh is among those who have called attention to the increased competition with Russia, including the fact that Iran has been forced to discount its oil in China in the face of increased competition from Russia. "Two countries, China and Russia, have taken extreme advantage of Iran's foreign policy and turned Tehran into a hostage to their interests," he declared in an interview in January 2023.[43]

Falahatpisheh's comments reflect suspicions among some Iranian politicians that Russia has made a political decision to take advantage of Iran—although official statements suggest otherwise. Indeed, the state continues to play a significant role in Russian economic policy,

---

[40] Mark Trevelyan, "Putin Says Russia Will Fight Sanctions with Shift in Trade and Energy Flows," Reuters, December 15, 2022, https://www.reuters.com/markets/putin-says-russian-gdp-fall-25-2022-2022-12-15/.

[41] Bijan Khajepour, "Decoding Iran's 'Resistance Economy,'" Al Monitor, February 24, 2014, https://www.al-monitor.com/originals/2014/02/decoding-resistance-economy-iran.html.

[42] "Rial-Ruble Share Exceeds 60% in Iran-Russia Trade," *Tehran Times*, January 24, 2023, https://www.tehrantimes.com/news/481213/Rial-Ruble-share-exceeds-60-in-Iran-Russia-trade.

[43] "Forsat-Suziyy-Hâ va Ziyan-e Manafe-e Melliy [The Opportunity Lost and Costs for National Interests]," *Shargh*, January 8, 2023, https://www.sharghdaily.com/خبر-منازو-ه-100/866493-تصرف-سوزی-های-ان-منفعت-ملی.

and therefore, the degree to which competition or cooperation comes to define the economic relationship with Iran will reflect state priorities. Russian officials may be making a genuine push for cooperation. But the decisions of individual firms matter as well, especially under conditions in which those firms are adjusting to sanctions-related headwinds. In this context, market forces will also play a role in determining whether cooperation can overcome competition. Reports of price wars between Russian and Iranian firms demonstrate how these forces can undercut moves toward greater cooperation.

As stated in the introduction to this chapter, Russia-Iran economic relations will only deepen if the two countries can overcome banking, logistical, and institutional constraints, while limiting the detrimental effects of increased competition. A review of the constraints facing bilateral trade and investment reveals significant physical and nonphysical barriers that will prove difficult to overcome, especially in the face of Western sanctions. An assessment of the available trade data suggests that the composition of the Russian and Iranian economies limits the scope for bilateral trade. The two countries, seeking to export and import many of the same goods, have been thrust into intensified competition. Russia is seeking to shift trade toward the same partners on which Iran has been dependent for the last decade. So far, Russia appears to be expanding trade with those partners, including China and Turkey, at Iran's expense. For these reasons, the prospects for Russia-Iran economic relations are dim. While Russian and Iranian policymakers have envisioned a future of greater cooperation, continued competition will likely prevent the formation of a true economic partnership.

Bibliography

Azer News. "Fleets of the Caspian amid Emerging Profitable Trends." March 15, 2019. https://www.azernews.az/nation/147380.html.

Badawi, Tamer. "Iran's Economic Leverage in Iraq." *Carnegie Endowment for International Piece. Sada* (blog), May 23, 2018. https://carnegieendowment.org/sada/76436.

Batmanghelidj, Esfandyar. "The Ins and Outs of Iranian Industrial Resilience under Sanctions." *The Muslim World* 111, no. 1 (February 1, 2021): 96–112. https://doi.org/10.1111/muwo.12374.

Batmanghelidj, Esfandyar. "There Is No Russia-Iran Partnership." Bourse and Bazaar Foundation, July 17, 2022. https://www.bourseandbazaar.com/articles/2022/7/17/there-is-no-russia-iran-partnership.

Berg, Matt. "Iran Preparing to Send 'Several Hundred' Drones to Russia, Sullivan Says." Politico, July 11, 2022. https://www.politico.com/news/2022/07/11/iran-uav-drones-russia-00045195.

Bloomberg. "Russia, Iran Tighten Trade Ties amid US Sanctions." May 22, 2022. https://www.bloomberg.com/news/articles/2022-05-25/russia-iran-tighten-trade-ties-amid-us-sanctions-interfax-says.

Bne Intellinews. "Russia's VTB Bank Defies US Sanctions on Iran with Cross-Border Iranian Rials Transfers." December 19, 2020. https://www.intellinews.com/russia-s-vtb-bank-defies-us-sanction-on-iran-with-cross-border-iranian-rials-transfers-265582/.

Cohen, Brett, and Garrett Nada. "Raisi in Russia." Iran Primer, January 21, 2022. https://iranprimer.usip.org/blog/2022/jan/21/raisi-russia.

DeYoung, Karen, and Joby Warrick. "Russia-Iran Military Partnership 'Unprecedented' and Growing, Officials Say." *Washington Post*, December 9, 2022. https://www.washingtonpost.com/national-security/2022/12/09/russia-iran-drone-missile/.

DeYoung, Karen. "U.S. Says Latest Iranian Nuclear Response Is 'Not Constructive.'" *Washington Post*, September 2, 2022. https://www.washingtonpost.com/national-security/2022/09/02/us-says-latest-iran-nuclear-response-is-not-constructive/.

Donya-e Eqtesad. "Aghaz-e b-e Kar-e Shura-Ye Tijari-Ye Iran va Rusiyye [Iran-Russia Trade Council Starts to Work]." December 6, 2022. https://donya-e-eqtesad.com/خبش-و یژ-نامه-63/3923371-آغاز-ب-ه-راه-اروش-یارجت-ی نار ی-هیسو ر.

Donya-E Eqtesad. "Se Galogâh-e Tijârat-e Iran-Rusiyye [Three Chock Point of Russia-Iran Trade]." November 16, 2022. https://donya-e-eqtesad.com/خبش-ص نعت-مع دن-3/3917517-س ه-گول-هاگ-تراج ت-ی نار ی روس هی.

El Khoury, Chady Adel. "Impediments to Correspondent Banking in Iran." International Monetary Fund, February 27, 2017. https://www.elibrary.imf.org/downloadpdf/journals/002/2017/063/article-A001-en.xml.

Etemad Online. "Rusiyye Ejaze-Ye Afzayesh-e Navagan-e Daryai-Ye Iran Dar Khazar Ra Namidahad [Russia Does Not Allow Increase in Iran's Shipping Fleet in Caspian Sea]." March 25, 2022. https://www.etemadonline.com/خبش-اق تصاد ی-22/564913-هیسو ر-هزاج ا-فا زاش ی-ناگوا ن-د ر ی ای ی-ی نار ی-در-خز ر-ار-ی من-ده د.

Eurasian Development Bank. "International North–South Transport Corridor: Investments and Soft Infrastructure." 2022. https://eabr.org/en/analytics/special-reports/international-north-south-transport-corridor-investments-and-soft-infrastructure/ (accessed January 30, 2024).

Financial Tribune. "Iran's Caspian Sea Ports Record 52% Rise in Container Throughput." November 26, 2022. https://financialtribune.com/articles/domestic-economy/116145/iran-s-caspian-sea-ports-record-52-rise-in-container-throughput.

Financial Tribune. "Iranian Ports Show 17% Rise in Throughput in Fiscal 2021–22." April 4, 2022. https://financialtribune.com/articles/112991/iranian-ports-show-17-rise-in-throughput-in-fiscal-2021-22.

Grajewski, Nicole. "As the World Shuns Russia over Its Invasion of Ukraine, Iran Strengthens Its Ties with Moscow." Atlantic Council, March 7, 2022. https://www.atlanticcouncil.org/blogs/iransource/as-the-world-shuns-russia-over-its-invasion-of-ukraine-iran-strengthens-its-ties-with-moscow%ef%bf%bc/.

Gross, Anna, and Max Seddon. "Everything Is Gone: Russian Business Hit Hard by Tech Sanctions." *Financial Times*, June 2, 2022. https://www.ft.com/content/caf2cd3c-1f42-4e4a-b24b-c0ed803a6245.

Hafezi, Parisa, and Francois Murphy. 'Russia's Demand for US Guarantees May Hit Nuclear Talks, Iran Official Says'. Reuters, March 5, 2022. https://www.reuters.com/article/us-iran-nuclear-idCAKBN2L207J.

Hafezi, Parisa. "Iran-U.S. Nuclear Talks to Resume in Coming Days: Tehran and EU Say." Reuters, June 25, 2022. https://www.reuters.com/world/middle-east/iran-nuclear-talks-with-us-resume-soon-tehran-eu-say-2022-06-25/.

Haidar, Jamal Ibrahim. "Sanctions and Export Deflection: Evidence from Iran." *Economic Policy (CEPR)* 32, no. 90 (2017): 319–55.

Iran Chamber of Commerce Newsroom. "Iran, Eurasian Economic Union to Sign FTA on January 18." December 26, 2022. https://en.otaghiranonline.ir/news/44343.

Iran Chamber of Commerce Newsroom. "Russia Says $40 Billion Trade with Iran Achievable." December 5, 2022. https://en.otaghiranonline.ir/news/44279.

Iran Primer. "Year One: Raisi on the U.S. & the West." September 14, 2022. https://iranprimer.usip.org/blog/2022/sep/14/year-one-raisi-us-west.

IRNA. "Tabdil-e Arz-e Saderat-i Ruble Dar Bazar-e Moteşakkel-e Nazdik-b-e Nerkh-e Bazar-e Azad [The Exchange of Ruble in State Market Is Close to Free Market Price]." December 13, 2022. https://www.irna.ir/news/84973305/تبدیل-ارز-صادراتی-روبل-در-بازار-متشکل-نزدیک-به-نرخ-بازار-آزاد.

IRNA English. "Iran, Russia Exchange Rial, Rouble for the First Time to Trade." August 24, 2022. https://en.irna.ir/news/84864149/Iran-Russia-exchange-rial-rouble-for-the-first-time-to-trade.

Kent, Lauren, and Salma Abdelaziz. "Iran Has a Direct Route to Send Russia Weapons—and Western Powers Can Do Little to Stop the Shipments." CNN, May 26, 2023. https://edition.cnn.com/2023/05/26/europe/iran-russia-shipments-caspian-sea-intl-cmd/index.html.

Khajepour, Bijan. "Decoding Iran's 'Resistance Economy.'" Al Monitor, February 24, 2014. https://www.al-monitor.com/originals/2014/02/decoding-resistance-economy-iran.html.

Knights, Michael, and Alex Almeida. "What Iran's Drones in Ukraine Mean for the Future of War." Washington Institute for Near East Policy, November 10, 2022. https://www.washingtoninstitute.org/policy-analysis/what-irans-drones-ukraine-mean-future-war.

Kozhanov, Nikolay. "Iran and Russia: Between Pragmatism and Possibilities of a Strategic Alliance." In *Foreign Policy of Iran under President Hassan Rouhani's First Term (2013–2017)*, edited by Luciano Zaccara, 131–56. Singapore: Springer Singapore, 2020. https://doi.org/10.1007/978-981-15-3924-4_7.

Kremlin. "Meeting with President of Iran Sayyid Ebrahim Raisi." January 19, 2022. http://en.kremlin.ru/events/president/news/67608.

Lyrchikova, Anastasia. "Russia Wants to Cooperate with Iran on Gas Turbines." Reuters, December 20, 2022. https://www.reuters.com/world/russia-wants-cooperate-with-iran-gas-turbines-2022-12-20/.

Moroor. "Jang-e Qiyamat-Ha; Navagan-e Daryai-Ye Khazar Nakar-Amad Ast? [Price War: Caspian Fleet Is Non Efficient]." November 24, 2022. https://www.iranchamber.com/calendar/converter/iranian_calendar_converter.php.

Reuters. "Iran and Russia's Gazprom Sign Primary Deal for Energy Cooperation." July 19, 2022. https://www.reuters.com/business/energy/iran-russias-gazprom-sign-primary-deal-energy-cooperation-2022-07-19/.

RFE/RL. "Iran's Top Automaker Eyes Russian Market Following Western Pullout." August 14, 2022. https://www.rferl.org/a/iran-khodro-russia-market/31988299.html.

Rome, Henry. "Iran and Russia: Growing Economic Competition." Iran Primer, July 18, 2022. https://iranprimer.usip.org/blog/2022/jul/18/iran-russia-growing-economic-competition.

Russia Matters. "Russia and Iran Get Closer While Still Competing, amid Balancing Act with Turkey." August 5, 2022. https://www.russiamatters.org/analysis/russia-and-iran-get-closer-while-still-competing-amid-balancing-act-turkey.

Shagina, Maria. "Own Goods, New Markets: Russia's Adjustment to Western Sanctions." *Zeitschrift Osteuropa* 71, nos. 10–12 (2021): 221–34. https://doi.org/10.35998/oe-2021-0089.

Shargh. "Forsat-Suziyy-Hâ va Ziyan-e Manafe-e Melliy [The Opportunity Lost and Costs for National Interests]." January 8, 2023. https://www.sharghdaily.com/خبر-شمانزمه-100/866493-تصرف-یزوس-ها-نایز-منافع-یلم.

Stecklow, Steve, David Gauthtier-Villars, and Maurice Tamman. "The Supply Chain That Keeps Tech Flowing to Russia." Reuters, December 13, 2022. https://www.reuters.com/investigates/special-report/ukraine-crisis-russia-tech-middlemen/.

Tasnim. "US Dollar Ditched in Iran's Trade with Russia, Turkey: CBI Chief." September 25, 2019. https://www.tasnimnews.com/en/news/2019/09/25/2104766/us-dollar-ditched-in-iran-s-trade-with-russia-turkey-cbi-chief.

TASS. "Russia, Iran Discussing Connection of Shetab, Mir Payment Systems, Says Deputy PM Novak." May 25, 2022. https://tass.com/economy/1455687.

Tehran Times. "Rial-Ruble Share Exceeds 60% in Iran-Russia Trade." January 24, 2023. https://www.tehrantimes.com/news/481213/Rial-Ruble-share-exceeds-60-in-Iran-Russia-trade

TINN. "Amalkard-e Banadar-e Tijar-i Shamali-e Iran Dar Haft Mahe-Ye Sepri-Shode Az Sal-e 1401 [The Performance of Northern Ports in the First 7 Months Passed from 1401]." December 22, 2022. https://www.tinn.ir/-بخش آمار-اطلاعات250/77--260عملکرد-بنادر-تجاری-شمالی-ایران-در-هفت-ماه-سپری-شده-از-سال (accessed January 30, 2024).

Trevelyan, Mark. "Putin Says Russia Will Fight Sanctions with Shift in Trade and Energy Flows." Reuters, December 15, 2022. https://www.reuters.com/markets/putin-says-russian-gdp-fall-25-2022-2022-12-15/.

Watson, Ivan, and Gul Tuysuz. "Iran Importing Gold to Evade Economic Sanctions, Turkish Official Says." CNN, November 29, 2012. https://edition.cnn.com/2012/11/29/world/meast/turkey-iran-gold-for-oil/index.html.

9 WILL IRAN CHALLENGE RUSSIA'S POSITION AS A MAJOR GLOBAL ENERGY PLAYER?

Jakub M. Godzimirski

The main goal of this chapter is to examine whether Iran can use the ongoing war in Ukraine as a window of opportunity to replace Russia as a supplier of energy to markets from which Russia is being pushed out after the imposition of various restrictive measures by the West. Both Russia and Iran are major energy producers and, as such, have a mix of overlapping and contradicting strategic energy interests. Until the outbreak of the war in Ukraine, Russia played a vital role as a supplier of energy to the European Union (EU). Iran also used to play a role as an energy supplier to the EU market before the EU imposed sanctions on its oil exports in January 2012,[1] when almost 20 percent of oil exports from Iran went to the EU. The 2015 deal on the Joint Comprehensive Plan of Action (JCPOA) reached by Iran with China, France, Russia, the UK, the United States, Germany, and the EU resulted in the reopening of dialogue on the energy sector between Iran and the EU.[2] However, Iran has not returned as a major energy supplier to the EU after the reimposition of US sanctions

---

[1] "Council Conclusions on Iran," Council of the European Union, January 23, 2012, https://www.consilium.europa.eu/uedocs/cms_data/docs/pressdata/EN/foraff/127446.pdf.
[2] "Joint Statement by the High Representative/Vice-President of the European Union, Federica Mogherini and the Minister of Foreign Affairs of the Islamic Republic of Iran,

following the US withdrawal from the deal. Will the Russian invasion of Ukraine help Iran return as a major energy supplier to Europe by filling the energy vacuum created after Russia's forced withdrawal from this attractive energy market? This is the main question addressed in this chapter.

However, to provide an informed answer to this question, we need to dig deeper into the bilateral relations between Russia and Iran and map their positions as energy actors. We also need to understand how the two countries' common challenge of facing restrictive measures imposed by the West—and, in the case of Iran, by the international community—has shaped their bilateral relations and their attitudes to cooperation. Russia's invasion of Ukraine in February 2022 has resulted in the imposition of a new set of restrictive measures on Russia, including on the Russian energy sector. At the same time, Iran was involved in complicated negotiations on the revival of the JCPOA, which sets out rules for international monitoring of the country's nuclear program.[3] A positive outcome of these negotiations could also result in lifting or waiving the various sanctions imposed on Iran. It was, therefore, expected that such a positive outcome, combined with the global impact of the energy sanctions imposed on Russia, could help Iran reestablish itself as a major energy supplier to markets from which Russia was being pushed out. However, after initial optimism, negotiations on the JCPOA became difficult. The prospects of reaching an agreement were viewed as unrealistic after the brutal onslaught against the anti-regime protesters in Iran in the second half of 2022 and military support for Russia's war in Ukraine. In the meantime, Russia and Iran have taken several steps to strengthen their bilateral relations and form an anti-Western coalition in close cooperation with China. These political factors and developments must also be considered when assessing the long-term prospects of Iran becoming a major energy supplier to markets vacated by Russia.

This chapter will, therefore, be divided into several sections. In the first section, we present the official Russian narrative on Iran. In the second section, we assess the role of Russia and Iran as energy actors

---

Javad Zarif," European Commission, April 16, 2016, https://ec.europa.eu/commission/prescorner/detail/en/STATEMENT_16_1441.
[3] "Additional Effort and Patience Needed to Revive Iran Nuclear Deal," UN, December 14, 2021, https://news.un.org/en/story/2021/12/1107922.

prior to the outbreak of war. The third section examines the impact of war on the relations between Russia and Iran. In the fourth section, we present some considerations on how the war and the changing pattern of relations between Iran and Russia can influence Iran's choices in a situation when the country can be tempted to fill the gap left by Russia's forced withdrawal from the European energy market.

Russia's Official Narrative on and Interests in Iran

To examine how the relations between Russia and Iran can change after the outbreak of the war, we must understand how these relations had been developing before the war broke out and in the broader regional context.[4] To do this, we examine the official Russian narrative on Iran as presented on the official website of the Russian Ministry of Foreign Affairs (MFA 2021), containing short texts on various countries and Russia's bilateral

---

[4]For more on this context, see Alex Vatanka, "Iran's Russian Conundrum," in *Russia in the Middle East*, edited by Theodore Karasik and Stephen Blank (Washington, DC: Jamestown Foundation, 2018), 87–104; Dimitry Trenin, *What Is Russia up to in the Middle East?* (Cambridge: Polity, 2017); Becca Wasser, "The Limits of Russian Strategy in the Middle East," RAND Corporation, 2018, https://doi.org/10.7249/PE340; Dimitar Bechev, Nicu Popescu, and Stanislav Secrieru, *Russia Rising: Putin's Foreign Policy in the Middle East and North Africa* (London: I.B. Tauris, 2021); Chiara Lovotti, Eleonora Ambrosetti, Christopher Hartwell, and Alexandra Chmielewska, eds., *Russia in the Middle East and North Africa: Continuity and Change* (London: Routledge, 2020); Irina Zvyagelskaya, Anastasiya Bogacheva, Aleksey Davydov, Ibragim Ibragimov, Stanislav Lazovsky, Lyudmila Samarskaya, Irina Svistunova, Nikolay Surkov, and Tatyana Tyukaeva, "Rossiyskaya politika na Blizhnem Vostoke. Perspektivy i vyzovy [Russian Policy in the Middle East: Perspectives and Challenges]," *Svobodnaya Mysl* 6 (2021), 71–86; Mark N. Katz, "Iran and Russia," in *Iranian Foreign Policy since 2001: Alone in the World*, edited by Thomas Juneau and Sam Razavi (London: Routledge, 2013), 181–92; Omid Shokri Kalehsar and Azime Telli, "The Future of Iran-Russia Energy Relations Post-Sanctions," *Middle East Policy* 24, no. 3 (2017), 163–70, https://doi.org/10.1111/mepo.12297; Abdolrasool Divsallar, "The Pillars of Iranian-Russian Security Convergence," *The International Spectator* 54, no. 3 (2019), 107–22, https://doi.org/10.1080/03932729.2019.1586147; Elaheh Koolaee, Hamid Mousavi, and Afife Abedi, "Fluctuations in Iran-Russia Relations during the Past Four Decades," *Iran and the Caucasus* 24, no. 2 (2020), 216–32, https://doi.org/10.1163/1573384X-20200206. For the semi-official Iranian view on these relations on the eve of the war, see Ali Eghbalizarch, "Benefits of Promotion of Tehran-Moscow Relations: At a Time When Russia and America Are Distancing," ISPI, January 2022, https://ipis.ir/en/subjectview/675251/Benefits-of-Promotion-of-Tehran-Moscow-Relations-At-a-time-when-Russia-and-America-are-distancing.

relations with them.[5] We treat this official MFA representation of Iran as a convenient point of departure for an official presentation of the state of relations before the war. This examination, together with a short review of the set of current Russian doctrines on national security, foreign policy, defense-related matters, and energy presented on the official website of the country's Security Council as core documents on security[6] will also be used to establish Iran's place on the Russian interest map.

The examined version of this official MFA presentation of Iran and Russia-Iran relations is a short 2,700-word-long document updated on April 4, 2021, providing basic information about the country and mapping the critical developments in Moscow's bilateral ties with Iran.[7] In addition, it contains information about the demographic, political, religious, and economic aspects of Iranian policy as well as a relatively detailed overview of the most recent developments in bilateral relations.

What are the main features of Iran presented in this official Russian narrative? The first lines show that the country's geopolitical position is of high interest as Iran historically occupies an important position at the crossroads of the Middle East, Transcaucasia, Central Asia, and South Asia. In addition, the country "has an ancient and rich history and culture that has strongly influenced many countries and peoples of the Near and Middle East." Another important feature is its location and its endowment with natural resources as "Iran is located at the crossroads of strategically important trade routes between Europe and Asia, ranks third in the world in terms of proven oil reserves and second in natural gas reserves, is one of the largest oil exporters in OPEC, and is also rich in minerals such as coal, chromium, copper, iron ore, lead, manganese, zinc and sulphur."

According to this official Russian narrative, since 1979, the economic and social development of the country has been strongly and negatively influenced by what is referred to as illegal sanctions imposed by the United States and its allies, culminating with Donald Trump's administration's decision to withdraw from the JCPOA. In addition to sanctions, the Covid-19 pandemic has had a disastrous impact on the

---

[5]"Ministerstvo Inostrannykh Del. Islamskaya Republika Iran [Islamic Republic of Iran]," Russian Ministry of Foreign Affairs, May 2, 2021, https://www.mid.ru/ru/maps/ir/.
[6]All these documents are available at http://www.scrf.gov.ru/security/docs/.
[7]"Ministerstvo Inostrannykh Del. Islamskaya Republika Iran."

situation in Iran, and the combination of these external shocks led to "further deterioration of the socio-economic situation in Iran in 2020." One of the Covid-19–related negative factors was the dramatic fall in the price of oil on the global market, which dealt a heavy blow to the country's economy, reducing its export revenues.

In the part of the Russian MFA document on the developments in bilateral relations,[8] these relations are described as being based on "the coincidence or proximity of the positions of the two countries on most issues of the world and regional agenda" and interest in the building of a multipolar world order based on international law, with strengthening the role of the United Nations (UN) in international affairs and countering new challenges and threats being listed as the most important common interests. To illustrate the importance of bilateral relations, the document mentions that President Vladimir Putin paid official visits to Iran three times—in 2007, 2015, and 2017—and received his Iranian counterparts in Moscow on three occasions—in 2014, 2015, and 2017. In addition, the national leaders of Russia and Iran also meet regularly in other such meetings as the Astana Format, where the focus is on finding a solution to the conflict in Syria, or the meetings of the Shanghai Cooperation Organization in which Russia is a full member, and Iran is an observer but aims to become a full-fledged member.

Iran is mentioned as one of the key countries with which Russia develops bilateral relations in the official Russian Foreign Policy Concept from 2016 that describes these relations in the following manner:[9]

> Russia is pursuing a policy of comprehensive development of cooperation with the Islamic Republic of Iran and is also seeking the consistent implementation of a comprehensive agreement to resolve the situation around the Iranian nuclear program on the basis of UN Security Council Resolution 2231 of 20 July 2015, the relevant decisions of the IAEA Board of Governors, and is giving its full support to the process.

---

[8] Ministerstvo Inostrannykh, 2021.
[9] *Kontseptsiya vneshnei politiki Rossiiskoi Federatsii* [*Foreign Policy Concept of the Russian Federation*], Kremlin (Moscow: President of the Russian Federation, 2016), http://www.scrf.gov.ru/security/international/document25/.

The Russian Energy Strategy until 2030[10] contains two mentions of Iran—as one of the countries in addition to Algeria, Central Asian countries, and others—in which Russian companies will actively cooperate. The possible areas of cooperation are listed as participation in the development of the gas fields and the construction of new interregional gas pipelines, particularly, as well as the coordination of export policies. According to the same document, Iran is also to play a role in the Russian efforts to consolidate the main regional gas production centers (Central Asian countries, Iran) around its gas transportation infrastructure and form the Eurasian integrated gas transportation system to ensure export and transit flows between Europe and Asia (in particular, the completion of the construction of the South Stream gas pipeline).

In addition to examining this short official Russian MFA account, one could get a better understanding of the relative importance of Iran in the Russian context by conducting a quantitative examination of the position of Iran in the broader regional Middle East and North Africa (MENA) context on the map of Russian official interests. For example, this could be done by examining how often and in what context Iran is mentioned in the key speeches of the Russian presidents and by comparing the number of direct references made to Iran at the websites of the Russian Ministry of Foreign Affairs and the website of the president of the Russian Federation.[11]

The most important speeches the Russian presidents give are Presidential Addresses to the Federal Assembly (PAFAs). In the period between 2000 and 2023, Iran is mentioned in these speeches a total of eight times. In 2009, in a PAFA given by President Medvedev, Iran was mentioned together with North Korea as a country whose nuclear program poses a challenge to the international community that must be dealt with through collective action.[12] In the 2010 PAFA, given by President

---

[10]*Energeticheskaya strategiya Rossii na period do 2030 goda* [*Energy Strategy of Russia through 2030*] (Moscow: Government of the Russian Federation 2009), http://scrf.gov.ru/security/economic/document122/.

[11]These quantitative examinations were conducted in August 2021 at the website of the Ministry of Foreign Affairs (https://mid.ru/ru/maps/ir/), where there were 1,029 documents referring directly to the Russian-Iranian relations, and in February 2022 before the outbreak of the war in Ukraine on the website of the Russian president (http://www.kremlin.ru/events/president/news/71451), where there were 121 documents tagged officially as being Iran-relevant.

[12]"Presidential Address to Federal Assembly," Kremlin, November 12, 2009, http://eng.kremlin.ru/transcripts/297.

Medvedev, Iran was also mentioned in the nuclear context as one of the countries with which Russia works together on the development of their nuclear industries, the other ones being India and China.[13] President Putin paid more attention to Iran in his 2013 PAFA.[14] In this speech, Putin referred to the problems related to the Iranian nuclear program and said that this situation demonstrates that any international problem can and should be resolved exclusively through political means, without resorting to forceful actions. He added that there was a breakthrough with the Iranian nuclear program that makes it imperative to continue patiently searching for a broader solution to guarantee Iran's inalienable right to develop peaceful nuclear energy. Putin also linked the situation in Iran to the development of a US missile defense system in Europe that he deemed important, saying that while the Iranian nuclear issue was being resolved, the US missile defense system developed in Europe to counter the possible Iranian threat remained a challenge. Finally, in his 2023 speech to the Federal Assembly,[15] President Putin listed Iran as one of the important partners—together with India, Pakistan, and the Middle Eastern countries—with whom Russia plans to work together to develop the international North-South Transit Corridor.

The results of the quantitative examination of the relative importance of Iran in the broader regional context are presented in Figure 9.1, and the main conclusion is that Iran is relatively very important to Russian policymakers as it is "ranked" third both by the MFA (behind Syria and Israel) and by the Russian president (after Turkey and Israel).

Russia's Economic Interests in Iran: What Role for Energy?

According to the data from Iranian customs quoted in the Russian MFA short note on Iran,[16] by December 20, 2020, Iran's non-oil exports decreased by 20 percent to $25.1 billion, while imports fell by 16 percent

---

[13]"Presidential Address to Federal Assembly," Kremlin, November 30, 2010, http://eng.news.kremlin.ru/news/1384.
[14]"Presidential Address to Federal Assembly," Kremlin, December 12, 2013, http://en.kremlin.ru/events/president/transcripts/messages/19825.
[15]"Presidential Address to Federal Assembly," Kremlin, February 23, 2023, http://en.kremlin.ru/events/president/news/70565.
[16]"Ministerstvo Inostrannykh Del. Islamskaya Republika Iran."

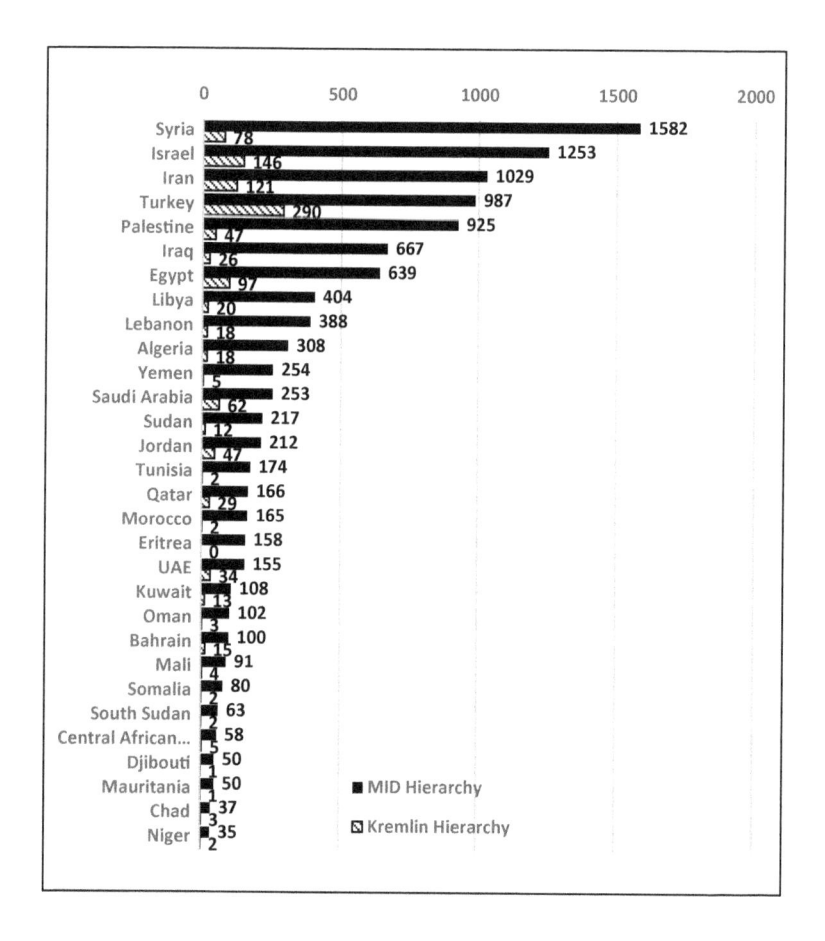

Country	MID Hierarchy	Kremlin Hierarchy
Syria	1582	78
Israel	1253	146
Iran	1029	121
Turkey	987	290
Palestine	925	47
Iraq	667	26
Egypt	639	97
Libya	404	20
Lebanon	388	18
Algeria	308	18
Yemen	254	5
Saudi Arabia	253	62
Sudan	217	12
Jordan	212	47
Tunisia	174	2
Qatar	166	29
Morocco	165	2
Eritrea	158	0
UAE	155	34
Kuwait	108	13
Oman	102	3
Bahrain	100	15
Mali	91	4
Somalia	80	2
South Sudan	63	2
Central African...	58	5
Djibouti	50	3
Mauritania	50	3
Chad	37	3
Niger	35	2

Figure 9.1 The relative importance of Iran in the broader MENA context on the Russian map of interests as measured by the references to Iran-related documents on the Russian MFA (MID Hierarchy) and the president of the Russian Federation (Kremlin Hierarchy) websites.

to $26.8 billion. Over a quarter of Iranian exports in this period went to China, which bought Iranian products worth $6.4 billion, Iraq ($5.9 billion, 23 percent), the United Arab Emirates ($3.3 billion, 13 percent), Turkey ($1.8 billion, 7.1 percent), and Afghanistan ($1.7 billion, 6.8 percent). Seventy percent of the exports were crude oil, natural gas, gas condensate, oil products, and mining ore. Among the main import partners were China ($7 billion), UAE ($6.3 billion), Turkey ($3 billion), India ($1.6 billion), and Germany ($1.3 billion).

This overview of official Iranian trade data demonstrates that Russia plays a relatively marginal role in Iran's trade. The situation is similar from a Russian perspective, as shown in Table 9.1, where a historical overview of the level of economic exchange between these two countries is presented.

There could be several explanations as to why the volume of trade between these two countries is relatively small, their geographical proximity notwithstanding. Lack of proper banking and financial connections was one crucial factor, and international sanctions against Iran also played a part, together with weak historical economic ties and logistical and bureaucratic problems as additional factors hampering their economic cooperation. Another possible explanation is the size of their national economies and their structure, as demonstrated in Chapter 8 of this book. Emma Ashford classifies both Russia and Iran as oil-dependent and oil-wealthy states that are also super-producers and super-exporters of oil in which petroleum resources play an important part and are also the primary source of export and budget revenues.[17] This can also explain why the volume of trade between them is low. For instance, in 2011, mineral fuels represented 66.8 percent of Russia's and 79 percent of Iran's exports. In 2019—the last pre–Covid-19 year—these shares also remained very high—60 percent in the case of Russia and 53.1 percent in the case of Iran.[18]

Keeping in mind the dominant role of hydrocarbons in both Russia and Iran's national economies and international trade, one could expect that they could perceive each other as competitors or even rivals in the global energy markets. However, the fact that their economies and exports are dominated by hydrocarbons can also mean that these two countries have some overlapping energy interests as critical producers and exporters of energy resources. In other words, energy can play a central role in shaping their bilateral relations.

To gauge the role of energy in their bilateral relations, we briefly examine how the energy-related questions figure in the official Russian MFA narrative.[19] Energy-related issues are treated in the official MFA narrative in a rather marginal way—нефт (oil) is mentioned seven

---

[17] Emma Ashford, *Oil, the State and War: The Foreign Policies of Petrostates* (Washington DC: Georgetown University Press, 2022).
[18] Data on the share of mineral fuels in Russian and Iranian exports in 2011 and 2019 has been extracted from The Observatory of Economic Complexity at www.oec.world.
[19] "Ministerstvo Inostrannykh Del. Islamskaya Republika Iran."

Table 9.1 Key Indicators of Russia's Trade with Iran in 2011–20 in Billion US$

	2011	2012	2013	2014	2015	2016	2017	2018	2019	2020
Export from Russia	3.406	1.902	1.168	1.326	1.016	1.881	1.314	1.205	1.518	1.423
Import from Iran	0.351	0.428	0.428	0.355	0.268	0.303	0.393	0.539	0.585	0.796
Russia's trade surplus	3.054	1.473	0.740	0.971	0.749	1.578	0.922	0.666	0.933	0.627
Iran share export (%)	0.66	0.36	0.22	0.27	0.30	0.66	0.37	0.27	0.36	0.42
Iran share import (%)	0.11	0.14	0.14	0.12	0.15	0.17	0.17	0.23	0.24	0.34

Source: Russian Customs Service data from https://customs.gov.ru/, extracted in 2021.
Note: These data are no longer available online due to restrictions introduced by the Russian authorities after the outbreak of war against Ukraine in February 2022.

times, газ (gas) four, ядер (nuclear) two, and энерг (energy) two times. However, Iran is also described as an important actor and exporter in the global energy context as it has the third largest reserves of oil and the second largest reserves of natural gas in the world. The document also mentions that questions related to energy cooperation between Russia and Iran are dealt with in the Permanent Russian-Iranian Commission for Trade and Economic Cooperation, which by the end of 2019 had fifteen meetings. The work of this body is coordinated by the Russian and Iranian energy ministers—N. G. Shulginov and Javad Owji—which somehow underlines the importance of energy in their bilateral economic relations.

As mentioned earlier, Russia and Iran, as major producers and exporters of fossil energy, have partly overlapping and partly conflicting energy interests. However, there is one energy dimension where Russia and Iran have developed mutually beneficial cooperation.[20]

In 1992, Russia and Iran signed a cooperation agreement on the development of civilian nuclear energy, and Russia also decided to help Iran complete the construction of a nuclear reactor at Bushehr. The work on this project started in 1975 under the Pahlavi monarchy, and the German company Siemens was to play a key part in this undertaking. However, the project was stopped after the 1979 Revolution, and it was first in 1992 with the signing of the Iranian-Russian agreement on cooperation in the field of nuclear energy that the work resumed. The agreement on Russian participation in constructing this nuclear power plant was finally signed in 1995 between *Atomstroyexport* and Iranian authorities. In September 2011, after several delays and technical problems, the plant was connected to the Iranian national grid, reaching its full capacity in August 2012. On November 11, 2014, Iran and Russia signed a new agreement to build two new nuclear reactors at the Bushehr Nuclear Power Plant (NPP) and possibly six other locations.

However, the cooperation on the Bushehr NPP has also caused some problems in the bilateral Russian-Iranian relations, as well as in the broader international context. What marred the bilateral cooperation

---

[20]Robert O. Freedman, "Russia, Iran and the Nuclear Question: The Putin Record," in *Russia: Re-emerging Great Power*, edited by Roger E. Kanet (London: Palgrave Macmillan, 2007), 195–221; see also R. Barari,"Nuclear Power as a Locomotive of Russian-Iranian Energy Cooperation," *Asia and Africa Today* 8 (2014), 32–4.

were various technical and economic problems that drove the costs up and soured relations between the involved partners. According to the most recent data, by the end of 2021, Iran had not paid all its Bushehr-related debts and still owed Russia approximately US$500 million.[21] Despite these difficulties, in January 2022, both countries discussed an extension of their nuclear cooperation and joint construction of new nuclear facilities in Iran.

Russia and Iran as Global Energy Players

Russia and Iran are important global and regional energy players.[22] But the tension between Russia and the West caused by the Russian military intervention in Ukraine can change Moscow and Tehran's positions in the global energy market and impact their energy cooperation, or even initiate their rivalry. To provide a better understanding of this issue, it is crucial to present more details on the two countries' roles as global energy players in the pre-conflict context. These details are provided in Table 9.2, where their positions are shown in the last pre–Covid-19 year 2019.

The main reason why this analysis focuses on the 2019 statistics is that in the two ensuing years, the situation in the global energy market was distorted. First, because of the Covid-19 pandemic, which reduced the global demand for energy resulting in much lower prices for energy commodities. And second, due to market manipulation caused partly—at least in Europe—by the growing political tensions in relations between Russia and the West, which was at that time Russia's main energy customer.[23]

---

[21]For more details on this Iranian debt, see https://www.rbc.ru/rbcfreenews/60d7edd59 a79471d490ef7ba, https://ria.ru/20211225/toplivo-1765442011.html, and https://tass.ru/ekonomika/14732653.

[22]Gawdat Bahgat, "Iran's Role in Europe's Energy Security: An Assessment," *Iranian Studies* 43, no. 3 (2010), 333–47, https://doi.org/10.1080/00210861003693869; IEA, *Key World Energy Statistics 2020* (Paris: International Energy Agency, 2020); Jakub. M. Godzimirski, "Russian Grand Strategy and Energy Resources: The Asian Dimension," in *Russian Energy Strategy in the Asia-Pacific*, edited by Elizabeth Buchanan (Canberra: Australian National University Press, 2021), 57–83, https://press.anu.edu.au/publications/russian-energy-strat egy-asia-pacific.

[23]On the role of the EU in Russian energy trade, see Szymon Kardaś, "The Twilight of the Oil Eldorado: How the Activity of Russian Oil Companies on the EU Market Has Evolved,"

Table 9.2 Russia and Iran as Global Energy Players

	Russia	Iran
Energy production (mtoe*) (IEA 2020)	1484.1	406.3
Energy consumption (mtoe) (IEA 2020)	759.3	265.7
Energy export dependence[†]	47.25% of production/ 701.3 mtoe	34.08% of production/ 138.5 mtoe
Oil production/net export (mtoe) (IEA 2020)	560/260	146/106
Oil production, global share (IEA 2020)	12.6	3.3
Oil reserves/global share 2019/R/P rate (BP 2020)	14.7/6.2%/25.5	21.4/9%/120.4
Gas production/export (bcm) (IEA 2020)	750/265	232/
Gas production, global share (IEA 2020)	18.3	5.7
Gas reserves TCM/global share/ R7P rate (BP 2020)	38/19.1%/55.9	32/16.1%/131.1
Russia/Iran in EU crude oil and petroleum products import 2019 (mtoe and share)[‡]	195.2/23%	1.02/0.12%
Russia/Iran in EU gas import 2019 (bcm/share)	168.9/38.3%	0/0%
Russia/Iran in EU LNG import 2019 (bcm and share)	14.6/16.7%	0/0%
Share of EU/Europe in Russia/Iran oil export (BP 2020)	53.5%/153 mtoe	0%/0
Share of EU/Europe in Russia/Iran export of piped gas (BP 2020)	86.5%/188 bcm	0%/0
Share of EU/Europe in export of Russia/Iran LNG (BP 2020)	52%/20.5 bcm	0%/0
Share of Russia/Iran in China crude oil import 2019/value in US$ billion (OEC)	16.4%/33.7	3.07%/6.3

	Russia	Iran
Share of Russia/Iran in China piped gas import 2019/volume of piped gas import to China (bcm; BP 2020)	0%/47.7	0%/47.7
Share of China in Russia/Iran oil export/value in US$ billion 2019 (OEC 2019)	27.4%/123	50.9%/12.4
Share of crude oil in Russia/Iran export to China 2019/value in US$ billion (OEC)	58.1%/33.7	52.1%/6.3
Share of China in Russia/Iran export of piped gas/export (bcm; BP 2020)	0%/217.2	0%/16.9
Share of China in export of Russia/Iran LNG/total LNG export (bcm; BP 2020)	8.6%/39.4	0/0
Share of petroleum revenues in Russian/Iranian state budget 2019	45%	25%[§]
Share of mineral fuels in Russia/Iran exports 2019 (OEC)	60%	53.1%
Value of export of mineral fuels Russia/Iran in 2019 US$ billion (OEC data)	249	13.9
Value of export of mineral fuels Russia/Iran 2020 in US$ billion (OEC data)	161	1.7

Source: Data in the table are from BP 2020 = *Statistical Review of World Energy*, 69th edn (London: British Petroleum, 2020); IEA 2020 = International Energy Agency, *Key World Energy Statistics 2020* (Paris: International Energy Agency, 2020); OEC = The Observatory of Economic Complexity at www.oec.world.

[*] mtoe = million tons of oil equivalent.

[†] Data on Russia's and Iran's export dependence—author's calculation based on International Energy Agency, *Key World Energy Statistics 2020*.

[‡] Data on shares of Russia and Iran in EU import of crude oil extracted from Eurostat database at https://ec.europa.eu/eurostat/databrowser/view/NRG_TI_OIL__custom_4076641/default/table?lang=en.

[§] Henry Rome, *Sanctions 1: Impact on Iran's Oil Export* (Washington: United States Institute of Peace, 2021), https://iranprimer.usip.org/blog/2021/feb/10/iran-struggles-under-oil-sanctions.

This 2019 energy snapshot can help us draw some preliminary conclusions on Russia and Iran's roles in the global energy context that can also help assess the impact the ongoing war may have on their energy cooperation or rivalry.

First, both countries depend on access to external markets as they must export huge volumes of energy produced within their borders—34.08 percent in the case of Iran and 47.25 percent in the case of Russia.

Second, both Russia and Iran have vast reserves of oil and gas. However, due to higher levels of production, these reserves will be depleted much quicker in Russia than in Iran.

Third, notwithstanding its huge oil and gas reserves, Iran seems to play in another energy "league" than Russia. This is because Iranian oil production is almost four times lower (3.3 percent vs. 12.6 percent of global oil production) while its gas production is almost three times lower than that of Russia (5.7 percent vs. 18.3 percent of global gas production).

Fourth, for various geographical, political, and infrastructural reasons, in 2019, Russia played a very prominent role in the European energy market while Iranian supplies of oil and gas to this market were almost nonexistent.

Fifth, both countries are seemingly interested in building stronger energy relations with China, where energy demand is expected to grow, contrary to Europe, where it is expected to stagnate—or even disappear for fossil fuels that can be phased out if the green transition is completed.[24] As a result, they both have aimed at increasing their shares of oil exports to China. The Chinese market received 27.4 percent of Russian and 50.9 percent of Iranian crude oil exports. These volumes, which generated huge revenues for exporters ($33.7 billion for Russia and $6.03 billion for Iran), represented 16.4 percent and 3.07 percent, respectively, of all oil imports reaching China. Oil exports from

---

OSW Studies, 2016, https://www.osw.waw.pl/sites/default/files/prace_55_ang_eldorado_net.pdf; Szymon Kardaś, "At Crossroads: Current Problems of Russia's Gas Sector," OSW Studies, 2017, https://www.osw.waw.pl/sites/default/files/prace_63_ang_at-crossroads_net.pdf; Jakub M. Godzimirski, "Russia–EU Energy Relations: From Complementarity to Distrust?" in *EU Leadership in Energy and Environmental Governance? Global and Local Challenges and Responses*, edited by J. M. Godzimirski (London: Palgrave Macmillan, 2016), 89–112.

[24]Morena Skalamera, "Understanding Russia's Energy Turn to China: Domestic Narratives and National Identity Priorities," *Post-Soviet Affairs* 34, no. 1 (2018), 55–77, https://doi.org/10.1080/1060586X.2017.1418613.

Russia and Iran to China represented at the same time 58.1 percent and 52.1 percent, respectively, of all exports to China coming from Russia and Iran, demonstrating the dominant role oil plays in their trade with China. The situation was completely different when it came to gas supplies as neither Russia nor Iran had the infrastructure to send huge volumes of gas to China through pipelines in 2019. Russia managed, however, to export some of its LNG to China (8.6 percent of its total LNG exports of 39.4 bcm). Still, these Russian LNG supplies (3.4 bcm) represented only a tiny 2.6 percent share of China's 2019 gas imports of 132.5 bcm and only slightly more than 1 percent of gas consumption of 307.3 bcm. However, since the opening in December 2019 of its Power of Siberia pipeline, Russia has increased its export of LNG to China, reaching 10.4 bcm in 2021.[25] It is also clear that Russia does not face any gas competition from Iran in the Chinese market as no gas supplies are reaching China from Iran either through the pipe or as LNG.

Sixth, the data presented in Table 9.2 also demonstrate the economic importance of energy in both countries and their apparent dependence on the price of oil in the international markets.[26] In 2019, 45 percent of the Russian and 25 percent of the Iranian state budget revenues came from the petroleum sector. In the same year, exports of mineral fuels generated 60 percent of Russia's and 53.1 percent of Iran's export revenues. Russia's revenue from exporting its fuels reached $249 billion, while Iran's petroleum export revenues reached almost $14 billion in the same year. However, only one year later, in 2020, these revenues dropped substantially when the demand for energy in the world hit by the Covid-19 pandemic was reduced due to a lower level of economic activity. This fact resulted in much lower prices for oil and gas and thus in much lower export revenues—$161 billion in the case of Russia and only $1.7 billion in the case of Iran.[27]

---

[25] "Gazprom's Exports to China Rose 61% in 7M," Interfax, 2022, https://interfax.com/newsroom/top-stories/81826/.
[26] See Clifford G. Gaddy and Barry W. Ickes, *Russia's Addiction: How Oil, Gas, and the Soviet Legacy Have Shaped a Nation's Fate* (Washington, DC: Brookings Institution Press, 2020); Veli-Pekka Tynkkynen, *The Energy of Russia: Hydrocarbon Culture and Climate Change* (London: Edward Elgar Publishing, 2019).
[27] All data from OEC.

Energy and Politics: Strategic Dimension

When discussing Russia's energy relations with Iran and the impact of the ongoing war in Ukraine on the positions of these two actors in the global energy market, we need to consider not only market-related questions but also how these actors' energy policies are influenced by their own choices and external actors.

Having to do with two actors whose economies, trade, and political choices are strongly influenced by their endowment with colossal energy resources, we assume that they treat these energy resources as important in strategic terms. Russia and Iran are interested in strengthening their strategic footprint in the regional and global contexts. Some other members of the international community view both Russia and Iran as revisionist powers interested in remaking the rules of the international system and undermining what they see as the Western strategic and normative hegemony.[28] Over the past decade, Moscow and Tehran have played an important part in redrawing the geopolitical map of the Middle East that still plays a major role in the global energy context as the main area for the production and export of traditional fossil fuels that still dominate the global energy mix. As was shown in Table 9.2, both Russia and Iran have shown interest in redirecting their energy flows to Asia, primarily the Chinese market, to reduce their export dependence on the Western European market.

It can also be assumed that energy resources play a major role in these two authoritarian regimes' attempts at legitimizing and stabilizing their power on the domestic front.[29] For any authoritarian regime, and neither the Russian nor the Iranian regime seems to be an exception in this matter, the question of regime survival and stability is the top priority. Having at their disposal rents generated by the country's energy resources, authoritarian regimes may fund projects that can increase their chances of survival, and this rentier repertoire includes not only strategic

---

[28] For more, see Piotr Dutkiewicz, "The Grand Split," *Russia in Global Affairs* 21, no. 1 (2023), 92–110.
[29] For more on the role of energy as a factor improving the chances of authoritarian regimes to survive, see Jorgen Andersen and Silje Aslaksen, "Oil and Political Survival," *Journal of Development Economics* 100, no. 1 (2013), 89–106, https://doi.org/https://doi.org/10.1016/j.jdeveco.2012.08.008.

spending, subsidies, tax cuts, more investment in political oppression,[30] but also buying popular support by redirecting some of the money flows to the population.[31]

It is relatively easy to map the strategic importance of energy resources in the Russian context. In 2007, Kari Liuhto presented what could be termed a map of the strategic importance of the various sectors of the Russian economy.[32] He assessed their strategic importance along two axes—economic strategy and national security—and concluded that Russia's oil and gas sector played a key part in both contexts. When Russian authorities published their first long-term energy strategy in 2003,[33] the opening paragraph of this document stated: "Russia has abundant energy resources and a powerful fuel and energy sector that forms the basis of economic development and is an instrument in [the] realisation of domestic and foreign policy. The country's role at the global energy market in many respects defines geopolitical influence."

Vladimir Putin, the main shaper of Russian policy since 1999, shared his views on the importance of natural and energy resources in the Russian strategic context. In his widely commented PhD thesis,[34] he wrote the following on this topic:[35] "Mineral and raw materials represent the most important potential for the country's economic development. In the 21st century, at least in its first half, the Russian economy will preserve its orientation toward raw materials. Given its effective use, this resource potential will become one of the most important pre-conditions for Russia's sustainable entry into the world economy."

What is, thus, the long-term strategic importance of the Russian and Iranian energy sectors and how does this play out in the broader context?

---

[30] Andersen and Aslaksen, "Oil and Political Survival."
[31] On the social contract between the regime and the population in Russia in which the redistribution of oil rent plays a key role, see Aleksei Makarkin, "The Russian Social Contract and Regime Legitimacy," *International Affairs* 87, no. 6 (2011), 1459–75.
[32] Kari Liuhto, "A Future Role of Foreign Firms in Russia's Strategic Industries," *Electronic Publications of Pan-European Institute* 4, (2007), 43, https://www.utu.fi/sites/default/files/media/Liuhto04_07.pdf.
[33] *Energeticheskaya strategiya Rossii na period do 2020 goda* [*Energy Strategy of Russia through 2020*] (Moscow: Government of the Russian Federation, 2003).
[34] Harley Balzer, "The Putin Thesis and Russian Energy Policy," *Post-Soviet Affairs* 21, no. 3 (2005), 210–25.
[35] Quoted in Allen C. Lynch, *Vladimir Putin and the Russian Statecraft* (Washington: Potomac Books, 2011), 37.

First, the production and sales of energy commodities generate huge revenues for the Russian state, which has introduced new rules for taxing these revenues.[36] The Russian state depends on these revenues to be able to implement a range of budget-funded programs, including national defense and internal security that are crucial for Russia's ability to claim the status as a great power that other great powers must reckon with.

Second, the energy trade has helped Russia to establish strong economic and political ties with various regional and global actors who have traditionally depended on supplies of energy coming from Russia.[37] These relations have been used both to influence policies and to project economic and political power beyond Russia's borders and have generated huge revenues for producers who are directly and indirectly controlled by the Russian state and for the Russian state itself. For instance, between 2000 and 2019, the export of oil, petroleum products, and natural gas brought in $4.038 trillion, representing 61.7 percent of the total Russian export revenues in this prewar period.[38]

Third, the endowment with energy resources also helps to secure political stability and support for the increasingly authoritarian Russian regime. During Putin and Medvedev's presidencies, the regime channeled enormous energy profits to improve the economic situation of various groups in the Russian society to increase the level of popular support for the regime and increase its legitimacy and secure its stability and chances of survival. Revenues generated by Russia's energy resources have, therefore, been essential for the smooth functioning of the unwritten social contract between the Russian political class and the Russian citizens.[39]

In the case of Iran, energy resources have played a similar role in the national strategy. They have generated huge revenues for different Iranian governments, financing many of their strategic undertakings, including military capabilities. For instance, during the Pahlavi era, the share of oil revenues in the total government budget increased from 11 percent in

---

[36] Adnan Vatansever, "Taxing the Golden Goose: Reforming Taxation of the Oil Sector in Putin's Russia," *Europe-Asia Studies* 72, no. 10 (2020), 1703–27, https://doi.org/10.1080/09668136.2020.1798685.

[37] Nicole Peterson, ed., "Russian Strategic Intentions," Strategic Multilayer Assessment (SMA) White Paper, NSI, 2019, https://nsiteam.com/social/wp-content/uploads/2019/05/SMA-TRADOC-Russian-Strategic-Intentions-White-Paper-PDF-1.pdf.

[38] The author's calculation based on data from the Russian Customs Service.

[39] Tynkkynen, *The Energy of Russia*.

1954 to 45 percent in 1963, to 56 percent in 1971, and to 77 percent in 1977.[40] These shares remained relatively high after the 1979 Revolution. Depending on oil price, production, and export, it was estimated that oil revenues could make up to 50 percent of the state budget revenues. These revenues also improved the Islamic Republic's ability to strengthen its military footprint in the region, project its military power beyond its borders, and resist strategic pressures from regional and global levels.

The country's energy resources have also helped the Islamic Republic build some external energy relations, the most important of these being the energy relationships with Turkey and China.[41] Turkey competes with Iran for influence in the Middle East,[42] as exemplified by their positions in the Syrian conflict, where they have been supporting opposing parties, and the country is also an ally of the United States through its NATO membership. But, the two have managed to develop a relatively good and mutually beneficial energy relationship. The energy relationship between Iran and Turkey has, therefore, some structural similarities to the energy relationship between Russia and the EU, although there are also clear differences because Turkey has never become so dependent on energy supplies from Iran as the EU has made itself dependent on energy imports from Russia. The energy relationship with China has been important for Iran because it has helped the country to circumvent Western sanctions by embarking on closer energy cooperation with Chinese companies in what could be described as a "gray zone" where Iran is able, according to some estimates, to sell up to 1 million oil barrels per day.[43]

Finally, revenues from the energy sector have helped Tehran to share wealth among the population, which is an important element in securing the regime's stability. The energy subsidies reached impressive levels—in 2020, the Iranian government offered indirect subsidies of $5 billion in oil

---

[40] Hossein Bashiriyeh, *The State and Revolution in Iran 1962-1982* (London: St. Martin's Press, 1984).
[41] Bahgat, "Iran's Role," 333–47.
[42] Anoushirvan Ehteshami and Suleyman Elik, "Turkey's Growing Relations with Iran and Arab Middle East," *Turkish Studies* 12, no. 4 (2011), 643–62, https://doi.org/10.1080/14683 849.2011.624322; Andre Barrinha, "The Ambitious Insulator: Revisiting Turkey's Position in Regional Security Complex Theory," *Mediterranean Politics* 19, no. 2 (2014), 165–82, https://doi.org/10.1080/13629395.2013.799353.
[43] Dalga Khatinoglu, "Paper Says Iran Lost $450 Billion in Oil Exports over a Decade," Iran International, November 18, 2022, https://www.iranintl.com/en/202211189727

products, $12.5 billion in electricity, and $12.2 billion in natural gas.[44] At the same time, however, these subsidies remove incentives for improving energy efficiency in the national economy,[45] which results in very high domestic energy consumption. For instance, Iran is the third largest producer of natural gas but not among the ten most important natural gas exporters. Most of the gas production is consumed in the domestic market and is not exported to markets that would be willing to pay much higher prices.

To sum up, one can therefore argue, following the arguments presented by Megan O'Sullivan,[46] that from a grand strategic perspective of Russia and Iran, energy resources can be viewed as (1) a resource facilitating the achievement of other strategic goals—for instance, the reestablishment of Russia's position as a great power or Iran's position as a regional power; (2) an instrument that helps Russia and Iran to project their economic and political power onto areas that depend on energy supplies from Russia or Iran, as evident in the role that energy resources play in both Russian and Iranian exports; (3) an objective/goal of the Russian and Iranian regime, a resource that generates a substantial share of state revenues crucial for securing the stability and survival of the current regimes as well as their ability to project power beyond their borders.

It is, however, important to underline that in the case of both Russia and Iran, the use of energy resources as an instrument in the realization of a national grand strategy can be hampered by the decisions of other actors who can use their normative, regulatory, market, or economic power[47] to influence the ability of Russia and Iran to use their energy resources as political leverage. Over the past decade, both Russia and Iran have had to deal with sanctions imposed by most of the West, and in the case of Iran, those sanctions have been supported by the UN and the

---

[44] "Iran Spends Tens of Billions of Dollars a Year on Energy Subsidies," Iran International, February 4, 2022, https://www.iranintl.com/en/202202042437.
[45] When measured in total energy supply (TES)/GDP, the Iranian economy is much more energy-intensive than the global average, than the Chinese economy, and almost as energy-intensive as the Russian economy and also more energy-intensive than the average for the Middle East—for details, see *Key World Energy Statistics 2020*.
[46] Megan O'Sullivan, "The Entanglement of Energy, Grand Strategy, and International Security," in *The Handbook of Global Energy Policy*, edited by Andreas Goldthau (London: Wiley-Blackwell, 2013), 30–47.
[47] Andreas Goldthau and Nick Sitter, "Regulatory Power or Market Power Europe? Leadership and Models for External EU Energy Governance," in *New Political Economy of Energy in Europe: Power to Project, Power to Adapt*, edited by Jakub M. Godzimirski (London: Palgrave Macmillan, 2019), 27–47.

international community.[48] These sanctions have had a direct impact on the ability of both Russia and Iran to monetize their energy resources and to use them as leverage in the pursuit of their short-, mid-, and long-term strategic goals both in the domestic and in the international arenas.

As far as Iran is concerned, it is estimated that Iran has lost $450 billion in oil revenues in the past decade because of international and US sanctions, which have caused a serious economic crisis with some serious political implications. A fact noticed by Russians too as, for instance, mentioned in the short account on Iran presented by the Russian MFA.[49] Before the imposition of the most severe sanctions, Iran was a significant global energy player and the second largest OPEC oil exporter, exporting between 2.2 and 2.5 million barrels of crude oil per day. The imposition of sanctions made these volumes dwindle to 200,000 barrels per day by 2019,[50] although it is assumed that China has been importing much higher volumes of Iranian oil, circumventing the international sanctions.

When it comes to Russia, its war in Ukraine, launched in 2022, will most probably end a very lucrative energy trade between Russia and the members of the EU. Between 2000 and 2019, the export of oil, petroleum products, and natural gas brought in $4.038 trillion and represented 61.7 percent of the total Russian exports. According to both Russian official data and calculations provided by various experts, up to 65 percent of Russia's revenues from the export of crude oil and natural gas came from Russia's trade with the EU, and this market has gradually become much less accessible—or even completely inaccessible—for Russian energy commodities after the outbreak of the war in Ukraine in 2022. Since the key question addressed in this chapter is whether Iran will be willing and able to fill the energy gap in the EU market, where Russia, until recently, covered 40 percent of the EU gas imports and around 25 percent of the EU's oil imports, it is important to examine how this ongoing war has influenced Russo-Iranian relations in general. To provide an informed answer to this intriguing question, we, therefore,

---

[48]For the impact of sanctions on Iran, see Nikolay Kozhanov, "Iran's Economy under Sanctions: Two Levels of Impact," *Russia in Global Affairs* 20, no. 4 (2022), 120–40. On Russia under sanctions, see Ivan N. Timofeev, "Sanctions on Russia: A New Chapter," *Russia in Global Affairs* 20, no. 4 (2022), 103–19; Segey K. Dubinin, "Russia's Financial System under Sanctions: Logic of Confrontation," *Russia in Global Affairs* 20, no. 4 (2022), 82–102.
[49]"Ministerstvo Inostrannykh Del. Islamskaya Republika Iran."
[50]Khatinoglu, "Paper Says Iran Lost $450 Billion in Oil Exports."

need to examine how these relations have evolved during the first months of Russia's war in Ukraine.

The War in Ukraine and the Evolution of Russia-Iran Relations

When Vladimir Putin announced on February 24, 2022, that Russia was about to launch what he labeled a special military operation against Ukraine, the aim of this operation was, in Putin's own words, to "denazify and demilitarize Ukraine" and to "provide protection to ethnic Russians living in this country, and especially in the two self-proclaimed people's republics in Donbas—the Luhansk People's Republic (LPR) and the Donetsk People's Republic (DPR)."[51]

The Russian political leadership expected to achieve these goals relatively quickly and without having to pay too high a cost in economic, human, military, or political terms. Russian policymakers also expected that their non-Western partners would show more understanding of their choices and abstain from criticizing Russia or even provide some indirect and maybe direct support. Iran is one of the regional powers operating in the Middle East, where Russia decided in 2015 to intervene militarily on the side of Bashar Assad's regime, also supported by Iran. The two countries could, therefore, even before the outbreak of the war in Ukraine, view each other as strategic partners confronting the West not only in the Middle East but also globally. Russia was, therefore, interested in strengthening its relations with Iran in a situation when its relations with the traditional enemy of both Russia and Iran were expected to worsen after Russia's attack on Ukraine.

Table 9.3 presents a timeline of the key developments in Russian-Iranian relations in 2022, starting with the visit of Iran's president Ebrahim Raisi to Moscow in January 2022, where he held talks with his Russian counterpart, and ending with deputy defense minister of the Russian Federation Aleksandr Fomin's visit to Iran in December 2022, where he met the chief of staff of the Iranian Armed Forces Mohammad Hossein Bagheri, apparently to discuss military cooperation between the two countries.

---

[51]Vladimir Putin, "Speech on Launching of the Special Military Operation in Ukraine," Kremlin, February 24, 2022, http://en.kremlin.ru/events/president/news/67843.

Table 9.3 Key Developments in Russian-Iranian Relations, 2022

Date	Short description
2022/1/19	Iran's president Ebrahim Raisi visits Moscow, meets with President Putin
2022/2/14	Telephone conversation between MFA S. Lavrov and his Iranian counterpart H. Amir-Abdollahian in which JCPOA and Ukraine-related questions were discussed
2022/2/24	Telephone conversation between V. Putin and Iran's president E. Raisi in which JPCOA and Ukraine conflict were discussed
2022/3/3	Iran's supreme leader Ali Khamenei argues that the war in Ukraine is the result of the US policy, and the United States was described as a mafia state
2022/3/3	Russia's ambassador to Iran L. Djagarian gives a lengthy interview to the Mehr press agency in which he discusses the goals of the special operation in Ukraine
2022/3/7	Telephone conversation between Russian Minister of Foreign Affairs S. Lavrov and his Iranian counterpart H. Amir-Abdollahian with focus on JCPOA-related questions, touching also upon the Ukraine conflict
2022/3/15	Iran's minister of foreign affairs Amir-Abdollahian pays a visit to Moscow, meets with S. Lavrov
2022/3/30	Russian MFA S. Lavrov meets Iran's MFA Amir-Abdollahian at the meeting of Afghanistan's neighboring states in Tunsi (China) where comments on Ukraine are also made
2022/5/4	Russia's ambassador to Iran L. Djagarian gives a lengthy interview to Izvestiya
2022/5/13	Russia's ambassador to Iran L. Djagarian comments on Russian-Iranian relations on the channel Russia 24, focusing on questions related to JCPOA
2022/5/19	Telephone conversation between Russian MFA S. Lavrov and Iran's MFA H. Amir-Abdollahian during which both JCPOA and Ukraine are discussed
2022/5/26	Russian deputy prime minister A. Novak pays a visit to Iran to discuss questions related to bilateral relations and economic cooperation

2022/6/22	Russia and Iran sign a memorandum of understanding on road transportation following a Road Transportation Joint Committee meeting in Moscow
2022/6/22	Russian MFA S. Lavrov provides introductory comments at a meeting with Iran's president E. Raisi in Tehran
2022/6/24	S. Lavrov meets his Iranian counterpart Amir-Abdollahian in Tehran
2022/6/28	At the meeting of the ministers of foreign affairs of the Caspian Littoral States, Russian MFA S. Lavrov announces that Russia will welcome Iran and Argentina as new members of the BRICS group
2022/6/30	Presidents of Russia V. Putin and Iran E. Raisi meet at the Caspian Summit
2022/7/19	Russia's president V. Putin paid a working visit to Iran and met with his Iranian counterpart E. Raisi and Supreme Leader A. Khamenei to discuss bilateral relations and conflict in Syria. A three-party meeting in Astana Format was organized during this visit to Tehran, which Turkish President Recep Tayyip Erdogan joined Gazprom and NIOC signed a US$ 40 billion memorandum on cooperation in developing Iranian gas and oil resources*
2022/8/31	Russian and Iranian MFA S. Lavrov and H. Amir-Abdollahian meet in Moscow
2022/9/15	Russia's president V. Putin meets with Iran's president Raisi in Samarkand
2022/10/9	Russia's minister of economic development Maksim Reshetnikov takes part in a conference on transit cooperation between Iran, Central Asian states, Russia, and Azerbaijan in Tehran
2022/11/10	Secretary of the Security Council of the Russian Federation N. Patrushev visits Iran and holds talks with Iranian decision-makers, including secretary of the Supreme National Security Council Ali Shamkhani, to discuss various security-related questions

Date	Short description
2022/12/03	Russia's deputy minister of defense A. Fomin visits Iran and meets with M. H. Bagheri, the chief of Iranian Armed Forces general staff, most probably to discuss deliveries of Iranian weapons to Russia†

Source: Based mostly on listings in *Russian Embassy to Teheran* Telegram channel at https://t.me/s/russianembassytehran.

* "Iran and Russia's Gazprom Sign Primary Deal for Energy Cooperation," Reuters, July 19, 2022, https://www.reuters.com/business/energy/iran-russias-gazprom-sign-primary-deal-energy-cooperation-2022-07-19/.

† ISW (@TheStudyofwar) "Iranian Armed Forces General Staff Chief Major General Mohammad Bagheri Reportedly Met with Russian Deputy Defense Minister," December 4, 2022, https://twitter.com/thestudyofwar/status/1599234351610241024.

This brief overview demonstrates the relatively high intensity of contact between the Russian and Iranian policymakers in 2022. Also, the Russian Ministry of Foreign Affairs' overview of bilateral Russian-Iranian relations[52] seems to confirm such a high intensity as there were (by December 20, 2022) sixty-eight references to documents covering these relations in 2022, which is much higher than forty-nine records per year, which was the average for the period 2000–22.

A quick examination of the records from the Telegram channel of the Russian Embassy in Iran seems to indicate that energy-related questions have played a marginal role in these relations in 2022. Key words such as газ*/gas were mentioned only once, нефт/oil only two times, while there are no mentions of ядер*/nuclear or энерг*/energy in the news covering bilateral relations in 2022.

This apparent lack of interest in energy-related questions in this official Russian diplomatic Telegram channel is worth noting, considering President Putin's visit to Tehran on July 19, 2022. On that occasion, the two countries' state-controlled energy champions, Gazprom and NIOC, signed a US$40 billion memorandum on cooperation in the development of Iranian gas and oil resources. There have been various interpretations of this agreement. Some observers presented it as a nonlegally binding but highly symbolic memorandum, while others argued that it represented

---

[52] "Ministerstvo Inostrannykh Del. Islamskaya Republika Iran."

the opening of a new chapter in energy cooperation between Iran and Russia.[53] However, by the beginning of 2024, it is difficult to assess what the real impact of this agreement on the bilateral energy cooperation is going to be. Its implementation will depend on many factors, such as the political will, the availability of funding, economic incentives and hindrances, and not least, the state of Iran and Russia's relations with other actors. Also, the possible effect of sanctions on the practical implementation of this deal should be factored in.

In November 2022, TASS announced that Gazprom and Iran were about to sign agreements on projects worth US$40 billion by the end of December 2022, but nothing happened by the end of the year.[54] The signals coming from both Iran and Russia instead suggest that the two countries are considering the introduction of some energy (gas and oil) swaps to alleviate structural problems related to energy supply in the region. Also, in this way, Iran could become a more important transport corridor or even a hub for Russian supplies of energy to other actors in the region, such as Pakistan or the Gulf countries, provided the plans for the construction of the North-South Transport Corridor are successfully realized.[55]

What is very clear is that the two visits of Russian officials in Tehran—the one paid in November by the secretary of Russia's Security Council Nikolay Patrushev and that of the deputy minister of defense Aleksandr Fomin in December 2022—seemed to focus more on security-related cooperation than on strengthening energy ties.[56] Also, information coming from the battleground in Ukraine where swarms of Iranian drones inflict damage on critical Ukrainian infrastructure indicates that security is the top priority. This military cooperation can have implications for the energy sector in Iran as the supply of Iranian weapons to Russia

---

[53]Vali Kaleji, "Capacities and Dimensions of Russian Investment in Iranian Oil and Gas Fields," *Eurasia Daily Monitor* 20, no. 7 (2023), https://jamestown.org/program/capacities-and-dimensions-of-russian-investment-in-iranian-oil-and-gas-fields/.

[54]"Iran nameren v dekabre zaklyuchit' s Gazpromom soglasheniya na $40 mlrd [Iran Intends to Conclude Agreements with Gazprom for $40 Billion in December]," TASS, November 2, 2022, https://tass.ru/ekonomika/16227489.

[55]See "Ekspert: Iran mozhet stat' khabom dlya tranzita nefti i gaza iz Rossii v drugiye strany [Expert: Iran Can Become a Hub for the Transit of Oil and Gas from Russia to Other Countries]," TASS, October 17, 2022, https://tass.ru/ekonomika/16073605; "V Irane zayavili, chto 'Gazprom' imeyet perspektivy tranzita gaza cherez respubliku [It Was Said in Iran That Gazprom Has Prospects for Gas Transit through the Republic]," TASS, October 13, 2022, https://tass.ru/ekonomika/16042559.

[56]Divsallar, "The Pillars of Iranian-Russian Security Convergence," 107–22.

could be interpreted as a breach of the JCPOA agreement and could, therefore, delay the lifting of sanctions against Iran or even result in the introduction of more sanctions in addition to those hitting the country's energy sector and trade.[57]

A fear of the West's reaction can also partly explain Iran's reluctance to provide direct political support to Russia's war in Ukraine on the international stage as exemplified by Iran's position during voting on Ukraine-related questions in the UN General Assembly. On March 2, 2022, Iran decided to abstain; on April 7, 2022, Iran decided to vote together with twenty-three other states against the proposal to suspend Russia from the human rights body; on October 12, 2022, when the UN General Assembly voted on Russia's annexation of four regions of Ukraine, Iran was not present, while during the vote on making Russia accountable for the war in Ukraine, it voted against, together with Russia and twelve other countries.

Conclusion: Iran Won't Replace Russia

One of the almost immediate consequences of Russia's aggression against Ukraine was the imposition by the West of various types of sanctions against Russia that have affected Russia's energy sector. Responding to these sanctions, Russia itself introduced some "punitive" countermeasures that reduced the supplies of Russian energy commodities to the EU. The future of energy cooperation between Russia and the West, first and foremost the EU, looked grimmer than ever when the EU in close cooperation with the G7 decided to introduce the eighth round and the ninth round of sanctions that targeted the Russian energy sector more directly, imposing a price ceiling for supplies of Russian gas and oil.[58]

---

[57] Sabine Siebold and Ingrid Melander, "EU Imposes New Iran Sanctions, No Deal yet on New Russia Package," Reuters, December 12, 2022, https://www.reuters.com/world/europe/eu-discuss-russia-iran-sanctions-top-up-ukraine-arms-fund-2022-12-12/.

[58] For more details on this, see "Council Agrees on Temporary Mechanism to Limit Excessive Gas Prices," Council of the EU, December 19, 2022, https://www.consilium.europa.eu/en/press/press-releases/2022/12/03/russian-oil-eu-agrees-on-level-of-price-cap/, https://www.consilium.europa.eu/en/press/press-releases/2022/12/19/council-agrees-on-temporary-mechanism-to-limit-excessive-gas-prices/, and https://home.treasury.gov/news/press-releases/jy1141.

The overall objective of the EU and the West could be read in Moscow as a wish to force Russia completely out of the very lucrative EU energy market.

How could this dramatic change in the pattern of energy relations between Russia and the West incentivize other major producers and exporters of energy to try to fill this export-import gap? Would Iran be willing and able to use this energy opportunity to replace Russia as one of the major energy suppliers to the West? To provide an informed answer to this last question, we decided to examine how the relations between Iran and Russia evolved after the outbreak of the war in February 2022 and to consider what impact this evolution could have on Iran's choices in this new situation.

Russian-Iranian political relations amid the war have developed into what remains to be a convenient and at least partly mutually beneficial strategic partnership aimed against the West that both Russia and Iran present as the main culprit and conflict instigator. Iran provides Russia with political, though reluctant, support on the international stage, as witnessed by the mixed record of Iran in the UN voting on Ukraine-related questions. But even more importantly, Iran provides Russia with direct military support in its war in Ukraine by supplying the Russian Army with weapons and shares Russia's view on the negative role played in this conflict by the West. The fact that the political leadership of the two countries—their presidents, ministers, and military leaders—have developed stronger ties during the war in Ukraine can bear witness to the two countries treating each other as strategic partners in their ongoing confrontation with the West. This may mean that the Iranian leadership will most probably not demonstrate the political will to help the West deal with the energy challenge caused by Russia's forced withdrawal from the Western energy markets. In other words, Iran will not opt to replace Russia as the leading supplier.

In addition, Iran's ability to fill the energy gap in Western Europe left by Russia will also depend on developments in the relations between Iran and the West. The future of the JCPOA agreement that could reopen Iran's access to the Western energy markets seems to be jeopardized by Iran's support of Russia's war effort in Ukraine. One could also wonder whether Western policymakers would be interested in making their energy markets more dependent on supplies from another authoritarian regime currently involved in the brutal quelling of domestic protests. Therefore, it could be concluded that even if Iran were to be willing to step in and fill the energy gap in the Western markets, its ability to do so would depend not only on Iran's choices but also on the decisions taken by the Western policymakers who could be reluctant to let Iran in.[59]

Finally, Iran's ability to fill the gap after Russia's withdrawal would also depend on some structural- and market-related factors. It would be much easier to replace Russia as an important exporter of crude oil to the Western markets as Iran seems to be able to increase its production and legal export of crude oil. However, the most pressing question the EU energy consumers must deal with is finding alternative supplies of gas to fill the gas gap on the European gas market left after Russia's withdrawal. And here, Iran's ability to play a positive part in this "filling the gas gap in Europe" game is minimal because most of the gas produced in Iran is used to cover Iran's own energy needs. In addition, as demonstrated in the section on Iran and Russia's global energy roles, Iran is not directly connected to the gas markets in Europe through an existing pipeline and has not developed LNG export capabilities to supply gas to other markets, including Europe's, that way.

One can conclude that Iran seems to lack the political will and structural ability to play an essential part in the evolving energy landscape undergoing profound changes in the wake of the war in Ukraine. Even before the war, the West had begun a deep structural change in its energy policy motivated by climate-related concerns. After the outbreak of the war in Ukraine, the same Western countries have finally realized that relying on energy coming from nondemocratic authoritarian states, including Russia and most probably also Iran, is not the best solution to the energy trilemma. As a result, this may effectively close the door for energy supplies to Europe from Russia and Iran. These developments could mean that Moscow and Tehran will compete for access to the still-growing energy markets in Asia, where they both are already present. The big question is, therefore, what effect this potentially growing competition for market shares in the Asian market will have on the relations between Russia and Iran. But this is a completely different story.

---

[59]For more on how the EU views the possible role of Iran in addressing its energy dilemma, see Alexandra Maria Bocse, "EU Energy Diplomacy: Searching for New Suppliers in Azerbaijan and Iran," *Geopolitics* 24, no. 1 (2019), 145–73, https://doi.org/10.1080/14650 045.2018.1477755. See also Bahgat, "Iran's Role."

Bibliography

Andersen, Jorgen, and Silje Aslaksen. "Oil and Political Survival." *Journal of Development Economics* 100, no. 1 (2013): 89–106. https://doi.org/https://doi.org/10.1016/j.jdeveco.2012.08.008.

Ashford, Emma. *Oil, the State and War: The Foreign Policies of Petrostates*. Washington, DC: Georgetown University Press, 2022.

Bahgat, Gawdat. "Iran's Role in Europe's Energy Security: An Assessment." *Iranian Studies* 43, no. 3 (2010): 333–47. https://doi.org/10.1080/00210861003693869.

Balzer, Harley. "The Putin Thesis and Russian Energy Policy." *Post-Soviet Affairs* 21, no. 3 (2005): 210–25.

Barari, Reykande. "Nuclear Power as a Locomotive of Russian-Iranian Energy Cooperation." *Asia and Africa Today* 8 (2014): 32–4.

Barrinha, Andre. "The Ambitious Insulator: Revisiting Turkey's Position in Regional Security Complex Theory." *Mediterranean Politics* 19, no. 2 (2014): 165–82. https://doi.org/10.1080/13629395.2013.799353.

Bashiriyeh, Hossein. *The State and Revolution in Iran 1962–1982*. London: St. Martin's Press, 1984.

Bechev, Dimitar, Nicu Popescu, and Stanislav Secrieru. *Russia Rising: Putin's Foreign Policy in the Middle East and North Africa*. London: I.B. Tauris, 2021.

Bocse, Alexandra Maria. "EU Energy Diplomacy: Searching for New Suppliers in Azerbaijan and Iran." *Geopolitics* 24, no. 1 (2019): 145–73. https://doi.org/10.1080/14650045.2018.1477755.

British Petroleum. *Statistical Review of World Energy*, 69th edn. London: British Petroleum, 2020.

Council of the EU. "Council Agrees on Temporary Mechanism to Limit Excessive Gas Prices." December 19, 2022. https://www.consilium.europa.eu/en/press/press-releases/2022/12/03/russian-oil-eu-agrees-on-level-of-price-cap/.

Council of the EU. "Council Conclusions on Iran." January 23, 2012. https://www.consilium.europa.eu/uedocs/cms_data/docs/pressdata/EN/foraff/127446.pdf.

Divsallar, Abdolrasool. "The Pillars of Iranian-Russian Security Convergence." *The International Spectator* 54, no. 3 (2019): 107–22. https://doi.org/10.1080/03932729.2019.1586147.

Dubinin, Sergey. "Russia's Financial System under Sanctions: Logic of Confrontation." *Russia in Global Affairs* 20, no. 4 (2022): 82–102.

Dutkiewicz, Piotr. "The Grand Split." *Russia in Global Affairs* 21, no. 1 (2023): 92–110.

Eghbalizarch, Ali. "Benefits of Promotion of Tehran-Moscow Relations: At a Time When Russia and America Are Distancing." IPIS, January 2022. https://ipis.ir/en/subjectview/675251/Benefits-of-Promotion-of-Tehran-Moscow-Relations-At-a-time-when-Russia-and-America-are-distancing.

Ehteshami, Anoushirvan, and Suleyman Elik. "Turkey's Growing Relations with Iran and Arab Middle East." *Turkish Studies* 12, no. 4 (2011): 643–62. https://doi.org/10.1080/14683849.2011.624322.

"Energeticheskaya strategiya Rossii na period do 2020 goda [Energy Strategy of Russia through 2020]." Moscow: Government of the Russian Federation, 2003.

European Commission. "Joint Statement by the High Representative/Vice-President of the European Union, Federica Mogherini and the Minister of Foreign Affairs of the Islamic Republic of Iran, Javad Zarif." April 16, 2016. https://ec.europa.eu/commission/presscorner/detail/en/STATEMENT_16_1441.

Freedman, Robert O. "Russia, Iran and the Nuclear Question: The Putin Record." In *Russia: Re-emerging Great Power*, edited by Roger E. Kanet, 195–221. London: Palgrave Macmillan, 2007.

Gaddy, Clifford G., and Barry W. Ickes. *Russia's Addiction: How Oil, Gas, and the Soviet Legacy Have Shaped a Nation's Fate*. Washington, DC: Brookings Institution Press, 2020.

"Gazprom's Exports to China Rose 61% in 7M." Interfax, 2022. https://interfax.com/newsroom/top-stories/81826/.

Godzimirski, Jakub M. "Russia–EU Energy Relations: From Complementarity to Distrust?" In *EU Leadership in Energy and Environmental Governance? Global and Local Challenges and Responses*, edited by J. M. Godzimirski, 89–112. London: Palgrave Macmillan, 2016.

Godzimirski, Jakub. M. "Russian Grand Strategy and Energy Resources: The Asian Dimension." In *Russian Energy Strategy in the Asia-Pacific*, edited by Elizabeth Buchanan, 57–83. Canberra: Australian National University Press, 2021. https://press.anu.edu.au/publications/russian-energy-strategy-asia-pacific.

Goldthau, Andreas, and Nick Sitter. "Regulatory Power or Market Power Europe? Leadership and Models for External EU Energy Governance." In *New Political Economy of Energy in Europe: Power to Project, Power to Adapt*, edited by Jakub M. Godzimirski, 27–47. London: Palgrave Macmillan, 2019.

Government of the Russian Federation. *Energeticheskaya strategiya Rossii na period do 2030 goda* [Energy Strategy of Russia through 2030]. Moscow: Government of the Russian Federation, 2009. http://scrf.gov.ru/security/economic/document122/.

Institute for the Study of War. "Iranian Armed Forces General Staff Chief Major General Mohammad Bagheri Reportedly Met with Russian Deputy Defense Minister." December 4, 2022. https://twitter.com/thestudyofwar/status/1599234351610241024.

International Energy Agency. *Key World Energy Statistics 2020*. Paris: International Energy Agency, 2020.

Iran International. "Iran Spends Tens of Billions of Dollars a Year on Energy Subsidies." February 4, 2022. https://www.iranintl.com/en/202202042437.

Kalehsar, Omid Shokri, and Azime Telli. "The Future of Iran-Russia Energy Relations Post-Sanctions." *Middle East Policy* 24, no. 3 (2017): 163–70. https://doi.org/10.1111/mepo.12297.

Kaleji, Vali. "Capacities and Dimensions of Russian Investment in Iranian Oil and Gas Fields." *Eurasia Daily Monitor* 20, no. 7 (2023). https://jamestown.org/program/capacities-and-dimensions-of-russian-investment-in-iranian-oil-and-gas-fields/.

Kardaś, Szymon. "At Crossroads: Current Problems of Russia's Gas Sector." OSW Studies, 2017. https://www.osw.waw.pl/sites/default/files/prace_63_ang_at-crossroads_net.pdf.

Kardaś, Szymon. "The Twilight of the Oil Eldorado: How the Activity of Russian Oil Companies on the EU Market Has Evolved." OSW Studies, 2016. https://www.osw.waw.pl/sites/default/files/prace_55_ang_eldorado_net.pdf.

Katz, Mark N. "Iran and Russia." In *Iranian Foreign Policy since 2001: Alone in the World,* edited by Thomas Juneau and Sam Razavi, 181–92. London: Routledge, 2013.

Khatinoglu, Dalga. "Paper Says Iran Lost $450 Billion in Oil Exports over a Decade." Iran International, November 18, 2022. https://www.iranintl.com/en/202211189727.

Koolaee, Elaheh, Hamid Mousavi, and Afife Abedi. "Fluctuations in Iran-Russia Relations during the Past Four Decades." *Iran and the Caucasus* 24, no. 2 (2020), 216–32. https://doi.org/10.1163/1573384X-20200206.

Kozhanov, Nikolay. "Iran's Economy under Sanctions: Two Levels of Impact." *Russia in Global Affairs* 20, no. 4 (2022): 120–40.

Kremlin. "Presidential Address to Federal Assembly." December 12, 2013. http://en.kremlin.ru/events/president/transcripts/messages/19825.

Kremlin. "Presidential Address to Federal Assembly." February 23, 2023. http://en.kremlin.ru/events/president/news/70565.

Kremlin. "Presidential Address to Federal Assembly." November 12, 2009. http://eng.kremlin.ru/transcripts/297.

Kremlin. "Presidential Address to Federal Assembly." November 30, 2010. http://eng.news.kremlin.ru/news/1384.

Liuhto, Kari. "A Future Role of Foreign Firms in Russia's Strategic Industries." *Electronic Publications of Pan-European Institute* 4, (2007): 43. https://www.utu.fi/sites/default/files/media/Liuhto04_07.pdf.

Lovotti, Chiara, Eleonora Ambrosetti, Christopher Hartwell, and Alexandra Chmielewska, eds. *Russia in the Middle East and North Africa: Continuity and Change.* London: Routledge, 2020.

Lynch, Allen C. *Vladimir Putin and the Russian Statecraft.* Washington: Potomac Books, 2011.

Makarkin, Aleksei. "The Russian Social Contract and Regime Legitimacy." *International Affairs* 87, no. 6 (2011): 1459–75.

Ministry of Foreign Affairs. "Ministerstvo Inostrannykh Del. Islamskaya Republika Iran [Islamic Republic of Iran]." May 2, 2021. https://www.mid.ru/ru/maps/ir/.

O'Sullivan, Megan. "The Entanglement of Energy, Grand Strategy, and International Security." In *The Handbook of Global Energy Policy*, edited by Andreas Goldthau, 30–47. London: Wiley-Blackwell, 2013.

Observatory of Economic Complexity, www.oec.world.

Peterson, Nicole, ed. "Russian Strategic Intentions." Strategic Multilayer Assessment (SMA) White Paper. Boston: NSI, 2019. https://nsiteam.com/social/wp-content/uploads/2019/05/SMA-TRADOC-Russian-Strategic-Intentions-White-Paper-PDF-1.pdf.

President of the Russian Federation. *Kontseptsiya vneshnei politiki Rossiiskoi Federatsii* [Foreign Policy Concept of the Russian Federation]. Moscow: President of the Russian Federation, 2016. http://www.scrf.gov.ru/security/international/document25/.

Putin, Vladimir. "Speech on Launching of the Special Military Operation in Ukraine." Kremlin, February 24, 2022. http://en.kremlin.ru/events/president/news/67843.

RBC. "Iran zadolzhal Rossii €500 mln za stroitel'stvo AES 'Busher' [Iran Owes Russia €500 Million for the Construction of the Bushehr Nuclear Power Plant]." June 27, 2021. https://www.rbc.ru/rbcfreenews/60d7edd59a79471d490ef7ba.

Reuters. "Iran and Russia's Gazprom Sign Primary Deal for Energy Cooperation." July 19, 2022. https://www.reuters.com/business/energy/iran-russias-gazprom-sign-primary-deal-energy-cooperation-2022-07-19/.

RIA Novosti. "V Tegerane zayavili, chto Iran vyplatil dolg Rossii po AES v Bushere [Tehran Says Iran Has Paid Russia's Debt on Nuclear Power Plant in Bushehr]." December 25, 2021. https://ria.ru/20211225/toplivo-1765442011.html.

Rome, Henry. *Sanctions 1: Impact on Iran's Oil Export*. Washington, DC: United States Institute of Peace, 2021. https://iranprimer.usip.org/blog/2021/feb/10/iran-struggles-under-oil-sanctions.

Siebold, Sabine, and Ingrid Melander. "EU Imposes New Iran Sanctions, No Deal yet on New Russia Package." Reuters, December 12, 2022. https://www.reuters.com/world/europe/eu-discuss-russia-iran-sanctions-top-up-ukraine-arms-fund-2022-12-12/.

Skalamera, Morena. "Understanding Russia's Energy Turn to China: Domestic Narratives and National Identity Priorities." *Post-Soviet Affairs* 34, no. 1 (2018): 55–77. https://doi.org/10.1080/1060586X.2017.1418613.

TASS. "Ekspert: Iran mozhet stat' khabom dlya tranzita nefti i gaza iz Rossii v drugiye strany [Expert: Iran Can Become a Hub for the Transit of Oil and Gas from Russia to Other Countries]." October 17, 2022. https://tass.ru/ekonomika/16073605.

TASS. "Iran nameren v dekabre zaklyuchit' s Gazpromom soglasheniya na $40 mlrd [Iran Intends to Conclude Agreements with Gazprom for $40 Billion in December]." November 2, 2022. https://tass.ru/ekonomika/16227489.

TASS. "Iran pogasil chast' dolga pered Rossiyey za stroitel'stvo AES [Iran Repaid Part of the Debt to Russia for the Construction of the Bushehr Nuclear Power Plant]." May 22, 2022. https://tass.ru/ekonomika/14732653.

TASS. "V Irane zayavili, chto "Gazprom" imeyet perspektivy tranzita gaza cherez respubliku [It Was Said in Iran That Gazprom Has Prospects for Gas Transit through the Republic]." October 13, 2022. https://tass.ru/ekonomika/16042559.

Timofeev, Ivan N. "Sanctions on Russia: A New Chapter." *Russia in Global Affairs* 20, no. 4 (2022): 103–19.

Trenin, Dimitry. *What Is Russia Up to in the Middle East?* Cambridge: Polity, 2017.

Tynkkynen, Veli-Pekka. *The Energy of Russia: Hydrocarbon Culture and Climate Change.* London: Edward Elgar, 2019.

UN. "Additional Effort and Patience Needed to Revive Iran Nuclear Deal." December 14, 2021. https://news.un.org/en/story/2021/12/1107922.

Vatanka, Alex. "Iran's Russian Conundrum." In *Russia in the Middle East*, edited by Theodore Karasik and Stephen Blank, 87–104. Washington, DC: Jamestown Foundation, 2018.

Vatansever, Adnan. "Taxing the Golden Goose: Reforming Taxation of the Oil Sector in Putin's Russia." *Europe-Asia Studies* 72, no. 10 (2020): 1703–27. https://doi.org/10.1080/09668136.2020.1798685.

Wasser, Becca. *The Limits of Russian Strategy in the Middle East.* Santa Monica: RAND Corporation, 2018. https://doi.org/10.7249/PE340.

Zvyagelskaya, Irina, Anastasiya Bogacheva, Aleksey Davydov, Ibragim Ibragimov, Stanislav Lazovsky, Lyudmila Samarskaya, Irina Svistunova, Nikolay Surkov, and Tatyana Tyukaeva. "Rossiyskaya politika na Blizhnem Vostoke. Perspektivy i vyzovy [Russian Policy in the Middle East: Perspectives and Challenges]." *Svobodnaya Mysl* 6 (2021): 71–86.

10 IRAN AND RUSSIA IN SYRIA: A CHANGING ALLIANCE AMID THE WAR IN UKRAINE

Hamidreza Azizi

According to the neorealist school of thought in International Relations (IR), one of the main reasons that states form alliances is to counter common threats or those perceived to be a threat. From this standpoint, forming alliances is driven by a desire to repel common threats and strike a balance against the perceived adversary. At the same time, neorealist scholars view alliances as temporary arrangements that may change or dissolve when the shared threat is eliminated or when there is a shift in power dynamics, such as a change in the balance of power. This has been the case with the Iran-Russia alliance in Syria. This chapter shows that the strength or weakness of the Tehran-Moscow alliance in Syria over the last decade has always been a function of their common threat perception. Consequently, the coalition between the two nations initially established as a diplomatic and then a military response to prevent the downfall of their common ally, Bashar al-Assad's regime, gradually evolved into a competition for increased influence within Syria's political, economic, and security structures. Nonetheless, due to Russia's involvement in the Ukraine war and the resulting implications for Moscow's position in Syria and the broader Middle East, Russia has once again been compelled to pursue closer collaboration with Iran in Syria.

By February 2022, Russia's intervention in Syria was the most significant case of the Kremlin's military adventurism outside the Russian borders since the collapse of the Soviet Union. But since then, Russia's war of aggression against Ukraine began to overshadow all other direct and indirect Russian military activities abroad, and Syria was no exception. The war in Ukraine, which has led to the most serious confrontation between Russia and the West since the end of the Cold War, potentially affects Russia's capacity for diplomatic maneuvering in the international arena, including on the Syria issue. Shortly after the start of the Ukraine war, and as the Russians began to realize that their military plans were not proceeding as expected, reports started to emerge that Russia was reconsidering its military role in Syria.[1] As the Russians evacuated some of their positions in eastern and central Syria, Iranian and Iran-backed forces took over, expanding Iran's territorial reach across the Arab country. The development was interpreted as Russia withdrawing parts of its forces from Syria and redeploying them to the Ukrainian front.[2] At the same time, signs began to emerge that Assad might be willing to compensate for a possible decline in Russian political support by attracting more support from Iran. Assad's visit to Tehran in May 2022 was widely seen in this context, sparking speculations that Iran might be trying to take advantage of Russia's obsession with Ukraine to expand its political role in Syria as well.

This chapter examines how the war in Ukraine has impacted Iran-Russia relations in Syria and what implications it may have for the IR surrounding the Syrian conflict and the overall stability in the Arab country. The first section of this chapter examines the main drivers of the Iranian-Russian partnership in Syria since the beginning of the crisis in this country. The aim is to clarify the main areas of common interest between Tehran and Moscow before the war in Ukraine. The second section deals with the key differences in Iranian and Russian approaches to the Syrian crisis, which had already introduced a serious element of

---

[1] Hari Prasad, "Russia's Invasion of Ukraine Complicates the Situation in Syria," The Carter Center, June 7, 2022, https://www.cartercenter.org/news/features/blogs/2022/russias-invasion-of-ukraine-complicates-the-situation-in-syria.html.
[2] Walid Al Nofal, "Amid War in Ukraine, Russia Withdraws and Iran Expands in Syria," Syria Direct, May 4, 2022, https://syriadirect.org/amid-war-in-ukraine-russia-withdraws-and-iran-expands-in-syria/.

competition to Iran-Russia relations before February 2022. The third section, the main part of this chapter, looks into how Russia's war in Ukraine has affected the areas of convergence and divergence between Iran and Russia in Syria and what implications it may have for their relations in that country.

The chapter argues that the new equations emerging in the aftermath of the Russian invasion of Ukraine could potentially help Iran strengthen its political and military influence in Syria. However, this will not necessarily result in heightened competition between Tehran and Moscow. On the contrary, Russia's need to focus on Ukraine leads to closer military coordination, if not cooperation, between Iran and Russia in Syria. Also, from a long-term perspective, Russia is not expected to give up its core strategic interests in Syria, especially its military presence in the Mediterranean, in Iran's favor. Meanwhile, continuous domestic unrest and public protests in Iran may also limit Tehran's capacity to expand its influence in Syria.[3] At the same time, the potential reaction of other actors, especially Israel, to the changing Russian and Iranian roles, has increased the potential for tensions in Syria that could threaten the interests of Tehran and Moscow alike. The revival of ISIS or a reinvigorated insurgency against Assad could also bring about a similar outcome.

Shared Threat Perceptions and the Formation of the Iranian-Russian Axis in Syria

The neorealist school of thought in IR maintains that tackling common threats—or perceived common threats—leads states to ally with each other. From this perspective, repelling common threats and balancing against the threatening actor is the main logic behind forming alliances.[4] Neorealism assumes governments to be rational actors that, in case of any threat, calculate their gains and losses and, based on expediency, build alliances with their peers who are also exposed to the same threats.

---

[3]See Hamidreza Azizi, "The International Relations of Public Protests in Iran," Sharq Forum, October 19, 2022, https://research.sharqforum.org/2022/10/19/the-international-relations-of-public-protests-in-iran/.
[4]Colin Elman, "Realism," in *International Relations Theory for the Twenty-First Century: An Introduction*, edited by Martin Griffiths, 1st edn (London: Routledge, 2007), 11–20.

Consequently, alliances are mechanisms to fend off threats and establish a balance of power against the threatening actor.[5] According to Glenn Snyder, in analyzing the formation of alliances, two key factors should be taken into account: first, identifying the nature of the threat, and second, determining whether it is necessary to ally with others in response to the threat; and if so, with whom?[6] Stephen Walt introduces the "Balance of Threat" concept, arguing that alliances entail an obligation to provide mutual military support against other actors considered a threat.[7] According to the balance of threat theory, the threat that states perceive from other states/actors determines their alliance behavior.[8]

From this point of view, it can be argued that what put Iran and Russia on a united front in the Syrian war alongside the Assad government was their common perception of the threats that the fall of the Damascus regime could bring to them. Indeed, in this case, the balancing alliance that Tehran and Moscow formed was not against a specific actor but against a set of potentially threatening factors arising from the crisis and instability in Syria. But in any case, common threat perception is the key concept and the most crucial driver of the close partnership between Iran and Russia in Syria.[9]

Russia's Threat Perception in Syria

Russia's growing rivalry with the West, on the one hand, and the potential political, security, and economic risks of a regime change in Syria for Moscow's interests, on the other hand, were the main elements shaping

---

[5] Elham Rasooli Sani Abadi, "mahiyat e etelaf dar khavar e miyane: ghodrat va hoviya [The Nature of Alliances in the Middle East: Power or Identity]," *Strategic Studies Quarterly* 17, no. 3 (2014), 199.
[6] Glenn Snyder, "Alliance Theory: A Neorealist First Cut," in *The Evolution of Theory in International Relations: Essays in Honor of William T.R. Fox*, edited by Robert Rothstein (Columbia: University of South Carolina Press, 1992), 83–104.
[7] See Stephen Walt, *The Origins of Alliances (Cornell Studies in Security Affairs)*, new edition (Ithaca, NY: Cornell University Press, 1990).
[8] Stephen M. Walt, "Why Alliances Endure or Collapse," *Survival* 39, no. 1 (March 1997), 158–60, https://doi.org/10.1080/00396339708442901.
[9] Some scholars argue that shared threat perception is a mega-driver of Russian-Iranian relation in general beyond the specific case of Syria. See, for example, Alex Vatanka and Abdolrasool Divsallar, "Can the West Stop Russian-Iranian Convergence?" Middle East Institute, April 3, 2023, https://www.mei.edu/publications/can-west-stop-russian-iranian-convergence.

the Russian threat perception of the Syrian conflict at its early stages. Russia's position in the first four years of the Syrian crisis can be best described as an *active observer*. In fact, apart from expressing political support for the Syrian regime, contributing to a few peace proposals, and cooperating with Washington in eliminating Syria's stockpile of chemical weapons in 2013, Moscow did not take any direct, that is, military, steps in supporting Assad—except for the regular arms export to Syria that was already ongoing for decades. However, following the 2014 annexation of Crimea, when the US and the European Union introduced sanctions against Russia, Moscow started to reevaluate its international standing based on the presumption of deteriorating relations with the West.[10] In other words, the Ukraine crisis of 2014 was a milestone in Russia and the West seeing each other as a threat, adjusting their foreign policies in different parts of the world accordingly.[11]

Syria was one of the first places where the renewed rivalry between Russia and the West was put on display. Considering the unified Western support for the Syrian opposition and the international pressure to remove Assad from power, a successful Russian intervention to save the Damascus regime could provide Moscow with a precious balancing tool vis-à-vis the West. In a way, Russia could move the boundaries of competition with the West from its western borders with Ukraine to hundreds of kilometers away in the Middle East. On the contrary, considering Moscow's close economic and political partnership with Damascus, there seemed to be a concern in the Kremlin that one of the main reasons behind the Western attempts at regime change in Syria might be to hit Russia's interests. After all, the Russians had not forgotten how their green light to NATO for a military intervention in Libya only a few years before had negatively affected Russia's economic and strategic interests in North Africa.[12] Therefore, Russia's perception of the increasingly threatening nature of the West's role in the Middle East and North Africa fundamentally changed Moscow's calculations and, subsequently, its military intervention in Syria.

---

[10]Riccardo Alcaro, *West-Russia Relations in Light of the Ukraine Crisis* (Ciudad de México, Mexico: Fondo de Cultura Económica, 2015), 24–8.
[11]Paul Rogers, "The Ukraine Crisis in Relation to Syria and Iran," Oxford Research Group Monthly Global Security Briefing, March 2014, https://www.files.ethz.ch/isn/178662/MarchEn14_0.pdf.
[12]"Russia Steps up Criticism of NATO Libya Campaign," Reuters, May 20, 2011, https://www.reuters.com/article/us-russia-libya-idUSTRE74J5K820110520.

Also related to the Russia-West rivalry was Moscow's interpretation of the international system, international rules, and Russia's status in the global arena as a great power. Contrary to the case of Ukraine, whose territorial integrity has been constantly challenged by the Russians since 2014, Moscow has advocated for respect for the principles of state sovereignty and noninterference in other states' internal affairs. In practice, this position has been translated into Russia opposing foreign intervention and threats to use force against the country.[13] Some believe that Russia's emphasis on the abovementioned principles in the case of Syria stemmed from its concern that an excessive resort to military intervention against suppressive regimes might someday come back to haunt its other close allies, especially those among the former Soviet republics, many of which categorized as undemocratic and prone to Syria-like instabilities. From this perspective, opposing Western interference—broadly speaking—in Syria has been primarily an attempt by Moscow to guarantee the continuation of its influence over the former Soviet territories.[14]

The international factor aside, there was simply too much at stake for Russian control in Syria to let a regime change happen. It would be safe to argue that what convinced the Russian leaders to elevate their support for Assad to the military level was to maintain—and even expand—their military presence in the Mediterranean. In mid-2015, when the Syrian rebels appeared determined to march toward western Syria, Russia started to worry about the fate of its naval facilities in Tartus.[15] The facilities are located in an important strategic position and could be used as a base for potential Russian military operations in the Middle East, North Africa, and even in Europe.[16] Also, after the start of their military intervention, the Russians showed their desire to establish military control all over the Syrian side of the Mediterranean by developing an air base at Hmeimim, near Latakia.

---

[13]See Richard Sakwa, *Russia against the Rest: The Post-Cold War Crisis of World Order* (Cambridge: Cambridge University Press, 2017).
[14]Vladimir Troyansky, "Russia's Support for al-Assad's Syria: Reasons Old and New," *Syrian Studies Association Bulletin*, May 11, 2012, https://www.syrianstudiesassociation.org/ssa-bulletin (accessed January 30, 2024).
[15]"Russia Launches Air Attacks in Syria," The Economist Intelligence Unit, October 1, 2015, http://country.eiu.com/article.aspx?articleid=1123554496.
[16]Roy Allison, "Russia and Syria: Explaining Alignment with a Regime in Crisis," *International Affairs* 89, no. 4 (July 2013), 807–8, https://doi.org/10.1111/1468-2346.12046.

In the period between 2011 and 2015, the emergence of radical armed groups, mainly the Islamic States (ISIS) and Jabhat al-Nusra, became another source of grave concern for Moscow, especially since those groups had managed to attract a significant number of militants from the Muslim-populated regions of the Russian Federation and other former Soviet republics.[17] In a way, the idea was that Russia should eliminate those radicals while they were still in Syria or they would soon bring their battlefield experience back home and become a more significant security threat. But broadly speaking, the Russian leaders have always taken seriously the potential spillover of radical Islamist ideas from the Middle East into Russian territory and its post-Soviet neighborhood, especially after the two bloody wars with the Islamists in Chechnya and the broader North Caucasus region.[18]

The potential risk of a regime change in Syria for Russia's economic interests formed another aspect of Moscow's threat perception. Traditionally, Syria has been a lucrative market for Russian arms and military equipment. According to a report by the Stockholm International Peace Research Institute (SIPRI), between 2007 and 2011, that is, right before the Syrian uprising, Russian arms exports to Syria increased by 580 percent compared to the 2002–6 period. The report also indicates that in 2011, Syria was the fifth biggest customer of Russian arms, with contracts worth about 3.5–3.8 billion dollars. Also, Moscow accounted for 78 percent of Syrian arms imports over the five years prior to 2012.[19] Arms export aside, a regime change in Syria could also jeopardize Russia's regular business interests. In 2009, Russian investments in Syria amounted to 19.4 billion dollars. In 2005, Russia had written off 13.4 billion dollars of Syria's debts. The move brought lucrative contracts to Russian companies, particularly in the energy and arms industries.[20] Therefore, it would be safe to argue that Russia's threat perception

---

[17]Dina Gusovsky, "Russian Fighters Are Joining ISIS in Record Numbers," CNBC, December 9, 2015, https://www.cnbc.com/2015/12/09/russian-fighters-are-joining-isis-in-record-numbers.html.
[18]Allison, "Russia and Syria," 819.
[19]"Trends in International Arms Transfers, 2012," SIPRI, March 18, 2013, https://www.sipri.org/publications/2013/sipri-fact-sheets/trends-international-arms-transfers-2012.
[20]Margarete Klein, "Russia and the Arab Spring: Foreign and Domestic Policy Challenges," StiftungWissenschaft Und Politik, February 2, 2012, https://www.swp-berlin.org/en/publication/russia-and-the-arab-spring.

of the Syrian crisis was a combination of international, geopolitical, ethnoreligious, and economic factors.

Iran's Threat Perception in Syria

If it took more than four years for Russia to decide on direct military intervention in Syria, for Iran, it was only a matter of a few weeks. The reason for this was the significant importance of Syria for the Islamic Republic from geopolitical and ideological points of view. As Iran's only state ally in the Arab world, Syria has always been of great strategic value to the Islamic Republic. Also, since the fall of the Saddam regime in Iraq in 2003, Syria has served as a geopolitical bridge that allows Iran to project its power all the way westward to Lebanon and the Mediterranean. A regime change in Syria would not only deprive Iran of this unique geopolitical advantage, but it could also boost Iran's regional rivals, especially Turkey and Saudi Arabia, thereby effectively isolating Tehran in the region.

In other words, for Iran, Syria is considered a foothold to expand its influence in the region and a strategic shield whose presence would make it difficult for adversaries, especially Israel, to target the Iranian mainland without facing grave consequences. This is what the concept of "forward defense" in Iran's military thinking has indicated. Also, the Alawite regime in power in Syria, as non-Sunnis, would prevent the country from joining any Sunni-Arab regional front against Shiite Iran. Therefore, as the majority of the Syrian population is also Sunni, any alternative for the Assad regime would endanger cooperation and strategic ties between Iran and Syria and boost Sunni powers like Turkey and Saudi Arabia. That could also explain Tehran's contradictory response to the 2011 Arab Spring developments, calling the regime change in countries like Egypt and Tunisia an "Islamic Awakening" while rejecting the same outcome in Syria.[21] Therefore, Iranian leaders saw the uprising in Syria as a zero-sum game, believing that, should the Assad regime in Syria be overthrown, plenty of geopolitical challenges would arise for Iran in the region.[22]

---

[21] Shahram Chubin, "Iran and the Arab Spring: Ascendancy Frustrated," Carnegie Endowment for International Peace, September 27, 2012, https://carnegieendowment. org/2012/09/27/iran-and-arab-spring-ascendancy-frustrated-pub-49626.
[22] Jubin Goodarzi, "Iran and Syria at the Crossroads: The Fall of the Tehran-Damascus Axis?" Wilson Center, August 2013, https://www.wilsoncenter.org/publication/iran-and-syria-the-crossroads-the-fall-the-tehran-damascus-axis.

Iran was also worried that Assad's fall could weaken its network of regional allies, that is, the so-called axis of resistance. Although this concept has increasingly assumed a geopolitical meaning over the past decade, it is a fundamentally ideological notion. The Islamic Republic considers Syria a member of that axis, which also includes the Lebanese Hezbollah, the Houthis in Yemen, and a number of nonstate-armed groups in Iraq and Palestine. What unites the members of this axis is a fundamentalist reading of political Islam and an uncompromising opposition to Israel and the United States.[23]

In fact, Iranian leaders often describe the developments in Syria as a plot by the United States and its regional allies to weaken and dismantle the axis of resistance.[24] According to Iranian supreme leader Ayatollah Seyyed Ali Khamenei, Iran "will support any nation and government across the world that fights against the Zionist regime [Israel]." This statement and a lot of similar expressions by senior Iranian officials explain Iran's support for the Syrian regime from the perspective of confronting Israel.[25] In the same vein, senior advisor to the supreme leader, Ali Akbar Velayati, who is also a former Iranian foreign minister, said at the beginning of the Syrian crisis that "Although what is happening in Syria is an internal affair, it is basically a confrontation between the axis of resistance and its enemies in the region and worldwide, and Iran will not tolerate, in any form, the breaking of the axis, of which Syria is also a part."[26]

Finally, Iran was also concerned about the rise of extremist and terrorist groups in Syria and Iraq, especially ISIS, which took control of significant parts of both countries from 2014 onward. Therefore, although Iran's military intervention in Syria had already started before the rise of those groups, their potential threat gave Iran a new incentive to increase its direct and indirect military presence. Iranian authorities mainly saw ISIS as a real threat, as, at some point, ISIS managed to expand the areas

---

[23]Nancy Ezzeddine and Hamidreza Azizi, "Iran's Increasingly Decentralized Axis of Resistance," War on the Rocks, July 14, 2022, https://warontherocks.com/2022/07/irans-increasingly-decentralized-axis-of-resistance/.
[24]Erik Mohns and André Bank, "Syrian Revolt Fallout: End of the Resistance Axis?" Middle East Policy Council (MEPC), 2012, https://mepc.org/journal/syrian-revolt-fallout-end-resistance-axis.
[25]Frederic Wehrey and Karim Sadjadpour, "Elusive Equilibrium: America, Iran, and Saudi Arabia in a Changing Middle East," Carnegie Endowment for International Peace, May 22, 2014, https://carnegieendowment.org/2014/05/22/elusive-equilibrium-america-iran-and-saudi-arabia-in-changing-middle-east-pub-55641.
[26]Goodarzi, "Iran and Syria at the Crossroads."

under its control in Iraq to areas close to the Iranian border. In fact, one of the main arguments put forward by the Iranian leaders to justify a military presence beyond the country's borders was that "if we don't confront the terrorists in Iraq and Syria, we will soon have to fight them inside Iran."[27] Also, the anti-Shiite tendencies of those groups, especially ISIS, were a cause of concern for Iran as they seriously threatened the Islamic Republic's Shiite allies throughout the region.

As such, one can argue that by 2015, some of the main aspects of the Iranian and Russian threat perception toward the Syrian crisis overlapped with each other. For both countries, the role of the West in the Syrian crisis and the potential negative implications of Assad's fall for the regional and international balance of power were among the primary motivations for supporting Assad militarily. Besides, they had shared views on the threats posed by the extremist and terrorist groups in Syria and the necessity to confront them. As for other aspects, that is, economic interests for Russia and ideological considerations for Iran, there was also a common perception that maintaining Assad's rule was a necessary precondition for achieving those objectives—even if Tehran and Moscow did not necessarily see eye to eye on those issues. In any case, a common threat perception and a common understanding of the urgent need to protect Assad were the main factors that brought Iran and Russia together as allies in Syria.

Competing Interests and Conflicting Agendas

Neorealist IR scholars consider alliances as essentially temporary phenomena that could undergo changes or break down when the common threat has been removed or the patterns of power distribution, that is, the balance of power dynamics, have been transformed.[28] The Iran-Russia alliance in Syria was no exception to this rule. In 2017, the self-proclaimed ISIS caliphate in Iraq and Syria collapsed, eliminating one

---

[27]Maysam Behravesh, "How Iran Justifies Its Costly Syria Intervention at Home," Middle East Eye, March 23, 2017, https://www.middleeasteye.net/opinion/how-iran-justifies-its-costly-syria-intervention-home.

[28]Kenneth N. Waltz, "The Origins of War in Neorealist Theory," *Journal of Interdisciplinary History* 18, no. 4 (1988), 615–17, https://doi.org/10.2307/204817.

of the main common threats against Iran and Russia. Later, throughout 2018, major battles in the Syrian war between the Syrian Army and the opposition ended in favor of the Assad regime. In other words, by that time, it was already clear that the main common goal of Tehran and Moscow, that is, keeping Assad in power, had been achieved to a large extent. Since then, serious elements of political, economic, and even military-security competition entered the Iran-Russia relations in Syria. Of course, the roots of those competitions would go back to the two sides' different views and interests on some key issues.

Assad's visit to Russia in May 2018 and his meeting with Russian president Vladimir Putin in Sochi were an indicator of the changing Iran-Russia alliance in Syria. At the meeting, Putin called for the withdrawal of "all foreign forces" from Syria. The following day, referring to what Putin had said, the Russian president's special envoy to Syria, Alexander Lavrentiev, stated, "What he said applies to all foreign forces in Syria, including the Americans, the Turks, Hezbollah of Lebanon, and of course, the Iranians."[29] Immediately after that, Iranian officials reacted by saying that the Iranian forces would leave Syria only at the request of the Syrian government.[30] The main areas of disagreement between Iran and Russia in Syria before the Ukraine crisis were as follows.

Competing Views of Security Assistance to the Assad Regime

Conflicting views on the role of Hezbollah and other militia groups affiliated with Iran in Syria have been a principal point of dispute between Tehran and Moscow. Russia's close relationship with Israel has been the primary factor making Moscow sensitive to those groups. Israel has been highly concerned over the presence of Iran-backed militias in southern Syria, close to the Israeli borders, which would enable them to use Syria as a base for attacking Israel. Trying to mitigate Israeli concerns, in August 2018, Moscow promised to keep Iranian and Iran-backed

---

[29]"Russia Calls for Foreign Troop Pullout from Syria Including Iran, Hezbollah," Al Arabiya English, May 20, 2020, https://english.alarabiya.net/News/middle-east/2018/05/19/Russia-calls-for-foreign-troops-pullout-from-Syria-including-Iran-Hezbollah-.
[30]Ahmad Majidyar, "Tehran Rejects Putin's Call for Troop Withdrawal from Syria," Middle East Institute, May 21, 2018, https://www.mei.edu/publications/tehran-rejects-putins-call-troop-withdrawal-syria.

forces at least 80 kilometers away from the Israeli borders.[31] Another Israeli concern regarding Syria, which also caused friction between Iran and Russia, was the alleged transfer of Russian arms from the Syrian Army's depots to Hezbollah. Damascus had promised not to hand over the advanced military equipment it received from Russia to Hezbollah. However, Israeli sources claimed that Iran had intervened and transferred Pantsir-S1 (SA-22 Greyhound NATO code name) surface-to-air missiles to Hezbollah. This has been a consistent concern for Israel, and, upon Israel's requests, Russia has asked Iran several times to prevent Russian arms transfer to Hezbollah.[32] Putin has also tried to assure Tel Aviv that Russian presence in Syria and its cooperation with Iran would not increase Israel's susceptibility to Hezbollah's missiles.[33]

Also related to the Iranian and Russian patterns of security assistance in Syria are their competing plans for the Syrian armed forces. The Syrian Arab Army has traditionally been greatly dependent on Moscow. As such, Moscow's plan for the postwar reconstruction of the army has included preserving its status as a centralized and secular entity. In contrast, instead of trying to create strong state institutions in Syria, the Islamic Republic has worked on strengthening its nonstate militias, including the National Defense Forces (NDF) and Local Defense Forces (LDF), and integrating them into the Syrian armed forces.[34] The Islamic Republic's main aim has been to form paramilitary structures parallel to the Syrian Army, establishing a loyal military force within the Syrian state structure that would guarantee Iran's interests in the long run. This is similar to Iran's strategy in Lebanon and Iraq, where Hezbollah and the Popular Mobilization Forces (PMF), respectively, emerged as robust Iran-backed military structures that could even challenge the state's authority. In fact, Tehran's intention in this sphere is also part of the ideological aspect of its Syria strategy, which fundamentally differs from that of Russia.

---

[31]Nikolay Kozhanov, "As Ringmaster, Russia Runs Israel-Iran Balancing Act in Syria," Al-Monitor: Independent, Trusted Coverage of the Middle East, August 6, 2018, https://www.al-monitor.com/originals/2018/08/russia-syria-israel-iran-golan-heights.html.

[32]Itamar Eichner, "Russia Promises to Keep Weapons Out of Hezbollah's Hands," *Ynetnews*, February 9, 2017, https://www.ynetnews.com/articles/0,7340,L-4919806,00.html.

[33]David Halbfinger and Ben Hubbard, "Netanyahu Says Putin Agreed to Restrain Iran in Syria," *New York Times*, July 13, 2018, https://www.nytimes.com/2018/07/12/world/middleeast/syria-israel-putin-netanyahu.html.

[34]See Hamidreza Azizi, "Integration of Iran-Backed Armed Groups into the Iraqi and Syrian Armed Forces: Implications for Stability in Iraq and Syria." *Small Wars and Insurgencies* 33, no. 3 (January 4, 2022), 499–511, https://doi.org/10.1080/09592318.2021.2025284

The Iran-Russia competition for military and security influence is not limited to ideas and agendas. During more than a decade of conflict in Syria, different parts of the Syrian armed forces have displayed conflicting loyalties. Iran already has loyal elements in the Syrian Air Force Intelligence, the 4th Division, and the Republican Guard.[35] In contrast, other units, such as the 5th Corps and the Tiger Forces, have fully coordinated with Russia.[36]

Syria's Political Future

The Syrian government's future political and ideological orientation has been another disagreement between the Iranian and Russian approaches. Iran wants to keep Syria within the "axis of resistance," which means that there won't be any normalization between Syria and Israel and that Damascus will continue to assist Iran and its allied militias in their persistent confrontation with Israel. However, as mentioned earlier, Russia is not willing to get involved in ideologically driven disputes and has been actively trying to assure the Israelis that the activities of Iran and its allied groups in Syria will not pose a threat to Israel.[37] In return, unlike many of its Western allies, Israel has never publicly opposed Russia's involvement in the Syrian conflict.

Iran and Russia have also shown diverging views on the potential establishment of a federal or decentralized government in Syria. While Iran has always emphasized the need to preserve the centralized structure of the Syrian government, Russian officials have now and again alluded to the idea of federalism.[38] For Moscow, federalism might be a midway solution to initiate some kind of meaningful political transition

---

[35] Jonathan Spyer, "What Does the Deraa Surrender Mean for Iran and Russia in Syria?" *Jerusalem Post*, September 9, 2021, https://www.jpost.com/middle-east/what-does-the-deraa-surrender-mean-for-iran-and-russia-in-syria-679086.
[36] Gregory Waters, "From Tiger Forces to the 16th Brigade: Russia's Evolving Syrian Proxies," Middle East Institute, September 12, 2022, https://www.mei.edu/publications/tiger-forces-16th-brigade-russias-evolving-syrian-proxies.
[37] "Russian Envoy Says Moscow Working to Prevent Transfer of Weapons to Hezbollah," i24NEWS, February 9, 2017, https://www.i24news.tv/en/news/international/137186-170209-russian-envoy-says-moscow-working-to-prevent-transfer-of-weapons-to-hezbollah.
[38] Mohammad Bassiki, "Syrian Kurds Focused on Federalism," Al-Monitor, October 27, 2017, https://www.al-monitor.com/originals/2017/10/syria-federal-state-kurds-turkey-russia.html.

in Syria while making sure that Russian geopolitical interests in western Syria, where its main military facilities are located and is the home to Syria's Alawite minority, would remain intact. At the same time, Russia promoting the idea of federalism would also elevate Moscow's position among other actors in Syria, that is, parts of the Syrian opposition, who would see Moscow as an honest broker and a force to reckon with to achieve their demands.[39] In contrast, Tehran has been opposing the idea of federalism in Syria,[40] as it would automatically diminish the influence of the Alawites in Syrian politics and empower the Sunnis. Iran has also been worried that further autonomy for the Syrian Kurds would generate similar demands among the Iranian Kurdish minority.

In any case, well before the start of its Ukraine invasion, Russia also stopped mentioning the idea of decentralization, at last publicly. One reason might be the firm opposition of not only Iran but also Damascus and Ankara to the notion of federalism, especially regarding the Kurdish areas. At the same time, one of Moscow's aims was to drive a wedge between the Syrian Kurds and the United States, thereby undermining American influence in the country. When that did not happen, Moscow presumably changed course and preferred not to alienate those other actors, that is, Iran, Turkey, and Assad.

Economic Competition

Competing agendas for Syria's postwar economic reconstruction was another feature of Iran-Russia relations that was already in place long before the start of the war in Ukraine. Since mid-2018, Iran has shown a strong interest in getting involved in the transport, mining, oil and gas, and electricity sectors in Syria. However, by then, the Russians had already gained the upper hand in many of those areas, for example, an agreement with Assad that would allow them to invest in Syria's phosphate and other mining resources.[41] Additionally, on January 31, 2018, Moscow

---

[39]Leonid Isaev and Andrey Zakharov, "A Russian Constitution for Syria?" Intersection, March 16, 2017, https://www.hse.ru/mirror/pubs/share/217044052.
[40]"Federalism suriye va amniyat e iran [Federalism in Syria and Iran's National Security]," *Taadol Newspaper*, September 1, 2016, http://www.taadolnewspaper.ir/fa/tiny/news-50492.
[41]Julia Sveshnikova, "Russia, Iran Compete to Reconstruct Syria," Al-Monitor, September 24, 2018, https://www.al-monitor.com/originals/2018/09/russia-iran-syria-economics-grievances.html.

and Damascus signed an energy cooperation agreement that could give Russia a dominant role in extracting and producing Syrian oil.[42]

Reacting to those agreements, Yahya Rahim Safavi, senior advisor to Iran's supreme leader, said what Russia has achieved in Syria should be a model for the Islamic Republic to pursue its interests in that country. "The Russians concluded a 49-year deal with Syria. They took a military base, as well as economic and political points. Iran could also have long-term political and economic agreements with Syria and return its expenses [in Syria]," Safavi said.[43] In the same vein, while downplaying the extent and severity of a potential rivalry between Tehran and Moscow, the then foreign minister Mohammad Javad Zarif also admitted that "there absolutely will be economic competition" in the process of Syria's reconstruction.[44] It should be noted that the US sanctions against Iran under the "Maximum Pressure" campaign, which began in May 2018, was another factor that reduced Iran's ability to compete economically with Russia in Syria. By reducing Iran's financial resources, the sanctions made it impossible for Tehran to realize its plans, even in those areas where the Iranian and Syrian authorities had agreed to cooperate.

The War in Ukraine: A New Turning Point in the Iran-Russia Axis

As discussed earlier, despite their common threat perceptions at the beginning of the Syrian crisis, Tehran and Moscow have had fundamentally different interests and agendas, especially when it comes to the future of Syria's political, economic, and military structures. Therefore, it came as a little surprise that after attaining its primary objectives, that is, maintaining its military presence in the Mediterranean, defeating ISIS, and successfully proving its role as an indispensable external power in the

---

[42]"Russia, Syria Ink Energy Cooperation Agreement—Ministry," Reuters, January 31, 2018, https://www.reuters.com/article/russia-syria-energy-idAFL8N1PQ7GE.
[43]"Rahim Safavi: Like Russia, Iran Should Gain Its Share in Syria," RFI Persian, February 18, 2018, https://shorturl.at/dkqrD.
[44]"be mokhalefan e barjam migoim titrhaye kayhan ra bekhanand [We Tell to Opponents of the JCPOA to Read Kayhan's Titles]," Azadi Today, March 12, 2019, https://azaditoday.ir/fa/news/4456.

Middle East, Russia began seeking to limit Iran's influence in Syria.[45] In contrast, Iran's ultimate success in preserving its goals in Syria, especially in terms of keeping Damascus in the axis of resistance, would require Tehran to be the dominant actor on the Syrian military and political stage. In this way, one might argue that as far as Russia is concerned, by February 2022, the war in Syria had already ended, and the focus had to be on stabilization and reconciliation—indeed, on Russia's terms. But for Iran, the war was still ongoing, albeit in a different form and at a different level.

However, Iran and Russia's mutual need for each other was the primary factor that allowed them to manage their competition and not let it get out of hand so that they continued to work together as partners. First and foremost, although the major battles between the Syrian Army and the opposition had subsided, this did not mean the actual end of the war. On the one hand, the situation in Idlib in northwestern Syria, which gradually became the center of armed extremist groups, remains unclear. The Assad regime insists that, sooner or later, using military force to retake the area will be inevitable. On the other hand, although ISIS does not control any specific region in Syria, there is still a risk that the terror group's sleeper cells may regroup and resume their activities. Therefore, there is still the possibility that new military campaigns against ISIS will become necessary. In this case, as has been the case before, there will be a division of labor between Iran and its proxies on the one hand and Russia on the other. During the major military campaigns in Syria since 2015, the former has been usually tasked with providing ground forces, while the latter has provided air support.[46]

The second factor is the uncertain state of the balance of power between the different foreign actors in Syria. Apart from Iran and Russia, Turkey and the United States have also had a direct military presence in Syria. While the Turkish Army and its proxy groups control significant parts of northern Syria bordering Turkey, the US and its allies in the form of the Syrian Democratic Forces (SDF) have been stationed to the east of the Euphrates. In such a situation, the withdrawal of either Iranian

---

[45]Nicole Grajewski, "The Evolution of Russian and Iranian Cooperation in Syria," Center for Strategic and International Studies, November 17, 2021, https://www.csis.org/analysis/evolution-russian-and-iranian-cooperation-syria.

[46]Emmanuel Karagiannis, "How and Why the Russian-Iranian-Hezbollah Axis Has Won the War in Syria," *Georgetown Journal of International Affairs*, November 12, 2019, https://gjia.georgetown.edu/2019/05/05/russian-iranian-hezbollah-axis/.

or Russian forces from Syria would drastically change the balance to the detriment of the other partner. Even in the Astana Format, whose founding members were Iran, Russia, and Turkey, the balancing acts between Tehran, Moscow, and Damascus, on the one hand, and Ankara and the Syrian opposition, on the other hand, have always been evident.[47] As a result, on military and political issues, continued cooperation has been more beneficial for Tehran and Moscow. Finally, one should not ignore the fact that Assad, in pursuit of his interests, has, from time to time, played the Iranians and Russians off against each other, trying not to allow one of the two powers to dominate Syria and be able to dictate its terms to his regime. As such, on the eve of the Ukraine war, the partnership between Iran and Russia was very shaky, but it was far from collapse.

But Russia's war in Ukraine was a new turning point in the Iranian-Russian partnership in Syria. The war and its consequences, on the one hand, closed the widening gap between the Iranian and Russian threat perceptions in Syria and, on the other hand, caused them to put aside some of the most significant areas of their dispute and competition to be sidelined, at least temporarily.

Russia's failure to secure a quick victory in Ukraine, as the Russian leaders seemed to have expected, and the unprecedented confrontation between Moscow and the West that came as a result of the Russian invasion started to affect some of the elements that had shaped Moscow's perception of victory in Syria. Since 2015, Russia has increasingly used its influence in Syria as a tool for diplomatic maneuvering in the Middle East and beyond. In line with their desire to restore Russia's role as a great influential power, Russian leaders largely succeeded in projecting the image that security and stability in Syria—and, by extension, the Middle East—would not be possible without Moscow's role and positive contribution. Initiatives such as the New Security Architecture for the Persian Gulf, put forward by Moscow in recent years, should be interpreted in this context.[48] However, the post–Ukraine War international atmosphere, the most important indicator of which being

---

[47]See Hamidreza Azizi, "Will Iran-Turkey-Russia Cooperation in Syria Survive Biden?" Amwaj Media, March 8, 2021, https://amwaj.media/article/ir-article-will-iran-turkey-russia-cooperation-in-syria-survive-biden.

[48]Nikolay Kozhanov, "Russia and the Issue of a New Security Architecture for the Persian Gulf," LSE Middle East Centre, August 5, 2021, https://blogs.lse.ac.uk/mec/2021/08/04/russia-and-the-issue-of-a-new-security-architecture-for-the-persian-gulf/.

the West's determination to isolate Russia, has made any effective and meaningful cooperation between Russia and the West in the Middle East all but impossible. Besides, Russia's failures in Ukraine have severely damaged its international credibility as a major power.

Under these circumstances, if the situation in Syria, which has so far been considered the main symbol of the post-Soviet restoration of Russian military power, also shifted to Moscow's detriment, the consequences for Russia's international image would be beyond repair. Here, Russian leaders faced a dilemma. On the one hand, in order to achieve at least a minimum of their strategic goals in Ukraine, they had to allocate the maximum possible amount of Russia's military resources to the war in Ukraine. On the other hand, any significant troop withdrawal from Syria could jeopardize all of Russia's achievements there in the past seven years. What further complicated matters was that other external and internal actors involved in the Syrian conflict were already seeking to exploit Russia's obsession with Ukraine to their benefit. After Turkish president Recep Tayyip Erdogan revealed his plans to repatriate one million Syrian refugees, it became clear that Ankara has new plans—potentially military ones—for Syria.[49] This could upend the status quo in northern Syria and, consequently, the overall balance of power in the country, to Russia's detriment. At the same time, terrorist and radical armed groups, particularly ISIS, began trying to seize the opportunity to regroup and resume their activities.[50] Similarly, there was a concern that if the Syrian opposition forces managed to form a new alignment and resume armed insurgency, the Assad regime and its allies would be in for tough times ahead.

In these circumstances, reports appeared that Russian troops were withdrawing from some of their positions in Syria, handing them over to the Iranian and Iran-backed forces. Since the start of the Ukraine war, Iran reactivated its forces in vast areas of the Homs and Deir ez-Zor provinces while equipping its proxy forces in various parts of Syria with new quality weapons. Iranian and Iran-backed forces also expanded their presence in al-Hasakah. Therefore, it soon became apparent that Russia

---

[49] Salim Çevik, "Turkey's Military Operations in Syria and Iraq," StiftungWissenschaft Und Politik, May 30, 2022, https://www.swp-berlin.org/publikation/turkeys-military-operations-in-syria-and-iraq.

[50] "Anti-IS Coalition Meets on Countering Jihadists' Revival," France 24, May 11, 2022, https://www.france24.com/en/live-news/20220511-anti-is-coalition-meets-on-countering-jihadists-revival.

was reconsidering its Syria strategy and, as a result, its partnership with Iran in the country.[51] That said, speculations about Russia's "withdrawal" from Syria were soon proven to be exaggerated. In fact, in response to such assumptions, Russian foreign minister Sergey Lavrov stated that Russian forces would remain in Syria, although their mission would be primarily "advisory"—a reference to the fact that Russia still sees that its military objectives are met.[52]

As such, facing actual and potential new challenges in Syria and elsewhere, Russia decided to roll back the policy of expanding military influence in Syria to once again focus on preserving its fundamental interests in the country. From this perspective, the withdrawal of Russian forces from their position in central Syria was apparently aimed at concentrating them at the main Russian bases in the west. At a time when Russia's military leadership is essentially preoccupied with the war in Ukraine, overstretching Russian forces throughout Syria would have exposed them to attacks by local militias. One can argue, therefore, that the developments on the ground point to a new division of labor between Tehran and Moscow, according to which the Iranian forces are in charge of confronting the revival of radical armed groups and maintaining pro-Assad positions in eastern and central Syria. However, a similar trend cannot be expected in the west, where Russia's vital interests, that is, its Mediterranean bases, are located. Besides, there have been no reports of the Russian air force being redeployed from Syria to Ukraine. Since Russia's main military contribution to the war in Syria has been providing air cover for the Syrian Army and pro-Assad militias, Moscow maintains the ability to support the Assad regime should the situation deteriorate. In the meantime, Iran and its allied forces play a more significant role on the ground. Indeed, this could give Iran a free hand to expand its geographical reach, but it helps Russia ensure that its primary interests in Syria are not jeopardized.

This apparent coordination at the military level is less the case in the political and economic spheres. In fact, Iranian leaders already sought to take advantage of Assad's concerns about Russia's changing role and

---

[51] Sinem Adar, Muriel Asseburg, Hamidreza Azizi, Margarete Klein, and Mona Yacoubian, "The War in Ukraine and Its Impact on Syria," StiftungWissenschaft Und Politik, April 28, 2022, https://www.swp-berlin.org/en/publication/the-war-in-ukraine-and-its-impact-on-syria.

[52] "Lavrov to RT: Russian Forces to Stay in Syria," RT Arabic, May 26, 2022, https://shorturl.at/egkTW.

increase their political leeway in Syria. On February 27, 2022, Assad's special security adviser, Ali Mamlouk, traveled to Tehran to meet with senior Iranian officials. One month later, on March 28, Iranian foreign minister Hossein Amir-Abdollahian visited Syria. Those diplomatic exchanges were a prelude to Assad's visit to Tehran on May 8, during which he met with Khamenei and President Ebrahim Raisi. Assad's visit to Tehran—only the second time since the start of the Syrian conflict—was an initiative by Tehran to reassure the Syrian president that, regardless of Russia's role, he could still count on Iran's total support.[53] Iran also tried to take advantage of the circumstances in the economic sphere. Iranian leaders were probably hopeful that Russia's economic woes as a result of Western sanctions, on the one hand, and the prospect of lifting the Iran sanctions with the potential revival of the 2015 nuclear deal (JCPOA), on the other, might give Tehran greater room for maneuvering in Syria's postwar economic reconstruction—where it has been increasingly marginalized by the Russians over the past four years.

But as the Islamic Republic also began to hurtle down on a collision course with the West over providing Russia with military drones for its war in Ukraine and the brutal suppression of public protests at home, a restored JCPOA got increasingly elusive. Therefore, Iran will have a difficult time advancing its economic ambitions. The lack of sufficient capital prevents Iran from playing a significant role in Syria's economy and infrastructure. Still, the role of China and Beijing's relations with Tehran and Damascus could be a way for Iran to stay relevant in Syria's economy. Iran has shown great interest in assuming a central role in China's Belt and Road Initiative (BRI), presenting itself as the central hub for East-West transit. At the same time, Iranian officials have repeatedly spoken of their desire to connect the BRI to Syria and the Mediterranean.[54] If the Chinese show seriousness about involving Iran in the BRI and, at the same time, decide to extend the project to Syria through the Iranian territory, Tehran could play a role as China's partner—albeit the junior one—in the Syrian economy, even in the absence of the JCPOA. But the more recent trend in China's warming ties with Iran's Arab neighbors, on

---

[53]Hamidreza Azizi, "5 Messages Projected by Assad's Visit to Iran." Amwaj.media, May 19, 2022, https://amwaj.media/article/5-messages-projected-by-assad-s-visit-to-iran.
[54]"Iran Planning Super-Highway to Connect with Mediterranean," Silk Road News, April 9, 2018, https://silkroadnews.org/en/news/iran-plans-to-build-a-highway-to-the-mediterranean-sea-al-quds-al-arabi-reports (accessed January 30, 2024).

the one hand, and the increasing chances of the BRI's "middle corridor," on the other, that would bypass Iran to go through Turkey to Europe has made even that scenario a distant possibility.

All in all, the war in Ukraine has started to affect the role of Russia and Iran in Syria and their interactions in the context of the Syrian conflict. Russia's need to focus its military apparatus on Ukraine makes Moscow reluctant to take on any new military adventures in Syria. It also increases coordination on the ground between the Iranian and Russian forces. In the meantime, Russia maintains its air force preparedness to face potential threats while maintaining its bases in the Mediterranean. But in the long run, Iran can be expected to increase its political influence in Syria. In the economic sphere, the most probable long-term scenario is for both countries to lose ground to China.

Meanwhile, there is an important factor making the new status quo quite fragile. As Russia focuses on securing its basic interests, Iran sees the conditions as conducive to pursuing a maximalist strategy. Iranian leaders might be convinced that after a decade of active involvement in Syria, now is the time to achieve the ideological goal of their intervention, which is to solidify the "axis of resistance." At least since 2018, Israel has been counting on Russia to keep Iran away from its borders with Syria. But various reports since the start of 2022 have indicated that in addition to central and eastern Syria, Iran has also been increasing its presence in the southern areas, close to the Israeli border.[55] This led the Israelis to expand the frequency and scope of their attacks against Iranian positions. If Iran shows a direct military response to Israel at some point, Syria may become a battleground between Tehran and Tel Aviv. Such a scenario would be in stark contrast to Moscow's desire to maintain calm in Syria to safely pursue its plans in Ukraine.

In fact, the war in Ukraine and Israel's reactions to it also affected Russian-Israeli relations, creating tensions between the two sides. However, both sides have been careful not to let those tensions turn into a real confrontation. For example, despite repeated requests from Kyiv, Israel has refused to provide advanced missile systems such as the "Iron Dome" to Ukraine. In turn, the Russians continued to decline to activate

---

[55] "Massive Iranian Reinforcements to Southern Syria," *The Syrian Observer*, February 14, 2022, https://syrianobserver.com/news/73479/massive-iranian-reinforcements-to-southern-syria.html.

their S-300 air defense systems in Syria against Israeli strikes.[56] Although Moscow's need for Tehran's assistance, especially in providing drones and other types of military equipment, has made it more tolerant of Tehran's expansionism in Syria, this does not mean that the Russians are willing to see a military conflict between Iran and Israel.

As for the other influential foreign actor in Syria, namely Turkey, there has been no immediate sign that Iran might be willing to take advantage of Russia's obsession with Ukraine to act against Ankara's interests in Syria. In fact, since February 2020, when Iran-backed forces, for the first time, engaged extensively in fighting in the Turkish zone of influence in northern Syria, Iran has limited its presence in north and northwestern Syria in general. However, if Moscow-Ankara relations start to deteriorate due to the war in Ukraine and, at the same time, the increasing rivalry between Tehran and Ankara in Iraq, the South Caucasus, and other places gets out of control,[57] Iran may encourage the Syrian regime to conduct a military operation in Idlib to increase pressure on Turkey. But given the risks of an all-out confrontation with Turkey, as well as Iran's own increasingly limited bandwidth due to the prolonged protest movement at home, Tehran has been quite cautious in dealing with the Turks.

Finally, concerning the US factor in Syria, it should be mentioned that Iran's opportunism in expanding its influence in eastern Syria right after the start of the Ukraine war, as mentioned earlier, brought the Iranian forces closer to the American and US-allied positions than at any time in the past. Throughout 2022, Iran also tried to make life difficult for Washington in eastern Syria by siding with the Arab tribes of Deir ez-Zor and inciting them against the US-backed Kurdish forces. At the same time, American positions have been repeatedly targeted by attacks believed to have been carried out by Iran-backed forces.[58] In this sense, the risk of conflict between Iran and the United States in Syria increased. However, as both Russia and Iran enter a period of heightened tensions with the West, the Russians do not appear to be displeased with Iran's

---

[56]Steve Hendrix, "As Missiles Strike Ukraine, Israel Won't Sell Its Vaunted Air Defense," *Washington Post*, October 12, 2022, https://www.washingtonpost.com/world/2022/10/12/ukraine-russia-israel-iron-dome/.

[57]Mehmet Emin Cengiz, "The Future of the Iranian-Turkish Relationship: A Contained Geopolitical Rivalry or a Possible Escalation," Al Sharq Strategic Research, September 30, 2022, https://research.sharqforum.org/2022/09/20/iranian-turkish-relationship/.

[58]Seth Frantzman, "Are There New Iranian-Backed Attacks on US Forces in Syria?" *Jerusalem Post*, January 5, 2023, https://www.jpost.com/middle-east/article-726727.

moves against American interests in Syria. In fact, when Putin met with Khamenei in Tehran in July 2022, the two leaders showed considerable agreement on confronting the United States in Syria.[59] In other words, the United States is now perceived to be a common threat by Iran and Russia more than at any time in the past.

Conclusion

The war in Ukraine has once again given rise to common elements in the Iranian and Russian threat perceptions in Syria. First of all, Russia's aggression against Ukraine has turned tension and confrontation into the main feature of relations between Moscow and the West, undermining the possibilities for any meaningful cooperation between the two sides. As far as Russia's role in Syria is concerned, this means that, in the foreseeable future, we cannot expect the Russians to cooperate constructively with the West, like they did, for example, in 2013 to destroy Syria's stockpile of chemical weapons. In fact, this new confrontational atmosphere has already started to affect international initiatives involving Russia and the West. Russia's opposition to a long-term extension of the humanitarian corridor from Turkey to northern Syria was a case in point.[60] Also, Russia has reportedly prevented a new round of Syrian Constitutional Committee talks from convening in Geneva.[61]

The Russians once again see diplomatic initiatives on Syria as a zero-sum game vis-à-vis the West, whose role in Syria, especially that of the United States, is increasingly perceived as a threat by Moscow. At the same time, the suspension of the nuclear talks with the West alongside the European and American support for the protests in Iran have caused the relations between Tehran and the West to experience one of its most tense periods. Even before these developments, Tehran used to consider attacking American interests in Syria as a way to force the United

---

[59]Guy Faulconbridge and Parisa Hafezi, "Putin Forges Ties with Iran's Supreme Leader in Tehran Talks," *Reuters*, July 20, 2022, https://www.reuters.com/world/putin-visits-iran-first-trip-outside-former-ussr-since-ukraine-war-2022-07-18/.
[60]Karen DeYoung, "U.N. Deadlocked on Mandate for Last Humanitarian Corridor into Syria," *Washington Post*, July 9, 2022, https://www.washingtonpost.com/national-security/2022/07/08/syria-humanitarian-corridor-un/.
[61]Ibrahim Hamidi, "Why Does Russia Want to Remove the Syrian Political Process from Geneva?" *Asharq AL-awsat*, July 18, 2022, https://english.aawsat.com/home/article/3764461/why-does-russia-want-remove-syrian-political-process-geneva.

States out of the country. In these circumstances, the Western factors have unsurprisingly become an incentive for enhanced Iran-Russia partnership in Syria.

More broadly speaking, following the Russian invasion of Ukraine, anti-Americanism has emerged as the primary characteristic of Iran-Russia relations in the Middle East. This has led to similar views on security cooperation in the region. While anti-Americanism has been an integral part of Iran's foreign policy for over four decades, it holds a different meaning for Russia, as it stems mainly from Moscow's broader confrontation with the West in the global arena. Nonetheless, Tehran and Moscow share a greater level of harmony now than ever before in their opposition to the US presence in the Middle East, including in Syria.

At the same time, Russia's eroding potential for maintaining an active military presence in Syria due to its involvement on the Ukraine front has created the concern that anti-Assad armed groups might try to capitalize on the opportunity and start to threaten Moscow's interests. This could come, for example, in the form of regaining control of some areas they have lost to the Syrian Army and its allies in recent years. This factor is also a common potential threat for Iran, Russia, and, of course, the Assad regime. Therefore, it has already led to a new division of labor between Tehran and Moscow, according to which Iran and its proxy groups have become more active in parts of Syria.

The new division of labor has also marginalized one of the main reasons for dispute between Tehran and Moscow in the past few years, that is, the role of Iran-backed militias in Syria. Russia knows that maintaining positions taken back from the insurgents, as well as preventing the reemergence of extremist groups, requires a combat-ready ground force. This is not something that Russia can handle in the short term, given its preoccupation with Ukraine. This set of developments, along with Israel's position on Ukraine, has caused the Israeli factor not to be an obstacle to cooperation between Tehran and Moscow in Syria as strongly as it was in the past. Although this does not mean that Russia will be willing to enter into a confrontation with Israel for the sake of Iran, the change in Russia's position in this regard is undeniable.[62] Finally, economic competition between Iran and Russia in Syria no longer seems as relevant as in the

---

[62]See Hamidreza Azizi, "Why Russia Is No Longer Iran-Israel De-escalator in Syria," Amwaj Media, March 9, 2023, https://amwaj.media/article/why-russia-is-no-longer-iran-isr ael-de-escalator-in-syria.

past. Severe sanctions against both countries have drained the financial resources needed for an effective economic engagement in Syria. But still, all these will not guarantee the long-term stability of the Iranian-Russian partnership in Syria. Alliances are temporary and prone to change as actors' threat perceptions change. This is a factor to be taken into account when analyzing the longer-term prospects of Iran-Russia relations in Syria.

The evolving dynamics in the region, from the Arab-Israeli normalization to Iran's recently emerged desire to mend fences with its Arab neighbors, are also likely to have an impact on Russia's role, contingent upon the duration of the conflict in Ukraine. The outcome of this process will naturally impact the Iranian-Russian partnership in Syria and the broader region as well. So far, the enhanced collaboration between Tehran and Russia has been mainly limited to the military-security sphere. In this vein, Iran-manufactured drones have been heavily utilized by Russia in its attacks on military and civilian targets in Ukraine. As a reciprocal measure, Moscow is anticipated to furnish Iran with numerous Sukhoi Su-35 fighter jets, in addition to advanced missile systems, air defense systems, and helicopters. But when it comes to the economy, the Arab states of the Persian Gulf continue to offer a better alternative to Moscow. A similar equation is expected to prevail in Syria. Tehran and Moscow may continue their close military collaboration on the ground and coordinate their security strategies in the Arab country, but their partnership is unlikely to be extended to the economic sphere. This single-dimensional nature of the Iranian-Russian partnership, generally speaking, can be considered its main weakness that casts doubt on its fate.

Bibliography

Adar, Sinem, Muriel Asseburg, Hamidreza Azizi, Margarete Klein, and Mona Yacoubian. "The War in Ukraine and Its Impact on Syria." Stiftung Wissenschaft Und Politik, April 28, 2022. https://www.swp-berlin.org/en/publication/the-war-in-ukraine-and-its-impact-on-syria.
Al Arabiya English. "Russia Calls for Foreign Troop Pullout from Syria Including Iran, Hezbollah." May 20, 2020. https://english.alarabiya.net/News/middle-east/2018/05/19/Russia-calls-for-foreign-troops-pullout-from-Syria-including-Iran-Hezbollah-.
Al Nofal, Walid. "Amid War in Ukraine, Russia Withdraws and Iran Expands in Syria." Syria Direct, May 4, 2022. https://syriadirect.org/amid-war-in-ukraine-russia-withdraws-and-iran-expands-in-syria/.

Alcaro, Riccardo. *West-Russia Relations in Light of the Ukraine Crisis*. Ciudad de México, Mexico: Fondo de Cultura Económica, 2015.

Allison, Roy. "Russia and Syria: Explaining Alignment with a Regime in Crisis." *International Affairs* 89, no. 4 (July 2013): 807–8. https://doi.org/10.1111/1468-2346.12046.

Azadi Today. "be mokhalefan e barjam migoim titrhaye kayhan ra bekhanand [We Tell to Opponents of the JCPOA to Read Kayhan's Titles]." March 12, 2019. https://azaditoday.ir/fa/news/4456.

Azizi, Hamidreza. "The Concept of 'Forward Defence': How Has the Syrian Crisis Shaped the Evolution of Iran's Military Strategy?" GCSP, February 3, 2021. https://www.gcsp.ch/publications/concept-forward-defence-how-has-syrian-crisis-shaped-evolution-irans-military-strategy.

Azizi, Hamidreza. "Integration of Iran-Backed Armed Groups into the Iraqi and Syrian Armed Forces: Implications for Stability in Iraq and Syria." *Small Wars and Insurgencies* 33, no. 3 (January 4, 2022): 499–511. https://doi.org/10.1080/09592318.2021.2025284.

Azizi, Hamidreza. "The International Relations of Public Protests in Iran." October 19, 2022, Sharq Forum. https://research.sharqforum.org/2022/10/19/the-international-relations-of-public-protests-in-iran/.

Azizi, Hamidreza. "5 Messages Projected by Assad's Visit to Iran." Amwaj Media, May 19, 2022. https://amwaj.media/article/5-messages-projected-by-assad-s-visit-to-iran.

Azizi, Hamidreza. "Will Iran-Turkey-Russia Cooperation in Syria Survive Biden?" Amwaj Media, March 8, 2021. https://amwaj.media/article/ir-article-will-iran-turkey-russia-cooperation-in-syria-survive-biden.

Azizi, Hamidreza. "Why Russia Is No Longer Iran-Israel De-escalator in Syria." Amwaj Media, March 9, 2023. https://amwaj.media/article/why-russia-is-no-longer-iran-israel-de-escalator-in-syria.

Bassiki, Mohammad. "Syrian Kurds Focused on Federalism." Al-Monitor, October 27, 2017. https://www.al-monitor.com/originals/2017/10/syria-federal-state-kurds-turkey-russia.html.

Behravesh, Maysam. "How Iran Justifies Its Costly Syria Intervention at Home." Middle East Eye, March 23, 2017. https://www.middleeasteye.net/opinion/how-iran-justifies-its-costly-syria-intervention-home.

Cengiz, Mehmet Emin. "The Future of the Iranian-Turkish Relationship: A Contained Geopolitical Rivalry or a Possible Escalation." Al Sharq Strategic Research, September 30, 2022. https://research.sharqforum.org/2022/09/20/iranian-turkish-relationship/.

Çevik, Salim. "Turkey's Military Operations in Syria and Iraq." Stiftung Wissenschaft Und Politik, May 30, 2022. https://www.swp-berlin.org/publikation/turkeys-military-operations-in-syria-and-iraq.

Chubin, Shahram. "Iran and the Arab Spring: Ascendancy Frustrated." Carnegie Endowment for International Peace, September 27, 2012. https://carnegieendowment.org/2012/09/27/iran-and-arab-spring-ascendancy-frustrated-pub-49626.

DeYoung, Karen. "U.N. Deadlocked on Mandate for Last Humanitarian Corridor into Syria." *Washington Post*, July 9, 2022. https://www.washingtonpost.com/national-security/2022/07/08/syria-humanitarian-corridor-un/.

The Economist Intelligence Unit. "Russia Launches Air Attacks in Syria." October 1, 2015. http://country.eiu.com/article.aspx?articleid=1123554496.

Eichner, Itamar. "Russia Promises to Keep Weapons Out of Hezbollah's Hands." *Ynetnews*, February 9, 2017. https://www.ynetnews.com/articles/0,7340,L-4919806,00.html.

Elman, Colin. "Realism." In *International Relations Theory for the Twenty-First Century: An Introduction*, edited by Martin Griffiths, 1st edn, 11–20. London: Routledge, 2007.

Ezzeddine, Nancy, and Hamidreza Azizi. "Iran's Increasingly Decentralized Axis of Resistance." War on the Rocks, July 14, 2022. https://warontherocks.com/2022/07/irans-increasingly-decentralized-axis-of-resistance/.

Faulconbridge, Guy, and Parisa Hafezi. "Putin Forges Ties with Iran's Supreme Leader in Tehran Talks." Reuters, July 20, 2022. https://www.reuters.com/world/putin-visits-iran-first-trip-outside-former-ussr-since-ukraine-war-2022-07-18/.

France 24. "Anti-IS Coalition Meets on Countering Jihadists' Revival." May 11, 2022. https://www.france24.com/en/live-news/20220511-anti-is-coalition-meets-on-countering-jihadists-revival.

Frantzman, Seth. "Are There New Iranian-Backed Attacks on US Forces in Syria?" *Jerusalem Post*, January 5, 2023. https://www.jpost.com/middle-east/article-726727.

Goodarzi, Jubin. "Iran and Syria at the Crossroads: The Fall of the Tehran-Damascus Axis?" Wilson Center, August 2013. https://www.wilsoncenter.org/publication/iran-and-syria-the-crossroads-the-fall-the-tehran-damascus-axis.

Grajewski, Nicole. "The Evolution of Russian and Iranian Cooperation in Syria." Center for Strategic and International Studies, November 17, 2021. https://www.csis.org/analysis/evolution-russian-and-iranian-cooperation-syria.

Gusovsky, Dina. "Russian Fighters Are Joining ISIS in Record Numbers." CNBC, December 9, 2015. https://www.cnbc.com/2015/12/09/russian-fighters-are-joining-isis-in-record-numbers.html.

Halbfinger, David, and Ben Hubbard. "Netanyahu Says Putin Agreed to Restrain Iran in Syria." *New York Times*, July 13, 2018. https://www.nytimes.com/2018/07/12/world/middleeast/syria-israel-putin-netanyahu.html.

Hamidi, Ibrahim. "Why Does Russia Want to Remove the Syrian Political Process from Geneva?" *Asharq AL-awsat*, n.d. https://english.aawsat.com/home/article/3764461/why-does-russia-want-remove-syrian-political-process-geneva.

Hendrix, Steve. "As Missiles Strike Ukraine, Israel Won't Sell Its Vaunted Air Defense." *Washington Post*, October 12, 2022. https://www.washingtonpost.com/world/2022/10/12/ukraine-russia-israel-iron-dome/.

i24NEWS. "Russian Envoy Says Moscow Working to Prevent Transfer of Weapons to Hezbollah." i24NEWS, February 9, 2017. https://www.i24news.tv/en/news/international/137186-170209-russian-envoy-says-moscow-working-to-prevent-transfer-of-weapons-to-hezbollah.

Isaev, Leonid, and Andrey Zakharov. "A Russian Constitution for Syria?" Intersection, March 16, 2017. https://www.hse.ru/mirror/pubs/share/217044052.

Karagiannis, Emmanuel. "How and Why the Russian-Iranian-Hezbollah Axis Has Won the War in Syria." *Georgetown Journal of International Affairs*, November 12, 2019. https://gjia.georgetown.edu/2019/05/05/russian-iranian-hezbollah-axis/.

Klein, Margarete. "Russia and the Arab Spring: Foreign and Domestic Policy Challenges." Stiftung Wissenschaft Und Politik, February 2, 2012. https://www.swp-berlin.org/en/publication/russia-and-the-arab-spring.

Kozhanov, Nikolay. "As Ringmaster, Russia Runs Israel-Iran Balancing Act in Syria." Al-Monitor, August 6, 2018. https://www.al-monitor.com/originals/2018/08/russia-syria-israel-iran-golan-heights.html.

Kozhanov, Nikolay. "Russia and the Issue of a New Security Architecture for the Persian Gulf." LSE Middle East Centre, August 5, 2021. https://blogs.lse.ac.uk/mec/2021/08/04/russia-and-the-issue-of-a-new-security-architecture-for-the-persian-gulf/.

Majidyar, Ahmad. "Tehran Rejects Putin's Call for Troop Withdrawal from Syria." Middle East Institute, May 21, 2018. https://www.mei.edu/publications/tehran-rejects-putins-call-troop-withdrawal-syria.

Mohns, Erik, and André Bank. "Syrian Revolt Fallout: End of the Resistance Axis?" Middle East Policy Council (MEPC), 2012. https://mepc.org/journal/syrian-revolt-fallout-end-resistance-axis.

Prasad, Hari. "Russia's Invasion of Ukraine Complicates the Situation in Syria." The Carter Center, 7 June 2022. www.cartercenter.org/news/features/blogs/2022/russias-invasion-of-ukraine-complicates-the-situation-in-syria.html.Rasooli Sani Abadi, Elham. "mahiyat e etelaf dar khavar e miyane: ghodrat va hoviyat [The Nature of Alliances in the Middle East: Power or Identity]." *Strategic Studies Quarterly* 17, no. 3 (2014): 199.

Reuters. "Russia Steps up Criticism of NATO Libya Campaign." May 20, 2011. https://www.reuters.com/article/us-russia-libya-idUSTRE74J5K820110520.

Reuters. "Russia, Syria Ink Energy Cooperation Agreement—Ministry." January 31, 2018. https://www.reuters.com/article/russia-syria-energy-idAFL8N1PQ7GE.

RFI Persian. "Rahim Safavi: Like Russia, Iran Should Gain Its Share in Syria." February 18, 2018. https://shorturl.at/dkqrD.

Rogers, Paul. "The Ukraine Crisis in Relation to Syria and Iran." Oxford Research Group Monthly Global Security Briefing, March 2014. https://www.files.ethz.ch/isn/178662/MarchEn14_0.pdf.

RT Arabic. "Lavrov to RT: Russian Forces to Stay in Syria." May 26, 2022. https://shorturl.at/egkTW.

Sakwa, Richard. *Russia against the Rest: The Post-Cold War Crisis of World Order*. Cambridge: Cambridge University Press, 2017.

Silk Road News. "Iran Planning Super-Highway to Connect with Mediterranean." April 9, 2018. https://silkroadnews.org/en/news/iran-plans-to-build-a-highway-to-the-mediterranean-sea-al-quds-al-arabi-reports (accessed January 30, 2024).

SIPRI. "Trends in International Arms Transfers, 2012." March 18, 2013. https://www.sipri.org/publications/2013/sipri-fact-sheets/trends-international-arms-transfers-2012.

Snyder, Glenn. "Alliance Theory: A Neorealist First Cut." In *The Evolution of Theory in International Relations: Essays in Honor of William T.R. Fox*, edited by Robert Rothstein, 83–104. Columbia: University of South Carolina Press, 1992.

Spyer, Jonathan. "What Does the Deraa Surrender Mean for Iran and Russia in Syria?" Jerusalem *Post*, September 9, 2021. https://www.jpost.com/middle-east/what-does-the-deraa-surrender-mean-for-iran-and-russia-in-syria-679086.

Sveshnikova, Julia. "Russia, Iran Compete to Reconstruct Syria." Al-Monitor: Independent, Trusted Coverage of the Middle East, September 24, 2018. https://www.al-monitor.com/originals/2018/09/russia-iran-syria-economics-grievances.html.

The Syrian Observer. "Massive Iranian Reinforcements to Southern Syria." February 14, 2022. https://syrianobserver.com/news/73479/massive-iranian-reinforcements-to-southern-syria.html.

Taadol Newspaper. "Federalism suriye va amniyat e iran [Federalism in Syria and Iran's National Security]." September 1, 2016. http://www.taadolnewspaper.ir/fa/tiny/news-50492.

Troyansky, Vladimir. "Russia's Support for al-Assad's Syria: Reasons Old and New." *Syrian Studies Association Bulletin*, May 11, 2012. https://www.syrianstudiesassociation.org/ssa-bulletin (accessed January 30, 2024).

Vatanka, Alex, and Abdolrasool Divsallar. "Can the West Stop Russian-Iranian Convergence?" Middle East Institute, April 3, 2023, https://www.mei.edu/publications/can-west-stop-russian-iranian-convergence.

Walt, Stephen M. "Why Alliances Endure or Collapse." *Survival* 39, no. 1 (March 1997): 156–79. https://doi.org/10.1080/00396339708442901.

Walt, Stephen M. *The Origins of Alliances (Cornell Studies in Security Affairs)*. New edition. Ithaca, NY: Cornell University Press, 1990.

Waltz, Kenneth N. "The Origins of War in Neorealist Theory." *Journal of Interdisciplinary History* 18, no. 4 (1988): 615–17. https://doi.org/10.2307/204817.

Waters, Gregory. "From Tiger Forces to the 16th Brigade: Russia's Evolving Syrian Proxies." Middle East Institute, September 12, 2022. https://www.mei.edu/publications/tiger-forces-16th-brigade-russias-evolving-syrian-proxies.

Wehrey, Frederic, and Karim Sadjadpour. "Elusive Equilibrium: America, Iran, and Saudi Arabia in a Changing Middle East." Carnegie Endowment for International Peace, May 22, 2014. https://carnegieendowment.org/2014/05/22/elusive-equilibrium-america-iran-and-saudi-arabia-in-changing-middle-east-pub-55641.

CONCLUSION

Abdolrasool Divsallar

The chapters in this book featured diverse contributors with different backgrounds who have used distinct analytical perspectives. Notwithstanding such diversity, looking back at the chapters, one can distinguish several common threads. The contributors to this volume were unanimously agreed that the war in Ukraine has impacted Russo-Iranian relations. The general belief is that Moscow and Tehran have substantially progressed in their relations and do not stand where they were before February 2022. The war initiated a process that has the potential to eventually give the relationship a strategic nature. While the authors agree that the war in Ukraine brought Moscow and Tehran closer, they also concur that its actual implications should be seen from a much broader historical perspective. This is because the scope and depth of recently witnessed trends differ across sectors and topics. At the same time, several factors negatively influence the sustainability of the recent dynamic in bilateral relations. Historically, it is not uncommon in Russo-Iranian relations that aspirations for a closer partnership quickly give way to frustration and backlash.

In its immediate impact, the war served as a catalyst for deepening the relations between the two states. It forged a strong political willingness and strategic sympathy to cooperate against challenges viewed to be rooted in the so-called unjust US-led international order, which is perceived as threatening the national security of both states. The view in Moscow and Tehran shifted to a common understanding that while the political-security aspects of the relationship have aligned and deepened strategically in recent years, other aspects of bilateral ties are underdeveloped and have not progressed as they should. While Iran's delivery of weapons to Russia grabbed public attention, the two states initiated a wave of efforts to expand non-security cooperation in such fields as economic, cultural, tourism, and people-to-people relations. That included a greater degree of connection at the different ministerial levels, agencies, and institutes that were often absent from relations in the past, including universities, private companies, and small businesses. The intensity of meetings, visits, and dialogues between Iranian and Russian state, private sector, and civil society actors since the outbreak of the war in Ukraine was unprecedented in the two countries' contemporary history. Such diverse interactions are certainly improving mutual understanding and building a new history of collaboration that had not been present in Iran-Russia relations before.

However, these actions seem to be only modestly successful in the short term. When compared to a huge surge in Russian investment, tourism, and trade with the UAE, Turkey, Egypt, and other countries in the Middle East, Russo-Iranian ties have improved moderately. It remains to be seen how long-term projects, such as the North-South Transit Corridor (NSTC), the implementation of a newly agreed free trade agreement (FTA) between the Eurasian Economic Union (EAEU) and Iran, agreements on oil and gas cooperation, Iran's membership in the Shanghai Cooperation Organization (SCO) and BRICS (Brazil, Russia, India, China, and South Africa), and inter-banking and other trade facilitation agreements, will impact mutual relations in the future. The truth is that all these initiatives face significant structural and bureaucratic barriers, which have proven difficult to overcome in the past. Now, resolving these barriers might become even more difficult in the face of Western sanctions that are forcing the two countries to compete in certain sectors, such as in the oil and gas market.

That being said, the driver of Russo-Iranian relations is neither economic benefits nor cultural attractions and people-to-people linkages. It is a choice at the political-security level favoring greater interdependence with the strategic objective of guaranteeing state security at its core. Moscow and Tehran share a range of threats to their security, including threats from the United States ranging from international sanctions to regime change, civilizational threats, and the threat of Islamic extremism. In this environment, an unbalanced interdependence is forming, in which security cooperation dominates the economic, cultural, and even political aspects. For elites in both capitals, the outcome of closer cooperation is perceived to be strategically important to enhance resilience to external pressures and guarantee state security. It is due to such an expected outcome that the Russo-Iranian partnership is not simply a transactional alliance of convenience. In fact, even a suboptimal advancement in non-security and nonpolitical cooperation will probably be viewed in both capitals as a success and as a contribution to state security. Thus, it is misleading to judge the depth of relations based on the state of trade, tourism, and people-to-people interactions, or any other nonpolitical security factor.

The relationship is also complemented by another critical reality. Neither Moscow nor Tehran has any other state that shares with them the fundamental elements of their political ideology. The political ideology of both states entails important elements of political messianism. A similar belief exists that Russia and Iran represent unique civilizations with a historical mission. These factors also shape the foundation of both sides' similar worldviews. The deep state in Moscow and Tehran, under the influence of eschatological approaches, shares animosity toward an unjust Western-led international order that is challenging their civilizational missions. In the eyes of Moscow and Tehran, the events after the war in Ukraine only better manifested common civilizational challenges when the "collective West" attempted to prevent the birth of a multipolar world by weakening Russia and Iran. This explains why both sides seek to strengthen shared identities, including Russia's encouragement of its Muslim minorities in building stronger ties with Iran.

In addition, several other factors have contributed to enhanced cooperation between Moscow and Tehran after the Russian invasion of Ukraine. First, the global condemnation of Russia reduced Putin's options for any normal partnership with the West in the near future. Turning to the East is no longer an option for Moscow but a necessity, despite representing a departure from five centuries of Russian tradition of focusing on European partners. Indeed, the tradition of Russia as a Eurasian power, trying to project power and influence in both Europe and Asia, is getting stronger. While Iran was in isolation for years and was constantly pushing Moscow to expand ties, political support from the Kremlin to improve ties emerged only when Russia found itself in a similar situation. Second, a lack of cooperation can prove costly for both sides. Urgency and a lack of options impose immediate political, economic, and security costs on noncooperation. Both sides feel in need of the other's political support on the international stage, on the battlefield, and for mitigating the economic damage caused by sanctions. Third, and most importantly, the war in Ukraine has changed the power dynamics between the two states. Russia is struggling to maintain a dominant position in the relationship because of the exhaustion of its resources in the war in Ukraine and the partial loss of foreign policy influence on the global stage. Russia's reliance on Iran has improved Tehran's bargaining position and confidence, contributing to a more equitable mutual dependency.

It is safe to argue that the relationship between the Kremlin and Tehran will grow as long as the existing political systems remain in place and shared strategic threat perceptions continue. However, no rapid transformation in Russo-Iranian relations should be expected, but rather a gradual and cautious process in the direction of finding strategic characteristics. Throughout this process, relations will still suffer from fluctuations, disputes, conflicting interests, situational decisions necessitated by urgencies, the influence of external factors, mutual cautiousness, and mistrust. Nor will opportunistic pragmatism disappear from bilateral relations easily; maintaining the relationship will be dependent on external factors. The Russo-Iranian partnership will remain vulnerable to fractures linked to changes in international relations and both countries' strategic environments. The improvement of relations after the war in Ukraine should be viewed as only one opportunity. But Russia and Iran will continue to struggle to forge an alliance in the years to come.

When considering the future sustainability of improvements in bilateral relations in the context of the war in Ukraine, one should keep an eye on the following variables as a barometer of Russo-Iranian ties.

Deliverables

The actual gains and benefits that closer ties can bring to each side remain the fundamental motivation behind future decisions. Moscow and Tehran are pragmatic actors, and the results of the partnership will remain at the top of the list of factors that shape their views. It is not difficult to imagine that if Tehran sees minimum gain from costly military support for Russia, its decisions toward aiding Moscow may change. For example, Russia's failure to deliver military hardware such as the SU-35 might raise internal debates in Iran about the value of having closer ties with Moscow, eventually leading to a new round of mistrust and cautiousness on the Iranian side. A similar pattern may be seen on the Russian side if a potential restoration of the JCPOA downgrades the prioritized position of Russia in Iran's foreign policy. Indeed, despite optimism about collaboration after the outbreak of the war in Ukraine, tangible results will be less than what both sides expected, and this may give rise to a new wave of frustration.

The US Factor

The state of each side's relations with the United States will remain the core issue in the future of Russia-Iran ties. If either side settles its disputes with the United States and Europe, it will impact relations in strategic ways. A destabilizing wave will affect bilateral ties if either side reaches an agreement with Washington or starts a normalization process with the United States that would distance it from an open confrontation with the West. Already, concerns about avoiding further antagonizing Europe have prevented Tehran from backing the Russian war objectives completely. Direct international costs and opportunity costs will persist as determining factors, preventing a fully committed alignment from emerging between Moscow and Tehran. At the same time, unlike with the Islamic Republic's eternal animosity with the West, there are doubts whether Russia's clash with the West will not resolve itself at some point in the future. In the event of a US-Russia agreement on Ukraine, Iran could find itself in a difficult position.

The Fate of the Ukraine War

The outcome of the war in Ukraine and how it ends will impact the two countries' relations too. Russia losing the war in Ukraine would make Moscow a less attractive international partner for Tehran and thus may initiate new debates within Iran about the reconfiguration of ties with Moscow. Although even a defeated Russia will remain a major power, such a scenario would impact Iran's strategic calculus toward the Kremlin. Tehran may reconsider the role of Moscow as a reliable partner in building a multipolar world order. But if Russia wins, then Iran's newly gained leverage due to Moscow's increased dependency on it during the war could be reduced or even lost. At the same time, Russia will emerge as a more assertive power and probably will find new points of leverage and reduce its reliance on Tehran. On the contrary, Iranian incentives to strengthen ties with Moscow may increase. In these ways, the outcome of the war and how it impacts the global balance of power will affect Moscow-Tehran ties.

Dispute Resolution Capacity

The evolution of relations will depend on the two states' capacity in managing their competition and conflicts of interest in areas where they have competed or may compete in the future. So far, competition has not resulted in a split because the security gains from cooperation are larger and the costs attributed to the deterioration of relations are estimated to be high, but also because the two sides enjoy intense military-security and political dialogues that assist them in resolving disputes. In the Syrian case, for example, the two sides have been able to compartmentalize competition and minimize its effects on their broader objectives. In another case, after the Russia-Gulf Cooperation Council statement about the Iranian islands in the Persian Gulf, and notwithstanding the summoning of the Russian ambassador, the multiple immediate high-level contacts helped resolve and contain the issue quickly. However, there is no guarantee in the event of a change in the presidency in Iran or the rise of new elites in Russia that the strategic cost-benefit assessment behind the existing flexibilities toward one another will remain intact. On that point, competition and conflicts of interest may become decisive obstacles to maintaining strong bilateral relations.

Persian Gulf Security Dynamics

Regional security dynamics in the Persian Gulf and the Arab-Israeli normalization process will continue to impact Moscow's Iran policy. For example, reports cited Israeli opposition to the delivery of SU-35 fighter jets to Iran as the main reason preventing it. Even the Saudi Arabia-Iran rapprochement is not going to meaningfully change Saudi and Emirati concerns about the regional balance of power. These concerns are directly channeled to the Russian side, given Mohammed bin Zayed and Mohammed bin Salman's warm personal relations with President

Putin. Besides, Moscow's growing dependency on the Arab states of the Persian Gulf since the start of the Ukraine war will cause Arab-Israeli considerations to continue to play a major role in Russian strategy toward Iran. That makes Moscow cautious and limited in what it can provide to Tehran.

Building Trust

The presence of past grievances and suspicions is a constant part of Russian and Iranian dialogues. Iranians, in particular, have not yet been able to overcome the memories of past Russian territorial aggressions in the 19th century, which led to the loss of Iranian provinces in the Caucasus and Moscow's negative influences on Iran's domestic politics during the Cold War. Thus, anything linked with Russia can quickly become a controversial public issue. The Russians too, aware of these negative perceptions, believe that Tehran's rapprochement is driven by pressing needs and that Iran will choose the West over Russia if that becomes possible. Regular state-level meetings have contributed to resolving parts of this mistrust among key decision-makers. However, mutual stereotypes and suspicions still exist in the strategic culture on both sides. Thus, it is difficult to imagine any strategic advancement in relations if Moscow and Tehran cannot come up with strategies to strengthen mutual trust.

Strategic Vision

Part of the situational nature of Russo-Iranian ties relates to the fact that they are not regulated by a set of principles and shared strategic objectives. It will be critical to see whether the momentum created by the war in Ukraine can push the two capitals toward a formal agreement that would give their relations long-term characteristics and principles to regulate bilateral ties. However, reaching a formal long-term agreement will be a difficult task too as the two states have different objectives in key areas where they tactically cooperate. Taking the example of Syria, Russia wants a centralized and de-ideologized armed forces in Syria, while Iran wants to maintain its influence through a network of ideologically driven militias. Besides, there is no domestic consensus among the elites in both capitals on the nature and future of relations. So far, no general agreement or binding mutual commitment exists, and it is difficult to imagine that one will emerge in the future. However, the extent to which each side can shape such principles, even if in the form of a tacit political commitment, will determine the fate of bilateral relations.

CONTRIBUTORS

Hamidreza Azizi is a visiting fellow at the German Institute for International and Security Affairs (SWP) and an associate researcher at Clingendael—the Netherlands Institute of International Relations. Azizi holds a PhD in regional studies from the University of Tehran and has worked as a lecturer at several Iranian universities, including the University of Tehran (2016–18) and the Shahid Beheshti University (2016–20). Azizi's research interests include security and geopolitical issues in the Middle East and Central Eurasia, Iran's foreign policy, and Iran-Russia relations.

Esfandyar Batmanghelidj is the founder and CEO of the Bourse and Bazaar Foundation, a think tank focused on economic diplomacy, economic development, and justice in the Middle East and Central Asia. He has published peer-reviewed research on Iranian political economy, social history, and public health, as well as commentary on Iranian politics and economics. He was a visiting fellow with the Middle East and North Africa program at the European Council on Foreign Relations.

Abdolrasool Divsallar is a senior researcher at the UN Institute for Disarmament Research and an adjunct professor at the Universita' Cattolica del Sacro Cuore in Milan, focusing on Iran's military affairs, Russia-Iran relations, and the Persian Gulf security architecture. He is also a nonresident scholar at the Middle East Institute in Washington. Divsallar cofounded and led the Regional Security Initiative at the European University Institute from 2020 to 2022. He has written and edited eight books, including *Stepping Away from the Abyss: A Gradual Approach towards a New Security System in the Persian Gulf* (2021), and has published numerous journal articles.

Diana Galeeva is a visiting fellow at the Oxford Centre for Islamic Studies and a nonresident fellow with the Gulf International Forum. She previously was an academic visitor to St. Antony's College, University of Oxford (2019–22). Galeeva is the author of two books, *Qatar: The Practice of Rented Power* (2022) and *Russia and the GCC: The Case of Tatarstan's Paradiplomacy* (2022). Galeeva was previously an intern at the president of Tatarstan's

Office for the Department of Integration with Religious Associations (2012) and the cabinet of ministers of the Republic of Tatarstan (2011) (Russia).

Jakub M. Godzimirski is a research professor at the Norwegian Institute of International Affairs (NUPI). He has been working on Russian foreign and security policy issues at NUPI for more than twenty years, paying special attention to the role of energy resources in Russian grand strategy. In addition, he has also worked on European policy and its impact on the developments in Central and Eastern Europe, including relations with Russia.

Nicole Grajewski is a Stanton Nuclear Security postdoctoral fellow with the Belfer Center for Science and International Affair's Project on Managing the Atom at Harvard's Kennedy School. She was previously a predoctoral fellow with the International Security Program at the Belfer Center. Nicole received a PhD in international relations and MPhil in Russian and East European Studies from the University of Oxford. Her research focuses on Russian and Iranian approaches to the international order, with particular emphasis on the global nuclear order.

Mark N. Katz is a professor of government and politics at the George Mason University Schar School of Policy and Government. He is also the chairperson of the Scientific Advisory Council of the Finnish Institute of International Affairs and a nonresident senior fellow at the Atlantic Council. Katz has received fellowships from the Brookings Institution, the Rockefeller Foundation, the Kennan Institute, and the US Institute of Peace. He has also been a Fulbright Scholar at the School of Oriental and African Studies and a Sir William Luce fellow at Durham University (both in the UK).

Anastasia Malygina is an associate professor at the School of International Relations at St. Petersburg State University. Malygina teaches courses on arms control, weapons of mass destruction (WMD) nonproliferation, and revolution in military affairs and has written extensively on the Russian approach to nuclear disarmament and nonproliferation.

Jeffrey Mankoff is a distinguished research fellow at the US National Defense University's Institute for National Strategic Studies. Mankoff is the author of *Empires of Eurasia: How Imperial Legacies Shape International Security* (2022) and *Russian Foreign Policy: The Return of Great Power*

Politics (2009, 2011). He frequently writes for *Foreign Affairs*, *War on the Rocks*, *CNN*, and other outlets.

Mahsa Rouhi is a research fellow for Iran, the Levant, and Turkey at the Institute for National Strategic Studies at National Defense University, and an associate fellow at the International Institute for Strategic Studies (IISS). Rouhi has written extensively on Iran's nuclear and military issues.

Mahmood Shoori is deputy director of the Institute for Iran and Eurasia Studies (IRAS) in Tehran and a former senior researcher at the Center for Strategic Studies. Shoori has held a senior advisory position at the Iranian government and has published dozens of books and articles on Iran-Russia relations.

INDEX

Abdi, Abbas 89, 90, 92
Abdollahian, Hossein Amir- 3, 18, 91, 304t–5t, 336
Afghanistan 21, 42 n.19, 81
Ahmad, Jalal al- 113
Ahmadinejad, Mahmoud 78, 83–4, 129, 223
Alaei, Hossein 92–3
alliances 317, 319–20, 326, 341
Amini, Jina Mahsa 112, 182–3, 211, 213
Amir-Abdollahian, Hossein 3, 18, 91, 304t–5t, 336
Anti-Access/Area Denial (A2/AD) 193
anti-Americanism 6, 24, 187, 340
Arab League 198
Arab Spring (2011) 130, 184, 324
Arab-Israeli normalization 352–3
Arab-Israeli War (1967) 131
Armenia-Azerbaijan conflict 139–40, 238
arms control. *See* strategic stability
arms transfers. *See* drones; military cooperation, Iran-Russia
Assad, Bashar al-
  Iran, visit to 318, 336
  Russia, visit to 327
Astana Framework 133, 199, 232–4, 333
Astrakhan region, Russia 110–11
Astra-Rasht railway project 17, 195
Atomstroyexport (Russia) 291
authoritarian governments
  global stability and 215–21
  public opinion and policy-making 74–6
  solidarity and learning 188–91, 225–7
  See also protective integration
Axis of Resistance
  purpose of 210, 212, 221
  Russia's stance toward 192
  Syria's role in 325, 329, 332, 337
Aymanabadi, Gholamali Jafarzadeh 90
Azerbaijan-Armenia conflict 139–40, 238

Bagheri, Mohammad Hossein 303, 306t
Baluchistan province, Iran 198
banking systems
  de-dollarization 118–19, 195
  Islamic collaborations 109–11
  limitations of 59–60, 255–8, 289
  sanction circumvention 191
barter cooperation 59
Barth, Fredrik *(Ethnic Groups and Boundaries)* 104
Belousov, Andrei 17
Belt and Road Initiative (BRI) 54, 231, 336–7
Bennet, Naftali 138
Biden, Joe 11, 129–30, 142, 171, 188
bilateral ties, Iran-Russia
  authoritarian solidarity 188–91, 225–7
  changing nature of 33–4, 62–3
  deliverables, importance of 350–1
  dispute resolution capacity 352

factors influencing 352–6
history of 2–4, 10–12, 79–86, 97–9, 114 n.33
identities, shared 104–5, 115–17, 119–20
limits to 196–202
motives for 7–8, 179–86, 348–50
mutual fear of "turn toward" US 117–18, 132, 197
as natural allies 40, 52, 202
nature of 55–7, 347–50, 353–4
regional security dynamics 352–3
shared identities 106–12
strategic logic of 179–81, 202
strategic vision for 353–4
timeline of key developments 304t–6t
trust and 79–86, 117–18, 120, 196–7, 353
Ukraine War, impacts of 4–7, 209–11, 234–7, 303–8, 347–8, 350
US role in 351
See also memoranda of understanding (MoU), Iran-Russia; protective integration; Syrian Civil War; Ukraine War (2022–); world order, multipolar
Black Sea 134–5, 260, 269
Brazil, Russia, India, China, and South Africa (BRICS) 153, 305t
Brezhnev, Leonid 128
Bush, George W. 46, 219
Bushehr nuclear power plant (NPP, Iran) 83, 157, 161–2, 291–2

Caspian Sea 44–5, 197, 259–61, 264–5
Caspian Summit in Turkmenistan (2022) 115, 133, 305t
Center for Energy and Security Studies (Russia) 159
Center for Strategy and Technology Analysis (CAST) 196–7
Chechnya 108–9

China
 BRI 54, 231, 336–7
 as counterbalance to West 144
 Great Firewall 227
 Russian partnership with 118, 151–6, 160, 217
 as trade partner 270t, 272t
China-Russia declaration on International Relations Entering a New Era 217, 220
civilizational essentialism and 116, 214–15, 239
Clinton, Bill 157
Cold War 90, 128, 215–17, 218, 353
Collective Security Treaty Organization (CSTO) 139, 231
color revolutions 46, 184, 213, 218–19
Commonwealth of Independent States (CIS) 41, 42 n.18, 43
Comprehensive Safeguards Agreement (CSA) 166, 173
Concept of Foreign Policy of the Russian Federation (CFP, 2016) 153–4
Concept of Foreign Policy of the Russian Federation (CFP, 2023) 155–6, 164, 168, 187
Conference on Security and Cooperation in Europe (CSCE) 234
Covid-19 pandemic 284–5, 292, 296
Crimea, Russian annexation. *See* Ukrainian crisis (2014)
currencies, national 59–60, 118, 195, 257–9. *See also* banking systems; economic ties, Iran-Russia
cybersecurity domain 190

de-dollarization 118–19, 195, 257–8. *See also* banking systems; economic ties, Iran-Russia
Deir ez-Zor province, Iran 334, 338
democratizing contagion 184. *See also* regime survival
Djagarian, L. 306t

Dolabi, Abdul Qasim 111
Donetsk People's Republic (DPR) 56, 303
drones
  aid as defensive pact 191–2
  Iran exports to Russia 19–20, 236
  Russian dependence 194
  use in Syria 61
  use in Ukraine 60, 61–2, 135–6, 341

"Eastern Excursion," 106, 117–19, 120
Eastern Ukraine. *See* Ukrainian crisis (2014)
economic resistance 57–60, 187, 224–5, 228–9
economic ties, Iran-Russia
  alternative financial structures 228–9
  banking constraints 257–9
  catalysts for 194, 253–4
  China, shift toward 54, 120, 262, 269, 276
  competition 255, 263–4, 269–75, 330–1
  constraints, overview of 198, 255–62
  energy sector and 287–92
  institutional constraints 261–2
  logistical constraints 259–61
  prospects for 253–5, 275–6
  protective integration and 194–5
  trade, rebalancing of 262–6
energy interests, Iran-Russia
  bilateral ties and 283–5, 308–10
  Chinese market 238–9
  competition in 269–75
  petroleum exports 132, 198, 295–6
  political leverage 303–4
  strategic dimension of 297–303
  Ukraine War and 254, 297–303
energy sector
  exports and imports, snapshot of 295–6
  Iran, strategic importance of 298–300

Iran-Russia ties 288t, 290t, 303–8
Russia, strategic importance of 298–300
Russia-Syria cooperation agreement 330–1
sanctions, impacts of 134, 301–2, 308–9
Ukraine War, impacts of 142, 308–10
Erdogan, Recep Tayyip 115, 137, 334
Ermakov, Vladimir 167
Esmailabad, Gholamali Jafarzadeh 92
Ethnic Groups and Boundaries (Barth) 104
Eurasia 53–5, 229–34
Eurasian Development Bank (EDB) 261
Eurasian Economic Union (EAEU) 54–5, 195, 256, 348
Eurasian regionalism 230–1
European Union (EU) 151, 171, 228, 263, 281, 300–2
extremist groups 325–6, 332, 340

Falahatpisheh, Heshmatollah 84, 89–90, 275
FIM-92 Stinger (missiles) 20
finance. *See* banking systems; economic ties, Iran-Russia
Finland 183
first strike, nuclear 155
Fomin, Aleksandr 303–6t, 307
Fordow Fuel Enrichment Plant (Iran) 168
foreign policy-making
  protective integration and 184–5
  trust at state level 197, 353
free trade zones 15, 54–5, 195

Ganji, Abdullah 88
gas. *See* energy interests, Iran-Russia; energy sector
Gazprom 195, 254, 305t–6
Georgia 56, 218–19
Gerasimov, Valery 221

global strategic stability. *See* strategic stability
Golestan, Treaty of (1813) 79, 196
Gorbachev, Mikhail 9
Gore-Chernomyrdin secret agreement 10, 97
gray zone operations 191
Greater Eurasia 53–5, 231
Green Movement (2009) 213
Gulf Arab states
  Chechnya, relations with 108
  Iran, reduced hostilities with 200
  Iran, territorial dispute 8, 198, 352
  positive neutrality policy 199
  Russia, relations with 130, 137–8, 198, 352–53
  Russian security initiative in 333–4
  security dynamics 352–3

Hemmati, Abdolnasser 257
Hezbollah
  Israel, conflict with 131, 138
  regional role 136, 223, 240
  role in Syria 327–29
Hizb ut-Tahrir 108
Homs province, Iran 334
Hosseinzadeh, Hossein 16

IAEA. *See* International Atomic Energy Agency (IAEA)
identity
  anti-Western, shared 34–7, 103, 115–17, 120, 181, 209–11
  Muslim, shared identity 106–12
  theoretical foundations of 104–6, 119–20
  "West-toxification," 112–15
ideology, political 225–6, 349
Imam Ali 107
India 14, 53–4, 55, 134, 192, 287
information sector
  control over 116, 188
  cybersecurity domain 190
  internet censorship 227–8

news media 78, 85–92, 163, 188
social media 75, 77, 190
Information Security Concept (Russia, 2016) 227
INSTC. *See* North-South Transit Corridor (NSTC)
Instrument in Support of Trade Exchanges (INSTEX) project, European Union 228
interdependence
  definition 180
  protective logic behind 193–5
  situational nature of 200–1
  trust and 196–7
International Atomic Energy Agency (IAEA)
  JCPOA implementation 165–8
  oversight of Iran program 45–6
  Rosatom and 157
  strengthening of 158
International North-South Transit Corridor. *See* North-South Transit Corridor (NSTC)
international order. *See* world order, liberal; world order, multipolar
International Relations Entering a New Era, China-Russia declaration on 217, 220
internet censorship 227–8
Iran
  Conference on Disarmament and Non-Proliferation 159
  as counterbalance to West 40–3, 47, 53, 56, 221–5
  deterrence strategy 192–3
  foreign policy, domestic debates 74–9, 86–96
  as global energy player 292–6
  Green Movement 213
  internet control 227–8
  Look to the East policy 120, 232
  NIMA 258
  nuclear program, Russian stance on 44–6
  policy, nonalignment 222–3

362 INDEX

public protests 78, 182–3, 213, 336, 339
Russia, public opinion of 185, 197
Russia, ties with 12, 129, 185–6
sanctions, impacts of 200
separatist movements in 198, 332
succession competition 185, 211
Syria, concerns for 326–8
Ukraine War, domestic debates 73–4, 86–92, 93–7, 188
Ukraine War, impacts of 133–44
See also bilateral ties, Iran-Russia
Iranian National Information Network (NIN) 228
Iranian Preferential Trade Agreement 195
Iranian Student Polling Agency (ISPA) 93–6
Iraq 219, 325–6
Iron Dome (missile system) 337
Islam 106–12, 120
Islamic Revolutionary Guard Corps (IRGC) 190
Islamic State in Iraq and Syria (ISIS)
  collapse of 326–7
  emergence of 323
  Iranian concerns about 325–6
  revival of 319, 334
isolation efforts. *See* sanctions
Israel
  Hezbollah, conflict with 131, 138
  Persian Gulf and 352–3
  Russia, ties with 130–1, 192, 352–3
  Syrian War and 20–1
  Ukraine War and 337–8
  Vienna Talks, role in 171
Ivanov, Igor 49–50

Jabhat al-Nusra 323
Jalali, Kazem 110, 257
Javelin (missiles) 20
Joint Comprehensive Plan of Action (JCPOA)
  adoption of 156
  GSS and 164–72
  Russia's role in 10–1, 84, 129–30
  sanctions linkage 161–4, 194
  Track II diplomacy 159–60
  Ukraine War, impacts of 150, 168, 172, 187, 308–9
  US withdrawal from 150–1, 160, 164–72, 201
  See also Vienna talks for reviving JCPOA
Joint Economic Commission, Iran-Russia (2022) 195
Juniper Oak (Israel-US joint military exercises) 171

Kadyrov, Ramzan 108–9
Karaganov, Sergey 53
Khamenei, Ali
  on decline of West 241
  Russia, ties with 133, 202, 339
  succession competition 185, 211
  on Ukraine War 186–7, 236, 305t
  on world order 213, 223–4, 325
Khatami, Mohammad 10, 78, 223
Khomeini, Ruhollah 9, 78, 222
Khorram, Ali 85
Khrushchev, Nikita 128
Kurds in Iran 198, 330
Kurds in Syria 330

Lapid, Yair 138
Latin America 47, 157, 158, 223
Lavrentiev, Alexander 327
Lavrov, Sergey 8, 119, 162, 218, 304t–5t, 335
Lenin, Vladimir 80
Levitin, Igor 14, 17, 195
Libya 158
linkage. *See* interdependence
Local Defense Forces (LDF) 328
Luhansk People's Republic (LPR) 56, 303

Majidi, Majid 108
Mamlouk, Ali 336

Maximum Pressure, US campaign
    103, 187–8, 331
Medvedev, Dmitry 158, 286–7
memoranda of understanding (MoU),
    Iran-Russia
  banking and energy 118
  energy sector 195, 306–7
  road transportation 305t
  security and law enforcement 190
  space cooperation 193
Middle East and North Africa
    (MENA), Russia policy
  balancing Iran and GCC 199–200
  historical overview 127, 128–32
  interests, map of 290t
  Iran, impacts on 129–31
  Syrian War and 20–1
  Ukraine War, impacts on
    Iran 133–40
  Ukraine War, potential
    impacts 140–4
  West's role in 323
military cooperation, Iran-Russia
  arms transfers as leverage 254
  conflicts of interest in 197–9
  core areas 17–20
  deliverables, importance of 350–1
  development of 11–12, 19–20
  external threat perception 182–4
  regime survival 184, 191–3, 348–50
  shared values as basis for 116
  in Syria 136–7, 317–19, 327–9
  in Ukraine 235–7
  Ukraine War, impacts of 60–2
  See also drones
militias, nonstate
  Iranian strategy in Syria 327–8, 335
  Israel, confrontation with 329
  Syria, role in 130, 136–7, 340
Minnikhanov, Rustam 110
Mir (payment card system)
    229, 258–9
Mirza, Abbas 79
Mishutshin, Mikhail 58
Mohajer-6 (drones) 19

Mohajerani, Attaullah 78
Mohammed bin Salman Al
    Saud 352–3
Mohammed bin Zayed Al
    Nahyan 352–3
Mostazafan Foundation (Iran) 111
Motahari, Ali 86–7
Mousavian, Hossein 89, 92
Muhammad: Messenger of God
    (film) 108
multipolar. *See* world order,
    multipolar
Munich speech (2007), Putin's 38,
    46, 217
Muslims, shared identity
    of 106–12

Naryshkin, Sergei 49
National Defense Forces (NDF) 328
National Iranian Oil Company
    (NIOC) 195, 305t, 306–7
NATO. *See* North Atlantic Treaty
    Organization (NATO)
Netanyahu, Benjamin 138
New Security Architecture for
    the Persian Gulf (Russian
    initiative) 333–4
news media 78, 85–92, 163, 188
NIMA (Iranian foreign exchange
    market) 258
9/11 terrorist attacks (2001) 46, 76
1979 Islamic Revolution (Iran) 128,
    210, 221–2
Non-Aligned Movement
    (NAM) 222–3
nonproliferation. *See* nuclear
    nonproliferation policy; Nuclear
    Non-Proliferation Treaty (NPT)
Noobari, Nasser 89
North Atlantic Treaty
    Organization (NATO)
  buffer zones 43
  expansion of 44, 86–8, 89, 91, 235
  Finland and Sweden's accession
    into 183

Libya, intervention in 321
Russian red lines 163, 186–7
Western hegemony and 113–14
Northern Alliance (Afghanistan) 42 n.19
North-South Transit Corridor (NSTC)
  Astra-Rasht railway project 17, 195
  economic linkage efforts 195, 231, 261–2
  plans for development 54, 111, 289
Novak, Alexander 40, 54, 59, 118, 258–9, 304t
Novorossiysk port (Black Sea) 260
NSTC. *See* North-South Transit Corridor (NSTC)
nuclear deal. *See* Joint Comprehensive Plan of Action (JCPOA); Vienna talks for reviving JCPOA
nuclear nonproliferation policy
  East-West relations 156–64
  Iran-Russia tensions 44–6
  Russian stance on 18–19, 149–50, 172–4
  See also strategic stability
Nuclear Non-Proliferation Treaty (NPT)
  Iranian violations 45
  JCPOA and 150
  1995 extension 156–7
  Review Conferences 156, 158, 162
  role in international security 154
Nuclear Security Summits 158–60

Obama, Barack 46, 158
Obydenov, Vladimir 59
Odessa, port of 134
1-2-3 Nuclear Cooperation Agreement 46
OPEC+ format 132, 138, 199
Owji, Javad 132 n.15, 291

Pahlavi, Mohammad Reza 7, 291
Pantsir S1 (SA-22 Greyhound, surface-to-air missiles) 328
paramilitary structures. *See* militias, nonstate
partnership. *See* bilateral ties, Iran-Russia
Patrushev, Nikolay 39, 57, 305t, 307
Permanent Russian-Iranian Commission for Trade and Economic Cooperation 291
Persian Gulf, Shahid Rajaee port 260
Persian Gulf countries. *See* Gulf Arab states
Peskov, Dmitry 62
petroleum. *See* energy interests, Iran-Russia; energy sector
Popular Mobilization Forces (PMF) 328
Presidential Addresses to the Federal Assembly (PAFAs, Russia) 286–7
Primakov, Evgeniy 37
Proliferation Security Initiative 163
protective integration
  accommodation of 184–5
  knowledge exchange 189–91, 225–7
  limits to 196–202
  mutual security assistance 191–3
  regime survival and 180–1, 182
  solidarity against isolation 188–9
  strategic sympathy 186–8
  See also authoritarian governments; bilateral ties, Iran-Russia; regime survival; world order, multipolar
Pushkov, Vasily 188
Putin, Vladimir
  Assad, meeting with 327
  Bush, phone call 46
  on energy resources 298
  foreign policy, MENA 128–32, 202
  Iran ties 34, 47, 133, 188, 235, 285
  Israel ties 131, 138
  Khamenei, meetings with 133, 339
  on new world order 213
  PAFA 287
  policy decision-making 38–9, 44–6
  policy of self-sufficiency 58

Raisi, ties with 3, 92, 113, 115,
   253–4, 304t
 on sanctions 274
 on Ukraine War 236
 2007 Munich speech 217
 uprisings against 213
 West, stance on 201, 218
 on West, decline of 240–1

Radan, Ahmadreza 190
Rafsanjani, Ali Akbar Hashemi 9,
   78, 81, 83
Raisi, Ebrahim
 foreign policy 4, 113, 115, 186
 on liberal world order 224
 Putin, meetings with 3, 133,
   235, 253–4
 Putin, phone call 92, 304t
regime survival
 as driver for bilateral ties 179–82,
   184, 348–9
 interdependence 193–5
 intrastate linkage and 184
 Syria, Iran's concerns for 324–7
 Syria, Russia's concerns for 320–4
 Ukraine War as lesson on 90
 See also protective integration
regional security. *See* security, regional
regionalism, Eurasian 230–1
resiliency. *See* regime survival
Rosatom 157–8, 160–1, 170
Rosoboronexport 46
Rouhani, Hassan 76–7, 186, 190, 223
RUnet (Russian internet) 227
Russia
 energy policy 134, 283–7
 foreign policy-making 38–40, 283–7
 as global energy player 292–6
 as great power 43–5, 215–21, 322
 great power status project 47–9, 216
 Information Security Concept 227
 internet control 227–8
 Iran, domestic discourse on 49–52,
   196–7
 Iran, elite's views on 41–9

Iran, policy toward 11–13, 34–8,
   42–3, 283–7
 Israel, ties with 352–3
 NATO expansion 163, 186–7, 235
 New Security Architecture for the
   Persian Gulf 333–4
 nuclear policy 149–50, 157, 160–1
 PAFAs 286–7
 policy, Turn to the East 53–5,
   349–50
 policy oscillations 41–9
 public protests 183, 213
 sovereignty, stance on 216–7,
   219, 322
 Syria, concerns for 320–4
 2016 Concept of Foreign
   Policy 153–4
 2023 Concept of Foreign Policy
   155–6, 164, 168, 187
 Vienna talks 18–9, 136, 164–73
 See also relations, Iran-Russia;
   Soviet Union
Russian-Iranian Intergovernmental
   Commission on Trade and
   Economic Cooperation in
   Grozny 108–9
Russian-Israeli deconfliction
   agreement in Syria (2015) 138
Ryabkov, Sergei 163

S-300 (air defense systems) 60, 338
SA-22 Greyhound (Pantsir S1,
   surface-to-air missiles) 328
Safavi, Yahya Rahim 331
Sanaei, Mehdi 4
sanctions
 on agricultural production 134–5,
   137
 as catalyst for cooperation 13–21,
   49
 collaboration against 113, 117–18,
   188–9, 191
 economic isolation 262–6
 economic resistance 57–60, 187,
   224–5, 228–9

366   INDEX

on energy exports 134, 137–8
energy landscape, impacts on 284, 308–10
GCC and circumvention of 199
JCPOA linkage to 161–4, 194
policy responses to 191, 194–5, 348–50
Russian stance on 46–7, 275
strategic empathy against 49–52
unilateralism and 221
Saudi Arabia 84–5, 192
security, regional
  Astana Framework 233–4
  Iran-Russia differences over 131–2
  power dynamics 194, 332–4, 334, 352–3
  threat perception in Syria 320–4
security cooperation. *See* military cooperation, Iran-Russia
Shahed (loitering munitions) 19, 236
Shahid Rajaee port (Persian Gulf) 260
Shahriyari, Hamid 112
Shamkhani, Ali 14, 57
Shanghai Cooperation Organization (SCO) 117, 133, 153, 229–30, 232
sharp power 115–16
Sherbank (Russian state bank) 110
Shetab (payment card system) 258–9
Shia Muslims 107–9, 131
Shulginov, N.G. 293
social media 75, 77, 190
Soleimani, Ghasem 198–9
Sources of the Self (Taylor) 105
"sovereign democracy," 219
Soviet Union 41–2, 113, 128. *See also* Russia
Soyuz (spacecraft) 193
Stalin, Joseph 80
state security. *See* regime survival
Stinger (missiles) 20
Stockholm International Peace Research Institute (SIPRI) report 323
strategic empathy 34, 50–2, 62–3, 86–92

strategic stability
  classic concept, aspects of 154–5
  as global framework 150
  JCPOA and 164–72
  key principles 152–4
  Russia-China joint statements on 151–2, 155–6
  See also nuclear nonproliferation policy
strategic sympathy (protective integration) 186–8
SU-35 (Sukhoi aircraft) 20, 192, 237, 341
Supreme Council for Cyberspace (Iran) 228
Surkov, Vladislav 219
Sweden 183
SWIFT payments 228–9, 258–9
Syria
  Assad, regime survival 320–6
  political future 329–30
  postwar reconstruction 330–31, 336
Syrian Civil War
  Astana Framework and 232–4
  balance of power in 332–3, 334, 339–41
  competing interests in 326–9
  Iran-Russia axis 194, 319–26, 340–1
  power dynamics in 317–19, 326
  regional impacts 11, 20–1, 40
  Russia, pivot to Ukraine 139–40, 318, 333–6
  Ukraine War, impacts of 317–18
  West, role of 320–1, 326
Syrian Constitutional Committee talks in Geneva 339
Syrian Democratic Forces (SDF) 332–3
System for Transfer of Financial Messages (SPFS) 229, 258

Tajikistan 43 n.21
Tatarstan 109–10
Taylor, Charles (*Sources of the Self*) 105

INDEX 367

Telegram (messaging app) 308
territorial integrity 4, 56–7, 79, 140, 198
terrorist groups 327–8, 336
Track II diplomacy 157, 159–60, 165, 167
trade relations, Iran-Russia
  barter cooperation 59
  compatibility of markets 266–9
  competition 269–75
  intergovernmental commission 108–9
  Muslim ties 107, 109
  Permanent Commission for Trade and Economic Cooperation 291
  rebalancing of 14–15, 262–6, 272–3
  sanctions 52, 54–5, 58–60, 118–19, 191
  strategic partnership 253–4
  transit routes 134, 284
  trends in 263t, 265t, 267t–8t, 290t
  before Ukraine War 10
Treaty of Golestan (1813) 79, 196
Treaty of Turkmenchay (1828) 79, 196
Treaty on Conventional Forces in Europe 46
Trump, Donald 11, 34, 150, 164, 270
Tsygankov, Andrei 36
Tudeh Party (Iran) 80–1, 114 n.33
Turkey
  energy relations 300
  Iran-Russia conflicts of interest 131
  in Syria 137, 324, 330–3, 337–9
  trends in trade relations 269–74, 273t, 274t, 276, 288
Turkmenchay, Treaty of (1828) 79, 196

Ukraine
  color revolution 218–19
  Western military aid 183
Ukraine War (2022–)
  bilateral ties, impacts on Iran-Russia 1–8, 234–7, 303–8
  bilateral ties, historical 8–13

as catalyst for Iran-Russia relations 7–8, 180, 253–4
conflicts of interests in 198
immediate impacts of 13–21, 347–8
impacts on Russia's MENA policy 133–40
Iranian domestic discourse 73–4, 86–92, 93–7
Iranian support for Russia 56, 133, 186–7
Iran-Russia axis in 331–9
JCPOA, impacts on 173
nuclear talks, impacts on 93, 150
outcomes, potential scenarios 94–5, 140–4, 351–2
power dynamics, Iran-Russia 350
Russian view of Iran following 50–2
strategic stability, impacts on 151
Syrian war, impacts on 319–20, 333–6
See also drones
Ukrainian crisis (2014)
  Iranian stance on 56
  Nuclear Security Summits 159
  Russian shift away from West 53–5, 151
  sanctions following 49–50, 57–8
Ulyanov, Mikhail 187
UN. *See* United Nations (UN)
unipolar world order. *See* world order, liberal
United Arab Emirates (UAE) 192, 198, 201
United Nations (UN) Charter 152, 155
United Nations Conference on Trade and Development (UNCTAD) 266
United Nations General Assembly (UNGA), vote on Ukraine War 189, 308
United Nations Security Council (resolution 1929) 99
United Nations Security Council (resolution 2231) 165, 167, 285

United Nations Security Council
    (UNSC) 45 n.26, 212, 217, 218
United States (US)
    containment strategy 13
    counterproliferation initiatives
        158, 160–1
    democracy promotion as
        tool 218–19
    Iran, policy toward 103, 132, 187–8,
        331, 338
    liberalism 212–13
    role in Iran-Russia relations 351
    Russia, relations with 45–7
unmanned aerial vehicles. *See* drones
USSR. *See* Soviet Union

Vardanian, Soren 259
Velayati, Ali Akbar 14, 186–7,
    199, 325
Vienna talks for reviving JCPOA
    Iran-Russia interdependence in 194
    Russian stance 18–19, 136, 164–72
    suspension of 161–2
Volga-Don canal (Russia) 261
Volodin, Vyacheslav 275
VTB Bank (Russia) 118, 258

Wagner mercenaries 139
Warsaw Pact states 44
Western hegemony
    counterbalance efforts against
        55–7, 158
    erosion of 47–8, 221–2, 240–1
    support for Ukraine 93–4, 183, 185
    Ukraine War, impacts on 209–11
    "West-toxification" identity 112–
        15, 120

world order, liberal
    emergence of 217
    Iran-Russia cooperation
        against 225–37
    opposition to 103, 115–17, 239–40,
        349
    Ukraine War, impacts of 180–1,
        235–6
world order, multipolar
    anti-Western identities 36–7, 115–
        17, 120, 181
    authoritarian solidarity 225–7
    counter-hegemony aspects
        187, 221–5
    emergence of 47–9
    energy strategy and 298–303
    framework and development 55–7,
        181–2, 229–34
    fundamental premise 50–1
    Iran-Russia shared mission 211–15,
        237–41, 349
    Russian role in 43–4, 48–9, 322
    stability, global strategic 45,
        152, 215–21
    Ukraine War, potential impacts
        of 351–2
    See also protective integration

Xi Jinping 217

Yeltsin, Boris 41, 44, 141–2, 156

Zaporizhzhia nuclear power plant
    (NPP, Ukraine) 162
Zarif, Mohammad Javad 10, 84, 331
Zelensky, Volodymyr 87–8
Zolotov, Viktor 190